# THE RHETORIC (
## LITERATURE A.

MW01240448

Why did eighteenth-century writers employ digression as a literary form of diversion, and how did their readers come to enjoy linguistic and textual devices that self-consciously disrupt the reading experience? Darryl P. Domingo answers these questions through an examination of the formative period in the commercialization of leisure in England, and the coincidental coming of age of literary self-consciousness in works published between approximately 1690 and 1760. During this period, commercial entertainers tested out new ways of gratifying a public increasingly eager for amusement, while professional writers explored the rhetorical possibilities of intrusion, obstruction, and interruption through their characteristic use of devices like digression. Such devices adopt similar forms and fulfil similar functions in literature to those of diversions in culture: they "unbend the mind" and reveal the complex reciprocity between commercialized leisure and commercial literature in the age of Swift, Pope, and Fielding.

DARRYL P. DOMINGO is Assistant Professor of English at the University of Memphis. His research focuses on the often subtle ways in which eighteenth-century cultural phenomena – urbanization, entertainment, advertising – both represent and are represented by the devices of literary texts. Darryl has published essays in such journals as *Eighteenth-Century Studies*, *Eighteenth-Century Fiction*, *Journal for Early Modern Cultural Studies*, and *The Review of English Studies*.

# THE RHETORIC OF DIVERSION IN ENGLISH LITERATURE AND CULTURE, 1690–1760

DARRYL P. DOMINGO

*University of Memphis*

CAMBRIDGE
UNIVERSITY PRESS

# CAMBRIDGE
## UNIVERSITY PRESS

University Printing House, Cambridge CB2 8BS, United Kingdom

One Liberty Plaza, 20th Floor, New York, NY 10006, USA

477 Williamstown Road, Port Melbourne, VIC 3207, Australia

314-321, 3rd Floor, Plot 3, Splendor Forum, Jasola District Centre, New Delhi - 110025, India

79 Anson Road, #06-04/06, Singapore 079906

Cambridge University Press is part of the University of Cambridge.

It furthers the University's mission by disseminating knowledge in the pursuit of education, learning and research at the highest international levels of excellence.

www.cambridge.org
Information on this title: www.cambridge.org/9781316509456

© Darryl P. Domingo 2016

First published 2016
First paperback edition 2018

*A catalogue record for this publication is available from the British Library*

*Library of Congress Cataloging in Publication data*
Domingo, Darryl P., author.
The rhetoric of diversion in English literature and culture, 1690–1760 / Darryl P. Domingo.
Cambridge ; New York : Cambridge University Press, 2016. | Includes bibliographical references and index.
LCCN 2015042968 | ISBN 9781107145801
LCSH: English literature – 18th century – History and criticism. | Recreation in literature. | Recreation – Great Britain – History – 18th century.
LCC PR448.R44 D66 2016 | DDC 820.9/3579–dc23
LC record available at http://lccn.loc.gov/2015042968

ISBN 978-1-107-14627-3 Hardback
ISBN 978-1-316-50945-6 Paperback

# THE RHETORIC OF DIVERSION IN ENGLISH LITERATURE AND CULTURE, 1690–1760

DARRYL P. DOMINGO

*University of Memphis*

CAMBRIDGE
UNIVERSITY PRESS

# CAMBRIDGE
## UNIVERSITY PRESS

University Printing House, Cambridge CB2 8BS, United Kingdom

One Liberty Plaza, 20th Floor, New York, NY 10006, USA

477 Williamstown Road, Port Melbourne, VIC 3207, Australia

314-321, 3rd Floor, Plot 3, Splendor Forum, Jasola District Centre, New Delhi - 110025, India

79 Anson Road, #06-04/06, Singapore 079906

Cambridge University Press is part of the University of Cambridge.

It furthers the University's mission by disseminating knowledge in the pursuit of education, learning and research at the highest international levels of excellence.

www.cambridge.org
Information on this title: www.cambridge.org/9781316509456

© Darryl P. Domingo 2016

First published 2016
First paperback edition 2018

*A catalogue record for this publication is available from the British Library*

*Library of Congress Cataloging in Publication data*
Domingo, Darryl P., author.
The rhetoric of diversion in English literature and culture, 1690–1760 / Darryl P. Domingo.
Cambridge ; New York : Cambridge University Press, 2016. | Includes bibliographical references and index.
LCCN 2015042968 | ISBN 9781107145801
LCSH: English literature – 18th century – History and criticism. | Recreation in literature. | Recreation – Great Britain – History – 18th century.
LCC PR448.R44 D66 2016 | DDC 820.9/3579–dc23
LC record available at http://lccn.loc.gov/2015042968

ISBN 978-1-107-14627-3 Hardback
ISBN 978-1-316-50945-6 Paperback

*For S. M. G., my most gratifying diversion*

# Contents

List of figures                                                          *page* viii
Acknowledgements                                                                   x

"Unbending the mind": introduction by way of diversion                             1

1  "The *predominant* taste of the present age": diversion
   and the literary market                                                        26

2  "Pleas'd at being so agreeably deceiv'd": pantomime
   and the poetics of dumb wit                                                    81

3  "Fasten'd by the eyes": popular wonder, print culture,
   and the exhibition of monstrosity                                            122

4  "Pleasantry for thy entertainment": novelistic discourse
   and the rhetoric of diversion                                                178

"The soul of reading": conclusion by way of animadversion                       214

Notes                                                                           223
Bibliography                                                                    276
Index                                                                           295

vii

# Figures

1  James Ralph, *The Touch-Stone* (1728), title page. Photo courtesy of   *page* 29
   the Newberry Library, Chicago (Case V 1845.735).
2  Marcellus Laroon, *The Cryes of the City of London* (1711), plate 68.   38
   Courtesy of the William Andrews Clark Memorial Library,
   University of California, Los Angeles.
3  Ad for "FAWKES's *Theatre*," *The Daily Post* No. 2302 (February 8,   41
   1727). Courtesy of the Bodleian Library, University of Oxford (John
   Johnson Collection: London Play Places, Box 7, No. 35).
4  *The Fair in an Uproar: or, The Dancing-Doggs* (1707). Photo courtesy   46
   of the Newberry Library, Chicago (Broadside in Luttrell Collection
   Centre Case 6A 159 No. 65).
5  James Ralph, *The Touch-Stone* (1728), p. 155. Photo courtesy of the   61
   Newberry Library, Chicago (Case V 1845.735).
6  Anonymous print of John Rich as Harlequin Doctor Faustus   88
   (c. 1720s). Courtesy of the Harvard Theatre Collection, Houghton
   Library, Harvard University.
7  James Miller, *Harlequin-Horace: or, The Art of Modern Poetry* (1731),   116
   frontispiece. Reproduced from the Author's Collection.
8  *The Odes and Satyrs of Horace* (1715). Reproduced from the Author's   117
   Collection.
9  Broadside ad for "Mr. Matthew Buchinger" (1724). Courtesy of the   124
   Bodleian Library, University of Oxford (John Johnson Collection:
   Human Freaks, Box 2, No. 48).
10  *The Works of Mr. Thomas Brown, Serious and Comical*, 5th edn.   132
   (1719–20), frontispiece to vol. 3. Reproduced from the Author's
   Collection.
11  *The Philosophical Transactions (From the Year 1732, to the Year 1744)*,   151
   ed. John Martyn, Vol. IX (1747), fig. 145. Courtesy of the William
   Andrews Clark Memorial Library, University of California, Los
   Angeles.

12 Jonathan Swift, *A Tale of a Tub*, 5th edn. (1710), p. 42. Reproduced      162
   from the Author's Collection.
13 Handbill for "ONE of the greatest Curiosities in Nature" (c. 1736).        164
   © British Library Board (B. L. N. Tab.2026/25 No. 42).
14 John Dunton, *A Voyage Round the World: or, A Pocket Library* (1691),       168
   title page. Photo courtesy of the Newberry Library, Chicago (Case Y
   1565.D925).
15 Thomas D'Urfey, *An Essay Towards the Theory of the Intelligible*          173
   *World* (1708), pp. 162–63. Photo courtesy of the Newberry Library,
   Chicago (Case Y 145.D94).

# *Acknowledgements*

This book began, appropriately enough, with an idle claim made in a Toronto coffeehouse: eighteenth-century digressions *are pleasurable*. Over the course of the last decade, many friends and colleagues – pleasure seekers, all – have encouraged me to test this claim and challenged me with their demanding questions: Why did eighteenth-century writers employ digression? Did their readers actually enjoy it? Why did digressive wit become so pervasive during this period? How is it conceptualized? In what ways is eighteenth-century digression different from early modern or medieval or classical digression? Why do twenty-first-century readers have a distaste for devices that divert them from the straight-and-narrow of discourse? *The Rhetoric of Diversion* is a modest attempt to answer some of these questions and, more importantly, to repay the generosity of many people from whom I have received instruction and delight.

I was first introduced to the pleasures of eighteenth-century literature and culture at the University of Toronto, where the earliest drafts of this book were written. Brian Corman, John Baird, and Susan Lamb read my work with rigour and good humour, restraining my youthful sallies into self-parody and preventing me from being diverted from my discussion of digression or digressing too far from my study of diversion. Deidre Lynch suggested that I analyse the dead metaphor of "unbending" and consider the role of the passions in the experience of pleasure. Simon Dickie forced me to rethink many of my naïve assumptions about reason, order, and propriety in the English Enlightenment. Paul Stevens helped me to navigate the perils of "professionalization." And Tom Keymer offered essential feedback at various stages in the long researching, writing, and revising process. His friendship and exacting scholarship remain one of my most valuable resources. Thanks as well to Piers Brown, Christopher Hicklin, Katie Larson, Roderick McKeown, and Rebecca Tierney-Hynes – Toronto colleagues, past and present – for their intellectual and emotional support.

I am fortunate to work in a field that seems constitutionally dedicated to conversation, and I have benefited greatly from exchanges at conferences, in libraries and archives, and during workshops where, like James Ralph's coffeehouse, "all critical Affairs are bandy'd *pro* and *con*." I am sincerely grateful for the kindness and collegiality of, among many others, Misty Anderson, Andrew Bricker, Frans DeBruyn, Christopher Fanning, Katie Gemmill, Michael Genovese, Sören Hammerschmidt, Tonya Howe, Heather Ladd, Tom Lockwood, Holly Luhning, Jack Lynch, Don Nichol, Hugh Ormsby-Lennon, Brad Pasanek, Carol Percy, John Richetti, Pat Rogers, Seth Rudy, Peter Sabor, Betty Schellenberg, Laura Stenberg, Eugenia Zuroski-Jenkins, &c. Thanks particularly to those colleagues who read the prospectus and portions of the manuscript, sharing vital insights that have made the published book immeasurably better. Lisa Freeman encouraged me to sharpen my analysis of literary self-consciousness and to refine my treatment of the commodification of reading. Rob Hume gave me excellent advice on how to avoid the pitfalls of historical scholarship. And Barbara Benedict read an early version of the manuscript, providing thoughtful commentary on almost every page and suggesting revisions that I am confident have made my "rhetoric" more *persuasive*.

I am very happy to have found an academic home in the Department of English at the University of Memphis, where I get to work every day with a talented group of scholars, teachers, and administrators. Special thanks are due to Cristina Maria Cervone, Shelby Crosby, Donal Harris, Carey Mickalites, John David Miles, Joshua Phillips, Jeffrey Scraba, Stephen Tabachnick and Laura Wright, none of whom study eighteenth-century England, but all of whom took a keen interest in my research and contributed in important ways to the completion of this book. Thanks as well to R. Scott Garner, at Rhodes College, for his expert assistance in putting together an expansive index that ranges between the learned (Pausanias) and the leisurely (Pinkethman). And thanks to my research assistant, Jenni Nettleton, who skilfully edited my unwieldy notes and compiled my bibliography. Finally, thanks to the students in my spring 2014 graduate seminar on "Leisure and Literature in the Long Eighteenth Century," whose unexpected observations complicated my views and inevitably taught me new things about the period.

At Cambridge University Press, I have been privileged to work with an editor who is also a distinguished scholar in my own field. Linda Bree saw enough potential in this book project to take it to readers and before the Press Syndicate, and I am deeply appreciative of her guidance, patience, and sound judgement. Thanks as well to Anna Bond at CUP, who cheerfully dealt with middle-of-the-night messages about matters of production, and helped ease the book's transition from manuscript to print. Thanks, finally, to the anonymous readers for the press, who said some nice things and prevented me from saying some foolish things. The readers engaged seriously with my study of amusement and challenged my arguments in productive ways. The book is very much improved for having passed through their hands.

Research for *The Rhetoric of Diversion* has been generously funded through fellowships and grants from the University of Toronto, the Social Sciences and Humanities Research Council of Canada, the Canadian Society for Eighteenth-Century Studies, the American Society for Eighteenth-Century Studies, the UCLA Center for Seventeenth- and Eighteenth-Century Studies, and the College of Arts and Sciences at the University of Memphis. Much of the research in this book is based upon readings of rare primary sources, and I am enormously grateful for the assistance of the librarians and staff at some of the world's great repositories of eighteenth-century print culture: the Thomas Fisher Rare Book Library at the University of Toronto, the British Library in London, the Bodleian Library at the University of Oxford, the Folger Shakespeare Library in Washington, the Houghton Library at Harvard University, the Newberry Library in Chicago, and the William Andrews Clark Memorial Library at UCLA. Thanks especially to Paul Gehl and Jill Gage at the Newberry, who directed me to the Luttrell collection of broadsides and chatted with me at length about Pinkethman's "Dancing Doggs." Thanks as well to Scott Jacobs and the staff at the Clark, who made my time in LA as pleasurable as the diversions in my book.

Material from the Introduction and Chapter 1 appeared, in a rather different form, as "Unbending the Mind: Commercialized Leisure and the Rhetoric of Eighteenth-Century Diversion," first published in *Eighteenth-Century Studies* 45.2 (2012): 207–36. Portions of Chapter 2 appeared as "'The Natural Propensity of Imitation': or, Pantomimic Poetics and the Rhetoric of Augustan Wit," first published in the *Journal for Early Modern Cultural Studies* 9.2 (2009): 51–95. I would like to acknowledge the Johns Hopkins University Press and the University of Pennsylvania Press, respectively, for permission to reprint this material here.

Last, but never least, thank you to my parents, Ian and Christine; my siblings, Janice, David, and Teresa; and my in-laws, Robert, Marilyn, and Patrick, whose enthusiasm for my enthusiasms pervades every page of this book. Without their unflagging support, *The Rhetoric of Diversion* would not have been possible. Most profoundly, thank you to Suzanne Grégoire, whom I met just as I was beginning this study and whom I married just as I was completing it. It is Suzanne who reminded me that my book would be dull indeed were I not to unbend my own mind every now and then. She has made my life happier and healthier and ever more diverting. This book is dedicated, with all my love and admiration, to her – though she would probably prefer that I simply take a weekend off from work.

# "Unbending the mind": introduction by way of diversion

I div'd not into the political Principles of any State, but knew to a Tittle, what City had the most elegant Buildings, the best judg'd Amusements, or the finest Women. I troubled not my Head about the endless Controversies in Religion, nor enquir'd where I came, which flourish'd, which was tolerated, or which oppress'd: But I narrowly inspected the Architecture and Ornaments of their Churches; observ'd how the Rules of the Antients and Moderns agreed, and compar'd the Beauties and Proportions of the several Orders. I never sought the Conversation of their Divines, Philosophers, or Astrologers; but became intimate with every Poet, Critick, Painter and Statuary, each different Country call'd eminent. In short, I principally study'd the Fundamentals of the publick Amusements most follow'd, wherever I came; I judiciously weigh'd the minutest Particulars in all Entertainments exhibited in OPERA or PLAY-HOUSES; both on this, and t'other Side the Alps. I read attentively all the French and Italian Criticks: I could repeat the greatest Part of three hundred and thirteen German Commentators; and went to the Bottom of all the Low-Dutch Authors who commented upon them. Then considering that Speculation is but barely a Foundation in every thing, which Practice can only compleat, I sung the chief Part of an OPERA, at Paris, a whole Winter, and with equal Applause appear'd as the Hero of a Tragedy at Amsterdam. Thus loaded with critical Learning, and cloath'd with necessary Experience, I return'd to my native Country, and have, since that Time, liv'd in publick, yet unknown, making my Studies my Amusements, always pleasing and improving my Mind by the noted Entertainments of the Town.
– Ralph, *The Touch-Stone: or, Historical, Critical, Political, Philosophical, and Theological Essays on the Reigning Diversions of the Town* (1728)

Like *The Touch-Stone*, this book is a study of amusement which makes an amusement out of study. Endeavouring to delight and instruct as well as to "unbend" the mind, it describes the anxious fascination of eighteenth-century writers with the "Reigning Diversions of the Town," while

attempting to account for the enormous pleasure eighteenth-century readers seem to have taken in the characteristically digressive representation of
these diversions. The book surveys conceptions of diversion during a
particularly dynamic period of English cultural history, in which leisure
was being produced in entirely new ways and consumed on an increasingly
commercial basis. Commercialized leisure was one of the "incontestable
signs" of growing affluence that historians since J.H. Plumb have identified
with the birth of a consumer society in England. According to Plumb,
commercialization "can be discerned in the 1690s, and in 1750 and 1760
leisure was becoming an industry with great potentiality for growth."[1]
Following Plumb, I analyse the years between approximately 1690 and
1760, not simply because I too am interested in the discovery that "*leisure
could be turned to profit*," but because this formative period in the "commercialization of leisure" coincided with a range of related shifts which, as a
number of more recent scholars have observed, brought about significant
changes in the relationship between English literature and culture –
changes exemplified by my epigraph's pairing of "Authors" and
"Criticks" with "the Fundamentals of the publick Amusements."

For Lawrence Klein, the period witnesses the advent of a "bourgeois
public sphere," created by print, cultivated in coffeehouses, and constituted by "polite" and inclusive discussion of aesthetics, policy, natural
philosophy, and social life. For Harold Love, the period is marked by an
antagonism between "polite" and "popular," which materializes in
response to the transition from an aristocratic scribal culture to a more
democratic print culture. For Brean Hammond, the expansion of print
during this period facilitates, and is facilitated by, the growth of a professional class of writers who unabashedly seek to supply the demands of a
market of readers. And this market, as J. Paul Hunter argues, necessarily
altered the modes of literary production by rejecting conventional genres
and styles in favour of "news and new things" – the recognized speciality of
Grub Street. According to Erin Mackie, the period sees the emergence of a
new mode of being as well, a nascent sense of self that was ironically
realized through social consumption – staring in shop-windows, wearing
hoop-petticoats, perusing fashionable literature, and paying for pleasure –
in a maturing market economy. William B. Warner associates this commercial demand for pleasure with the "elevation" of novel reading from
1684 to 1750, in that the eponymously "new" genre seemed shamelessly to
appeal to public taste and threatened, in turn, to recast all poems, plays,
periodicals, and prose works as a "mode of entertainment." In the opinion
of John O'Brien, the modern conception of entertainment itself, as a "form

of diversion directed to a mass culture," develops in the closing years of the seventeenth century and the first half of the eighteenth century. And, finally, for Patricia Meyer Spacks, the roughly seventy-year period culminates with the invention of "boredom" as a psychological category denoting a failure to entertain or engage the attention, and thereby claiming "interest" as the sine qua non of all pleasurable discourse.[2] The commercialization of leisure therefore coincides with the cultural moment at which writing began self-consciously to resist boredom and reading began to expect it to do so. While showmen and impresarios actively catered to the eclectic and often eccentric desires of England's pleasure seekers, professional authors "to be lett" looked for innovative ways to gratify a reading audience increasingly avid for diversion.

Taken together, these shifts comprise what has been seen as a "cultural revolution" in England between the lapse of the Licensing Act (1695) and the case of *Donaldson vs. Beckett* (1774); between the opening of Don Saltero's coffeehouse of curiosities (1695) and the foundation of the British Museum (1753); between Collier's attack on theatrical entertainment (1698) and Zoffany's commemorative portrait of *David Garrick as Sir John Brute* (1765); and between the "Glorious Revolution" (1688) and the accession of the George III (1760), whose wide reading and interest in theatre and sport made him peculiarly appreciative of the pleasures of the imagination.[3] What has less often been noticed is that this broad revolution in culture also coincided with something of a "discursive revolution" in English literature, since this was also the historical context in which popular writing came to be distinguished by its propensity for disruption and by a fashion for what Wayne Booth identified in the 1950s as "intrusive play" and "self-conscious narration."[4] The period between the experiments of John Dunton (1690s) and the extravagancies of Laurence Sterne (1760s) is characterized by an increasing awareness of the rhetorical possibilities of devices usually perceived to go beyond mimetic decorum and to flout the prevailing standards of English neoclassicism, devices associated with false, abusive, or catachrestic wit, textual and typographical play, and, most pervasively, digression. This "genealogy" was in fact recognized during the period itself. In the wake of *Tristram Shandy* (1759–67), where Sterne famously described digression as the "the life, the soul of reading," an enterprising publisher "revised," "corrected," and reprinted Volume I of Dunton's self-reflexively rambling prose narrative, *A Voyage Round the World* (1691), as *The Life, Travels, and Adventures of Christopher Wagstaff, Gentleman, Grandfather to Tristram Shandy* (1762).[5] Claiming plausibly that Sterne is "under *some obligations*" to the author of the earlier work, the editor of the reprint identifies several similarities in "the general turn of the stile" and in "the method of *protraction*, or art of *continuation*, where by either performance might be *lengthened out* to the utmost extent of the reader's *patience*, or author's *imagination*." Yet because each "motley production" engages primarily "by its singularity," the editor ultimately argues that both works are "chiefly calculated" for "the amusement and entertainment of such as are willing to be pleased they care not how, or why."[6] *The Rhetoric of Diversion* seeks to account for why authors "calculated" their writing for "amusement and entertainment," and how the "motley productions" they published "pleased" readers. The book opens by asking why the period during which the pursuit of pleasure for its own sake was gradually legitimized happens also to be the period during which intrusion, obstruction, and interruption first began to thrive as conspicuous aesthetic techniques. It answers this question through a series of close readings that reveal the complex reciprocity between commercialized leisure and commercial literature in late seventeenth- and early eighteenth-century English culture.

In discussing what I view as the coming of age of devices like digression, I do not of course mean to suggest that digressive wit was invented, much less perfected, in the seventy or so years between Dunton and Sterne. Indeed, following in the oratorical tradition of Cicero and Quintilian, early modern rhetoricians like George Puttenham had sanctioned tropes and figures of "tollerable disorder" as a convenient way of giving pleasing variety to a work and of surprising through the "noueltie" of expressions distinct from the "ordinary and accustomed." Versatile devices such as the *hyperbaton* and the *parenthesis* were a constitutive part of what was then conceived of as "ornament poeticall," in that they adorned a work while providing "fresh objects of interest" to divert the active mind.[7] Critics have long been interested in understanding the meaning of the "Taffeta phrases" and "Figures pedantical" that feature in Shakespeare's comedies, the bookish copia that structures Burton's *Anatomy of Melancholy* (1621–38), and the "digressive voices" foregrounded in Marvell's *Upon Appleton House* (c. 1651), Browne's *Garden of Cyrus* (1658), and Milton's *Paradise Lost* (1667–74).[8] More to the point, they have demonstrated the deep influence on eighteenth-century English writers of Thomas Shelton's early edition of Cervantes (1612–20), Charles Cotton's popular translation of Montaigne (1685), and Urquhart and Motteux's textually exuberant edition of Rabelais (1708), each of which provided an important pattern for digressive writing.[9] But under a new literary-critical regime, influenced by the linguistic proscriptions of the Royal Society and distinguished by a shift in taste from rhetorical display to formal unity and harmony, the tolerability of "disorder" came to be a subject of discourse in its own right.[10] What changes, therefore, is the degree of "self-consciousness" with which these kinds of devices are treated, both by writers who brazenly defend their refusal to be restrained and by readers who comment upon their experience of "over-strained" metaphors, "*typographical* figures," "digressions upon digression," or, as Dunton's eighteenth-century editor puts it on his title page, "OUT-OF-THE-WAY" writing.

### Reading and diversionary rhetoric, 1690–1760

Ever since the publication of *The Rhetoric of Fiction* (1961), Booth's seminal study of literary self-consciousness, scholars have taken for granted that although such devices may seem "disruptive and inartistic," they are paradoxically but precisely what gives many of the works published during this period their "formal coherence."[11] Discussion of disruption has thus routinely focused on the methods through which a real or fictional "author" makes known his meaning and draws attention to the "written-ness" or "printed-ness" or "crafted-ness" of his own work. Expanding upon Booth's emphasis on the "notion of function," scholars have stressed the purported epistemological motives for linguistic and textual disruption, and have argued for the critical importance of laying bare the artificiality of literature and, by extension, of social and political institutions – of "consciousness-raising." The result has been a tendency to place literary self-consciousness, as Christina Lupton has wryly warned, "on the side of the critic who exposed the true operation of discourse, typically in spite of an author's attempt to use words as transparently as possible."[12] So, for instance, Garry Sherbert contends that the figurative excess that usually distinguishes the learned "Anatomy" or Menippean satire foregrounds the arbitrariness of language and "symbolizes, ironically, the difficulty of communication." Christopher Flint identifies the rows of asterisks that frequently punctuate eighteenth-century works as a passionate resistance to the "alienation" and "anonymity" imposed by the "mechanics of the print industry." And J. Paul Hunter explains the obtrusiveness of many of the period's narrators as an attempt to control "the process of creation" and "the nature of response."[13] Drawing compelling evidence from the reflexive asides of authors who apologize for their disruptive rhetoric, such arguments point to important critical cruces. Yet in giving priority to the reasons why a writer might *employ* the devices of digressive wit, scholars have neglected to ask how a reader might *enjoy* them. Just as significantly, they have failed to recognize a feature of these devices that might help to

answer this question as well as account for their ascendance at this particular time and place: the fact that self-conscious authors regularly describe
their intrusions, obstructions, and interruptions through the language of
contemporary diversion.

   While rambling, for example, through the streets of turn-of-the-century
London, Tom Brown excuses the digressions in his *Amusements Serious and
Comical* (1700) on the grounds that they "properly belong to my Subject,
since they are all *nothing but Amusements.*" John Dunton compares the
narrative enigmas of his *Voyage Round the World* (1691) to playing "at *Bob-
cherry*" and his mischievous conceits to the antics of a "*Merry Andrew,*
clapping his Conjuring-Cap on." The Grub Street speaker of Jonathan
Swift's *A Tale of a Tub* (1704–10) identifies the paratextual conventions of
"*Prefaces, Epistles, Advertisements, Introductions, Prolegomena's, Apparatus's,*
[and] *To-the-Reader's*" with the commercial tactics of "*Monster-mongers*
and other *Retailers of strange Sights.*" Richard Blackmore justifies the
extended similes in his epic poetry by asserting that the "Exercise of Wit"
excels "all other Recreations," including "Country Sports" and the "politer
Diversions of Balls and Operas." A "good sizable *Hiatus*" in the text of
Thomas D'Urfey's *An Essay Towards the Theory of the Intelligible World*
(1708) is made an occasion for wonder and delight by being associated with
the "private Aperture" in a Savoyard's raree-show. In the preface to his
scandal narrative, *All for the Better; or, The World Turn'd Up-Side Down*
(1720), Charles Gildon disclaims that he has interspersed his
"Argumentations with several Fables or Novels, which, like the Musick
between the *Acts* of a *Play*, serve to relieve the Mind from less agreeable
Pursuits." Alexander Pope has Martinus Scriblerus draw an analogy
between the popular appeal of bathetic tropes and figures and the ballyhoo
of a "Master of a Show in Smithfield." Colley Cibber likens a "Rhapsody"
that distracts him from the "Historical View of the Stage" in his autobiographical *Apology* (1740) to a "Dance between the Acts," which makes up
"for the Dullness of what would have been by itself only proper." Henry
Fielding has the impertinent narrator of *Tom Jones* (1749) refer to his
rhetorically inflated and mock-heroic passages as a "mental
Entertainment." And in *The Touch-Stone: or, Historical, Critical,
Political, Philosophical, and Theological Essays on the Reigning Diversions of
the Town* (1728), James Ralph, popular journalist, pamphleteer, and eventual assistant manager of the Little Theatre in the Haymarket, digresses
from his survey of what he calls the "most taking" of London amusements
in order to comment self-consciously on what he acknowledges to be his
oddly singular style: "as no Author can pretend, in Writing, to please the

various Humours and Desires of Mankind; let him but leave some Parts of his Work imperfect, and every Man, in finding out the Meaning, will undoubtedly strive to please himself."[14]

In manner, if not necessarily in matter, Ralph's digression exemplifies the subject of his series of essays, even as it seems to stray from the "Reigning Diversions." For digression, as *The Touch-Stone* appears to suggest, has a similar effect on readers as diversion was believed to have on eighteenth-century pleasure seekers. As a noun "diversion" refers to any pastime, sport, or recreation that is engaged for the purposes of "entertainment" (*O.E.D.* 4.b). But as a derivative of the verb "divert," the term also denotes a "turning aside" from "a settled or particular course of action," from "the business in hand," or from "one's regular occupation" (*O.E.D.* 2).[15] The fact that *The Touch-Stone* turns aside from its apology for the "noted Entertainments" in order to defend the pleasures of "imperfect" writing points to a semantic overlap between what I classify as "cultural diversion" and "discursive diversion" – between social amusements which provide relief from the serious concerns of daily life and rhetorical devices which characteristically disrupt so much of the discourse of the period. Writers of the period not only recognized this overlap, but exploited it in order to satisfy the new cultural demand for diversion by way of the formal idiosyncrasies of their work: through, for example, luxuriant, illogical, and mixed metaphors, typographical blanks and lacunae, interpolated tales, burlesque erudition, and the devices of digressive wit. Such devices enact at the linguistic and textual level the nature and purpose of eighteenth-century diversion: they "unbend the mind," to use Samuel Johnson's definition, "by turning it off from care," and thereby achieve an ironic verisimilitude through a kind of formal parody of the "Reigning Diversions of the Town."[16] As Paul Keen has recently demonstrated, eighteenth-century debates over literature were "necessarily embedded" within the proliferation of commercial spectacles and entertainments.[17] The harlequinades mounted by John Rich and John Thurmond, the human and animal oddities exhibited at Bartholomew Fair, and, in general, the busy round of amusements offered around every corner and in every street and "*over-against*" every London establishment provided a useful context in which writers could negotiate the difficulties of communication, the problems associated with the explosion of print, and the relationship between aesthetic creation and reader-response. But they also served as a rhetorical model whose form and function reminded writers of their obligation to distract readers temporarily from any such serious issues, to refresh and invigorate the minds of those bored or wearied by straightforward discourse in the same way as contemporary diversion relieved those exhausted by the severity and monotony of routine labour.

Baroque literary theory had located the motive for "distraction" in what Robert L. Montgomery describes as "our impatience and our boredom, in our need for entertainment and diversion."[18] In the period between approximately 1690 and 1760, this traditional motive is re-configured by market-savvy writers who boldly associate the "pleasures of the text" with the actual "pleasures of the town," and who identify the threat of boredom as the main impetus behind disruptive ornament. Commercialization brought about a higher valuation of work as an important activity in itself, and of leisure as a "differentiated psychic space" which served as a foil to the tedium of progress and an alternative to work's forward momentum.[19] Commercial literature did something of the same by providing for "differentiated discursive spaces," time away from plot, character, or thematic argument in which readers could also have their minds unbent. Devices like digression played to both the material and mental needs of a pleasure-seeking public, furnishing a market that was actively assimilating contemporary theories of mind as a justification for commercial diversion. However, as this book will demonstrate, digressions were able to do so because the self-conscious authors who employed them took for granted a reading public who expected intrinsic leisure for their literature. As James Ralph puts it: "to ride Post thro' any Treatise, without Stop, Guess-work, scratching the Noddle, or grope in the Dark, is as insipid as a Fox-chace without Fatigue" (xxiv). Literature, like life, becomes dull without occasional diversion. Far from being out of place, therefore, Ralph's digressions ensure that his readers will be entertained, that their varied interests will be engaged, and, consequently, that they will be persuaded to continue reading.

In delineating a rhetoric of diversion, this book says something new about the material pleasures of art, by bringing together two previously distinct fields of critical inquiry: the history of English leisure and the development of self-conscious literature. Along the way, it re-evaluates some of the assumptions of cultural historians *and* literary historians who have tended to employ overwrought methodologies that, in my opinion, separate diversionary rhetoric from the "Reigning Diversions," and the "Reigning Diversions" from their original function as pleasurable amusement. When, in 1986, Terry Castle published her enormously influential study of the masquerade motif in eighteenth-century English fiction, she could claim that "the history of human pleasures has seldom met with the same dignified attention accorded to the history of human suffering." With

the obvious exception of theatre, Castle argued that cultural and literary history has tended to deny "intellectual significance" to such activities as "festivity, games, jokes, and amusements."[20] The past twenty-five years, however, have more than made up for this deficiency: pleasures as diverse as curiosity collecting, freak shows, pantomime, jest-books, opera, social clubs, coffeehouses, organized sports, ballooning, scientific exhibitions, pleasure resorts, waxworks, puppet shows, window-shopping, and novel reading, to name just a few, have received extensive and conspicuously "intellectual" treatment from scholars in a wide range of disciplines. In fact, so intellectual has much of this research proven that the pleasure of the original activities has seemed sometimes in danger of being overwhelmed by heady scholarly fireworks – the academic equivalent of another favourite diversion. Eighteenth-century amusement has been particularly receptive to elaborate New Historicist readings that have discovered in London's leisure activities an important site of ideological conflict and modern identity formation.

For example, in his important book on the development of pantomime and its influence on eighteenth-century British culture, John O'Brien emphasizes the anxiety produced by "pantomime's populist impulses," demonstrating how and why, in a culture of increasing censorship and surveillance, the antics of Harlequin could provide subversive commentary under the guise of disinterested entertainment. Eliding the more "local pleasures" of, say, the Lincoln's Inn Fields production of *Perseus and Andromeda: or, The Spaniard Outwitted* (1730), O'Brien explains pantomime's potential threat to "the state's power" while championing Harlequin as "a point around which vectors of deference and resistance gather." O'Brien takes the genre's "ideological" implications so seriously that he organizes the argument of his book around discussions of what he views as "pantomime's *unconscious*." Yet, as even O'Brien concedes, it is difficult to pursue such an argument "without some equivocation," given that it was obviously pantomime's very "conscious" elements – the raucous dances, elaborate stage effects, mechanical tricks, sudden appearances and disappearances, and startling transformations – that tended to seize the attention of audiences.[21] To speculate on the ways in which Harlequin undermined hegemonic authority is thus to overlook somewhat the most likely reasons for which the English public flocked to see John Rich, as Harlequin, transform himself into a spaniel or a "Statue of MERCURY."

In a similar manner, Dennis Todd explains away some of the wonder and delight of the fairground "freaks" he treats in his book on eighteenth-century monstrosity, by implicating them in learned debates over the power of imagination and the problematic nature of human identity. Todd explores the mental and physical "*frisson*" between "the monstrous" and "the normal," arguing that the dynamics of sightseeing made the viewer who gazed, stared, and gaped at monsters on display "mindful of the very mindlessness the spectacle produces in him."[22] But were the sightseers who crowded, in 1736, into "the *Rummer* in *Three King Court*, Fleet-Street" to gawk at "a BOY and GIRL, WITH two distinct Heads and Necks, and but one Body, three Arms, and three Legs, and Feet, and 1 Foot with six Toes" really so self-aware? And to what extent can erudite treatises on philosophy, embryology, or ontology help to account for how the ordinary Londoner would actually have experienced "ONE of the greatest Curiosities in Nature"?

In her fascinating study of early modern inquiry, Barbara M. Benedict attempts to answer such questions by analysing "curiosity" itself, showing how and why the "passion" and its related "habits" came to function as an index to many of the cultural anxieties of the English during the seventeenth and eighteenth centuries, anxieties related to rapid urbanization and commercialization, the institutionalization of empirical science, the democratization of print, the infringement of women into the public sphere, and the topographical and temporal expansion of leisure. Benedict discusses the gradual commoditization of curiosity and its reifying effects on curious men and women, whose unbridled enthusiasm for the "Rarities" and "Novelties" on display at Gresham College or the performance of a "Bottle Conjuror" at Covent Garden, threatened to turn them into objects of curiosity.[23] Yet like O'Brien and Todd, Benedict uses her substantial research into the "Reigning Diversions of the Town" as a means to some other critical end. Instead of treating diversion as a subject that is valuable in its own right, Benedict moves in short order from a provocative material reading of how curiosity was perceived and consumed by "The Curious Eye" to complicated conceptual readings of "Women as Closeted Curiosities" and "Curiosity in the Mental Cabinet."

Julie Park does much the same in her recent book on the "correspondences" between the emergence of the genre of the novel and the fashion for new diversions and "novel objects" in eighteenth-century Britain. Park ingeniously analyses the meaning of novelty, tracing its development during the period as a "general aesthetic category," a "psychological stimulant," and, most importantly, a "feature of consumer experience." Drawing together these strains of novel discourse, she explains the multiple ways in which lifelike commodities such as dolls and popular entertainments like waxworks, automata, and puppet-shows simulated the lived reality of readers and, in so doing, provided writers with "complex mimetic strategies." Park, however, goes even further to suggest that the "mere imitations" exhibited at, for instance, Charlotte Charke's puppet theatre in James Street or James Cox's Museum in Spring Gardens contributed vitally to the rise of "modern subjectivity." Indeed, as if to exemplify Castle's concern that amusements are rarely perceived to be sufficiently "dignified" to warrant scholarly "attention," Park hyperbolically treats contemporary discussion of the "allure" of mechanical entertainments as "a rich and exotic idiom of selfhood." As a result, what begins as an original discussion of the undeniable pleasures of "consuming novelty" ends as yet another study in which "metropolitan scenes of pleasure and leisure" are used primarily to explore eighteenth-century "models of the self."[24]

Brian Cowan uses his detailed study of British coffeehouse culture as a context through which to debate the efficacy as a concept of the Habermasian "bourgeois public sphere." Rather than focussing on the supply end of the "commodity chain," Cowan explores "the subjective motivations for consumption expressed by the consumers themselves." However, these consumers, in Cowan's analysis at least, tend to be "polite" and "enlightened" individuals who appear less interested in the commodity as such than in its increasing cultural capital during the period. Cowan wishes to see the coffeehouse as a hub of intellectual and political activity, but this obliges him to assume that consumers drank deep with their minds at the expense of their bodies. Although his concern is to explain why precisely coffee was desirable, Cowan often neglects the physiological and psychological effects of a caffeinated beverage that was ultimately addictive. Consequently, popular coffeehouses like Bridge's, White's, and Button's cease to be recognizable as "Reigning Diversions," becoming instead "Penny Universities" that necessarily stressed "profit" over "pleasure."[25]

Even Terry Castle, whose book on masquerade demonstrates the critical usefulness of applying a cultural history approach to literary analysis, is vague about exactly why eighteenth-century pleasure seekers would have been willing to pay a great deal of money to attend one of "Count" Heidegger's "Midnight Masques" in the Haymarket. Castle brilliantly illustrates how English novelists exploited masquerade scenes as a titillating plot device, but her discussion of the features that made masquerades appealing to both readers and pleasure seekers has recourse to needless abstractions about "symbolic inversion," "*temps perdu*," "sexual frisson," and "the utopian space of the assembly room." By the end of her book, the masquerade is no longer a particular diversion held in a particular place at a particular time, but is rather a conceptual category synonymous with "the carnivalesque."[26]

Each of these studies of eighteenth-century amusement is engaging and critically important. And, as the following chapters will make clear, each has influenced my thinking and this book's treatment of its subject. But I have never been able to shake the sense that something – namely pleasure – is being lost in the translation from the "Reigning Diversions of the Town" to the reigning trends in scholarship. The same is true of the professed "pleasures of the text," which have frequently been analysed by way of abstract philosophical epithets borrowed from "Capital-T" theorists: through Derrida's ideas about "catachresis" or Barthes' conception of "*jouissance*" or, perhaps more usefully, Genette's description of *description* as a "recreational pause in the narrative."[27] Yet readers do not experience literature in abstract and philosophical ways, but in material and, I would like to think, historically identifiable ways. The purpose of this study is precisely to identify these ways, to account for how and why readers derive pleasure from certain kinds of linguistic and textual devices. Rather than placing self-consciousness "on the side of the critic," it will examine the digressiveness of eighteenth-century literature as the product of a specific cultural milieu.

*The Rhetoric of Diversion* thus contributes to the history of reading an explanation of the passions, habits, and desires of a very particular set of English readers. As recent historians of reading have reminded historians of writing, the activity of reading is as culturally specific as those of theatre-going, scientific experimentation, and even printing.[28] Modern readers cannot always assume that their response to devices like digression is comparable to that of their forebears, since attitudes towards the reading of printed texts in the eighteenth century were fundamentally different from those of the twenty-first century. This book aims to reproduce these attitudes by reproducing the commercial context that informed and shaped them. Building upon important research into the consumption of culture during the seventeenth and eighteenth centuries, the book analyses traditional literature alongside contemporary puffs and playbills, handbills and newspaper advertisements, theatre reviews, scrapbooks and diaries, graphic prints, bills of fare, question-and-answer sheets, "Trips Through the Town," and surveys of diversion like *The Touch-Stone*. In the process, it seeks to exemplify what I view as the interrelatedness during the period of cultural and literary forms, not in order to de-essentialize the boundaries between the literary and nonliterary, but to demonstrate what a new generation of Historical Formalists have identified as "the mutual interrogation of form and history."[29] Instead of relying upon the inherently conservative truisms that underlie both ideological and aesthetic analysis, *The Rhetoric of Diversion* responds to a call for a New Historicism that is sensitive to matters of form, and a Formalism that appreciates that literary devices and techniques are historically determined. The book is a "rhetoric" in the sense that it encompasses both the persuasive language used by pleasure-mongers to market commercial amusement to diverse pleasure seekers, and the techniques through which professional authors used diversion *as a rhetoric* to secure diverse readers in the commercial literary marketplace. What I hope to persuade my readers of is that the "diversions" of the late seventeenth and early eighteenth centuries were, first and foremost, diverting. If diversion signifies a delightful avocation of ordinary life, I argue that deviations from the straightforward representation of this life correspondingly mark a pleasant interval in conventional literary discourse.

## The pleasures of satire

In discussing the relationship between the period's cultural and discursive diversions, I do not seek simply to elucidate topical allusions or oblique references to the relative *content* of late seventeenth- and early eighteenth-century amusement. Rather, I reveal the degree to which the *format* of works published in the late seventeenth and early eighteenth centuries reproduces the modes of presentation peculiar to the "Reigning Diversions of the Town." The book is thus less interested in *who* played the role of Scaramouch in *Apollo and Daphne: or, Harlequin's Metamorphoses* (1726), *where* in London the curious "Hedge-hog Boy" was exhibited, or *when* Martin Powell moved his "Punch's Theatre" to the Little Piazza in Covent Garden, than in *how* and *why* such genres of amusement influenced the devices of literary genres and *what* this suggests about the sorts of diversion eagerly consumed by English pleasure seekers and readers.

Cultural and literary historians from Austin Dobson and Walter Besant to Ronald Paulson and Pat Rogers have presumed that a knowledge of popular amusement is vital to a thorough understanding of the complex "Augustan" response to popular literature.[30] This is primarily because standard satiric works like *A Tale of a Tub*, *The Dunciad* (1728–43), and *The Author's Farce* (1730, 1734) associate the commercialization of literature with the increasing commercialization of leisure, identifying the spread of pleasure-resorts and the success of professional entrepreneurs with a broader decline in cultural values. Rogers, for example, makes much of the observation that "the lifespan of the great Augustan satirists coincides with the period when sights and shows were promoted as never before," implying that, when confronted with a burgeoning leisure industry, Swift, Pope, and Fielding, like Juvenal, believed that they had no choice but to write.[31] Rogers discusses masquerade, opera, rope-dancing, posture-making, triumphal processions, puppet theatre, and fairground comedy and tragedy, all by way of contextualizing the typical subject matter of Augustan satire. What Rogers neglects, however, is the manner of this satire, as well as that of the "hack" writing it generally satirized. Certainly, the literature produced in Grub Street had its counterpart in the low diversions of London, but this, I argue, had as much to do with the fact that writers often nominated "popular" incorporated the formal contrivances of contemporary diversion into the rhetoric of their works as with the fact that the works of writers like John Dunton, Ned Ward, and Charles Gildon are largely the result of commercial opportunism. Far from simply being an idle witticism, *The Dunciad*'s prognostication that authors-turned-entertainers will bring the "Smithfield Muses to the Ear of Kings" hints at one of the reasons for the popularity of so-called popular literature: because it mimicked discursively the types of diversion being offered at Drury Lane or Bartholomew Fair or "*Fleet-Street*, just through *Temple-Bar*."[32] In turn, it suggests why Pope and other satirists of the period had frequent recourse to the "Reigning Diversions of the Town" when ridiculing the contemporary literary scene. By parodying the distinctive devices of Grub Street writers, the Augustans at once catered to and censured the new cultural demand for diversion, drawing in pleasure-seeking readers and then chiding them for their susceptibility – for the very fact of their being drawn in.

The commonplace Horatian dictum, *aut prodesse volunt aut delectare*, applied equally to leisure as to literature.[33] Just as London entertainers operated under the pretence that their sights and shows were in some way edifying, so too were satirists obliged to entertain the public if they ever hoped to edify them. For all of its didactic vigour, the efficacy of Augustan satire depended upon a certain degree of condescension to popular taste, which is why *A Tale of a Tub*, *The Dunciad*, and *The Author's Farce* seem to celebrate what they actually mean to criticize, diverting readers at the linguistic and textual level while reproaching them at the thematic level. Swift's digressions and his rows of asterisks, Pope's forced conceits and his hectoring footnotes, Fielding's off-stage commentary on his on-stage performance distract from their respective satires because distraction itself helps to communicate their meaning and message. "[S]uch is the Depravity of human Nature," explains James Ralph, "that if we are not pleas'd, we will not be instructed" (129). Part of the purpose of this book is to demonstrate the ways in which Augustan satirists achieved instruction through pleasures of a discursive kind – how they entertained their readers, engaged their interests, and persuaded them to continue reading, even while attacking their reading habits.

Recent studies of eighteenth-century satire have problematized traditional critical distinctions between "high," "middle," and "low," illustrating the deep implication of satirists in that which they satirize.[34] I expand upon this research in order to show not just that the Augustans found in commercial amusement a provocative object of satire, but that the "Reigning Diversions" gave structure and shape to their works. Responding to anxieties over shifting or collapsing boundaries in literature and culture, satirists used diversion to produce the kind of "difference" that, as Frederic V. Bogel and others have contended, could no longer be taken for granted.[35] If they wished convincingly to make their point, critics of diversion, like diversion's apologists, had to acknowledge, as Ralph does when describing "the additional Ornaments to *Stage-Entertainments*," that pleasure seekers and readers alike will "never sit out a tedious Lecture of Morality" (129–30). What both critics and apologists offered instead was a literature with its own entr'acte divertissements that served to unbend the mind whenever complications of plot, character, or argument threatened to become tiresome. In calculatedly "turning aside" from these time-honoured foci of literary analysis, *The Rhetoric of Diversion* provides an alternative account of the various consequences of commercialized leisure, one that emphasizes the forms of diversion over the mere fact of it.

The commercialization of leisure was one of the most controversial manifestations of the broader "consumer revolution" in England, which provided the economic and material basis upon which pleasure was demanded and eventually supplied. However, political barriers to retail trade and cultural prejudices against consumption meant that this process did not actually reach maturity until the third quarter of the eighteenth century, and towards the end of the period that I discuss in this book. According to Neil McKendrick, "the embryonic development" of a consumer society was under way by the late seventeenth century, but "the pregnancy had still had some way to go." Although McKendrick discovers "new consuming tastes" in England as early as the 1690s, he explains that it was only in the 1760s and 1770s that the idea of conspicuous consumption came to assume "its rightful place in models of economic growth."[36] England was not a sophisticated commercial nation until *after* 1760, and this is exactly why I examine the seventy or so years *before* 1760. It is during the period in which Plumb sees growing "signs" of commercialized leisure that commentators first begin to struggle with the perceived effects of the "Reigning Diversions" on English literature and culture. I have adopted the dates 1690–1760 because I wish to focus on a cultural context in which diversion had yet to be widely accepted or fully institutionalized and, in turn, in which it provoked the most considerable amount of anxiety and the most extensive commentary. The book demonstrates how and why anxiety itself came to be constitutive of the modern consumer economy. While satirists like Pope represent commercialization in apocalyptic terms, author-entertainers like Cibber and apologists like Ralph describe the productive *work* of leisure and attempt to legitimize it by illustrating its unbending function. I argue that it is the vigorous debate over the production and consumption of leisure during the late seventeenth and early eighteenth centuries that, in many ways, cultivated the habits of mind that made possible the consolidation of England's consumer economy in the later eighteenth century.

## The topography of pleasure

The history of commercialized leisure is necessarily also a history of London, which, during the lifetime of Swift, Pope, and Fielding, was very much a city in flux – a city expanding demographically and topographically. While the population of the rest of England stagnated, due to high mortality and low fertility rates, the population of London multiplied exponentially. In 1600 there were approximately 300,000 people living in the metropolis. By 1700, the population had grown to over 600,000 people, representing 10 per cent of the entire population of England. By 1800, London was the largest city in the world, with a population of over one million people.[37] A large number of these people were migrants from the provinces, who came to the capital in search of professional opportunities and gainful employment. In order to accommodate this growing population, the physical scale and structure of London had to change as well. The historic "City of London" comprised the square mile within the old walls, and small districts to the west at Blackfriars and to the south, across London Bridge, at Southwark. By the second half of the seventeenth century, the built-up area covered by the capital had outgrown its medieval limits, spreading westward towards the Court, eastward past the Tower and across Spitalfields, northward into rural Middlesex, and southward into Surrey. In the literary and cultural imagination, this entire urban and suburban area came to signify a single sprawling metropolis.[38] The suburbs, also known as "the Town," comprised the space between the Roman city of *Londinium* and the Danish foundation at Westminster, where the rich and aristocratic lived and took their leisure. In conscious imitation of their social betters, the middle classes were moving west as well, commuting to the Royal Exchange and Cheapside in the centre of the commercial city. Meanwhile, the poor migrated east along the river or north into St Giles-in-the-Fields or Farringdon-Without, settling in densely populated extra-mural communities and working in the precarious shipping or service industries of the capital.

Unlike other European capitals, London was at once the social, political, administrative, religious, legal, and economic centre of England's emerging empire, and these diverse institutions were inscribed in the very topography of the city. The monarchy was established at the Palace of Whitehall and Parliament sat at nearby Westminster Hall, both on the banks of the Thames. The spiritual life of the English was supervised from Lambeth House, Westminster Abbey, and St Paul's Cathedral, which had been rebuilt by Christopher Wren in the wake of Great Fire of 1666. Barristers pleaded their cases at the Inns of Court, including Temple Bar, and were trained up for the profession at Gray's Inn and Lincoln's Inn, in the vicinity of Chancery Lane and a short ride from Bridewell, Newgate, and the Old Bailey. Merchants and financiers inhabited the city centre, wheeling and dealing to supply the overseas goods and domestic manufacture that Londoners desired. In addition to being England's principal port, with safe harbour for sea-going vessels along the Thames, London was England's main manufacturing city, with a near monopoly over the luxury trades and the brewing, distilling, sugar processing, and textile industries. While the developing potential *to earn* attracted many people to the city, so too did the increasing opportunities *to spend*. As McKendrick explains, London served as "the shopwindow for the whole country."[39] The commodities of merchants, shippers, and manufacturers were seen at Smithfield, Covent Garden, Billingsgate, and a plethora of smaller markets, as well as in the upscale shops along the Strand, Oxford Street, and Paternoster Row – where consumption first became conspicuous.[40]

With so much "business" daily going on in London, and so many Londoners working to earn a living, "pleasure" was an industry as vital to the prosperity of the city as any other. Perhaps the most characteristic manifestation of the rapid urbanization of the period was the institutiona-lization of diversion into the "built environment" of the hectic metropolis, what Roy Porter describes as the "pleasure machines" through which London consumers found recreation and amusement.[41] Although commercialization had an impact outside of the metropolis, most significantly in large provincial towns such as Norwich, Bristol, Scarborough, York, and Bath, the most important developments took place in London, which was the locus of both cultural and discursive diversion – a city obsessed with pleasure and saturated by print.[42] Certainly, there were places of pleasure and printing presses elsewhere in England, but it was those that operated within the "Meridian of London" that largely defined the nature and established the tenor of the amusements it was desirable to pursue.[43] Bull-baiting in Birmingham owed something to the "sundry diversions" of Hockley-in-the-Hole. The *al fresco* tea gardens and assembly rooms at Tunbridge Wells borrowed extensively from the fashionable "West End" entertainments at Mulberry, Vauxhall, and Pall Mall. And successful provincial booksellers like William Bonny, Felix Farley, and Henry Crossgrove derived their publishing practices from Jacob Tonson, Bernard Lintott, Edward Cave, James Dodsley, and London's other leading publishers.[44]

Moreover, the hack writer was part of a peculiarly urban demographic that included theatre managers, street performers, showmen, taverners, mountebanks, fairground conjurors, and the many entrepreneurs and impresarios who purveyed pleasure to the public at large. Grub Street, after all, was situated in a topographically specific and thematically significant locale in Moorfields, in the shadow of some of London's most popular but least reputable sites of entertainment: the Windmill Tavern, where strong-man acts were often mounted; the Old Canon Foundry, which provided stages for itinerant preachers; the Flying Horse, which was celebrated for music, merry andrews, and cudgel play; and, notoriously, Bethlehem Hospital, or "Bedlam," where pleasure seekers could gawk at madmen – for a price.[45] Writing to the perceived "*Humour of the Age*," hacks frequently took London and its diversions as their subject, and exemplified this subject through their digressive style, producing what Swift summarily derides as "those monstrous Productions, which under the names of *Trips, Spies, Amusements*, and other conceited Appellations, have over-run us for some Years past." That the concurrent proliferation of actual amusements had an impact upon broader language and literature is suggested by Swift's further claim that those writers who produce "*Trips, Spies*, [and] *Amusements*" often borrow "odd Words" and "Flowers of Style" from the "Coffee-House" and the "Gaming Ordinary."[46] By the middle of the eighteenth century, London had grown large enough to support a wider range of permanent places of pleasure than previous centuries had known. And these pleasures were open to a broader spectrum of the population. While other urban industries tended to be tied to certain districts, diversion existed virtually everywhere, which is why most contemporary surveys of the "Reigning Diversions" imply the modifier "*of the Town.*" Given that London is almost inevitably the backdrop to the period's conceptualization of diversion, it is likewise the backdrop to this book, which confines itself to the "Meridian of London" because Londoners themselves could or would not confine their diversions.

Drawing upon the evidence of street literature published in the late seventeenth and early eighteenth centuries, Clare Brant and Susan E. Whyman conclude that "London's urban way of life was heady and intense, exhilarating and exasperating, but never dull."[47] The same is true of the experience of reading works that represent this way of life and that seek to stave off dullness through divertissement. If London was a locus of eighteenth-century diversion, it was also the focus of some of the most digressive writing of the period. The chapters of this book broadly discuss contemporary writing about London, explaining why the city gives such frequent occasion to digression and how these digressions effectively *write* London, capturing what might be viewed as the "cultural attention deficit disorder" of Londoners rambling the streets, reading advertisements for amusement, and looking alternately to bend or unbend their minds. The condition is summarized well by John Dunton in his *Voyage Round the World*, which is more accurately a reflexive "ramble" through "the famous *Metropolis of England*": "*like Bees in a Garden we hum and rove about from Flower to Flower, and as soon as we have tasted one and exhausted its sweetness, we leave it and fly away to another, seeking in vain to eternise our Pleasures, by a continued circle of Varieties*" (1.141). In an effort to do justice to a city notable for its "*circle of Varieties,*" authors who write about London conventionally parody its frenetic pace through a loosely digressive style that vacillates from subject to subject in much the same manner as Londoners moved from one "*Flower*" to the next. Motion and mobility fascinated the eighteenth-century imagination, and, as a means of moving freely and without an intended destination, the London ramble served as a particularly useful means of chronicling, organizing, and narrating the life of the metropolis.[48] Published works that are structured around rambling carry the implication that they will only provide readers with a small sampling of commodities, brief sketches of characters, and mere glimpses of amusements as they set out in search of business or pleasure. Yet the fleeting nature of the observations is what makes them realistic, since they represent through narrative form the miscellaneousness of the urban experience. Although Dunton's narrator boasts that his account of London will be "the *best Flower* in the Book" (1.126), he refuses to follow the example of John Stow or James Howell, and to "drudge on at the old *Hum-Drum* way of describing Cities, begin at one end and go to the other" (141). Instead, he allows his long-deferred "*Description of London*" to be interrupted by extended digressions on such whimsical topics as the lust after "*Gold*," "*Old Harry's Codpiece*," the power of man "over his *own Life*," "*Sodom* and *Gomorrha*," the "*Tricks*" of the contortionist Joseph Clark, the "Diversion of Gentlemen," the antics of a popish "Puppet-show," and the pleasures of digression itself :

> [D]on't let the Reader trouble me with so many impertinent Objections, for that unavoidably leads a man into *Digressions* from the main subject, and then these *Digressions* lead a Man further into *Digressions*, for *Error is infinite*, and the longer you wander in a wrong Path, my Shoes to yours, the further you go from the right, if they are opposite to t'other: Not but that *Digressions* are so far from being always a fault, that they are indeed often pardonable, and sometimes, a *great Beauty* to any discourse —— but then they must be well turn'd and managed, they must come in naturally and easily, and seem to be almost of a piece with the main Story, tho never so far distant from it —— *I love a Digression*, I must confess with all my heart, because 'tis so like a *Ramble* — but all this while what's *Digression* to *Westminster* — very much, for that it self's but one great *Digression from* London. (1.142)

Even while acknowledging in traditional terms the danger of too many digressions, Dunton's narrator implies that his are "well turn'd and managed" because digression achieves in form what his rambles pursue in content. It is thus precisely because he digresses "*from* London" that his readers arrive safely at "*Westminster*." "Let no body insist upon the *Matter* I write," the narrator demands, "but my *Method* in writing" (3.24). Though they purport to offer an arm's-length view of the city, works like Dunton's *Voyage* ironically bring readers into closer proximity with the streets by way of rhetorical flowers that engage the attention while interrupting forward momentum. In such a way, I argue, digressions "*eternise*" London pleasures, diverting readers by introducing them intermittently to novel objects of interest. Applying to the "Reigning Diversions of the Town" contemporary theories regarding the aesthetic appeal of the "*new or uncommon*," this book illustrates the many ways in which digressive wit keeps writing fresh, doing to discourse what the expansion of the urban leisure industry was believed to have done to the cultural character of London.

## Bill of fare

This book is about diversion and about England's dual cultural and discursive revolution. Its central claim is that, in the face of a broad expansion in the number and notoriety of commercial amusements, commercial authors internalized diversion as a constitutive aspect of their writing. The intrusion, obstruction, and interruption peculiar to this writing represent, in effect, an attempt by writers to co-opt the energy of extra-textual diversion for their readers' pleasure and their own profit. By thus analysing literary performances through culture and cultural performances through literature, the book explains the pervasiveness in the eighteenth century of devices like digression in a way that is grounded in and consistent with the spirit and flavour of the period. English writers of the late seventeenth century and the first half of the eighteenth century recognized a correspondence between cultural and discursive diversion. *The Rhetoric of Diversion* maintains that modern readers should as well, since the suggestion that devices like digression might be *"nothing but Amusements"* has significant implications for both the history of English leisure and the development of self-conscious literature.

In order fully to explore the "Reigning Diversions of the Town," each chapter of this book juxtaposes cultural and discursive diversion in such a way as to reinforce their reciprocity during the period. Chapter 1 establishes the pattern through a discussion of the relationship between the increasing cultural demand for amusement and the new discursive supply of devices like digression, a relationship mediated through the dual meanings of the term diversion and epitomized by digressive surveys of London amusement that I punningly dub "animadversions upon diversion." Beginning with an examination of the commercialization of leisure, and taking into consideration the gradual legitimization of pleasure, the rise of a professional class of entertainers, the expansion of pleasure-resorts across the topography of London, and the marketing of urban amusement, the opening chapter goes on to trace the parallel development of indirect literary techniques aimed at the unbending of individual minds. In the period between approximately 1690 and 1760, writers such as Tom Brown, Colley Cibber, and James Ralph experiment with linguistic and textual devices that simulate the specific effects of London amusements, entertaining pleasure-seeking readers by giving them the opportunity to experience commercialized leisure discursively: *to read* pantomimes and freak-shows and what Ralph calls "the Circle of the Town-Diversions" (87). In its broad analysis of early eighteenth-century debates over taste and audience psychology, Chapter 1 connects digressive wit to the rhetoric of diversion and points towards a new way of comprehending the pleasure readers have often received from devices that appear to stand in the way of their enjoyment of a well-developed plot, a series of well-drawn characters, or a coherent and well-structured argument.

The two subsequent chapters exemplify this rhetoric through comparative case studies in diversion, each of which illustrate the formal analogies between a particular mode of linguistic or textual disruption and the material conventions of a particular amusement. Chapter 2 attempts to account for the enduring attractions of "false wit," by likening its characteristic verbal devices to the tricks and transformations of English pantomime. Poets and critics of the 1720s, 1730s, and 1740s frequently invoke the antics of Harlequin as a visual way of proscribing the excesses of extravagant wit and of satirizing writers who impose upon their readers through "catachresis" – the contemporary figure for the misuse or misapplication of language. At the same time, apologists for pantomime associate Harlequin's distinctive motions, gestures, and attitudes with truth, reason, and the pattern of nature, claiming that the genre's corporeality allowed it to transcend the limitations and equivocations of words and communicate to audiences through a kind of "dumb Wit." Analysing the surprising overlap between the rhetoric of critical arbiters like Alexander Pope and Joseph Addison and that of pantomime's apologists like John Weaver, the chapter argues that the popularity of pantomime re-contextualizes the Augustan reaction against false wit, in that it identifies a source of aesthetic pleasure in the public's eagerness to be duped by apparent sameness in difference. Although wit could be distracting and could obscure meaningful language, early eighteenth-century readers seem to have enjoyed luxuriant, illogical, and mixed metaphors, forced similes, and trifling jibes and quibbles for the same reason that early eighteenth-century theatre-goers delighted in the unexpected turns of pantomimic entertainment: in a world under the sway of Harlequin's magical slapstick, audiences derived satisfaction from being deceived.

Chapter 3 attempts to explain the appeal of printed ellipses and exaggerated paratext, by comparing these peculiar visual devices to the human and animal "monstrosities" exhibited throughout this period in taverns, coffeehouses, and itinerant booths at the London fairs. The chapter examines at length the popular "craze" for monsters through a critical study of handbills, pamphlets, and newspaper advertisements "Relating to Dwarfs, Giants, and Other Curiosities," analysing what made monsters so appealing, how they were marketed, and why they became a satiric figure for the defects and excesses of the print trade. Although it is difficult to determine how precisely London audiences responded to monster exhibitions, extant accounts tend to emphasize the way in which literal and figurative "sights" appealed to the senses at the expense of the mind, lulling the critical faculties with the grotesque or gaudy spectacle of physical abnormality. Chapter 3 relates the psychology of sightseeing to the epistemology of shallow reading, suggesting that audiences experienced the same wonder at the materiality of textuality that they did in staring at monsters in a booth, and that hacks like Thomas D'Urfey and satirists like Jonathan Swift often followed monster-mongers in catering to a pleasure that is taken in at the eyes. Benedict usefully describes the eighteenth-century monster as "an ontological transgression that is registered empirically."[49] By reading discourses of monstrosity into eighteenth-century literature, the chapter demonstrates that the same might be said of textual and typographical devices that exemplify "too little" or "too much," and that "fasten the eyes" of sightseeing readers on the visual and physical features of print culture.

The analogies that I draw between cultural and discursive diversion might at first seem arbitrary or idiosyncratic, but they take their precedent from the eighteenth century and from the rhetoric of commentators who animadvert upon diversion. Tom Brown and the author of *The Tricks of the Town Laid Open* (1747), for instance, exemplify the frenetic pace of London and its amusements through their rambling digressions, and I do the same. John Weaver and Alexander Pope compare true and false wit to "*Serious* pantomime" and "*Grotesque Dancing*," and I follow suit. Thomas D'Urfey and Jonathan Swift, among others, explore the ways in which the materiality of textuality might be related to the commercial exhibition of monstrosity, and I do so as well. And James Ralph, whose extensive experience as both theatrical impresario and hack writer made him familiar with the difficulties of reconciling taste with commercial demand, draws out parallels among all of these diversions, which is why I begin each chapter with a reading of *The Touch-Stone* intended, first, to ground the book's case studies in contemporary attitudes towards "the Circle of the Town-Diversions," and, second, to provide an imaginative model for analysis.[50] The book examines what Erin Mackie calls a "transgeneric stylistic influence" between literature and the rhetoric surrounding eighteenth-century amusement.[51] Chapter 1 therefore argues not that digression has to be contextualized in the diversions of commercial London, Chapter 2 contends not that catachrestic language should be likened to pantomime, Chapter 3 claims not that textual deficiencies and excrescences must be compared to monster exhibitions, but rather that it is critically illuminating to do so. Both apologists and critics of diversion consider the refreshment offered by digression as in many ways analogous to the novelty and variety of the itinerary of urban amusement; both see the pleasing deceits of "false wit" as somewhat akin to the delight theatre-goers took in the trademark tricks and transformations of Harlequin; and both perceive the blank wonder stimulated by printed ellipses and exaggerated paratext as comparable to the mindless speculation provoked in sightseers by fairground monstrosities. Though such devices disrupt the readerly experience and move away from what is typically conceived of as mimesis, Chapters 1–3 argue that discursive diversions are nonetheless mimetic insofar as they represent rhetorically the form and "unbending" function of cultural diversion.

In an effort to enlarge the scope and significance of the book, Chapter 4 extends the argument beyond satires and surveys of diversion to works that take relatively little interest in diversion as such. The chapter begins with a brief discussion of digression and the cultural problem of satiety, before touching upon why the rhetoric of diversion theorized in Chapter 1 and exemplified in Chapters 2 and 3 was appropriated by writers in miscellaneous genres, and how these writers exploited its devices to produce novelty and variety and unbend the minds of their readers. Given the mutual market for cultural and discursive diversion, it is not surprising to find examples of "pantomimic poetics" in an otherwise grave sermon, instances of "teratological textuality" in an ontological treatise, or a digressive "circle of Varieties" in a didactic novel. The novel, in particular, takes advantage of the possibilities of diversion because, perhaps more than any other genre, the constitutive length of its writing called for something to break the monotony of long reading. Yet if the very act of reading a novel was supposed to offer relief from the dullness and repetition of everyday life, how did novelists ensure that their own narratives did not become dull and repetitive? What made novelistic discourse pleasurable?

Picking up where the research of Warner and other recent scholars of the eighteenth-century novel leaves off, Chapter 4 examines the "modes of entertainment" *within* the novel, and relates these modes to the increasing demand for entertainment from without. Warner wishes to rewrite the literary history of the eighteenth-century novel so that "it becomes a subset of the cultural history of print entertainments."[52] I briefly reconsider the literary history of the "self-conscious" novel, in particular, so that its characteristically disruptive devices become a subset of the cultural history of diversion. While some novels of the period plot diversion, organizing their narratives around the sights and shows of the metropolis, others utilize diversion in a more rudimentary way through digressions that serve to unbend the mind when, for instance, the story of Tom Jones, with its requisite lessons in "PRUDENCE," begins to grow tedious or boring. The centrepiece of the chapter is an extended reading of Fielding's *Tom Jones* that aligns the characters' pursuit of diversion – their visit to a puppet show, participation in a Haymarket masquerade, and attendance at a performance of *Hamlet* at Drury Lane – with the intrusions of the self-conscious narrator, who explains that all such "poetical Embellishments" are designed "to refresh the Mind, whenever those Slumbers which in a long Work are apt to invade the Reader as well as the Writer, shall begin to creep upon him" (4.1.151–52). The chapter maintains that the basis of Fielding's claim that he is "the Founder of a new Province of Writing" lies in his realization that plot might not always be enough to keep a novel interesting, but that devices which "turn aside" might provide sufficient relief to make it so.

Boredom is the antithesis of interest, and, consciously or unconsciously, it is the state against which authors in the age of Swift, Pope, and Fielding could not help but write. If the literature of the late seventeenth century and the first half of the eighteenth century is frequently odd or extravagant, if it plays with the format of the printed book, and if it seems often to ramble away from coherence, it does so because of a persistent anxiety on the part of writers about the psychology of readers and the possibility, or probability, of their being bored. As only one of many amusements available for purchase, reading was necessarily volitional and provisional: the public had the choice to read or not to read, depending upon whether the diversion received was commensurate with the time and money expended. For all of the recent critical discussion of the ostensible "authority" of self-conscious writers, it was usually the market of readers who were in charge, who made demands, who required that a work remain interesting in order to retain their attention and keep them from moving on to one or another competing amusement. The amiable "acquaintance" that Wayne Booth and other critics have seen developing in the 1690s between the self-conscious writer and his "implied" reader had, by the 1760s, become a commercial relationship between producer and consumer, entertainer and entertained, performer and noisy "Crowd," who, Ralph jokes, are generally "the *tout ensemble* of Perfections in all public *Entertainments*" (234–35). Taken together, the chapters in this book should suggest some of the ways in which writers of the period provided for a "good read," and thereby gratified an audience who took their role as pleasure seekers as seriously as their role as readers.

CHAPTER I

# "The predominant taste of the present age": diversion and the literary market

I know some Divertisement is so necessary, both for the Body and Mind of a Man, that 'tis hardly possible for either of them to be at Ease without it: But that which I would reprehend, is the Excess and the Inordinacy of them; the making that a set and formal Business and Trade, which should be only used as a Diversion, and to fill up the idle Intervals.

– *The Tricks of the Town Laid Open* (1747)

The Melange of so many different Subjects, and such a Variety of Thoughts upon them (which, if I am not deceiv'd, give an agreeable Goût to the whole) may not satisfie you so well as a Composition perfect in its kind on one intire Subject; but possibly it may divert and amuse you better, for here is no thread of Story, nor connexion of one Part with another, to keep the Mind intent, and constrain you to any length of Reading.

– Bysshe, *The Art of English Poetry* (1702)

In *The Touch-Stone: or, Historical, Critical, Political, Philosophical, and Theological Essays on the Reigning Diversions of the Town* (1728), James Ralph surveys the most popular of London's contemporary amusements in an alternately earnest and facetious effort to vindicate them and to place them in a context both delightful and instructive – *dulce et utile*. Written and published under the waggish pseudonym of "A. Primcock," *The Touch-Stone* presents itself as the peculiar production of an author who plays "Hide and Seek with the World" and whose anonymity allows him to be an impartial and studious observer of all the "noted Entertainments" (XIV). Ralph characterizes Primcock as having "liv'd in publick, yet unknown," and the biographical preface to the work boasts of the substantial personal and professional credentials that make Primcock a dilettante of diversion. He is lineally descended from the illustrious family of "the Cocks," whose various branches have produced "Gentlemen" of "an

26

amorous Disposition" (Allcocks), amateur virtuosi "altogether given to the Study of *Physick* and *Surgery*" (Stopcocks), romps and rooks who are recognized as "the Inventors of the Game of *Hot-cockles*" (Laycocks), and castrati performers esteemed throughout England "for their fine Voices" (Nococks). Being born, as it were, into a life of leisure, Primcock has travelled abroad and examined "the Fundamentals of the public Amusements" in Paris and Amsterdam and all "those Parts of *Europe* which are most worthy a Traveller's Curiosity" (xiii–xiv). In his own "native Country," he has sought to attend every London "opera" or "play," has frequented "Coffee-Houses" and made regular visits to "*Fleet-Ditch, Moor-Fields* Rails, and *Holborn-Bars*," and has spent a considerable amount of time and money in "Booksellers Shops" (xv). Fancying himself both a "Scholar" and a "Man of the Town," he has read "all the *French* and *Italian* Criticks" and consulted "three hundred and thirteen *German* Commentators," but has discovered just as much of "Wit, Truth, and Reason" in the busy round of London pleasures (xiv–xv). Taking these pleasures as his precedent, Primcock confidently asserts that "by Genius, Study, and Experience," he is "sufficiently qualify'd to inspect, criticise, and determine upon the reigning Diversions of the town" (xvi).

Primcock's "Manner of Criticizing" these diversions is, he claims, unique in introducing both "Panegyrick" and "Censure" rather than one at the expense of the other. The ambivalence of his manner has accordingly made him an arbiter of taste in matters of amusement: he has given "Laws to the Realms of both theatres" and has been invoked as an "infallible Umpire" in disputes "betwixt Men or Brutes, at the bear-garden" (xvi). In *The Touch-Stone*, Primcock applies his expertise more broadly so as to reconcile two even more staunchly opposed camps – those quick to dismiss the reigning diversions and those all-too-ready to indulge them. To the "Reformers and Criticks" who would abolish all entertainments upon account of "some few bold Licences" (xvii), Primcock offers, for instance, an enthusiastic apology for the "Diversion of our cock pits," which, he muses, "may vie with any thing Antique or Modern, as to Humanity or Politeness" (222). At the same time, and as a potential corrective to more impertinent pleasure seekers, Primcock vigorously attacks a number of amusements that seem not to warrant such harsh treatment. Of the farces performed by "*Italian* Strollers," he declares that it is "impossible to enter into a regular Criticism, either on their Action, or *Drama*," since "to get thro' such Heaps of Rubbish, would require more than *Herculean* Help" (223). The inordinacy of this praise and blame is a function of Primcock's ···al role in *The Touch-Stone*: by having his pseudonymous author exaggerate both "Panegyrick" *and* "Censure," Ralph hints at a middle way between the social extremes of priggishness and voluptuousness.[1] Ralph's stated purpose is to encourage every diversion that is "Praise-Worthy" and to reform every "blameable" diversion, either by "turning its Bent towards somewhat perfectly harmless, or substituting in its Place, what may be render'd of Use to the World" (170). Distinguishing himself from Jeremy Collier, William Law, Arthur Bedford, and other equally sober critics, Ralph refuses to indict eighteenth-century amusements comprehensively, but rather has Primcock discriminate between the virtuous and the vicious, between those amusements that might conduce to public or private good and those that strain too much against standards of decency and decorum. He explains: "I am so far perswaded of the Innocence and Use of all our publick Diversions, that I shall endeavour to remove all Prejudices rais'd against them by unthinking Zealots" (XVII–XVIII). In thus setting out *to think* about diversions, Ralph takes for granted the cultural relevance, if not the cultural value, of activities as disparate as operas, ridottos, and masquerades, pantomimes, prize fights, and public auctions, bearbaitings, fairground exhibitions, and puppet shows, all of which are part of the purview of A. Primcock, "occasionally handled" in *The Touch-Stone*, and mingled together in its copious and zeugmatic title page (Figure 1).[2]

As the title page graphically implies, Ralph does not separate the "polite" from the "popular," amusements that reside at the higher end of the social scale from those which inhabit the lower, but rather evaluates all and sundry according to the degree to which they contribute to the "pleasing and improving" of the body or mind. The exact character of this pleasure and the precise nature of this instruction vary from diversion to diversion. Ralph has Primcock praise the power of Italian opera to move the passions, but has him argue that they would be more intelligible to English audiences if they took native and "traditionary" materials, such as "The London Prentice," "Whittington and His Cat," or "The Dragon of Wantcliff," as their topics (22ff). He acknowledges the numerous proscriptions against the masquerade by those who curse it "by Bell, Book and Candle," while contending that the liberty of the event carries out a civil service in allowing participants to "penetrate into the Excellencies of every one's hidden Talent" (169ff). When discussing the pantomimes mounted on the legitimate London stage, he likens the antics of Harlequin to the fairground performances of tumblers, posture-makers, and ropedancers, all of whom dazzle the eye while "speaking to the Mind without Words" (94ff). And he humorously claims that the bear garden satisfies "the great Design, of mixing Instruction with our Amusements," by exhibiting bravery, pride,

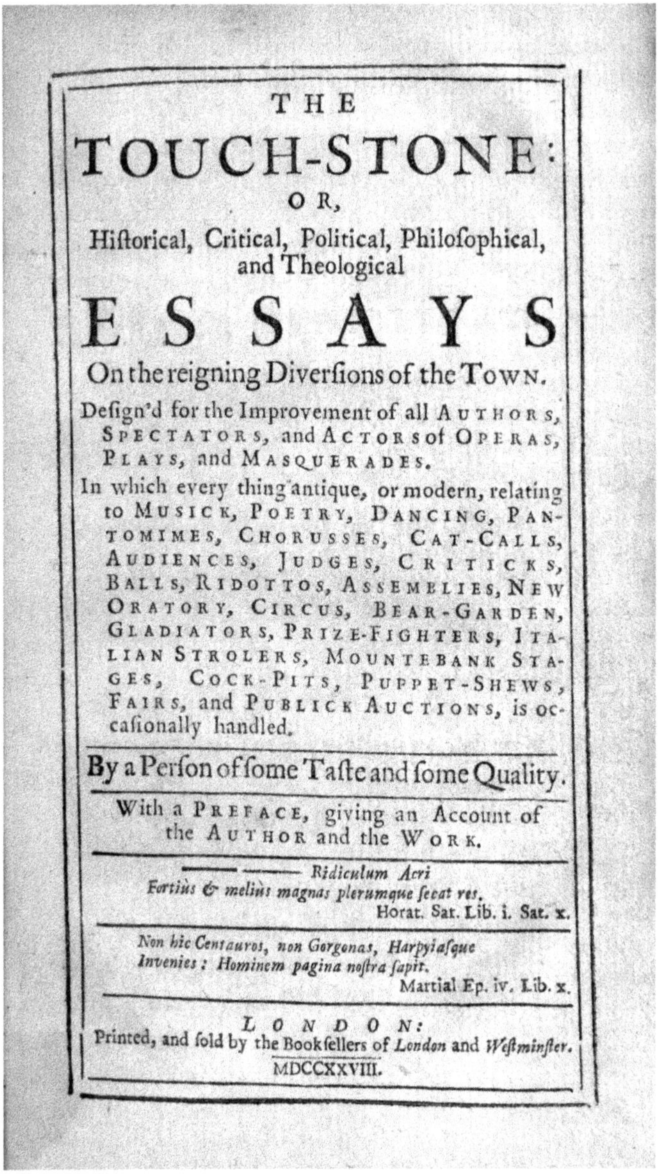

# THE
# TOUCH-STONE:
### OR,
#### Historical, Critical, Political, Philosophical, and Theological
# ESSAYS
#### On the reigning Diversions of the TOWN.

Design'd for the Improvement of all AUTHORS, SPECTATORS, and ACTORS of OPERAS, PLAYS, and MASQUERADES.

In which every thing antique, or modern, relating to MUSICK, POETRY, DANCING, PANTOMIMES, CHORUSSES, CAT-CALLS, AUDIENCES, JUDGES, CRITICKS, BALLS, RIDOTTOS, ASSEMBLIES, NEW ORATORY, CIRCUS, BEAR-GARDEN, GLADIATORS, PRIZE-FIGHTERS, ITALIAN STROLERS, MOUNTEBANK STAGES, COCK-PITS, PUPPET-SHEWS, FAIRS, and PUBLICK AUCTIONS, is occasionally handled.

## By a Person of some Taste and some Quality.

With a PREFACE, giving an Account of the AUTHOR and the WORK.

—————— *Ridiculum Acri*
*Fortius & melius magnas plerumque secat res.*
Horat. Sat. Lib. i. Sat. x.

*Non hic Centauros, non Gorgonas, Harpyiasque Invenies : Hominem pagina nostra sapit.*
Martial Ep. iv. Lib. x.

### LONDON:
Printed, and sold by the Booksellers of *London* and *Westminster.*
MDCCXXVIII.

Figure 1  Title page to James Ralph's *The Touch-Stone* (1728)

and courage, and animating audiences to do the same (221). Ranging from the exclusive setting of the King's Theatre in the Haymarket to Lincoln's Inn Fields to the pell-mell confusion of Smithfield or Southwark Fair, the seven essays that comprise *The Touch-Stone* enact the hierarchization of contemporary amusements, only to collapse it.[3] Ralph's playful programme of reform involves a levelling of high and low: polite diversions are invigorated by the popular, while popular diversions are tempered by the polite. In ironically recommending that the famous contralto Francesco Senesino sing the part of Dick Whittington or that army officers be stirred by the "daring Spirit" of bears and mastiffs, Ralph makes a connection between generic miscegenation and a decline of taste in English literature and culture. Like other characteristic works of Augustan satire, *The Touch-Stone* parodies the threat to traditional cultural forms by commercialization, novelty, print, and tawdry show. But, as with most parodies, *The Touch-Stone* cuts both ways, reproducing the energy of these threats while pretending to ridicule them.

The shifting perspective of Ralph's persona mimics the mixed character of diversion itself, which was theorized during the period as an agreeable activity with a serious social and, as this chapter will suggest, rhetorical purpose. The chapter explores the implication of the social in the rhetorical, demonstrating how and why the development of commercialized leisure came to influence the content and form of commercial literature and, specifically, works like *The Touch-Stone*. As with many other surveys of the "Reigning Diversions of the Town," *The Touch-Stone* treats "diversion" in both its nominal and verbal senses, in that its seven essays on London "entertainment" (*O.E.D.* 4.b) frequently and self-consciously "turn aside" from "the business in hand" (*O.E.D.* 2) by way of digression. These digressions reflect in surprising ways contemporary debates over diversion, the terms of which this chapter will rehearse in order to explain the resonances between the diverting and the digressive in a literary culture where commercial authors and entertainers came to share motivations, methods, and even markets. Ralph appears to make a case for diversion through Primcock's often ironic arguments in favour of the popular amusements English pleasure seekers most enjoy. I argue, however, that it is just as likely the digressive wit of Ralph and other apologists that persuades English readers of the cultural efficacy – the "Innocence and Use" – of diversion. In this context, Primcock's half-earnest and half-facetious proposals are not intended as a real alternative to contemporary amusements, but rather as an index of them. By identifying Italian opera *and* bearbaiting as diversions that, though incongruous, are nonetheless equally

"Reigning," Ralph has Primcock draw attention to the ubiquity and universality of diversion in eighteenth-century England. His point is not necessarily that the polite and the popular share the same diversions, that the former condescend to the amusements of the latter or that the latter frequent the pleasure-haunts of the former, but that polite and popular alike pursue some form of diversion. *The Touch-Stone* thus represents diversion as something that is available to people at large, and, in so doing, documents significant changes in the general attitude towards pleasure, in the economic and material basis of society, in the boundary between elite and mass art forms, and in the rhythm of work time and time set apart from work.

## The genealogy of commercialized leisure

Cultural historians identify these changes with the "commercialization of leisure," which had its formative period in England between approximately 1690 and 1760.[4] During this period, the pursuit of pleasure for its own sake was gradually legitimized as the routine entitlement of all people to seek entertainment, gratification, and relief from the ordinary or due course of things – from politics and study and business and from all earnest labour and employment. "I think it appears very plain," Ralph has Primcock remark, "that Nature requires a gentle raising of the Spirits, after the Fatigue of the Day; and the generality of People are agreed to have it one way or t'other" (71). Ralph does not confine this "raising of the Spirits" to the aristocratic and genteel, groups who customarily enjoyed the privilege of pleasure. Nor does he grant it to the rabble as an occasional and "carnivalesque" respite from drudgery and penury. Instead, Ralph conceives of diversion as a basic human desire for an intermittent mental, physical, and, most importantly, psychological time-out. As the structures of an increasingly individualized consumer society came to replace the traditional patterns of the agrarian economy and the liturgical calendar, an important division was established between regulated "work time" and what became known as "leisure time," a fixed interlude during which English men and women were not only permitted but were institutionally encouraged to choose their diversion. In contrast to the ritualized cycles of feast and rogation days, which had previously governed the when, where, and why of social recreation, eighteenth-century leisure was organized around the interaction of production and consumption and the well-defined pursuits of a winter or summer "season." Work and leisure ceased to be part of a unified continuum of shared obligation and celebration and became instead distinct kinds of time that defined themselves against one another and permanently altered attitudes towards temporality.[5] Leisure offered a conceptual break from the concerns of daily life, not so much a formal gap in normal time as a separate though synchronous kind of time in which people demanded diversion in both its nominal and verbal senses. What the verb added to the noun was affect: the experience of diversion was one of an emotional and psychic release in response to new and surprising objects of attention.[6] At this early stage in the history of commercialized leisure, the English public could be understood, more than ever before, to be diverted *by* diversions.

This is not to say that the English stopped participating in the diversions associated with seasonal holidays like Shrovetide or Michaelmas, but rather that some manner of festivity was now integrated into day-to-day life. Primcock is thus made to explain that in eighteenth-century England "*Carnival*" is kept "all the Year round" (192). The witty remark subtly evokes the familiar tradition of the "old holiday pastimes," while simultaneously illustrating the tone and tenor of the set of "new commercial diversions" that *The Touch-Stone* takes as its subject. The old holiday pastimes were a fundamental component of the rites of church and state in Renaissance England. Rural in nature and celebrated only during periods reserved for a sort of communal catharsis, these holidays provided a liminal context in which to relieve some of the pressures that almost inevitably built up in a fractious and highly stratified society. The English carnivalesque, like the European Carnival, was characterized by inversions of hierarchy that allowed ordinary men and women to express their distrust of the ruling elite and to rethink or revise cultural codes – to participate in what modern sociologists and anthropologists have called "rituals of rebellion." The Stuart monarchs gave their sanction to these rituals because they recognized their topsy-turvydom as essentially normative: morris dances, hobby-horses, May games, dramatic interludes, wassails, athletic sports and disports, mummings, tableaux vivants, and feasts of misrule helped to reinforce the established order by easing, at regular and predictable intervals, tensions that might otherwise erupt into a full-scale challenge of religious and political orthodoxy.

This theory received its definitive expression in James I's *Book of Sports* (1618), a controversial declaration that seemed to countenance public mirth by permitting the practice of the old pastimes after divine service on Sundays and on feast days. As a riposte to attacks on recreational activities by "*Puritans* and precise People," the king assumed the conventional role of the prudent patriarch supervising the playtime of his children, mandating that "our good People be not disturbed, letted or discouraged from any lawful Recreation," such as the setting up of maypoles, archery, dancing, leaping and vaulting, wakes, and "Whitson-Ales."[7] Making no secret of the ideological stakes of his declaration, James observed that any broad prohibition on traditional pastimes could not "but breed a great Discontentment in our Peoples Hearts," and incline those already discontented to change their faith or spread dissent through "idle Speeches" in their "Ale-houses" (A4r). In the face of even more virulent Puritan opposition, Charles I reissued his father's defence of diversion in 1633, out of what he described as "a like pious Care for the Service of God, and for suppressing of any Humours that oppose Truth, and for the Ease, Comfort and Recreation of our well-deserving People" (A5r). Charles' rider to the declaration makes explicit the claim that matters of no less consequence than piety and verity were at issue in debates over the legitimacy of festive "Gambols." It also prefigures later seventeenth- and eighteenth-century conceptions of "work" and "leisure" by distinguishing certain "Times" as set aside for the diversion of "the meaner Sort," who "labour hard all the Week" and who, every now and then, require something "to refresh their Spirits" (A3r). As both James I and Charles I understood, the old holiday pastimes did ideological work: they indulgently suspended authority, but only for a time and only within the "lawful" confines of the country and the carnivalesque. Far from being kept "all the Year round," seventeenth-century "*Carnival*" was a periodic and strategic condescension to the people's desire for a respite from their everyday lives. "By placing their official stamp of approval on the old pastimes," explains Leah Marcus, the Stuarts "attempted to extend royal power into an area of ambivalence and instability, to channel the equivocal status of popular festival into what we can perhaps call an official 'paradox of state'—a condition of happy ambiguity in which the license and lawlessness associated with the customs could be interpreted as submission to authority."[8] In the context of absolutist statecraft, *The Book of Sports* enabled the Stuart monarchs to counter potential threats while, at the same time, ingratiating themselves with the English population. Though they might have provided psychological release, the old holiday pastimes did not necessarily change anything since they tended to diffuse seditious impulses and were thus bound up with the maintenance of social order. "[I]nnocent Recreations" were therefore encouraged because, Primcock summarizes, "a most religious King, and zealous Metropolitan" knew that "the Genius of the Nation demanded this Relief on such Occasions." "For that reason," he concludes, "the *Book of Sports* after Divine Service was publish'd by Royal Authority, to prevent their running into greater Excesses" (71).

In having Primcock gloss the religious and political subtext of *The Book of Sports* and in referring to the tradition of old holiday pastimes, Ralph usefully historicizes the new commercial diversions of contemporary London. Describing what these pastimes were in order to analyse what they have become, he establishes a genealogy that proceeds from the ideological festivity of the past to the secular, urban, and radically individualistic "Reigning Diversions" of the present. During the late seventeenth century and the first half of the eighteenth century, the meaning of this shift from old to new provoked considerable critical discussion, as writers in different contexts with different interests offered their own take on the genealogy of diversion. In *A Discourse Concerning the Original and Progress of Satire* (1693), for example, John Dryden locates the origin of public entertainment in bacchanalian and saturnalian festivals that, he claims, had a "double Reason of their Institution: the first of Religion, the other of Recreation, for the unbending of our Minds."[9] Like the "Sports and Merriments" of the English Renaissance, those of classical Greece and Rome had an ideological function since they were usually accompanied by "Scoffs and Revilings," a formal custom allowing revellers to vent any discontent within the limited time and space of "these Holydays" (30). For Dryden, the institution of recreation is in turn bound up with the gradual development of "Satyr," which puts into perspective his well-known attack on the "multitude of Scriblers, who daily pester the World with their insufferable Stuff" (8). If both public activities derive from the same foundation, then the proliferation of "Lampoons and Libels" in 1690s England has, Dryden implies, as much to do with unregulated leisure as with the expansion of unlicensed print. Dryden rationalizes the edition of the *Satires* of Juvenal and Persius that his *Discourse* prefaces through the idea of leisure, comparing the competing literal translations of those who "wrote to Scholars" to the "Paraphrases" that he and his colleagues believe will be "far more pleasing to our Readers": "We write only for the Pleasure and Entertainment, of those Gentlemen and Ladies, who tho they are not Scholars are not Ignorant" (87). But even as Dryden pitches his edition to representative "Gentlemen and Ladies," he obliquely criticizes the misuse of power by the traditional leisure classes, including his patron and dedicatee, Charles Sackville, sixth Earl of Dorset, through self-conscious digressions that conceal an "undercurrent of hostility." According to Anne Cotterill, the digressive structure of the *Discourse* signifies a strategic effort by Dryden "to distract attention" from his attack on "a factious, illiberal court world neglectful of poets."[10] While exploring the "original and progress" of satire, and prescribing rules for the genre's modern usage,

Dryden thus takes advantage of the customary licence of leisure to engage in the very kind of political polemic that his *Discourse* problematizes.

Joseph Addison, on the other hand, sees leisure as one way of tempering the "relish for faction" that often gives rise to the sort of libellous satire that Dryden claims to disdain. In the thirty-fourth issue of *The Free-holder* (April 16, 1716), Addison presents a myth of origin for diversion that attempts to encompass the pastimes sanctioned by the Stuart monarchy, as well as those permitted by the modern Whig ministry:

> The institution of sports and shews was intended by all governments, to turn off the thoughts of the people from busying themselves in matters of state, which did not belong to them; to reconcile them to one another by the common participations of mirth and pleasure; and to wear out of their minds that rancour which they might have contracted by the interfering views of interest and ambition.[11]

Addison argues along traditional lines that "public diversions and entertainments" provide a useful distraction from political concerns, and should ideally be disinterested: "I do not find that either party has yet thrown themselves under the patronage of *Scaramouch*, or that *Harlequin* has violated that neutrality, which, upon his arrival in *Great-Britain*, he professed to both parties" (486). Yet his invocation of the old holiday pastimes, in a discussion of a modern theatrical entertainment, obscures the absolutist ideology behind this conception, displacing the source of authority from the Crown to the politician – from the governance of the past to the government of the present. As John O'Brien has shown, Addison cites and silently recasts the Stuart defence of diversion, presenting "sports and shews" as an alternative, not to the "Puritan conformity" of the seventeenth century, but to the "partisan bickering" of the early decades of the eighteenth century.[12] Given the unabashed Whig bias of *The Free-holder*, and the celebrated role of *The Tatler* (1709–11) and *The Spectator* (1711–14) in the creation of a "bourgeois public sphere," which encouraged the middle classes to debate moral, aesthetic, and political issues while taking part in commercialized social life, the claims of No. 34 are exaggerated and at least partly disingenuous.[13] Addison's genealogy nonetheless proposes that diversion can be a domain separate from politics, one that contributes to the good of the nation by removing itself and its participants from matters of state. He asserts that "it would therefore be for the benefit of every society, that is disturbed by contending factions, to encourage such innocent amusements as may thus disembitter the minds of men, and make them mutually rejoice in the same agreeable satisfactions" (487).

Addison's optimism about diversion's capacity to settle difference is qualified later in the century by Henry Fielding, whose *Enquiry into the Causes of the Late Increase of Robbers* (1751) laments that what had once been a method of assuaging political subversion has itself become subversive, due to the "vast Torrent of Luxury" that he sees as having lately "poured itself" into England.[14] Fielding traces diversion back to the ancient custom of putting "Seasons of Idleness" into the ritual calendar, broadening his genealogy to include the Old Testament's reservation of one day in seven for physical and mental rest (80). Citing Seneca, Macrobius, the books of Exodus and Deuteronomy, and a "Statute of *Hen*. VIII," he explains that "by divine as well as human Institution, as well as by our own Laws and those of other Countries, the Diversions of the People have been limited and restrained to certain Seasons" (81). According to Fielding, the purpose of such periods of diversion has always been to provide the "useful Part of Mankind" with a temporary "Relaxation from Labour," and so "Holydays" have historically been infrequent – an occasion to anticipate or remember fondly, but rarely to enjoy for long. In the modern metropolis, however, "where the Places of Pleasure are almost become numberless," diversion has advanced to "so scandalous an Excess" that the periodic is now continuous (81–2). People of "Fashion and Fortune" while away their time following the circuit of mid-century amusements: plays, operas, drums, routs, riots, masquerades, oratorios, ridottos, assemblies, hurricanes, and pleasure-gardens like Ranelagh and Vauxhall. Meanwhile, the "lower Order of People," whose desires exceed their means of supporting them, emulate the "Voluptuousness" of the rich and aspire to indulge year-round in what had been devised as occasional release. Fielding contends that such affectation is an incentive to crime, as workers steal in order to afford the pleasures belonging to other classes. The universal availability of amusement thus threatens to undermine the political order:

> To the upper Part of Mankind Time is an Enemy, and (as they themselves often confess) their chief Labour is to kill it; whereas, with the others, Time and Money are almost synonymous; and as they have very little of each to spare, it becomes the Legislature, as much as possible, to suppress all Temptations whereby they may be induced too profusely to squander either the one or the other; since all such Profusion must be repaired at the Cost of the Public. (84)

The fact that Fielding must exhort politicians to address the explosion of diversion across cultural boundaries emphasizes its increasingly apolitical status during the period. Contrary to the "institution" of diversion, the authorities have stopped paying close enough attention to the socioeconomic pragmatics of the people's pastimes: What specific kinds are available? Who exactly is attending them and how much do they cost? Where and when and how often are they offered?

Although the particular issues at stake necessarily change over the roughly seventy years encompassing Dryden's *Discourse*, Addison's essay, and Fielding's *Enquiry*, each of these writers identify diversion as a problem relevant to their own cultural moment and to their respective interests in satire, party politics, and criminal justice. And each of them revise the traditional genealogy of diversion in an attempt to reconcile the maxims of *The Book of Sports* with a newly urban and commercial context. But for Fielding in the 1750s, as for Dryden in the 1690s and Addison in the 1710s, the difficulty of regulating the "immense Variety" of London entertainments suggests that the pastimes of the people have been "grossly perverted" from their origin in ideological sport (82). Formerly a "Season of Idleness," diversion has come to exemplify idleness *out of season*.

### Advertising, audience, and individualized amusement

Irregular and unpredictable, the diversions of the late seventeenth and early eighteenth century eased tension in various ways at varying times, and were thus a challenge to control or to accommodate to any official purpose. Where the old pastimes provided for a "gentle raising of the Spirits" on Sundays and holidays and what Ralph designates as "*Idle days*" (70), the new diversions were available virtually daily. Moreover, where the old pastimes tended to be confined to rural areas or to a rustic ethos, the new diversions spread themselves throughout the dense topography of London, where opportunities for festive inversion multiplied and where the carnivalesque became popular commodity.[15] The specialization of function that urbanization and commercialization encouraged permanently changed the conduct of diversion by giving rise to a discernibly modern English leisure industry, managed by an ambitious class of entrepreneurs, showmen, and impresarios who operated in fixed sites in London and whose paradoxical business was pleasure. *The Touch-Stone* alludes to some of the most innovative and influential of these professionals: Martin Powell (d. 1725), the puppet-master who delighted audiences at Bath, Bristol, and Oxford, before moving his "Punch's Theatre" to the Little Piazza in Covent Garden; Joseph Clark (d. 1697), London's favourite "posture-master" or contortionist, who won applause for appearing "in all the deformities that can be imagined" (Figure 2); Christopher Preston (d. 1709), who ran the

CLARK the Englifh Pofture Mafter
Le Maistre des Postures Anglois
Postura de Matscini Ingleli

Figure 2  Joseph Clark in Marcellus Laroon's *The Cryes of the City of London* (1711),
plate 68

city's best-known bear-garden at Hockley-in-the-Hole, but who was killed
by his own bears when he fell into their enclosure; Mrs Salmon (c. 1670–
1760), whose popular waxworks held permanent residence in Fleet Street
just through Temple Bar; William Pinkethman (d. 1725), who began his

career as a straight actor at the patent theatres, but who became famous for his fairground drolls and for the "moving pictures" he mounted in and around London in coffeehouses and assembly rooms; Isaac Fawkes (d. 1731), the fairground conjurer and sleight-of-hand artist who eventually set up at James Street in the Haymarket; Christopher Pinchbeck (1669/70–1732), originally a clock- and toy-maker who rose to prominence because of the complex automata and feats of mechanical ingenuity that he exhibited under the sign of the "Astronomico-Musical Clock" in Fleet Street; Colley Cibber (1671–1757), whose long professional career included turns as comedian, playwright, co-manager at Drury Lane, poet laureate, and ironic hero of *The Dunciad in Four Books* (1743); Johann Jakob Heidegger (1666–1749), the opera impresario who introduced the masquerade into England, orchestrated public ceremonies for the Hanoverian monarchy, and was mocked as "*Surintendant des Plaisirs d'Angleterre*"; John Henley (1692–1756), whose eccentric lectures, sermons, and "academical orations" drew large audiences to his "ORATORY," first in Newport Market and then in Clare Market, and whose advertisements in London newspapers of the 1720s and 1730s were rhetorical performances in their own right; Samuel Johnson of Cheshire (1690/91–1773), the dancing master and playwright whose claim to fame was his ability to make love while playing the fiddle on stilts "about eight Foot high"; and John Rich (1692–1761), the manager of Lincoln's Inn Fields and, later, Covent Garden, who performed Harlequin under the stage-name of "Lun" and who was in many ways responsible for changing the format of English drama by establishing complex machinery, extravagant scenery, and entr'acte divertissement as integral parts of a full and pleasant evening at the theatre.[16] There was money to be made from diversion, as from other commercial endeavours, and these men and women – "new capitalists of cultural enterprise," as John Brewer calls them – were among the first to exploit the economic possibilities of providing entertainment for the public at large. "Their aim," according to Brewer, "was to appeal to the appetite, to cater to changing tastes, and to satisfy an audience eager to enjoy novelty and variety."[17]

Novel genres of amusement arose both at the margins and near the centre of a culture increasingly dominated by supply and demand, while time-honoured amusements were rendered more miscellaneous to make them more attractive to diverse pleasure seekers with what Ralph identifies as "a prodigious Tendency to every thing mighty new" (194). For instance, the London theatres began to supplement their five-act main pieces with "additional Entertainments" ranging from acrobatics and oddities to processions, burlettas, and comic or grotesque dances.[18] Puppet shows introduced life-sized marionettes with life-like features, gestures, and costumes.[19] The "antique" bear-garden varied its fare by covering its combatants with lighted fireworks in order to enrage them.[20] Even the traditional conjuring act was invigorated by sleight-of-hand artists who realized that the public wanted to be entertained by more than merely the pretence of magic. Isaac Fawkes offered his own innovative take on the repertoire of illusions familiar since the Renaissance, surprising and delighting London audiences of the 1720s by transforming playing cards into flying birds, and by making flowers, sweetmeats, and "Showers of real Gold and Silver" appear "out of nothing" – the "Egg-Bag Trick" for which he was famous. According to Simon During, Fawkes was the first English showman to build a successful "magic assemblage business" and to make "a good living on false mysteries."[21] But a significant part of the reason for Fawkes's success was that he calculatedly diversified his legerdemain with an assortment of entertainments borrowed from collaborators and competitors in the streets of London, including Powell and Pinchbeck. A 1727 newspaper ad for "FAWKES's *Theatre*" promises the usual tricks, as well as a "Posture-Master, who far exceeds all that ever perform'd in Europe," a "Musical Clock that plays Variety of Tunes on the Organ, Flute and Flagellet," a "Puppet-show, perform'd by Figures five Foot high," and an "extraordinary Piece of New Machinery, representing his sacred Majesty King George, with the most Illustrious House of Lords as sitting in Parliament"[22] (Figure 3). Fawkes's mixed programme allowed him to appeal to a mixed audience of high, middling, and low, to the curious as well as the credulous. And his three-tiered admission fee of two shillings, one shilling, or sixpence sought to ensure that no paying customer would be excluded from his show.[23] In fact, so willing was Fawkes to entertain his audience that he occasionally invited specific members to participate directly in the show: a February 1724 advertisement in *The Daily Post* explains that the artist "purposes to learn any Gentlemen and Ladies his Fancies by Dexterity of Hand for their own Diversion."[24]

As Fawkes's advertisements illustrate, one of the features that most distinguished the new commercial diversions from the old holiday pastimes was that they were marketed in new ways. Brewer observes that, in the early eighteenth century, "the marketing of culture became a trade separate from its production."[25] This was because the consumption of culture required that the public first be distracted from any competing activities. Entrepreneurs and impresarios continued to promote their amusements through traditional channels, hiring street-criers, posting

*1727*

At FAWKES's *Theatre adjoining to the Tennis-
Court in James-street near the Haymarket,* this
present Evening will be presented the following
Entertainments.

FIRST, his surpri-
zing Tricks with Cards,
as changing them into living
Birds, causing them to dance
upon the Table, blowing the
Spots off and on, commanding
a Card out of any Person's
Hand, changing them to all
Sorts of Pictures, and conveying a Card into an Egg:
He causes all Sorts of Fruits, Flowers, Sweet-meats, Birds
and Mice to appear, with several Showers of real Gold
and Silver; likewise a very fine Collection of Birds from
all Parts of the World to appear on the Table, as you'd
suppose out of nothing. 2. His famous Posture-Master,
who far exceeds all that ever perform'd in Europe; also his Musical Clock that plays Variety of Tunes on the
Organ, Flute and Flagellet, with Birds whistling and
singing as natural as Life. With his Puppet-show, perform'd by Figures five Foot high; being the Play of Pa-
tient Grissel, or the Woman never vex'd; with the comical Humours of Punch and his Wife Joan; concluding with an extraordinary Piece of New Machinery, representing his sacred Majesty King George, with the most
Illustrious House of Lords as sitting in Parliament.
  N. B. The Doors will be open'd at Five, and we shall
begin every Evening exactly at Six. Prices 2 s. 1 s. and 6 d.

Figure 3 Ad for "FAWKES's *Theatre*" in *The Daily Post* No. 2302 (February 8, 1727)

bills, and drumming up business through the ballyhoo of jack-puddings or
merry-andrews. But entertainers like Fawkes came increasingly to rely
upon the resources of print and, especially, the periodical press, which
gave them access to wider audiences of readers and pleasure seekers, and

made diversion as much a part of daily life as shipping news, bankruptcy notices, lost-property lists, and books "just published."[26] Fawkes made himself a fixture in the London newspapers of the 1720s, buying up advertising space in the *Daily Courant, Daily Post, Mist's Weekly Journal, Pasquin, Weekly Journal, London Journal,* and *Grub Street Journal.* He conducted a sustained marketing campaign in these papers that not only notified the public when, where, and what he would be performing, but also how each individual performance would be different from the last and why Londoners should pay to attend. For example, Fawkes ran the following advertisement in *The Daily Post* for December 17, 1723:

> This present Evening, In the Long Room, over the Piazza's, at the Opera House in the Hay Market, the famous FAWKES performs his most surprising Tricks by Dexterity of Hand, with several Curiosities of that Kind, being entirely new, and different to what has been shewn by any other Person; together with the wonderful Activity of Body by his Posture Masters, far exceeding all that ever performed in Europe before: Also besides their usual Performance, there will be two Dances by the two Posture masters in Metamorphosis. First, They come in and appear to be but 2 Foot high, and perform a Pigmy Dance; likewise, an Italian Scaramouch Dance, with 2 Heads, 4 Legs, and but one Body, to the Admiration of all Spectators. Note, There was a Mistake in the Advertisement Yesterday, for the Opera Nights being Wednesdays and Saturdays, and those Nights we shall not perform; but other Nights we shall begin precisely at 5 a-Clock, and again at 7.[27]

The ad is typical in several respects: it uses the "Admiration" of previous spectators in an attempt to win new ones; it teases these potential spectators with provocative details of performance; and it emphasizes the supposed novelty of Fawkes's programme in order to set it apart from the competition. The advertisement also suggests the ways in which diversion-mongers could exploit the inevitability of commercial competition as a subtle marketing technique, in that it implies that the sleight-of-hand artist shares with the rarefied London opera both space and an audience. Fawkes's ad is "rhetorical" in the sense that it seeks not only to inform audiences but also to persuade them to choose his show over others.[28] By January 2, 1724, Fawkes was advertising his intent to best his competitors by supplementing his season's programme with "vaulting and shewing of Postures upon the Slack Rope, in such a manner as was never performed by any other Person."[29] And by January 11, he was claiming a "commendatory Paragraph" in *The Weekly Journal,* and "all the Papers of the Week," to invite audiences who had been diverted by the magical devices in recent theatrical pantomimes to see their epitome in his own conjuring act:

Be it known therefore to our Customers, that whereas the two Entertainments of the Necromancer Dr. Faustus, and the Whim-Wham Jupiter and Europa, at the two Theatres, have lately tickl'd the Fancies of the Town, who resorted thither in prodigious Numbers; so the new Tricks and Conveyances brought to the utmost Perfection by Mr. Fawkes himself, and the most astonishing Shapes and Statues by his two Boys in Metamorphosis, wherein they form a Dance, and seem to be no more than two Foot high, must equally excite the Wonder and Encouragement of the whole Town, more especially when they shall be told that most of the Quality of the first Rank, and the prime Gentry, daily Favour them with their Company and Approbation.[30]

In a culture where the lower and middling classes were often criticized for aping the taste of their social betters, the "Approbation" of certain audiences could result in the "Encouragement" of "all Sorts and Conditions of Men, Women, &c." Yet as Fawkes understood, even relative discouragement could be productive. Within a few weeks, the conjuror was again playing with audience expectation by publishing a false report in *Pasquin* No. 105 (February 4, 1724) that "the Ingenious Mr. *Fawkes*," having been "out-done at both Play-Houses in the Mysteries of his own Art," has "form'd a Resolution, to which many other great Minds have been reduc'd, to abdicate the Administration in Favour of his powerful Competitors, and to retire altogether from publick Business, resolving to devote the Remainder of his Days to plain Dealing, and acting altogether above-board." This public-relations notice does not deal plainly, which is why it is effective. In disingenuously announcing his early retirement, Fawkes manipulates the medium of print to attract the very pleasure seekers he pretends to have lost – those anxious to, as twentieth-century showmen would put it, "catch him before he is gone!" In so doing, he ironically outdoes many of his competitors simply by acknowledging their own commercial success. The rhetoric of Fawkes's newspaper ads testifies to his desire to keep things fresh, as well as to raise the status of his "fringe" entertainment by comparing and claiming as competition to his sleight-of-hand tricks more legitimate arts. It is without exaggeration, therefore, that he concludes his "puff" in *Pasquin* with the inflated assertion that his decision to retire will not only leave a void in London's leisure industry, but will likely be "the finishing Stroke to the Ruin of Poetry."[31]

It is precisely this kind of commercial hyperbole that prompts Ralph to worry that readers of *The Touch-Stone* will expect him "to take Notice of every Mushroom Amusement in the way," including "Fawk's *Dexterity of Hand*, the *moving Pictures, Musical-Clocks*, Solomon's *Temple*, [and] the

*Wax-works, all alive*" (236). Fawkes was by no means unique in taking advantage of the periodical press and in using the expanding resources of commercial literature to market commercialized leisure. Indeed, most of the entertainers alluded to in *The Touch-Stone* advertised regularly in the London newspapers of the early eighteenth century. Martin Powell purchased space in *The Spectator* and *The Daily Courant* to promote his "Punches Theatre." John Henley published extravagant puffs for his popular oratory in *Mist's Weekly Journal* and several of the London "dailies." Fawkes's collaborator, Christopher Pinchbeck, advertised his mechanical entertainments in *The Daily Post, The Daily Courant, Fog's Weekly Journal,* and *The Daily Journal.* And William Pinkethman promoted his variety shows – as well as himself – in *The Tatler, The Spectator,* and *The Daily Courant,* where a 1710 ad for "a most surprising and magnificent Machine, call'd the Pantheon," celebrates him for having "ever made it his Study to invent something New and Excellent to please the World." The advertisement goes on to detail "14 several Entertainments and near 100 Figures, besides Ships, Beasts, Fish, Fowl, and other Embellishments" that feature in "Mr. Penkethman's Wonderful Invention."[32]

To many critics more conservative than Ralph, these kinds of diversions merely pandered to popular taste, indulging in the desires of the public for the strange and uncommon, for farce, spectacle, and sex, and for sound and show over sense. This is a common complaint in many of the period's vehement polemics against London's "Reigning Diversions." In a short pamphlet entitled *The Danger of Masquerades and Raree-Shows* (1718), the pseudonymous author "C.R." contends that the "degenerate State of the *Nation* in regard to *Wit*" has inevitably proceeded from the public's "attributing too much to the *Senses,* and too little to the *Judgement.*"[33] In a similar vein, the author of *A Letter to My Lord ******* On the Present Diversions of the Town* (1725) regrets the absence of "good Sense" and "TASTE" in English audiences whom, he claims, "are delighted with any thing that glitters."[34] Yet in an age of vigorous commercial consolidation, it was the public who were the arbiters of "TASTE" in amusement: they purchased tickets, filled theatres, pleasure-resorts, and fairgrounds, and participated, as audience, in the busy round of pleasure provided by a Powell, a Pinchbeck, or a Pinkethman. Pinkethman was especially adept at reading audience taste and adapting his offerings to the capricious demands of the London public. In 1707, the sometime-actor and theatre manager imported a pack of "Dancing Dogs" from France to perform in an operatic spectacle, first at May Fair and then at Bartholomew Fair in August.[35] The performance prompted a broadside satire entitled *The Fair in an Uproar: or, The Dancing-Doggs* (1707), in which the singularity of "Mr. *Pinkeman's* New OPERA" is mock-panegyrized in comparison to such run-of-the-mill entertainments as "*Tumblers*," "*Fidlers*," and "*Rope-Dancers*":

> 'Tis well we live in such a fickle Place,
> Where *Novelty* was ever follow'd more than Grace:
> (Strange Fancies take in these Unrighteous Days)
> But sure, of all the Whims with which we'ave met,
> We've ne'er had *Dancing Dogs* in OP'RAS yet.

The doggerel verse of the broadside is accompanied by an illustrated engraving of Pinkethman's dogs, dressed as Frenchified fops or *commedia dell'arte* characters (Figure 4). Like many of the period's other satires on commercial amusement, *The Fair in an Uproar* warns of the cultural consequences of condescending to the public's lust for "*Novelty*," suggesting that the popularity of Pinkethman's "OPERA" exemplifies the triumph of bestial entertainments over rational ones. "This is the Charm that gathers all the Town," the author complains, "Whil'st Ancient Drolling will no more go down." Yet for all of his distaste for the dancing dogs, the author rightly predicts that "*Pinkeman* ne'er can fail of good Success, / Whil'st *Dogs*, or *Apes*, or *Elephants*, can please."[36] Pinkethman proved so successful at pleasing London audiences that he was said by John Downes to have "gain'd more in Theatres and Fairs in Twelve Years, than those that have Tugg'd at the Oar of Acting these 50."[37]

Commercial entrepreneurs like Pinkethman appropriated the conventional role of the monarch, audaciously supervising the people's mirth and giving their special sanction to the new pastimes. In their turn, the people happily consumed what the entrepreneurs produced, but only if they enjoyed it, only if their peculiar desires were gratified, and only if they received sufficient diversion for their money. This explains why so many newspaper advertisements contextualize their descriptions of particular amusements in the individual experiences of pleasure seekers. Pinchbeck's ads, for instance, routinely invite prospective patrons to consult with those who have already enjoyed "The Grand Theatre of the MUSES," since the "general Satisfaction" of these audiences is ultimately more important to the diversion-monger than the specific reasons for their satisfaction. "No Idea of its Harmony and Beauty can be formed," according to one advertisement, "those who have seen it declaring, That the Entertainment surpasses Thought, and is not to be express'd by Words."[38] In a similar way, a "new moving Picture" to be exhibited by Pinkethman in

Figure 4 *The Fair in an Uproar: or, The Dancing-Doggs* (1707)

1710 "at the Duke of Marlborough's Head in Fleet-street" is advertised not by a summary of its "great Variety of curious Motions and Figures," but by an admission that "it has the general Approbation of all who see it."[39] In each of these advertisements, an audience of individual pleasure seekers – each person who has "seen it" – is invoked to testify to the appeal of a commercial amusement. It is the taste of this audience that, the ads suggest, determines the itinerary of London diversions. By calculating audience response and directly marketing to the perceived needs and wants of the English public, eighteenth-century entertainers reconfigure the social and political function of leisure, shifting the power to those who partake of the "Reigning Diversions" and who read about them in surveys like *The Touch-Stone* or satires like *The Fair in an Uproar*. The eighteenth-century *"Audience,"* as Primcock is consequently made to argue, "may be justly look'd upon as the *Primum Mobile* of all Diversions; by whose Generosity they are supported, and by whose Smiles, or Frowns, they flourish or languish" (136–7).

Ralph's circumlocution does little to disguise the fact that the audience's "Generosity" involves a commercial transaction and that the principal motivation of the entrepreneurs and impresarios is "profit" – not in the classical sense of *utile*, but in the more modern sense of *lucrum* or pecuniary gain. Rich is famous for having been worth £60,000 at his death; Heidegger is said to have earned £300 to £500 per masquerade and close to £5,000 each year; and even Fawkes was able to leave his wife an impressive legacy of £10,000, and to pass his conjuring business on to his son, whose ads of the early 1730s assure audiences that the "Young *Fawkes*" was "instructed by his Father in his Life-Time, in all those wonderful Secrets with which he so agreeably diverted the Publick."[40] Without a doubt, diversion could be profitable. But when it came to the moral value of the "Reigning Diversions of the Town," the entertainers were, in the opinion of Brewer, generally "agnostic."[41] While many of them claimed that their diversions were uplifting and instructive, emphasizing their affinities with tragedy, epic poetry, historical painting, and other elevated forms, cultural edification seems usually to have been secondary to commercial reward. John Rich's "long Apology" for his "*Pantomime* Entertainments" is representative of the typical apologia offered by the period's diversion-mongers: "I own my self extremely indebted to the Favour with which the Town is pleas'd to receive my Attempts to entertain them in this Kind; and do engage, for my own Part, that whenever the Publick Taste shall be disposed to return to the Works of the *Drama*, no one shall rejoice more sincerely than my self."[42] The entrepreneurs were in business to make money, even if their profit was perceived to come at the expense of that of their patrons or customers. The "profit motive" obliged them to give the public, both at the "polite" and the "popular" end of the market, whatever it wanted, regardless of how lavish or debased.[43] As the anonymous author of *The Tricks of the Town Laid Open* (1747) puts it, when satirizing the London theatre:

> *Players* like the Money of a Fool, as well as they do of a Man of Sense, and in some measure are as willing to please him with their Trifles and Baubles, as divert and instruct the other with their *Encomiums*, and *Satyrs*; tho' by the way, I must tell them, they had best take Care that by their *Farces* and *Drolls*, and their *Jack-Pudding* Tricks, they don't at last pull their Houses upon their Heads.[44]

Bemoaning the commercial opportunism that has come to characterize urban amusement, he adds that if "the Original Design of Play or Gaming was Diversion or Recreation," it has since "lost its native Property, and basely degenerated into a mechanical Trade and Occupation" (96). From the perspective of this commentator, at least, the new commercial diversions constituted a threat to English culture for the simple reason that they appeared to supplant cultural activity with commerce.

This did not mean, however, that they had no influence on the welfare of the nation, but rather that this relationship was now negotiated through the intricacies of the market. In England's nascent capitalist economy, fuelled by selfish interests and the satisfaction of material appetites, diversion could be both a catalyst to and an embodiment of commerce, insofar as it promoted, in the words of Primcock, the "Circulation of ready Money (which else would lie dead in Banker's Hands, or Iron-Chests)" (175). Forgoing its former function within absolutist ideology, diversion assumed an important financial function, bolstering the nation by stimulating trade and conspicuous consumption. Although the increased accessibility and availability of diversion had the potential to encourage recklessness, idleness, concupiscence, and luxury, for many these were somewhat grudgingly understood to be integral to a flourishing economy, necessary evils that ensured the demand for commercialized leisure would always equal or exceed the supply. Playing on the most notorious formulation of this "paradox of pleasure," Primcock jokes that "these Topicks" have been "learnedly and copiously handled in a wonderful Book, where *private Vices* are undoubtedly prov'd to be *publick Benefits*" (175). In citing as Primcock's specious authority Mandeville's *Fable of the Bees* (1714–34),

Ralph draws attention to, perhaps, the most significant consequence of the eighteenth-century consumer revolution: the fact that private individuals came to be responsible for their own particular use of time. Just as significantly, he implicates eighteenth-century diversion in contemporary debates over the abuse of time, insofar as any turning aside from the ordinary course of things could not help but distract individuals from their public responsibilities.

## Time and the attack on diversion

In the past, time was rationally ordered and expressed in calendrical rituals that fixed schedules and routines and insinuated that everyone should be doing the same thing at the same time. Individual men and women laboured together and took periodic pleasure together and in this togetherness were perceived to strengthen the community at large, ignoring their own "private inclinations and personal rhythms" in response to what cultural historian Edward Muir calls "the collective demand."[45] The new commercial diversions of the late seventeenth and early eighteenth centuries disrupted this traditional pattern by catering precisely to private inclinations and personal rhythms, to the desires of a mass urban audience who worked hard during hours defined by employers, but were otherwise left at liberty, Ralph boldly maintains, "to frequent all publick Amusements, to be instructed as well as delighted" (212). *The Touch-Stone* easily dismisses "*Collier*'s ill-grounded, dogmatical Zeal" and "*Bedford*'s and *Law*'s ignorantly pious Blunders" (43) as exorbitant and, to a certain degree, irrelevant to an English society absorbed by such worldly matters as foreign and domestic policy, the growth of empirical knowledge, and "the commerce of everyday life."[46] But Ralph has more trouble dealing with the criticism of those who censure the "Reigning Diversions" on secular grounds, and who identify them as potentially dangerous impediments to earnest labour and employment – to politics, study, and, especially, business.

The majority of these critics share Fielding's anxiety that diversion has transgressed topographical and temporal boundaries, promoting idleness in those determined for industry. In the modern metropolis, the consequences of idleness were greater than in the provinces, since the labour of individual tradesmen and apprentices had the real potential to bring reward. Work and leisure had high stakes. As Hogarth's *Industry and Idleness* (1747) would have Londoners believe, the industrious could expect to rise economically and socially, while the idle could only anticipate ignominy and ruin.[47] It was one thing to neglect the demands of the next world, but it was quite another to ignore the material responsibilities of this one. According to Daniel Defoe: "Pleasures at certain seasons are allow'd, and we may give our selves some loose to them; but business, I mean to the man of business, is that needful thing, of which it is not to be said it *may*, but it *must* be done."[48] In the ninth letter of *The Complete English Tradesman* (1726), Defoe draws out this distinction between the compulsory and the voluntary, as a way of exposing what he sees as the false paradox of so-called innocent pleasures:

> All manner of pleasures should buckle and be subservient to business; he that makes his pleasure be his business, will never make his business be a pleasure: Innocent pleasures become sinful, when they are used to excess, and so it is here; the most innocent diversion becomes criminal, when it breaks in upon that which is the due and just employment of the man's life. (123–4)

In contrast to that of Collier, Bedford, and Law, Defoe's criticism is temperate and pragmatic. Time itself is the measure which he uses to evaluate diversion: if it takes the "mind" or "delight" or "attendance" of the tradesman from his work, if it distracts him for an inordinate "length of time," then it cannot be innocent.

Defoe's concern is not with the bare exercise of diversion, which he admits might be necessary for "the unbending of the bow of the mind," but with the "immoderate" extent to which it is frequently carried in the modern metropolis, where he sees "other and new pleasures daily crowding in upon the tradesman, and some which no age before this have been in danger of" (128). The old holiday pastimes occupied the idle intervals in the year, but the new commercial diversions, presented at "unseasonable and improper hours," threaten to seduce the tradesman away from his vocation and apply his "hands and head" to the dubious business of "pleasures and diversions." Defoe's letter engages the entire semantic field of diversion. On the one hand, he ranges through the "unlawful" amusements of early eighteenth-century London, alluding to the tavern, the gaming-house, the ball, and the playhouse. On the other hand, he describes these amusements as one of "the many turnings and by-lanes which are to be met with in the straight road of trade" (118). It is not so much that these deviations represent a moral failing, as that they turn the tradesman away from "the one needful thing which his calling makes necessary" (118). For Defoe, that is, the "Reigning Diversions" are dangerous because they necessarily divert from positive labour, interrupting the hopeful progress from "Prentice" to "Master" to "Lord-Mayor of London."

Likewise for Samuel Richardson, whose own handbook (or "Pocket-Companion") for the urban working classes plays frequently upon the overlap between diversion's nominal and verbal senses. Midway through Part I of *The Apprentice's Vade Mecum* (1734), Richardson digresses from his treatment of the obligations of indentured servants in order to comment on the many "Mischiefs" to which "young Men" might be subject. Principal among these are London's popular amusements which, he remarks, "may be call'd literally *Diversions* from all useful Employments and Business."[49] Richardson, like Defoe, surveys a variety of diversions, observing the specific qualities that allow each to persuade apprentices from their "solemn Engagement" (17). Cards, dice, tables, and "*other unlawful Games*" teach apprentices to covet other people's goods, fixing them in a "*Habit*" which can only lead to "Ruin" (17). The "*haunting*" of "Publick-houses" subjects apprentices to expenses they cannot honestly afford, and provides them with a "great Temptation to ill Hours and ill Company" (18–19). Even the theatre, once "Second to the *Pulpit* itself" in the inculcation of virtue, is far from being managed in "an unexceptionable Manner" (19). In the first place, modern plays are generally calculated for "Persons in *upper Life*," appealing to the experiences of those in a different social situation than men of business. Indeed, men of business are often made the "Dupes and Fools" of such plays, a circumstance that inevitably places "the Tradesman's Sphere" in a ridiculous light (20). Where comedies and tragedies do take the lower and middling classes as their subject, they tend to disregard "Poetical Justice," celebrating "odious and detestable Characters" while punishing honest ones. The "Depravity of the British Stage" is evidenced by plays like John Gay's *The Beggar's Opera* (1728), as well by the "horrid Pantomime," the "wicked Dumb Shew," and the "infamous Harlequin Mimicry," all of which are "introduc'd for nothing but to teach how to cozen, cheat, deceive, and cuckold" (21). Add to this the fact that the performance of plays usually begins before the work day ends, and what had formerly been exhibited "to very good Purpose" becomes yet another instance of what Richardson indicts as "the Luxury of the present Age": "Instead of gently relaxing the Mind from the Fatigues of Business, which in many Cases gives it a greater Edge on the Return to it, a frequent visiting of a Play-house (were even the Company and Entertainment better suited to a young Man's Circumstances and Situation) must too much detach his Mind from his Business, and fill it with light and airy Amusements" (21).[50] The problem with contemporary play-going, as with most other forms of modern amusement, is that a little is never enough. One amusement leads to another and that to another in such a way as to "intirely unhinge" the apprentice's mind from serious matters. Music will constantly "play upon his Ears," dancers will always "swim before his Eyes," and the affective performances of actors will "perpetually take up his Attention" (21). The result is less a diversion of attention than a compulsive attention to diversion.

Critics throughout the period warn that the hectic world of London amusements has come to occupy too much of the public's time and consciousness. In response to this concern, London entertainers seek to reassure the public through newspaper advertisements that acknowledge contemporary anxieties over the misuses and abuses of time, and then casually dismiss them with an empty but conventional disclaimer. For example, Christopher Pinchbeck advises audiences that his "most excellent Performance" is "shewn to two, or more, any Time of the Day, without Loss of Time."[51] An ad in *The Daily Courant* inviting sightseers to gawk at an exhibition featuring, among other things, "An Ægyptian Panther, spotted like a Leopard" and "A little black Man but 3 Foot high," notes that "This Collection of Wonders are all alive, and are to be seen from 8 in the morning till 8 at Night, without any Loss of Time."[52] In the same way and for the same reason, Isaac Fawkes adds an addendum to his puff for a September 1725 performance at "*a large commodious Room at the Queen's Arms Tavern*": "N.B. We show from one in the afternoon till nine at Night without Loss of Time."[53] Given that each of these advertisements list hours of operation that run the better part of the workday, the disclaimer that the "wonderful Machine" or exhibition of "Rarities" or "surprizing Tricks by Dexterity of Hand" represents an appropriate use of time seems to redound ironically against the showmen. But as many critics observe, the time employed *in* pursuit of diversion is not the only time lost *by* it. In *The Female Spectator* (1744–46), Eliza Haywood turns again and again to what she derides as "those hurrying Pleasures" that seem "to monopolize our Time, and every busy Care."[54] Attacking "our modern Diversion-Mongers," who every day contrive new entertainments to encroach upon "those Hours which Reason and Nature require should be otherwise employed," she cautions that time may in fact be an inadequate measure of diversion's harmful consequences (1.263–4). "The Idea of it is apt to render us indolent in our Affairs," explains Haywood, "the darling Topic engrosses too much of the Mind, and occasions an Inattention to every Thing but itself" (1.301). When not being diverted by diversion, pleasure seekers are nonetheless thinking about it, looking forward to or backward from the "Chocolate-House," "*Goodman's-Fields*," "Masquerades, Balls, and Assemblies," since "where the Heart is the Thoughts will continually be when the Body is absent" (1.301). Echoing Richardson and Defoe, Hayward argues that diversion is both a physical and a psychological obstacle to politics, study, and business.[55] Notwithstanding the hazards associated with the topographical and temporal expansion of diversion during the late seventeenth and early eighteenth centuries, the real problem had to do with diversion's perceived effects on the individual mind.

## Mental unbending and the work of leisure

If critics were concerned that diversion had come to monopolize "every busy Care," their exuberant expression of this concern exemplifies in itself the pervasiveness of amusement in the public sphere. By dedicating chapters and letters, periodical issues, and entire treatises to the controversial topic of amusement, critics ironically show themselves to be as engrossed by the "Reigning Diversions of the Town" as were audiences and apologists. Simply by writing about diversion, critics imply that it is worth writing about. And although they typically characterize it as trivial or frivolous, critics clearly expect their readers to take diversion very seriously. They expect pleasure seekers to do the same, which is why even critics such as Defoe, Richardson, and Haywood acknowledge that *regulated* diversion might serve to refresh the mind when it most requires it. Critical attacks on the new commercial diversions thus have something in common with works, like *The Touch-Stone*, which attempt to defend these diversions at length and in earnest by professing the right of all English men and women "to unbend their Minds from the Cares of the World," as Ralph has Primcock express it, "and hunt out Amusements of some Sort or other" (70).

Most commonly used in reference to amusement, the dead metaphor of "unbending" provocatively embodies the shift from communal catharsis to a singular psychological release. Just as the tension in a bent bow is relieved by letting go of the string, so is the strain of daily life diverted by "innocent" pleasures which rejuvenate those fatigued by politics, study, or business, giving them the wherewithal to continue on in their earnest labour and employment and, in the process, reconciling *utile* with *dulce*. In early modern physiological terms, the tenor of this vehicle involved a series of corporeal phenomena that were believed both to stimulate and to respond to conceptual changes: the perception of pleasure causes a dilation of the blood and an expansion of the animal spirits which, flowing through the proper channels, titillate the cerebrum, invigorate the cerebellum, and thence unbend the mind.[56] These animal spirits – a "quasi-magical fluid secreted by the brain" – were conducted through fibrous networks of nerves, and were thus understood by natural philosophers to be responsible for connecting the mind and body and, just as importantly, for bridging emotion and action by moving the passions.[57] For moral and civil philosophers, occasional diversion was essential because it gave vent to these passions, which, as Susan James explains, were "liable to disrupt any civilized order," unless they were "tamed, outwitted, overruled, or seduced."[58] To unbend the mind meant therefore to turn it away from objects of inclination or aversion, either of which might dangerously fix the attention, causing the juices to flow slowly or stultify and the individual to grow weak or dull.[59] However, consistent with contemporary theories of mind, the metaphor also implied a straightening out of the mental faculties, which ironically suggests that unbending might in fact be the real mental exercise: not a diversion away from work, but a phenomena that in itself does vital psychological work. The frequency with which the "Reigning Diversions" come to be valued for their capacity to unbend indicates that, during the formative period in the commercialization of leisure, diversion has somewhat more to do with discourses of the passions than with discourses of policy, with the action of amusements on individual minds instead of on the body politic.

What the Stuarts had seen initially as the political expedience of the people's pastimes, later apologists identify as a psychic imperative. So, in his preface to *The Compleat Gamester* (1674), Charles Cotton takes it for granted that "there was never any Stoick found so cruel, either to himself, or nature, but at some time or other he would unbend his mind, and give it liberty to stray into some more pleasant walks."[60] Similarly, when attempting to validate his *Athenian Sport: or, 2000 Paradoxes Merrily Argued to Amuse and Divert the Age* (1707), John Dunton applies a maxim drawn from Richard Allestree's *Whole Duty of Man* (1653) to modern work and leisure: "Recreations are sometimes necessary to both the Body and Mind of Man, neither of them being able to endure a constant Toil, without somewhat of Refreshment in between; and therefore there is a very lawful Use of them."[61] In *Tatler* No. 112 (December 27, 1709), Richard Steele elaborates on what he calls "the idle Hour of a wise Man," claiming that "the Slackening and Unbending our Minds on some Occasions, makes them exert themselves with greater Vigour and Alacrity, when they return to their proper and natural State."[62] Even Henry Fielding qualifies the attack in his *Enquiry* on "Voluptuousness," and on the social problems that result from "*too frequent and expensive Diversions*," by calling upon no less of an authority than Seneca to prove that occasional amusement is "the necessary Temperament of Labour": "Some Remission must be given to our Minds, which will spring up the better, and more brisk from Rest" (81). For each of these commentators, as for James Ralph, the relative lawfulness of diversion derives from its very usefulness: diversion unbends the mind so as to bend it more effectively when the temporary "turning aside" comes inevitably to an end. The "Reigning Diversions" are thus paradoxically conducive to a more productive exercise of body and, especially, mind, in that the latter is refreshed by every turning towards an object that is, as Ralph explains, "new, or out of the Way" (62).

The almost-universal accessibility and availability of the new commercial diversions made them volitional as well: if pleasure seekers possessed the money requisite for a ticket to Heidegger's "Midnight Masque," a beverage at Don Saltero's, or a seat in the upper gallery of Rich's Covent Garden, then they were free to unbend their minds at will. It was therefore incumbent upon pleasure-mongers to find ways of keeping their audiences interested and their respective minds engaged. In an attempt to assess how his culture resists boredom, Ralph surveys the practices of London's most successful showmen and impresarios, eventually having Primcock endorse novelty as the characteristic feature of any "Diversion truly *English*" (198). Primcock praises dramatic entertainments that advance "some new Turn, or surprizing Thought" (53). He predicts that the polite part of the nation will "fix their Attention" upon the "Novelties" performed at Henley's "Or- - -ry in *N—rt—m—t*" (194). He censures theatre managers who begrudge the expense of amusing audiences with "a new Scene, or suit of Cloaths, a new Dance, or Piece of MUSICK" (67). And he takes pride in the fact that several of the most popular innovations of the London fairgrounds are distinctly modern and conspicuously English:

> Then our teizing of a tame Ass into Madness, with Dogs at his Heels, and lighted Squibs and Crackers all round him——the baiting of a wild Bear with Wheel-barrows, and teaching Horses to Dance, play at Cards, and tell Fortunes——are *Entertainments* of that Novelty, Beauty and Grandeur, as never were known to the most Expensive and Luxurious of the Old *Roman* Emperors. (212)

Convinced that such devices are the only thing that will sell among contemporary audiences easily wearied by the same old amusements, Ralph elides the distinction between novelty and substantial quality by making Primcock explain that he never misses any operas or plays "that are good, or new" (xv). However, the terminology that he employs demonstrates a considerably more complicated attitude towards the psychology of audience response, acquiescing to the needs of the market while analysing the wants of the public that supports it.

When Primcock invokes "Novelty, Beauty and Grandeur" in the context of London "*Entertainments*," he tellingly applies to the "Pleasures of the Town" the principles of Joseph Addison's *Spectator* series on the "Pleasures of the Imagination," an eleven-essay study of the aesthetic appeal of the "*Great, Uncommon,* or *Beautiful.*" And Addison, as it happens, had invited writers and pleasure-mongers to do exactly this. In *Spectator* No. 412 (June 23, 1712), he asserts that "[e]very thing that is *new* or *uncommon* raises a Pleasure in the Imagination, because it fills the Soul with an agreeable Surprise, gratifies its Curiosity, and gives it an Idea of which it was not before possest." Wishing to expand precept into practice, Addison goes on to provide a material basis for this pleasure in one of the period's most provocative treatments of audience psychology:

> We are, indeed, so often conversant with one Sett of Objects, and tired out with so many repeated Shows of the same Things, that whatever is *new* or *uncommon* contributes a little to vary Human Life, and to divert our Minds, for a while, with the Strangeness of its Appearance: It serves us for a kind of Refreshment, and takes off from that Satiety we are apt to complain of in our usual and ordinary Entertainments.[63]

Addison's theory of pleasure is remarkably consonant with the terms of the rhetoric of diversion: novelty facilitates variety, variety produces refreshment, and refreshment staves off boredom and satiety, preventing the mind from fixing upon any object for too long and, in so doing, diverting readers when they are believed to need it most. But Addison also has something to say about the "usual and ordinary Entertainments" of pleasure seekers. Although it is primarily concerned with aesthetics proper, the *Spectator* series opens with an important, if unexpected, discussion of broader material pleasures and the potentially deleterious consequences of a singular taste in "Diversion":

> There are, indeed, but very few who know how to be idle and innocent, or have a Relish of any Pleasures that are not Criminal; every Diversion they take is at the Expence of some one Virtue or another, and their very first Step out of Business is into Vice or Folly. A Man should endeavour, therefore, to make the Sphere of his innocent Pleasures as wide as possible, that he may retire into them with Safety, and find in them such a Satisfaction as a wise Man would not blush to take. Of this Nature are those of the Imagination, which do not require such a Bent of Thought as is necessary to our more serious Employments, nor, at the same time, suffer the Mind to sink into

that Negligence and Remissness, which are apt to accompany our more sensual Delights, but, like a gentle Exercise to the Faculties, awaken them from Sloth and Idleness, without putting them upon any Labour or Difficulty. (3.538–39)

Echoing contemporary commentary on diversion, and anticipating Addison's later remarks in *Free-holder* No. 34 on the cultural function of "sports and shews," *Spectator* No. 411 (June 21, 1712) advocates "innocent Pleasures" as a medium between "sensual Delights" and "serious Employments," while warning that a devotion to any one or too few of these pleasures might make this "Sphere" tediously sensual or serious – a kind of "Business" in itself.[64] Because there are right ways and wrong ways to be "Idle" and to spend leisure time, Addison points out that even unbending diversions require engagement and a certain "Bent of Thought." He therefore recommends variety over unity and encourages pleasure seekers to "Exercise" their "Faculties" in a wide range of amusements, so as to keep up the novelty and maximize the unbending effects of their respective pleasures. At the same time, by applying similar criteria to literary art and leisure activity, Addison opens up the possibility that the reading of imaginative literature might be able to supply the novelty and variety demanded by a public looking to divert their "Minds."

## Animadversions upon diversion

Taking up this possibility, Ralph has Primcock recommend only those diversions that, as he puts it, "amuse the Audience with an agreeable Variety" (123). He claims, for example, that London audiences visit the "THEATRE" because they expect to be charmed by the "Variety of MUSICK and DANCING" (130). He marvels at the "Variety of Spectators and Amusements" that attend the London fairs (231). He offers a fulsome account of the "Variety of Habits" on display at Heidegger's Haymarket masquerades (177). And he digresses to describe how these habits correspond to "the Characters of Life":

> The various Characters that are there seemingly represented; the different Inclinations, Desires and Interests that fill every Breast, and that Medley of Nations, Languages and Judgments, must form the most agreeable Mixture of Conversation imaginable, giving every one a true Taste of easy Dialogue, and of consequence inspiring them with a sprightly Turn, and fixing the Standard of each Member's talking pertinently in his Character or Profession. (188)

Even while interrupting the seeming "Subject" of his particular essays, Primcock's digressions vary his discourse by moving from "one Sett of Objects" to the next. And the self-conscious copia of *The Touch-Stone* ensures that, as Addison puts it in *Spectator* No. 412, "the Mind is every Instant called off to something new, and the Attention not suffered to dwell too long, and waste it self on any particular Object" (3.541). Ralph's digressive survey realizes the coalescence of leisure and literature suggested by the aesthetic theory of the "Pleasures of the Imagination." If Addison's series of essays propose that even diversions require diversion, *The Touch-Stone* demonstrates that surveys of diversion do as well. The 237 octavo pages that Ralph devotes to operas, ridottos, and masquerades, pantomimes, prize fights, and public auctions, bearbaitings, fairground exhibitions, and puppet shows at once take advantage of a growing public interest in diversion and bend the mind to unbending. In the process, *The Touch-Stone* discursively enacts Ralph's subject matter, straying from the sober and significant concerns of the world around him in order to give extended analytical treatment to contemporary diversion.

Yet Ralph frames his analysis in terms that appear initially to contradict the substance and spirit of all things diverting. "My design was," he reflects in the closing pages of his book, "to animadvert upon the Standard *Entertainments* of the present Age" (236–7). In the present age, "to animadvert" meant, in one sense, "to comment critically on" (*O.E.D.* 4), and in another, "to turn the mind or attention to" a particular subject (*O.E.D.* 1). Playing on the semantic ambiguity of this now obsolete verb, Ralph combines both senses of animadversion in such a way as to reinforce the fact that the chastisement or censure of any subject cannot help but also take cognizance of it. That Ralph's particular subject is diversion allows him to play as well on the ambiguity of animadversion's semantic opposite: *The Touch-Stone* turns the attention of its readers to something consciously intended to distract their attention. In animadverting upon diversion, therefore, Ralph is able to acknowledge what he calls "the most material Objections of Consciences truly scrupulous" (xviii), while assimilating the matter of these objections into a broad defence of a commercial culture in which the idleness, concupiscence, and luxury often associated with London amusements ironically help to focus the attention of modern pleasure seekers. Moreover, in directing the attention of modern readers to the itinerary of London amusements, Ralph follows Addison in deftly conflating within a single survey the activities of reading *and* pleasure seeking, implying, on the one hand, that these may both be classified as "reigning" modes of diversion, and, on the other hand, that the activities of writing *and* pleasure-mongering share a responsibility to unbend, to entertain, and to indulge the desires of a public ardent about diversion.

Part of the broad cultural response to the commercialization of leisure was that diversion became an important topic of discourse in commercial literature published in the closing years of the seventeenth century and the first half of the eighteenth century. As the number of works printed with the words "diversion," "amusement," or "entertainment" in their title suggest, in literature, as in culture, diversion was perceived *to sell*. A search of the English Short-Title Catalogue (ESTC) for the years 1690 to 1760 discovers 172 titles under the keyword "diversion," 114 titles under "amusement," and 469 titles under the keyword "entertainment." Plural forms of the nouns turn up an additional 313 titles. And this is to say nothing of many other possible synonyms such as "pleasure," "leisure," "play," "recreation," and "sport."[65] *The Touch-Stone* is only one of many dozens of works which animadvert upon contemporary diversion, but it is typical of this popular genre in several respects. It discusses the consequences of commercialization in its various manifestations; it documents the conflict between traditional pastimes and the fashionable new diversions of London; it alternately characterizes or caricatures the emerging class of professional entrepreneurs who purveyed pleasure to the mass public; and it makes exaggerated claims for its own usefulness – being, as its title page boasts, "Design'd for the Improvement," first and foremost, "of all AUTHORS." Finally, and as the title-page designation hints, *The Touch-Stone* is typical of the genre I dub "animadversions upon diversion" in its measured commitment to readers who are invariably also pleasure seekers.

Although other surveys of "diversion," "amusement," and "entertainment" were better known or more widely read, *The Touch-Stone* is an excellent representative of the genre both because of the wide scope of its treatment of the "Reigning Diversions of the Town" and because of the self-consciousness with which it employs disruptive or "diversionary" rhetoric as intrinsic leisure for commercial literature. Ralph expects his readers to be edified by his survey, but he is also aware that the "Generality of Mankind" will only be persuaded to swallow "the black Potion of *Instruction*" if first promised "the Sugar-Plumb of *Delight*" (130). *The Touch-Stone* is thus conventional in mingling a serious plea for the revival of the ancient "CHORUS" with a rollicking "CONSORT of CAT-CALLS" – instruction with delight. However, it also mingles straightforward analysis with linguistic and textual devices that, like the period's cultural diversions, exuberantly turn aside from the business in hand for the purposes of entertainment. Though Primcock is made to joke in his preface that his "Method of Writing will not be sufficiently surprizing, or out of the Way, to take with the English Nation" (xxii), the diversions of the ensuing seven essays demonstrate quite the opposite. For example, when describing the "Contrivance and Conduct" of the period's "puppet-shews," Primcock compares the "Mechanical Genius" of English puppet-masters to the life-giving power of mythic Titans:

> I confess, I cannot view a well-executed puppet-shew, without extravagant Emotions of Pleasure: To see our Artists, like so many *Prometheus's*, animate a Bit of Wood, and give Life, Speech and Motion, perhaps, to what was the Leg of a Joint-Stool, strikes me with a pleasing Surprize, and prepossesses me wonderfully in Favour of these little Wooden Actors, and their *Primum-mobile*. (228)

Usually thought of as the champion of humankind against the hostility of the gods, Prometheus was a favourite figure in epic poetry and tragedy. But for the hero who created men out of clay, taught them all kinds of arts and sciences, and provided them with fire stolen from heaven to be related to a popular puller-of-strings (who might, nevertheless, set bits of wood ablaze) points to wit's penchant for inordinacy. Whether Prometheus is thereby reduced or puppeteers are exalted, the extravagant metaphor stands out from the discussion of the development of English "puppet-shews" as a discrete linguistic unit, which interrupts narrative progress and redirects attention from the "Historical, Critical, Political, Philosophical, and Theological" content of *The Touch-Stone* to the high-flown rhetoric of its form. Yet in so doing, the form of *The Touch-Stone* ironically makes a case for its content in that the metaphor illustrates, through its "out of the Way" vehicle, exactly the kind of mental distraction peculiar to diversion. "ESSAY V," on the poor behaviour of London audiences, is similarly disrupted by a series of asterisked ellipses that stand out as discrete textual units and seem to take the place of what purports to be a "plan" to improve "the fashionable Way of judging": "I could enlarge mightily upon this Head; and tell how * * * * * and where * * * * * the greatest * * * * and wisest * * * * * do and say * * * * * a thousand * * * * * better or worse * * * * and thus * * * * Fame" (155) (Figure 5). Even "ESSAY VII," which describes not one but a "Variety of Amusements," and thus has the tacit sanction of a certain degree of copia, digresses from the "Reigning Diversions of the Town" in order to pre-empt readers who will criticize Primcock for having dedicated his study to amusements:

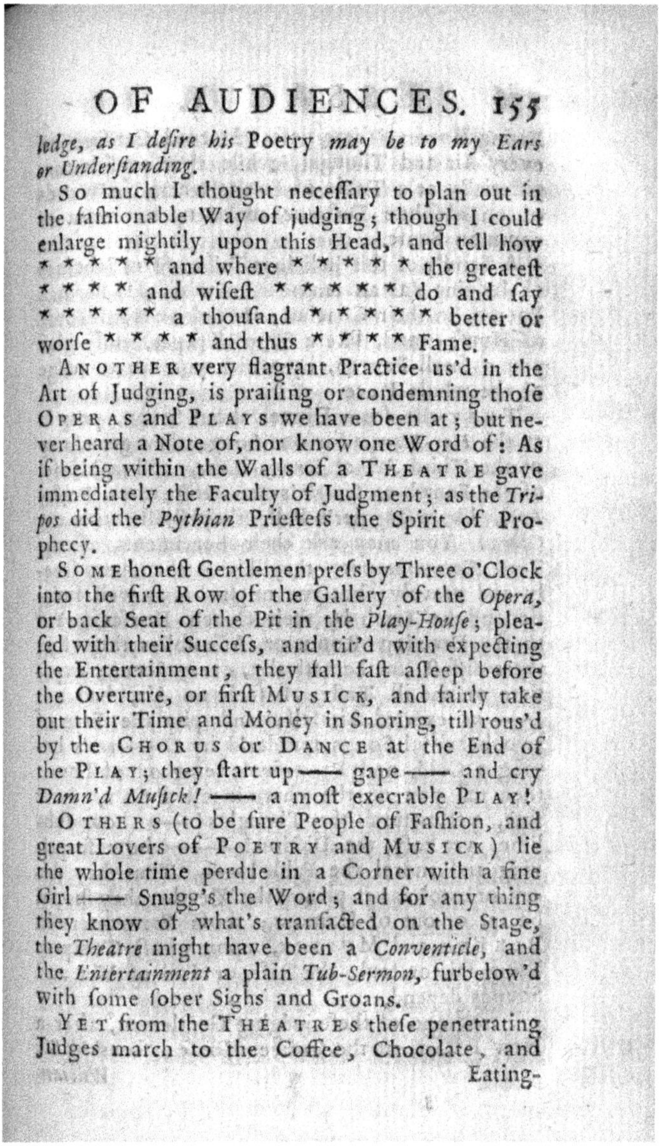

## OF AUDIENCES. 155

*ledge, as I defire his* Poetry *may be to my Ears or Underftanding.*

So much I thought neceffary to plan out in the fafhionable Way of judging; though I could enlarge mightily upon this Head, and tell how ✱ ✱ ✱ ✱ ✱ and where ✱ ✱ ✱ ✱ ✱ the greateft ✱ ✱ ✱ ✱ and wifeft ✱ ✱ ✱ ✱ ✱ do and fay ✱ ✱ ✱ ✱ ✱ a thoufand ✱ ✱ ✱ ✱ ✱ better or worfe ✱ ✱ ✱ ✱ and thus ✱ ✱ ✱ ✱ Fame.

ANOTHER very flagrant Practice us'd in the Art of Judging, is praifing or condemning thofe OPERAS and PLAYS we have been at; but never heard a Note of, nor know one Word of: As if being within the Walls of a THEATRE gave immediately the Faculty of Judgment; as the *Tripos* did the *Pythian* Prieftefs the Spirit of Prophecy.

SOME honeft Gentlemen prefs by Three o'Clock into the firft Row of the Gallery of the *Opera,* or back Seat of the Pit in the *Play-Houfe*; pleafed with their Succefs, and tir'd with expecting the Entertainment, they fall faft afleep before the Overture, or firft MUSICK, and fairly take out their Time and Money in Snoring, till rous'd by the CHORUS or DANCE at the End of the PLAY; they ftart up —— gape —— and cry *Damn'd Mufick!* —— a moft execrable PLAY!

OTHERS (to be fure People of Fafhion, and great Lovers of POETRY and MUSICK) lie the whole time perdue in a Corner with a fine Girl —— Snugg's the Word; and for any thing they know of what's tranfacted on the Stage, the *Theatre* might have been a *Conventicle,* and the *Entertainment* a plain *Tub-Sermon,* furbelow'd with fome fober Sighs and Groans.

YET from the THEATRES thefe penetrating Judges march to the Coffee, Chocolate, and Eating-

Figure 5 Asterisked ellipses in James Ralph's *The Touch-Stone* (1728), p. 155

The wise Cabals of our *News-mongers* (who feed upon our publick Papers, and gravely hold forth in the principal Corners of our top Coffee and Chocolate-Houses) will be struck with Amazement, that in the present Posture of Affairs, the State of *Europe* is not look'd into, War and Peace never mention'd, and the Ballance of Power forgot; when these Points, artfully vary'd, serve to amuse four Parts in five of the deepest heads in *Great-Britain*. (235)

In candidly acknowledging *The Touch-Stone*'s disregard for serious matters, this digression mimics diversion's delightful avocation of ordinary "Affairs." More than that, it treats the gravity of European power politics as merely another kind of diversion – something which might be discussed in a coffee or chocolate house and which might very well "amuse." The disruptive effects of the digression are thus mitigated by the self-consciousness of its association with the pleasurable effects of London amusement.

Not surprisingly, *The Touch-Stone* is self-conscious about almost all of its linguistic and textual diversions, Primcock's reflexive asides serving, like handbills and show-cloths and newspapers ads, to inform pleasure-seeking readers what kind of entertainment they are to expect. Ralph has Primcock expound upon "the Charms of the most beautiful Irregularities" (xvii); he discusses the usefulness of "half Blanks, whole Blanks, or mutilated Sentences" (xxiii); and he makes note of every instance in which his implied "Readers" compel him to address specific "*Entertainments*," even if, he confesses, "to touch upon them would be taking me out of my Way" (193). In another sense, however, these moments of self-consciousness are directly to the point, insofar as they reproduce discursively the psychological function of diversion: they "deviate" from what Primcock archly calls "the beaten Path of our public Diversions" in order to unbend the minds of individual readers and pleasure seekers who require occasional distraction if they are to remain attentive (43–44). *The Touch-Stone* takes the "Reigning Diversions of the Town" as its subject, and it represents this subject through a mischievously indirect style that characterizes luxuriant, illogical, and mixed metaphors, typographical blanks and lacunae, interpolated tales, burlesque erudition, and digressive wit as the tools-in-trade of any "AUTHOR" who intends for his "*Audience*" to enjoy vicarious pleasure. In this way, *The Touch-Stone* helps to gloss both why some of the period's most compelling defences of digressive wit appear within apologetics for amusement, and why some of the period's most idiosyncratic writers were among the most popular with pleasure-seeking readers.

## Leisure for literature

In the late seventeenth and eighteenth centuries, literary intrusions, obstructions, and interruptions gradually become "lawful" for the same reason as do the new commercial diversions: because they provide temporary relief to readers, allowing them to apply themselves with greater focus and force when they return to the literary business in hand. This mutual purpose is best exemplified by works, like *The Touch-Stone*, that animadvert upon diversion and that illustrate their cultural diversions through discursive ones. In a calculated attempt to secure an audience in the print marketplace, these works tend to debate the usefulness of amusement and the "tolerability" of linguistic and textual disorder in the same context and using a similar sort of rhetoric, entertaining in its means, if ultimately commercial in its ends. "This is the coquetry of a modern author," writes Anthony Ashley Cooper, 3rd Earl of Shaftesbury, "whose epistles dedicatory, prefaces and addresses to the reader are so many affected graces, designed to draw the attention from the subject towards himself and make it be generally observed not so much what he says as what he appears, or is, and what figure he already makes, or hopes to make, in the fashionable world."[66] The self-consciousness with which writers come to patronize readers – amusing, cajoling, and engaging them directly – ironically interrupts the very process of reading in which they are involved. Yet it is through these interruptions that readers are ingratiated and made to have a stake in the text in which they have invested their time and money. Taking a lesson from modern pleasure-mongers, commercial writers endeavour to show that they are doing all they can to unbend their readers' minds.

Authors who have traditionally been classified by critics as "popular" or as "hacks" routinely claim that they have adapted their works to the demands of the market and, more specifically, that they have pitched their digressive style at the easily distracted readers whom they expect will be their audience.[67] In the preface to the fourth volume of his collected *Writings* (1709), for example, Ned Ward boldly places the responsibility for the rambling discursiveness of his journalistic works on the reading public. Ward opens by self-identifying as one of those downtrodden gentlemen "who earn our Bread by the pointed end of a Gooses Feather."[68] He proceeds to express regret that the world is not as "full of Wise Men" as he would wish, but asserts that as a professional writer he is nonetheless willing "to descend so low as to tickle the giddy number, as well as the wiser few, or which of the two we shall think most conducing to either our

Credit or our Interest" (A1r–v). Ward's cynical use of economic language and his ambivalence about whom he pleases and whether he earns credit or interest registers the way in which the print trade is commoditizing traditional values: artistic skill becomes credit and literary esteem becomes interest. When he turns to the contents of the volume, Ward anticipates Addison's aesthetic theory in suggesting that the "Variety" of his works will recommend them to "the Taste of the Reader" (A4r). Arguing in defence of *The London Terræfilius*, a satirical survey of the commodities, character types, and entertainments of the metropolis, Ward writes that he "can assure the Reader, that the Style of the Prose is Laconick, and consequently not tedious."[69] The term "laconic" denotes an affected brevity of style, and Ward's description of his prose is ironic in that it achieves concision only because it treats each of its heterogeneous subjects briefly and discretely. In quick succession Ward satirizes "*Occasional Conformity*" (4), the trade of a "*Town-Strumpet*" (5), "*People-Plaguers*" at "*Westminster-Hall*" (10), modern hypocrisy (10–11), a "*Frenchify'd*" fop whose "whole Figure" resembles "a piece of *Salmon*'s Wax-work" (11), a city shrew (14–16), the atheism of a "Wavering *Anythingarean*" (23), and a "Fashionable *Lover*" whose favourite "Recreation" is "the *Play-House*" (26–27). Each of the six parts of the *Terræfilius* is interspersed with doggerel verse and each part closes with a series of mock-advertisements or "*Divertisements*," as Ward wittily calls them, that caricature the London public through an exposure of their habits of consumption:

> There is lately Erected, a little on this side *Islington*, a Famous *Dog-Academy*, where all sorts of *Puppies*, except those that keep 'em, may be Train'd up in the Diverting Sciences of *Ducking, Gunning, Hunting, Setting, Bull-baiting, Bear-baiting, Fighting, Thieving*, and all other Accomplishments that may fit 'em for any Station or Employment, from the *Ladies-Chamber* to the *Bear-Garden*, provided the Blockheads that own 'em will half starve their poor Families to pay well for their *Dogs* Board, and keep their Children from School, that they may be the better able to give to their four-Leg'd *Whelps* a more liberal Education. (Part 2, 37–38)

Howard William Troyer observes that Ward's unrelated vignettes produce a work that is lacking in "unity," but speculates that *The London Terræfilius* was enjoyed by contemporary readers who were "neither unduly distracted nor detained by the style."[70] In fact, Ward wagers that distraction is the very essence of modern literary style, and that his audience are looking to move casually from one "*Divertisement*" to the next. He therefore proposes that if the implied reader be "a lover of Humour … he may here be supply'd (if he pleases) with enough to divert himself at any time from a Fit of the Hypocondria" (A3v).

Another popular writer, Charles Gildon, appeals to the same demographic when he has the fictional editor of *The Post-Man Robb'd of his Mail* (1719) explain that since most readers "love not to dwell long on any thing," he has deliberately left his collection of "found" letters in a fragmentary and disjointed state. Gildon's work of early epistolary fiction comprises several "Packets" of "*Miscellaneous* LETTERS" that the aptly named "Sir Roger de Whimsey" discovers discarded in a ditch on the road from Paris to London. Prompted by a "Devil of Curiosity," he and his fellow travellers open the packets to read the letters in the hopes that they will receive "some sort of Diversion by the different Manners, Ways, Sentiments, Opinions, and the like, of the several Writers."[71] Whimsey decides to publish the "Epistles" for the same reason, informing "the Publick" that his book "consists of so great a Variety of Matter, as well as Manner, that I think there is something in some of them that will please you all" (xiv). The variety of manner is presented as the inevitable product of the disparate subject matter of the letters, which ranges from a pathetic exchange between pseudo-romantic lovers (153–78) to a disquisition on "*Pride, Modesty, Vanity, &c.*" (236–41) to a satiric letter of "*Advice*" to a would-be author, reflecting on the pitfalls of commercial success: "Never think of growing popular by Wit, good Sense, or solid Reason; there is a Burlesque Spirit that rules the Age, and a merry Buffoon is sure to carry the Prize" (147). Whimsey makes little effort to tie the letters together or to organize them along coherent structural or thematic lines, and the letters are introduced for seemingly arbitrary reasons. When Whimsey presents his fellows with "another Packet, though not so big as the last," and questions whether he should "break it open, and read the Contents, or pass on to the next," one of them encourages him to "read it in its turn, for I lik'd the last so well, that I am not frighted at the Bulk" (152). Yet notwithstanding the looseness of the narrative structure, the letters turn frequently to the literary and cultural market and to the issues of taste that appear to be Gildon's main theme. One fictional letter compares "Modern Dancers" to "the Mimes and Pantomimes of *Rome*," arguing vehemently that the popularity of "squeaking *Italians*" and "capering Monsieurs" is evidence of "*the Degeneracy of the Taste of our Great Men in their Pleasures*" (109–13).[72] Another ill-tempered letter complains of the mercenary habits of London booksellers who have "open'd the Door to all the abominable Scribblers that have so often won a Reputation from the Ignorance of the Town" (321). A series of letters evaluate the virtues (and vices) of such popular pastimes as the tavern, gaming table, assembly room, and playhouse, and describe the capriciousness of "the Publick Applause" (271). And a well-received letter from a "George Goodtaste" defends the necessity of "unbending Hours" in terms reflexive of Gildon's stated desire to please his readers: "you wou'd in vain perswade the People that they are free, while you depriv'd them of those innocent Diversions to which they [are] so inclin'd" (213–14). Gildon's epistolary novel is itself one of these "innocent Diversions," in that the miscellaneous content of the work caters to readers who would prefer not to be "always on the Bent" (214). *The Post-Man Robb'd of his Mail* plays to "the Gust of the Times" (xiv), exemplifying the pleasures of diversion through its juxtaposition of letters on incongruous topics. At the same time, the collection thematizes the proper uses of "Hours of Refreshment" and the right ways and wrong ways of distracting the English public from more serious concerns – from, as Goodtaste explains, "Study or Business" (215).

Tom Brown structures his popular survey of what he calls the "Meridian of London," *Amusements Serious and Comical* (1700), around a similar dichotomy between business and "Pleasantry."[73] Brown prefixes his book with a "long Preface," which he describes as a "true *Amusement*," intended to justify his "whimsical" style and distinguish the temper and character of "the generality of Readers." Addressing a prospective second-person reader, Brown predicts the reception of his work by imagining a mimesis of like-minded author and audience: "I have given the following Thoughts the Name of *Amusements*; you will find them Serious or Comical, according to the Humour I was in when I wrote them; and they will either *divert, instruct*, or *tire* you, after the Humour you are in when you read them" (3.1–3). As other hack writers, Brown acknowledges the cultural threat of boredom and strategically markets his *Amusements* to a public seeking relief from "serious Matters" (3.3). When he undertakes a discussion of the "surprizing Singularities" of London, he invites those who are too wrapped up in "Business" to "spare themselves the trouble of reading further in the Book," while encouraging more sympathetic readers who "are minded to amuse themselves" to "attend the Caprice of the Author" (3.13). The sudden and unpredictable change of mind denoted by "caprice" guides Brown's determination to set his "*Imagination* on the ramble" (3.13). Capriciousness takes Brown's narrator from a satire on "*News-mongers*" to commentary on "Matters of Gallantry" to a systematic anatomy of "the Circulation of *London*" (3.25). He portrays courtiers who "play at Bo-peep with Politicks" (3.11) and Cheapside shopkeepers who stand in the street "on purpose to be taken notice of" (3.21). And he employs humorous figures to represent the mental disposition of Londoners, as when he compares those who are "equally uncapable both of Attention and Patience" to "Moles" that "work in the Dark, and undermine one another" (3.25). Brown very quickly shifts his focus from London "*Amusements*" to the pleasure seekers who consume them, anticipating James Ralph in treating the audience as itself an object of diversion. Concluding his extended description of what he calls "*The City Circle*," the narrator is made to observe: "The *Publick* is a great Spectacle always new, which presents itself to the Eyes of private Men, and *Amuses* them. These private Men are so many diversified Spectacles that offer themselves to public View, and *divert* it" (3.93). Brown's suggestion that the habits of the public might be diverting to those in private (and vice versa) appears to apply particularly to London readers, whom he hopes will receive vicarious pleasure from his account of literal and figurative amusements. "I was amused in making these Reflections," he professes, "and I wish my Reader may amuse himself in Reading them" (5).

In the opinion of Benjamin Boyce, Brown's "realistic satiric 'journeys' about town" were popular with early eighteenth-century readers because they seem always "to afford some new entertainment." But if, as he claims, Brown was "the most successful hack of his day," it was also because he attempted to make the style of a work like *Amusements Serious and Comical* capture the pleasure of its subject.[74] Brown's narrator repeatedly digresses from his account of London amusements in order to reflect self-consciously on his penchant for digressing whenever the fancy strikes him: "I am so far from *confining* my self like a Slave to one particular Figure, that I will keep the Power still in my Hands, to change, if I think fit, at every Period, my Figure, Subject, and Stile, that I may be less tiresome to the Modern Reader" (3.45). To this end, Brown has his narrator take upon himself "the *Genius* of an *Indian*," a foreign observer who has "never seen any Thing like what he sees in *London*," and whose remarks upon the city, combined with the narrator's own remarks upon these remarks, comprise the substance of the work:

> LONDON is a World by it self; we dayly discover in it more new Countries and surprizing Singularities, than in all the Universe besides. There are among the *Londoners* so many Nations differing in *Manners, Customs,* and *Religions,* that the *Inhabitants* themselves don't know a quarter of 'em. Imagine then what an *Indian* would think of such a motly Herd of People, and what a diverting Amusement it would be to him to examine with a Traveller's Eye, all the remarkable things of this mighty City. A Whimsy now takes me in the Head, to carry this Stranger all over the Town with me: No doubt but his odd and fantastical Ideas will furnish me with *Variety,* and perhaps with *Diversion.* (3.13)

What is most striking about Brown's whimsical device is not its professed novelty, but the way in which it facilitates novelty, first, in the representation of all that is "new," "surprizing," "singular," or "remarkable" about London and, second, in the *"Diversion"* it purports to offer readers. Identifying novelty as at once the most distinctive feature of the city and the most avid desire of its "motly" inhabitants, Brown exploits the foreignness of his Indian to make the familiar seem startlingly fresh: "We shall see how he will be amazed at certain things, which the prejudice of Custom makes to seem reasonable and natural to us" (3.13).[75]

Once he has abruptly "dropt" his Indian "perpendicularly from the Clouds," Brown's narrator thrusts him into the winding streets of what he describes as a "prodigious and noisy City" (3.14). On their initial ramble through old London, the pair weave their way between "an infinite Number of different *Machines*, all in violent Motion" (3.14); they decline the "*Elixirs* and *Gallipots*" of a "Bookseller turn'd Quack" (3.14); they wonder at the "noble Edifice" of St Paul's Cathedral (3.18); they express sympathy for the "perfect Confusion" on display in Bedlam (3.32); and they eventually step inside a coffeehouse, as the narrator explains, to "rest our selves a little, and recover our Ears from the Deafness which the confused Noise of the Street had occasioned in 'em" (3.16). As they pass later through "*Cheapside*," on their way to "the great Place of Noise and Tumult, the *Royal Exchange*," the Indian is so overcome by the city and its sights and sounds that he succumbs to a kind of sensory overload:

> [M]y *Indian*, whether out of the several indigested Ideas he had receiv'd from the Diversity of Objects he met with, or a sort of a Surprize that had laid hold of him, at the first Sight of the Chimney-sweepers at the Conduit, that look'd so much like his own Country-men, was taken sick in an Instant, and I was forc'd to carry him to a Neighbouring Physician. (3.21)

When the Indian has sufficiently recovered, the narrator attempts to take stock of all that they have seen and heard, describing Londoners in terms ironically reflexive of his own narrative style: "Their Actions succeed one another with so much Rapidity, that they begin a Thousand things before they have finished one, and finish a Thousand others before they may properly be said to have begun them" (3.25). What Brown's narrator suggests about the overwhelming experience of turn-of-the-century London is also true of his book, which moves hastily from one "Amusement" to the next and thereby challenges readers to, as it were, "digest" the "Diversity of Objects" with which they are confronted. While the pair stroll the "*Walks* about *London*," an encounter with a "*Bevy of gallant Ladies*" provokes the narrator into a figuratively dense attack on the habits of modern women:

> They are fickle and light by Inclination, weak by Constitution, but never weary of Billing and Chirping. They never see the Day till the Sun is just going to set, and hop always upright with one Foot upon the Ground, and touch the Clouds with their proud Toppings. In a word, the Generality of Women are Peacocks when they walk; Water-Wagtails when they are within Doors, and Turtles whence they meet Face to Face.

Following this initial burst of misogyny, the narrator admits: "I have suffer'd my self to be carried too far by my Subject. 'Tis a strange thing that we cannot talk of Women with a just Moderation: We either talk too much or too little of them." Yet the narrator continues to talk "too much," discussing in turn the "Class of *Irregular* Women," the "Railing of the Men," and the most suitable punishment for "Defamation" and "Slander," before the Indian cuts him off: "Come, come, you ramble from your Subject; you speak of Back-biting in general, whereas at present we are only talking of that Branch of it, which belongs to Women" (3.49–51). Having been duly chastened, the narrator closes his digression upon women and from London walks with a concession that "I have made too long a Stay in this Part of my Voyage" (3.55) and a promise to "come back to my travelling Stile" (3.58).

Brown conflates form and content through the phrase "travelling Stile," implying that in his survey of the "Meridian of London" topographical and narrative rambling are one and the same thing. So as to reinforce this identity, Brown opens *Amusements Serious and Comical* with a digression that comments self-consciously upon his method of producing leisure for literature:

> There is no Amusement so entertaining and advantageous as improving some of our leisure time in Travelling, and giving a Loose to our Souls that have been upon the Stretch, by diverting 'em with agreeable Reflections on the *Manner* of the different Countries we journey thro', and the *Constitutions* of the several People, the Places we visit, are furnish'd with. If any Man therefore has an inclination to divert himself, and sail with me round the Globe, to supervise almost all the Conditions of human Life, without being infected with the Vanities and Vices that attend such a whimsical Perambulation, let him follow me, who am going to relate it in a Stile and Language proper to the Variety of the Subject: For as the *Caprichio* came naturally into my *Pericranium*, and I am as fond of what is the Product of my Fancy, as a young Woman of the Fruits of her lost

Virginity, I am resolv'd to pursue it thro' thick and thin, in order to enlarge my Capacity for a Man of Business. (3.6)

The irony of this digression is that Brown enlarges his capacity as a "Man of Business" precisely by abandoning what at first glance appears to be the business of his work. Under the rubric of "Perambulation," which implies both a fastidious journey on foot and an all-too-comprehensive account of this journey, Brown's narrator rationalizes digression as wholly appropriate to the dizzying "Variety" of a ramble across London.[76] And since he elsewhere portrays the "Hurry and Swiftness" of Londoners as they move from one thing to "a Thousand others," the narrator allows his narrative to do the same. When visiting the royal "*Court*," the narrator reflects upon the vicissitudes of "*Fortune*," the "Articles" of "*Transubstantiation, Nonresistance* and *Predestination*," and the apprehension of "being frightened from *flashing in the Pan* at Night with one's Mistress" (3.7–12). When attending the "*Play-House*," he wanders into a discussion of "Pippins, small Nuts and Gingerbread," the "*Humour*" of "*Primitive Christians*," and the "Difference" between "*Rhimes*" and "*solid Verse*" (3.37–43). And when rambling through the corridors of "*Westminster-Hall*," he digresses upon the transactions that typically take place within a "surly Judge's Chamber," the sale of "*Ribbons, Gloves, Towers* and *Commodes*," and the ins and outs of what he damns as "this cursed *Petty-fogging*" (3.43–47). This final digression he defends by way of yet another digression upon digressions: "Some pert Critick will tell me now, that I have lost my way in Digressions: Under Favour, this Critick is in the wrong Box, for Digressions properly belong to my Subject, since they are all *nothing but Amusements*; and this is a Truth so *uncontested*, that I am resolved to *continue* 'em" (3.44). If it is an "*uncontested*" truth that digression is the rhetorical equivalent of amusement, then Brown's "Perambulation" diverts readers in both form and content, satisfying his "Serious and Comical" purpose by turning intermittently aside from it. Like Ward, Gildon, and Ralph, Brown conceives of reading as one of London's primary amusements and of variety as the cultural quality most likely to produce amusement. He employs digression as the device best suited to the limited attention span of pleasure-seeking readers, altering his "Figure, Subject, and Stile" in an attempt to gratify the public's desire for variety in both diversion and discourse. "[F]or I know well enough," he remarks, "that Variety is the *predominant* Taste of the present Age" (3.45).

Although in certain cases ambivalent about the topic, each of these professional authors "to-be-lett" write about diversion because they realize that the English public wishes to read about it. And each of them stray from the straight-and-narrow of discourse because they understand their obligation not only to engage the interest of readers, but also to refresh them when and if they become tired of diversion after diversion. It is therefore important that Brown's implied reader is "Modern," since this situates him in commercial London, where he may choose to read about commercialized leisure in a work of commercial literature.[77] According to Christopher Flint, early eighteenth-century "hacks" were "renowned for writing in any style, regardless of what content a work might demand," and thus their publications materially illustrate "the market's influence upon literary works."[78] While it is certainly true that decisions regarding what and how to publish were shaped by trends in the "commercial culture industry," the digressive rhetorical asides and paratextual disclaimers characteristic of popular hack writing suggest that these authors were remarkably sensitive to the relationship between content and stylistic form.

Brown, perhaps the most brilliant and wily of all the Grub Street hacks, is also among the most honest about his mercenary motivations. He boasts in his preface that, despite the decline of the patronage system, his writing will inevitably thrive because of the general public's support of "AMUSEMENT":

> I am one of the first of the Suburban Class that has ventur'd out with an Amusement of this bulk, without making Application to a Noble-man's Porter, and tiring him out with shewing him his Master's Name. Which consideration I comfort my self with at no small rate; and if I have sent into the World what may divert the Pleasant, please the Serious, and instruct those that are willing to be advised, it's beyond my Expectance, and consequently must be an *Amusement* to my self as well as others. (3.6)

Brown's original epithet for London's professional class of writers ("Suburban") captures the awkward position of authors whose crass commercialism placed them outside of traditional literary culture, but whose condescension to the taste of pleasure-seeking readers allowed them to succeed almost in spite of themselves. Gildon, for example, opens his epistolary novel with a long-winded preface expressly intended to "pre-engage" the "good Will" of the "*Gentle Reader*" by forging an identity with his surrogate author-editor (IX). Ironically, in order to confirm his "Qualifications as a *Writer*," Gildon has Whimsey outline his own fashionable reading habits (XII), including his fondness for works that "entertain my Fancy" and distaste for "crabbed Tracts of Philosophy and Divinity" better suited to those "who have more Time on their Hands than

I have, and more Patience too" (IX). Declaring that "most Readers are of my Mind," Whimsey goes on to tease his audience with "the Entertainment I design for thee" (XIV–XVI). The preface keeps readers from this entertainment, yet Gildon nonetheless highlights the formal ends of his work out of a conviction that such self-consciousness is "in the Mode." So Whimsey is made to question "who wou'd be out of Fashion, when he may so easily avoid it, at the Expence of only a little perishable Paper?" (IX). In a similar way, Ward writes himself into fashion by addressing the preface to his *Writings* to the reading public rather than to "Powerful Friends and unprofitable Flatterers" (A2v). Like Brown, Ward seeks to bypass a patronage system that he maintains keeps writers in "in a starving condition" and "in precarious Dependencies" (A2r). He solicits instead the "suitable encouragement" of the publishing industry, whose representatives comprehend both how to market to readers who expect pleasure and support authors who desire profit:

> I shall not be ashamed to acknowledge, that the best Friends I have ever met with, have been my honest Chaps the Booksellers, tho some Authors, who have had but slender Dealings with that worthy Fraternity, have been pleased sometimes to brand them with too selfish a regard of their own Interest, which unfavourable suggestion, I am well satisfied, arises chiefly from an over-fondness of their own productions or from a false computation of the great hazard which Booksellers often run, for nothing more than an honest reasonable Profit. (A2v–A3r)

The notion that commercial profit is a "reasonable" motivation for publishing is one of the factors that necessarily set hack writers apart from those like Alexander Pope, whose crafty manipulation of the conventions of the print trade helped to establish, in the opinion of Flint, the "essential principles of modern authorship."[79] But these writers undeniably *sold*, and their success offers a different way of understanding the relationship between modernity and literary style. The posthumous four-volume *Works* of Brown went through an impressive nine editions between 1707 and 1760 due, in large part, to the author's ability to divert his readers through the shifting form and content of his miscellaneous *Amusements*. Gildon's *Post-Man Robb'd of his Mail* was the sequel to *The Post-Boy Robbed of his Mail*, a work that first appeared in 1692 and that sold so well that its author expanded it into a "Second Volume" in 1693 and published a "Second Edition" in 1706, with "the addition of many new and ingenious letters, never before published." Ward's *Writings* were among the most eagerly consumed of the early eighteenth century, miscellaneous volumes appearing in up to five different editions between 1700 and 1718. The marketability of such authors helps to account for what made popular literature *popular* in the first place. As pleasure-mongers start paying attention to the psychological state of pleasure seekers, so too do writers begin to regard more closely the psychological state of their readers – their needs and wants and their desire for diversion. The desire for diversion, after all, is a desire for change; and in wandering from Westminster Hall to the "Coffee-house" to Gresham College; in reflecting upon "Farcewrights," town sharpers, and the sales prospects of *The Complete Art of Poetry* (1718);[80] in describing "Doctor *Harlequin Paramount*," a group of "most fantastical Female Puppits," and the revival of "an Old *Pagan* Droll," Brown, Gildon, and Ward ensure that their pleasure-seeking readers will never become bored and, consequently, will buy the amusement they are selling.

In the process, works that at first appear to defend the usefulness of social amusement become as well apologetics for self-consciousness and for a rhetorical mode that separates disruptive writing from any purpose other than distraction. Colley Cibber's autobiographical *Apology* (1740) takes this one step further, defending the digressive style in a work designed to defend a life dedicated to defending commercial diversion. Cibber endeavours to account for his controversial career as "Theatrical Merchant," and for his promotion of "Farcical Folly" while co-manager at Drury Lane, declaring that he has simply followed the lead of men greater than himself, who have enjoyed the particular pleasure "of unbending into the very Wantonness of Good humour, without depreciating their Dignity" (16). Citing a canon of classical pleasure seekers that was becoming commonplace in eighteenth-century discussions of amusement, he argues that a readiness to take time out from serious matters is what qualifies men for greatness:

> He that is not Master of that Freedom, let his Condition be never so exalted, must still want something to come up to the Happiness of his Inferiors who enjoy it. If *Socrates* cou'd take pleasure in playing at *Even or Odd* with his Children, or *Agesilaus* divert himself in riding the Hobby-horse with them, am I oblig'd to be as eminent as either of them before I am as frolicksome? If the Emperior *Adrian*, near his death, cou'd play with his very Soul, his *Animula*, &c. and regret that it could no longer be companionable; if Greatness, at the same time, was not the Delight he was so loth to part with, sure then these cheerful Amusements I am contending for, must have no inconsiderable share in our Happiness; he that does not chuse to live his own way, suffers others to chuse for him. (16)[81]

In Cibber's opinion, diversion is democratizing insofar as a desire for "cheerful Amusements" is, perhaps, the one quality that the eminent and inferior have in common. This is why he endorses freedom in the choice of amusement, since to be proscribed or coerced to enjoy oneself is to lose the pleasure of the enjoyment. Cibber's emphasis on the subjective experience of diversion makes possible a different kind of genealogy of leisure, one that takes its precedence from the pastimes of famous individuals rather than those of historically distinguished cultures. Socrates, the Spartan king Agesilaus, and Emperor Hadrian provide Cibber with an exemplary pattern for imitation, both because of their individual achievements and because of their commitment to individualized amusements – the latter contributing materially to the former.

From the outset of his *Apology*, Cibber equates his dual role as writer and pleasure-monger, treating at one and the same time the effects of his prose and his reputation as player and theatre manager on "the Publick":

> This Work, therefore, which I hope, they will not expect a Man of my hasty Head shou'd confine to any regular Method: (For I shall make no scruple of leaving my History, when I think a Digression may make it lighter, for my Reader's Digestion.) This Work, I say, shall not only contain the various Impressions of my Mind, (as in *Louis the Fourteenth* his Cabinet you have seen the growing Medals of his Person from Infancy to Old Age,) but shall likewise include with them the *Theatrical History of my Own Time*, from my first Appearance on the Stage to my last *Exit*. (7)

Making a case for digression within a parenthesis, digression's grammatical double, Cibber interrupts his syntax in order to emphasize that all such interruptions function to relieve readers from the tedium of linearity. If the parenthesis does not divert the reader, then the strained metaphor will; and if this is still insufficient, then the digressiveness of Cibber's self-conscious aside will almost certainly unbend the mind. Although it makes a subject of the self, Cibber's *Apology* is remarkable for the attention it pays to the mental condition of the reader while reading. When attempting to return to a description of theatrical rivalries from a "short Digression" on the "Spirit of Patriotism," "*Sophocles*," and the taste of "Honest *John Trott*," Cibber thanks the indulgent reader for his patience:

> And this Crisis, I am myself as impatient, as any tir'd Reader can be, to arrive at. I shall therefore endeavour to lead him the shortest way to it. But as I am a little jealous of the badness of the road, I must reserve to myself the Liberty of calling upon any Master in my Way, for a little Refreshment to whatever Company may have the Curiosity or Goodness, to go along with me. (199)

Elsewhere, Cibber directly associates the time spent in reading a digression with leisure time: "All this I own, is leading my Reader out of the way; but if he has as much Time upon his Hands, as I have, (provided we are neither of us tir'd) it may be equally to the Purpose, what he reads, or what I write of. But as I have no Objections to Method, when it is not troublesome, I return to my Subject" (190–91). Cibber's actual method is to draw out a parallel between those social amusements that provide relief from the serious concerns of daily life and those linguistic and textual devices which occasionally disrupt plain discourse. The *Apology* animadverts upon both, using a rhetoric that is so similar as to become at times reciprocal. Having already contended that "cheerful Amusements" must have "no inconsiderable share in our Happiness," Cibber argues that the same maxim should apply to the pleasures of reading: "No, Sir, I am not for setting up Gaiety against Wisdom; nor for preferring the Man of Pleasure to the Philosopher; but for shewing, that the Wisest, or Greatest Man, is very near an unhappy Man, if the unbending Amusements I am contending for, are not sometimes admitted to relieve him" (19). Because this address to the reader immediately follows what Cibber characterizes as yet another "copious Digression," the amusements that he is here contending for are necessarily discursive – the rhetorical equivalent of the new commercial diversions. And they function, like other "unbending Amusements," as a kind of sorbet for the critical intellect, invigorating the mind, refreshing the senses, and staving off boredom and satiety. "Satiety," remarks Cibber, "puts an end to all Tastes, that the Mind of Man can delight in" (162). Just as he claims in the *Apology* that the "Novelties" he was responsible for mounting at Drury Lane prevented the repeated show of the same tired old plays, so too does the digressive style of his autobiography offer diversions to an audience unable or unwilling to read straight through forty years of "*Theatrical History*."[82] And just as "new-fangled Foppery" and "monstrous Medlies" (279) inevitably drew pleasure seekers to the theatre, so too did Cibber's *Apology* sell, going through five editions between 1740 and 1761, in oversized quarto, octavo, and, eventually, two-volume duodecimo format.

If the rhetoric of those who defend the usefulness of devices like digression echoes or even, in some cases, coalesces with that of the period's apologists for amusement, then the converse is also true: the rhetoric of those who proscribe the extravagance associated with linguistic and textual disruption resembles that of the period's opponents of diversion. "Overstrained" metaphors, "*typographical* figures," and "digressions upon digression" might be seen to unbend the minds of individual readers, but they might just as well confound these readers, engrossing their minds and causing them to waste away their time in pursuit of matter that is at best beside the point. Just as in social life, the problem is not with diversion itself, but with the "immoderate" extent to which the devices of digressive wit are frequently carried in modern literature and in works like *The Touch-Stone*. Although it has been treated in this chapter as a case study in the "profit" of diversionary rhetoric, it is noteworthy that *The Touch-Stone* does not appear to have been a commercial success: it reached a "Second Edition" in 1729, but was reissued in 1731 under the title *The Taste of the Town*, this purportedly new "Guide to All Publick Diversions" being composed of unsold sheets from the first press run. For all of Ralph's efforts to delight and instruct his pleasure-seeking readers, the fact that *The Touch-Stone* did not sell makes it clear that too much digression could be just as problematic as too much amusement, and that concerns over the efficacy of diversion could have an impact on the reception of animadversions upon diversion.

Ralph has Primcock return from one of his many self-conscious "*Side-Steps*" under the tongue-in-cheek assumption that he will be "pardon'd for such seasonable Digressions, without the Trouble of digressing any farther" (114). But Ralph's contemporaries were not always so optimistic about the rhetorical expedience of digressive wit. In *An Essay Upon Wit* (1716), Richard Blackmore acknowledges that the talents of witty writers "are very much to be esteem'd in their proper place; that is, as they unbend the Mind, relieve the Satiety of Contemplation and Labour, and by the Delight which they give, refresh the Spirits and fit them for the Returns of Study and Employment."[83] Like Ralph, Blackmore collapses the distinction between cultural and discursive diversion, treating witty writers as pleasure-mongers and weary readers as an audience fearful of satiety and avid for amusement. He goes so far as to argue that writers who "divert and entertain the Fancy" should claim "the highest Rank among those, who are Inventors or Ministers of Pleasure, and provide Amusements and Recreations for the Busy and the Wise" (214–15), suggesting a competition for audiences between imaginative writers and entertainers like Isaac Fawkes or John Rich. Yet the qualification of "in their proper place" implies that not all wit is true wit, that inordinate unbending compromises earnest labour and employment, and that digression *out of place* is analogous to idleness *out of season*. Blackmore observes:

> It is a meretricious Prostitution of Wit, when the Possessors of it can deny no Addresses, and refuse no Invitations and Appointments, but suffer

themselves to be shown at every Entertainment: Besides the gratifying of their Vanity, by a constant pursuit of Approbation and Praise, which is the Spring whence this prodigality of Parts and waste of facetious Humour chiefly arise: it is evident they spend a great deal of Time, of which a wise Man can give no Account, while Wit, which should in its proper place, renew and revive the Spirits for useful Employment, becomes a continu'd Diversion, and makes everlasting Idleness the Business of Life. (213)

Blackmore's anxieties about digressive wit reflect almost exactly Haywood's concern that amusement "occasions an Inattention to every Thing but itself," Richardson's warning against literal *"Diversions* from all useful Employments and Business," and Defoe's criticism regarding the "unseasonable and improper hours" of contemporary pleasures. And it parodies the popular commonplace of the wise or great man who routinely takes time out for diversion. Like cultural diversion, discursive diversion is irresponsible in "facetious" writers because it makes pleasure-seeking readers idle and lazy and causes them to neglect the "Business" of both life and literature.[84] Threatening to become one "continu'd Diversion," devices like digression imitate the expansion of commercial amusements across topographical and temporal boundaries.

But in transgressing mimetic boundaries, digression delights in the verisimilar reality of the busy round of London pleasures that even staunch critics could not help but describe in a digressively self-conscious way. In a short pamphlet on *The Regulation of Diversions* (1708), the Presbyterian minister Henry Grove sets out to codify for his audience "such Rules and Directions as regard the *Use* and *Enjoyment* of your Diversions."[85] He begins by defining the former (*"Use"*) in familiar terms that emphasize the psychological value of a certain sort of physical unbending:

> The general End of Diversions is, by invigorating *Nature*, and providing her with fresh Recruits of Spirit, to fit her for better and more cheerful Service; from whence it follows that all too violent and intense Exercises that exhaust the Spirits, over-strain our Powers, and crack the Sinews of the Constitution, are heedfully to be shunn'd. The particular and immediate End is, either to relieve the Mind under Melancholy, and then some Diversion that will amuse the Thoughts at the same Time that it employs the Body is best; or to cure it of a Fit of Dulness, and then bodily Exercise prudently manag'd will be of Use, leaving the Thoughts to rest themselves, I mean, as to any vigorous and close Application. (15–16)

He goes on to discuss the latter (*"Enjoyment"*) in equally familiar terms, warning that too much diversion is just as prejudicial to the well-being of pleasure seekers as too little, in that it makes an unproductive use of time and turns into an end in itself what should be a means:

> Let not your Diversions be too long and entrench upon your Time; as for certain they do when so much of the Day is allotted them that you're forc'd to crowd together in Haste your Devotions and Business, that they may come within the Compass of the little that is left, or perhaps, wholly neglect them. He is to be commended that knows when to leave off, who having stop'd and breath'd a while, and taken necessary Refreshment, pursues his Journey with fresh Vigour and Alacrity, and does not, as some others, make a tedious Stay at every *baiting* Place. (34–35)

Yet when Grove attempts to find a way of expressing both the possible dangers of "immoderate" diversion and the potential delights of "*seasonable*" diversion, he breaks with the familiar by drawing a simile from the rhetorical arts:

> Diversions in Life are not altogether unlike *Digressions* in a Book, things mighty serviceable to an *Author*, they relieve him in the Want of Matter, and, which is yet better, swell the Bulk and the Price of his Book; neither, if discreetly husbanded, are they unacceptable to the *Reader*; but if spun out to an unreasonable Length, they take up much more Room than the main Subject, we conclude the Author to have a wrong Idea of Digressions, or a very mean one of his Readers. (35)

Although his argument is essentially the same as that of critics such as Blackmore, and although it is analogous to that of apologists such as Brown and Cibber, Grove startlingly inverts the rhetorical pattern of his contemporaries: it is not that digression is like diversion, but that the "Reigning Diversions" are like a "continu'd *Digression*."

That tenor and vehicle might be interchangeable points to a perceived reciprocity between disruptive linguistic and textual devices and social amusement, as well as to an overlap between the activities of reading and pleasure-seeking. Grove implicitly directs his pamphlet to English pleasure seekers, yet he frequently addresses himself to English readers, or to "any such" who "happen to read this small Essay," regulating their social habits by cultivating their reading habits (38). At the same time, he exemplifies his proscriptions in occasional digressions that at once relieve the "*Reader*" and allow the "*Author*" to elaborate freely upon the causes and broader effects of unregulated diversion. For example, an off-handed attack on the leisured rich, who have time lying upon their hands and who "give it all to Recreation," provokes a three-page digression on the education of "Young Men that are Born to Estates," but who "miserably neglect their

Studies" (42). Wandering further and further away from his principal subject, Grove censures the rich for their neglect of the distresses of "the *Poor* and the Needy" (41), he comments upon the "Ignorance" of the "present Age" and "the Vices of the Tongue" (42), and he pursues the claim that making "a Jest of Damnation" has "almost become a set Diversion" among "*Men of Wit*" (43), before eventually concluding with a concession of digression: "In short, (that I may return from this little Digression) young Gentlemen will find enough to do to lay in Materials, that they may appear with Honour and Reputation when their *Queen* or *Country* shall call them into the Scene of Action" (43). Even though this digression is not strictly to the point, it helps to facilitate Grove's broader arguments about regulated diversion and digression by the very fact of its being, as Grove asserts, "little." And being "little," the digression ensures that pleasure-seeking readers will return to their task and his text with "fresh Vigour and Alacrity." If other authors write about diversion because they realize that the English public wishes to read about it, Grove reflects self-consciously upon digression because he realizes that he will not retain these readers unless he unbends them.

Whether bestowing "Panegyrick" or offering "Censure," the period's animadversions upon diversion seem to share a consensus that reading has become one of the most pervasive of the "Reigning Diversions of the Town." The many reasons for this shift are complex, but the consequences are not. If readers have become pleasure seekers, then writers – as pleasure-mongers – have a duty to refresh and invigorate their respective minds. In analysing the coincidental "individualization" of amusement and "subjec-tivization" of reading, works that survey the new commercial diversions record an emerging cultural interest in the psychology of audience response, an interest that is often manifested in a self-conscious rhetoric that expressly aims to divert pleasure-seeking readers by co-opting the energy of commercial leisure and internalizing diversion as a constitutive aspect of commercial literature. The evident pleasure that *The Touch-Stone* and other works expect these readers to take in devices like digression exposes the insufficiency of traditional critical assumptions of self-consciousness which, first, tend needlessly to "intellectualize" their subject and which, second, tend necessarily to privilege the authorial "self." But the frequency with which these kinds of devices are related to the "Reigning Diversions" suggests that they have as much to do with the recreations of a voluptuous society as with the lucubrations of a self-conscious mind. One of the most important ways in which writers of this period gratified a reading audience avid for diversion was through a variety of linguistic and textual devices that themselves diverted – that turned aside from plot, character, and argument in order to unbend the mind. And thus the valuable question of why the flourishing of literary self-consciousness coincides with the commercialization of leisure may be resolved through simple socio economics: "over-strained" metaphors, "*typographical* figures," and "digressions upon digression" develop as a way of supplying the demand for "*nothing but Amusements.*"

CHAPTER 2

# *"Pleas'd at being so agreeably deceiv'd": pantomime and the poetics of dumb wit*

Here you've a Dragon, Windmill, and a Devil,
A Doctor, Conjuror, all wond'rous civil;
A Harlequin, and Puppets, Ghosts, and Fiends,
And Raree-Show to gain some Actor's Ends:
So perfectly polite is grown this Town,
No Play, without a Windmill, will go down.
–Anon., The British Stage: or,
The Exploits of Harlequin (1724)

Take then no pains a Method to maintain,
Or link your Work in a continu'd Chain,
But cold, dull Order gloriously disdain.
Now here, now there, launch boldly from your Theme,
And make surprizing Novelties your Aim;
Bombast, and Farce, the Sock and Buskin blend,
Begin with *Bluster*, and with *Bawdry* end.
–Miller, Harlequin-Horace (1731)

The third essay of *The Touch-Stone* (1728) takes as its seeming subject the history and development of pantomime, one of the most contentious and, as James Ralph explains, most popular of the "Reigning Diversions of the Town." Tracing its origins back to the *mimi* and *pantomimi* of antiquity and through the tradition of Italian *commedia dell'arte*, Ralph attempts to determine the degree to which pantomime's current manifestation, in the two-part harlequinades mounted as afterpieces at Lincoln's Inn Fields and Drury Lane, may be "render'd of the utmost Consequence to the Republick of Letters" (103–04). The first or "serious" part of these panto-mimes made the most of their classical heritage by featuring a mythological story, most often taken from Ovid or from some other tale of magic and metamorphosis. This part was interspersed by a second or "comic" part that followed the frenetic efforts of Harlequin to dupe Pantaloon or Scaramouch and win the heart (and usually body) of Colombine.[1] The gods and goddesses, heroes and heroines of the serious part, typically represented their stories through song, dance, and occasional dialogue. But because the more entertaining comic part was usually mute, eighteenth-century pantomime came to be best known for the "silent *Rhetorick*" (101) of Harlequin, who managed to be persuasive without resorting to what Ralph describes as a "trifling Superfluity of Words" (108).

Here, as elsewhere in *The Touch-Stone*, Ralph's latent interest is in the relationship between English amusement and the state of native literature; consequently, his "Historical Account of MIMES and PANTOMIMES" (86) deals as much with contemporary poetics as it does with pantomimic art. Ralph learnedly discriminates between the Greek, Roman, and English pantomime, he analyses the contributions of "*J—n R—h*, Esq." (108) to the genre, and he variously defines "pantomime" as "that Supplement to a *Stage Entertainment*" (93), as a kind of "*Speaking Dance*" (95), and as a representation of "proper Fables by Motions, Gestures, Attitudes, &c." (93).[2] At the same time, he complains of "our present visible Decay of all Sense, especially *Poetick*" (104); he comments upon the low ebb of heroic poetry, elegy, pastoral, and satire; and he censures the "nonsensical *Jargon*" and "*Jack-pudding* Action" that have come to characterize the English stage (101). Setting himself, however, in ironic opposition to many of his contemporaries, Ralph does not view pantomime as symptomatic of or as a reason for this "Decay of all Sense," but as a potential corrective to it. Although pantomime was widely criticized as an unnatural, indecent, and irregular threat to polite standards and taste, Ralph claims that it might nonetheless help to rejuvenate poetry and bring it to a greater pitch of instruction and delight. "[S]ince Nonsense has so long usurp'd the Provinces of Tongue and Pen," he writes, "we may chance to improve, by dumb Wit" (104).

The tongue-in-cheek tone of this proposal, that literature might take a lesson from commercial entertainment, should not diminish the earnest, if unexpected, suggestion that poetical art has something in common with the "dumb Wit" of contemporary pantomime. Throughout *The Touch-Stone*, Ralph has his pseudonymous author, A. Primcock, draw analogies between the two, asserting, at one point, that pantomime is "the dumb younger Sister of Poetry" (100), and contending, at another point, that the "nimble Talents" of Harlequin are akin to those of modern poets (108). Ralph conceives of pantomime as an art of imitation comparable to poetry, but one that represents nature in its motley dress without the encumbrance of verbal wit. Where contemporary poetry has strayed from strict mimesis by indulging in what he deems "tedious" language (108), pantomime restores imitation to its natural origins, exploiting the physical movements of dancers to represent visibly "all Actions of Life" (98).[3] In, for example, John Thurmond's *Apollo and Daphne: or, Harlequin's Metamorphoses* (1726), a vigorous "nodding" of the head demonstrates Peneus's resolve to preserve his daughter from the rough "Insults" of the amorous god of "*Rhetorick.*" In *The Rape of Proserpine* (1727), by Lewis Theobald and John Rich, the sudden dispersion of a train of dancing nymphs signifies the confusion and disorder that immediately precedes Pluto's assault. And in the "*Comic Part*" of Theobald and Rich's *Perseus and Andromeda: or, The Spaniard Outwitted* (1730), the vanity and assurance of the Petit Maitre is discovered by his "admiring and adjusting himself with a Pocket Looking-Glass," while Harlequin's disdain for his romantic rival is made manifest by his running against him and striking him "upon the Back."[4] What Ralph finds attractive about such "silent *Rhetorick*" is its apparent proximity to truth, reason, and the pattern of nature: in conveying meaning by way of motion alone, pantomime avoids the "Nonsense" to which words had become prone and the stylistic excess with which rhetoric proper had come to be associated. For Ralph, the "Decay of all Sense" (104) is principally owing to language that allows manner to stand in the way of matter, directing attention to its own discursive status instead of the thing, idea, or action to which it refers. Pantomime, on the other hand, eschews the idiosyncrasies of manner in favour of a direct and sensible representation of matter. As these stage directions and scene descriptions suggest, physical antics might speak to the mind through the body, and thereby fulfil the communicative function of language without using any. In having Primcock promote contemporary pantomime at the expense of contemporary poetics, Ralph playfully participates in seventeenth- and eighteenth-century debates about the place of "additional Ornaments" (61) on the English stage, as well as critical discussion concerning the efficacy of verbal language, the relative value of rhetoric, and the nature of true and false wit. The extravagance of Primcock's own rhetoric indicates that these debates were separate but not mutually exclusive: "since Head-pieces are at a Loss in giving us proper Documents, we may look for Instruction from Arms and Legs" (104).

Like the third essay of *The Touch-Stone*, this chapter explores the meaningful association during the period between "dumb Wit" and verbal wit, between "silent *Rhetorick*" and the *ars rhetorica*, and between pantomime and poetics. It develops a parallel between two otherwise distinct topics for the simple reason that, during the 1720s, 1730s, and 1740s, pantomime and poetics came to share a critical vocabulary in theatrical performances that were preoccupied with language and expression, and rhetorical performances that were realized in conspicuously physical terms. All expressive arts overlap in various ways, but in the early eighteenth century the tricks and transformations of Harlequin and the characteristic turns of rhetorical wit were mutually allusive: where painting and sculpture and music were seen to reflect similar cultural norms, pantomime and poetics reflected one another by way of commentary that described each in the context of the other and in turn drew attention to wit's material aspect. As such, Chapter 2 is not solely concerned with what pantomime reveals about public taste during the period, nor is it merely about "Augustan" wit and its discontents. Rather, like Ralph's "Historical Account," it deals with the complex and often reciprocal relationship between pantomime and wit – one that is negotiated through the corporeal appeal of Harlequin's motions, gestures, and attitudes, and the corresponding visual appeal of elaborate tropes, figures, and similitudes.

Contemporary writers took for granted that they were living in an "Age of Wit," but they were far less certain what precisely wit was. They were considerably more certain about what wit *was not*. The critical essays and manuals of polite discourse of the period invariably define "true wit" negatively, by opposition to the perceived improprieties and unnatural deceits of what John Locke terms "*wilful Faults and Neglects*" in language, what Shaftesbury dismisses as little more than "jingling eloquence," what Pope satirizes as "One *glaring Chaos*," what John Oldmixon calls "a kind of counterfeit Money," and what Addison archly classifies as "Tricks in Writing."[5] Working from the theoretical high ground of authors such as Locke, Pope, and Addison, literary historians have generally treated all such epithets for "false wit" in terms of a broad cultural anxiety about the limitations and equivocations of verbal forms of rhetoric. In everyday practice, however, wit's semantic ambiguity allowed it to assume a variety of forms in a range of contexts – not all of which were verbal. This chapter will demonstrate that critical quarrels over the witty and witless could have as much to do with *things* as with *words* and, moreover, that apologies for and satires against pantomime could also have a stake in conceptions of language, rhetoric, and wit. Augustan poets and critics frequently employed visual analogy to describe the epistemological effects of wit: true wit made spectators out of readers, prompting them to picture in their mind's eye that which was represented, while false wit distorted this picture by inviting readers to gawk at grotesque mental monsters. Yet as Ralph's epithets for Harlequin's "*Speaking Dance*" imply, objects of analogy often took on rhetorical meaning in themselves, revealing the unexpected verbal significance of physically visible representation.

*The Touch-Stone* exemplifies what I call "pantomimic poetics" through metaphors that self-consciously strain sense while attempting to account for the origins of English pantomime, as when Ralph has Primcock declare that modern *"Arlequins, Scaramouches* and *Punchinello's"* have risen *"Phœnix-like"* out of the "old *Mimes"* of ancient Greece and Rome (100).[6] Though the ascendance of monarchs and the emergence of nations were sometimes likened to the red-and-gold plumed bird that lived for 500 years, burned itself on a funeral pyre, and then rose eternally from its own ashes, a comparison of the rising popularity of Harlequin to such an image is patently absurd. The mythological vehicle is so far removed from its trivial tenor that the object represented is obscured by the fact of its representation. As with Primcock's ironic comparison of English puppet-masters to Prometheus in Chapter 1, this figure stands out from *The Touch-Stone's* discussion of pantomime as a discrete linguistic unit, which diverts attention from Ralph's primary content to the facetiousness of his form. But the form of *The Touch-Stone* illustrates its "Historical, Critical, Political, Philosophical, and Theological" content through its parody of the very kind of language perceived by proponents of English neoclassicism to disturb meaningful communication, transgress mimetic decorum, and deviate from truth, reason, and the pattern of nature. Pantomime's *"Phœnix-like"* rise thus exposes the apparent abuses of rhetoric while hinting at the possibility of a language that exceeds the conventional uses of verbal wit. *The Touch-Stone* offers Harlequin's wordlessness as an alternative to a "trifling Superfluity of Words," and, indeed, to all words whatsoever. For "it is next to a Demonstration," Primcock concludes, "that the only Method of attaining an universal Language, is to be *Dumb"* (111).

### Augustan wit and the apology for pantomime

Given that Ralph is interested in the interaction of pantomime and poetics, this jocular allusion to "universal Language" is far from extraneous or hyperbolic. During the seventeenth century, universal languages emerged as a significant touchstone of the rationalizing programme of the New Science, which aimed to reform not only the methodology of natural philosophy, but also its modes of discourse through a "plain style" that shunned verbal ornament as well as the trivial play of wit.[7] Taking literally this demand for linguistic objectivity, universal language schemes went so far as to actually make a symbolic *object* out of language, thus levelling discourse and allowing it to communicate to all people in all places at all times.[8] Primcock's universal language scheme proposes to do much the same – to transcend the impostures and cheats of language by way of a nonverbal system of communication.[9] But pantomime, significantly, adopts the "silent *Rhetorick*" of dance instead of graphemic or phonemic emblems. When Primcock explains that harlequinades are "the *only* Method of attaining an universal Language," he at once parodies language reformers and intimates an historical truth: that other schemes have proven wrongheaded or impracticable.[10] Yet if the possibility of a universal language had been discredited, the motivations behind it remained relevant well into the eighteenth century, as poets and critics appropriated the well-known proscriptions of the Royal Society and adapted them to their own imaginative or analytical purposes. The empirical interest in unbiased description gradually gives way to an individual desire to express the intellectually and emotionally authentic through language that shows verbal restraint. Where, for the scientists, the plain style had been a way of representing nature as it really exists, rather than as words made it appear to exist, for neoclassical literati it facilitated the expression and appreciation of what Pope calls "*Unerring Nature*" – the foundation of ethics and aesthetics and, at once, "the *Source*, and *End*, and *Test of Art*" (*Essay on Criticism*, ll. 70–73). In associating pantomime with the schemes of language reformers, Ralph subtly links Harlequin's tricks and transformations to a recognized tradition of proscription of stylistic extravagance, ornamental rhetoric, and, to quote one such reformer, "*fine Metaphors* and *dancing periods*."[11] Just as importantly, Ralph plays on the claims of pantomime's apologists, who strove to distinguish Lincoln's Inn Fields and Drury Lane harlequinades as a context for what may be described as mute mimeticism: a representation of the universality of nature through the universality of motions, gestures, and attitudes.

Traditional rhetoric classifies motion, gesture, and attitude as devices of *actio* or delivery, which function to help animate discourse but which do less to express meaning than *elocutio* or style. Pantomime, however, expresses meaning through a kind of gestural *elocutio*, in which the antics of the body are not subservient to but are an embodiment of style. In his important study, *Harlequin Britain* (2004), John O'Brien argues that "embodiment" is precisely what allows pantomime to bypass "the distortions of speech and the vagaries of the text" (xxii). The physical movements of Harlequin's body communicate to diverse audiences because the body is "universally shared" (85), and thus constitutes a language in itself. O'Brien connects pantomime's apparent potential as a universal language to early eighteenth-century theories of spectatorship, which discovered meaning in the material and mimetic relationship between performer and audience, who are brought together by the commonality of their physical presence. Harlequin's expressive gestures encourage spectators "to feel" and in turn participate in what O'Brien calls "a concentrated engagement of the passions" (80–81).[12] The "dumb Wit" of pantomime is therefore made up of the contortions of Harlequin's limbs; the countenance of his face; the array of his checkered bodysuit, mask, cape, cap, and slapstick; the frenzied steps of his silent dances; and the audience's response to all of these.

In fact, the nuances of Harlequin's body are the aspect of eighteenth-century pantomime that seems most frequently to have attracted critical attention. Take, for example, a print that, in O'Brien's clever reading of it, reproduces graphically the physical dynamism of John Rich as Harlequin (he is depicted in motion), in order to identify "Wit corporeal" as the key reason for pantomime's appeal – the reason why, as the accompanying motto explains, the "crouding Audience draws" (Figure 6). The print presents the motions, gestures, and attitudes of Rich as not just comparable but as superior to the spoken dialogue of Robert Wilks, since it is now "Harlequin D$^r$. Faustus," not Sir Harry Wildair (the role for which Wilks was best known), who gains popular "applause." As the unanimous favourite of the "Genteels," a sarcastic term for the social rank between commonality and aristocracy, Rich appears twice in the image. In the background, Harlequin Doctor Faustus duels with a furious miller in a famous scene from *The Necromancer* (1723), the afterpiece often considered to have initiated the vogue for pantomime in England. But the parti-coloured Harlequin of the foreground dominates the background, revealing that the effect of the pantomime has more to do with the activity of Rich's body than with the thin plot of a sorcerer who sells his soul for magical powers, who uses these powers to make bumpkins dance minuets on their hands or to set a windmill a-going with a cuckold hanging from its sails, and who is ultimately devoured by a fire-belching "monstrous Dragon."[13] Transposing linguistic categories into perceptual ones, "Wit corporeal" becomes Rich's "darling Care" because, the print slyly proposes, the resources of verbal wit have proven insufficient in engaging the "Genteels."

For better or for worse, this was the main rationale for the promotion of pantomimic entertainments throughout the period. Thomas Davies accounts for Rich's popularity in particular, and the pervasiveness of pantomime in general, by claiming that the "gesticulation" of Rich's Harlequin "was so perfectly expressive of his meaning that every motion of his hand or head, or any part of his body, was a kind of dumb eloquence

Figure 6  Anonymous print (c. 1720s) depicting John Rich as Harlequin Doctor
Faustus

that was readily understood by the audience."[14] Like Ralph, Davies draws
attention to the gestural *elocutio* through which Harlequin makes his
meaning known, delighting while instructing audiences with the motion
of his body. A contributor to a 1737 issue of *The Grub Street Journal*, a
periodical that was generally hostile to Harlequin, is more specific about

the nature of this instruction, conceding that a "rightly managed" pantomime might be just as useful as a good play: "for as these improve our
discourse, so might those our carriage; and a well-chosen Subject, properly
represented by genteel action and graceful attitudes, would, I doubt not,
make a considerable alteration in the outward behaviour of the attentive
spectator."[15] The suggestion is that the body of Harlequin might produce a
figurative and literal impression on the body of the spectator, who is
necessarily attentive to representations that speak in universals and thus
bridge differences of culture, taste, and language. Indeed, as a telling review
in *Universal Journal* No. 1 (December 11, 1723) notices, language itself
might be inadequate even to describe pantomime: "in the Machinery
there is something so highly surprising, that Words cannot give a full
Idea" of a wordless performance at Drury Lane.[16] Of course, the displace-
ment of dramatic language by stage antics and mechanical effects was one
of the chief apprehensions about the genre, and so any such puff for
pantomime ironically rehearses the terms of contemporary critique. Yet
even Colley Cibber, who sheepishly states that he only mounted pantomimes at Drury Lane as "Crutches to our weakest Plays," acknowledges
that certain performances are able to make "something more than Motion
without Meaning." He cites John Weaver's *The Loves of Mars and Venus*
(1717) as a model of a pantomime in which "the Passions were so happily
express'd, and the whole Story so intelligibly told, by a mute Narration of
Gesture only, that even thinking Spectators allow'd it both a pleasing, and
a rational Entertainment."[17] In spite of the fact that speech was generally
thought to be the badge of reason, these and other commentators focus on
the centrality of Harlequin's physical motion to a pantomime's meaning,
and on the capacity of Harlequin's "dumb Wit" to go beyond verbal
language. From this perspective, Harlequin speaks most when he moves
mute.

But Cibber's praise of Weaver's *The Loves of Mars and Venus* suggests
that the communicative ability of pantomime might also be understood in
the context of a contemporary poetics of dance. Aside from being a
dancing-master and, by his own account, the inventor of the English
pantomime, Weaver was perhaps Harlequin's most ardent apologist.[18] In
a series of treatises that attempt to establish both dancing and pantomime
as "worthy the Regard and Consideration, as well as Reflexion of the
learned World," Weaver sets out a rigorously mimetic theory of stage
dancing.[19] Although the specific focus of each of these treatises is different,
they collectively emphasize the imitative quality of the dancing body, in
order to claim a formal affinity between the art of pantomime and other

more distinguished mimetic arts – especially poetry. Weaver self-consciously models his broad apologetic for dance on current assumptions about poetical art, and thus his not-so-modest defence of pantomime makes it a point of echoing the language and rhetoric of the recognized arbiters of Augustan literary taste. Doing in earnest what Ralph does in jest, Weaver draws out the relationship between pantomime and poetics in such a way as to place them on corresponding conceptual and critical grounds. Not surprisingly, given contemporary interest in the antiquity of the arts, Weaver argues from ancient authority, citing, among other sources, Cicero's analysis of the emotive force of gesture and Lucian's assertion that pantomimic dance, in its purest form, is a physical expression of mental activity.[20] But Weaver also employs the standard conventions of neoclassical literary apology, using Aristotle's theory of poetic imitation to put pantomime on par with poetry. In *An Essay Towards the History of Dancing* (1712), Weaver observes that "the natural Propensity of Imitation in Mankind gave Rise to *Poetry* and *Dancing*, and furnish'd them with their greatest Excellence and Beauty" (161).[21] For Weaver, this "Excellence and Beauty" is a physical equivalent of "true wit," which entails not, as Dryden puts it, a "propriety of thoughts and words," but rather a propriety of thoughts and motions that adapts bodily style to intellectual subject.[22] The true wit of pantomime unifies mind and body through meaningful movement in the same way as poetry represents the "*Actions, Manners,* and *Passions*" (160) through diction drawn from universal nature. In both modes of μίμησις or "*Imitation,*" the subject matter is plain and intelligible to the audience because the subject matter *is* the audience. For, as Pope explains in *An Essay on Criticism* (1711):

> *True Wit* is *Nature* to Advantage drest,
> What oft was *Thought*, but ne'er so well *Exprest*,
> *Something* whose Truth convinc'd at Sight we find,
> That gives us back the Image of our Mind. (ll. 297–300)

Literalizing Pope's suggestion that wit's relative truth or falsity is ascertained "at Sight," Weaver applies the traditional "mirror-up-to-nature" motif to pantomimic performances that, first, "must be every Thing exactly," and in which, second, "every Spectator must behold himself acted, and see in the *Dancer*, as in a Glass, all that he himself used to do and suffer" (*History*, 25). The uniquely comprehensive scope of pantomime requires that the stage dancer possess an equally comprehensive knowledge of all things in art and nature. To this end, Weaver encourages the pantomimist to draw upon the varied resources of music, arithmetic, geometry, natural and moral philosophy, and, above all, the "Art of Eloquence" or "RHETORICK" (*Lectures*, 144). In his *Anatomical and Mechanical Lectures Upon Dancing* (1721), Weaver submits rhetoric as an important vehicle to what sounds like a kind of pantomimic sublime:

> What *Rhetorick* is to the *Orator* in Speaking, is to the *Dancer* in Action; and an Elegance of Action consists, in adapting the Gesture to the Passions and Affections[;] and the *Dancer*, as well as the *Orator*, allures the Eye, and invades the Mind of the Spectator; for there is a Force, and Energy in Action, which strangely affects; and when Words will scarce move, Action will excite, and put all the Powers of the Soul in a ferment. (144)

For Weaver, "RHETORICK" is not merely a useful metaphor through which to account for the universal language of pantomime; rather, it is an actual qualification for a stage dancer, who, like a poet, must exploit the rhetorical arts in order to adapt his performance to the thing performed.[23] Boldly acknowledging, but refusing to give credence to, long-standing prejudices against dancing as a lewd or mechanical art devoid of wit, Weaver stresses the refinement of performers who manage to stimulate the mind and invigorate the passions through motions, gestures, and attitudes that truthfully represent powerful feeling. By applying such poetic common-places to the art of pantomime, Weaver expands the scope of neoclassicism by suggesting the insufficiency of any conception of wit that does not acknowledge the affective power of the active body. In turn, he encourages a more thorough identification between dancer and audience and a higher critical valuation of pantomime on account of its poetics.[24]

*The Loves of Mars and Venus* puts this theory of pantomime into practice, representing, as the preface to the printed text affirms, the "Manners, Passions, and Affections" of the characters through their "numerous Variety of Gesticulations." It was the first of Weaver's productions to be dubbed a "Dramatick Entertainment of Dancing," and the preface audaciously boasts that *The Loves of Mars and Venus* is also the "first Trial of this Nature that has been made since the Reign of *Trajan*."[25] Citing the apparent novelty of his enterprise as an excuse for pseudo-scholarly pedantry, Weaver transfers the observations made in his *Essay* to the critical paraphernalia of his entertainment, where they are made to justify the silent action of the mythological *ménage-à-trois*. Following in the well-established tradition of the Augustan *ars*, *The Loves of Mars and Venus* is a "how-to" guide, which simultaneously explains and exemplifies an idealized art of pantomime. Weaver's printed text intersperses slight scene descriptions with glosses which attempt to assign specific meanings to the motions, gestures, and attitudes represented. Take, for instance, the description of Scene II:

> ENTER *to* Venus, Vulcan: *They perform a* Dance *together; in which* Vulcan *expresses his* Admiration; Jealousie; Anger; *and* Despite: *And Venus shews* Neglect; Coquetry; Contempt; *and* Disdain. (20)

Although printed texts of eighteenth-century pantomimes are relatively scarce, extant examples of the genre are usually vivid and detailed in their descriptions of stage action and antics.[26] In contrast, Weaver's text puts the focus on the meaning expressed, and then works backward, through a sort of gestural shorthand, to determine exactly how this meaning is expressed. "This last *Dance* being altogether of the *Pantomimic* kind; it is necessary that the Spectator should know some of the most particular Gestures made use of therein; and what Passions, or Affections, they discover; represent; or express" (20). Weaver's key delineates twenty-one emotions and their representative actions. Vulcan's ill-requited "ADMIRATION" for Venus is "discover'd by the raising up of the right Hand, the Palm turn'd upwards, the Fingers clos'd; and in one Motion the Wrist turn'd round and Fingers spread; the Body reclining, and Eyes fix'd on the Object." Meanwhile, Venus's "scornful Smiles; forbidding Looks; tossing of the Head, filliping of the Fingers; and avoiding the Object" indicate her "CONTEMPT" for Vulcan (20–23). Venus's feelings towards her husband are foiled by her "reciprocal Love" for Mars, which is betrayed in Scene IV by exchanges of "Gallantry" and a close "embrace" between the illicit lovers (25–26). In Scene VI, after being caught in Vulcan's net in *flagrante delicto*, Venus expresses "GRIEF" by "hanging down the Head; wringing the Hands; and striking the Breast"; Mars shows "RESIGNATION" by holding out "both the Hands joyn'd together"; and Vulcan, by shaking "the given hand," demonstrates *"Friendship, Reconciliation,* and the like" (27–28).[27] Weaver does not explain what is happening in the pantomime, but, as it were, allows the stage dancer's body to do the talking. As is insinuated by the epigraph that he borrows from Cicero's *De Oratore*, the choreography of the characters is what carries the story and constitutes its drama: *"Sed Hæc Omnia perindè sunt, ut aguntur"* / "But the effect of all these oratorical devices depends on how they are delivered."[28] Weaver's epigraph contextualizes his "Dramatick Entertainment of Dancing" by collapsing the traditional distinction between *elocutio* and *actio*. The entertainment itself gestures towards the possibility of *actio* as *elocutio*. Both in theory and in practice, *The Loves of Mars and Venus* argues that the dancer's physical rhetoric communicates ideas "significantly and decently" because "Nature assign'd each Motion of the Mind its proper Gesticulations and Countenance, as well as Tone." In attempting to systematize and standardize these natural "Gesticulations," Weaver not only grants meaning to otherwise unmeaning motion, but advances pantomime as, in his words, an "Art or Science Imitative" (XII).

Moreover, Weaver recognizes that pantomime, like other arts and sciences, must be regulated if it is to satisfy its mimetic purpose. Like contemporary literati, Weaver conflates "true wit" with poetic invention and the truth of nature, but warns that wit becomes unnatural when it is exercised without judgement, the faculty responsible for restraining the excesses of both verbal and "dumb Wit." In *An Essay on Criticism*, poetic "RULES" are "*Nature* still, but *Nature Methodiz'd*" (ll. 88–89). Having a common basis in "*Nature*," Weaver claims that pantomime must also be subject to methodology, since "'tis plain, that without Rules there can be no Art" (*Lectures*, 131). As such, both Weaver's stage dancer and Pope's "winged Courser" are best able to represent nature when the poet or pantomimist "*check* his Course" (ll. 86–87). Weaver repeatedly alludes to the importance of "*Theory*," of "Order, Decency, and Measure," of "Rules and Conduct," and of the "regulated *Motions* of all Parts." His composite "whole Art of *Dancing*" is particular in its advice about what to do with the arms, hands, fingers, eyes, mouth, and head; about how to achieve a "Symmetry of the *Movements*"; about which steps are most communicative; and about how to give the works of nature their "proper and distinguishing Characters" (*History*, 22). Yet the very necessity of Weaver's proscriptions implies that while "silent *Rhetorick*," like rhetorical wit, might reach to the sublime, it might just as well tumble into the profound whilst striving to "put all the Powers of the Soul in a ferment" (*Lectures*, 144).

Weaver's *Essay* and *Lectures* argued that the corporeality of the dancer's body allowed pantomime to transcend the peculiarities of verbal language and communicate to audiences of all kinds, but his later *History of the Mimes and Pantomimes* (1728) qualifies this early optimism in the wake of the danced dramas of the 1720s, which seemed to follow no discernible rule and therefore lacked the art requisite of the classical genre:

> The Town having for some Years last past run into *Dramatick Entertainments*, consisting of *Dancing, Gesture,* and *Action,* intermix'd with *Trick* and *Show;* and to which they have given the Name of *Pantomimes*: I am apt to perswade my self, that an Historical Account of the ancient *Mimes* and *Pantomimes* of the *Greeks* and *Romans,* will, at this

Juncture, not only be acceptable and entertaining to the Publick, but will render the Spectator better capable of Judging of these modern Performances. (1–2)

Notwithstanding his seeming condescension to the evaluative skills of London spectators, Weaver makes it clear that contemporary harlequinades have fallen considerably short of the sort of "*Representative Dances*" (4) that he identifies with the true art of pantomime. Though the danced dramas mounted by Rich and Theobald at Lincoln's Inn Fields and Thurmond at Drury Lane are nominated *pantomime*, they are deficient in the "Excellency" that consists in "the Beauty of *Imitation*, and the Harmony of *Composition* and Motion" (2). The genre that Weaver had instituted in *The Loves of Mars and Venus* had developed successfully, but in ways that exaggerated the corporeal at the expense of the genuinely witty. The intrinsic materiality and physicality of what had emerged as English pantomime – the raucous dances, elaborate stage-effects, mechanical tricks, sudden appearances and disappearances, and startling transformations – predisposed the genre to a certain degree of extravagance, which necessarily problematized its claim as universal language. Indeed, in the opinion of many critics, the entertainments that had come to dominate London in the 1720s, 1730s, and 1740s were more often concerned with indulging the audience's desire for spectacle than with meaningfully adapting Harlequin's gestures to the "Passions and Affections" of nature. For Henry Fielding, "Pantomimical Farces" consist primarily of "a Set of People running about the Stage after one another, without speaking one Syllable, and playing several Juggling Tricks, which are done at *Fawks's* after a much better manner." The anonymous author of *Letters from a Moor at London* (1737) similarly stresses the mute physicality of Harlequin, who "[s]kips, dances, runs about, but says nothing," and whose "wooden actions" are "fit for nothing but to divert wooden heads." Ned Ward offers another counterpoint to ideals of "dumb Wit" by complaining of pantomime performances where "instead of Wit, we find / Dumb Shows, of an inferior kind."[29] Taking the claims of apologists at their own worth, such remarks acknowledge pantomime's corporeality as its most fundamental feature, only to point out that the body in motion is just as susceptible to excess as tropes, figures, and similitudes. Weaver wants to see pantomime as fulfilling the function that language is supposed to fulfil, but, as Richard Ralph notes, the entertainments that ended up winning public acclaim "put paid" to his "serious ambitions for a purely and expressively danced drama."[30]

Ironically, Weaver's apologetic contains within itself the egg out of which Harlequin was hatched. Having already observed that poetics and pantomime have a common origin in the "natural Propensity of Imitation," Weaver explains what happens when they deviate from mimesis proper:

> the first degenerates into *Anagrams, Acrosticks, Conceits, Conundrums*, and *Puns*, below the Dignity of Poetry, and the other into ridiculous senseless *Motions*, insignificant Cap'rings, and worthless *Agility*, tho' both of these are what the *English* have generally been too fond of in their *Poetry* and *Dances*; to the Scandal of the *English Wit* and *Ability*. (*Essay*, 138–39)

For all of his emphasis on the communicative value of pantomimic performance, Weaver concedes that, unless well conceived and suitably regulated, "dumb Wit" may turn out to be a physical equivalent of "false wit" – an *im*propriety of thoughts and motions. He makes his point by way of a tacit analogy between what poets and critics usually categorized as true and false wit, and what he designates as "*Serious*" pantomime and "*Grotesque Dancing*," of the kind regularly mounted on the eighteenth-century stage (*History*, 55–56). Weaver goes so far as to associate the actions and antics of pantomime with the specific devices that Addison had recently censured in his *Spectator* series on the "History of false Wit." In *Spectator* No. 61 (May 10, 1711), Addison explains that "Imitation is natural to us," but warns that "when it does not raise the Mind to Poetry, Painting, Musick, or other more noble Arts," it often results in pattern poems, rebuses, anagrams, acrostics, conceits, chronograms, puns, conundrums, and other species of wit that misrepresent the truth of nature by relying for their effect on seeming similitude (1.244ff).[31] False wit's mimesis involves a superficial kind of imitation that elides or suppresses actual differences between words and things. It delights instead in physical resemblances that foreground the materiality of language and seem to change words *into* things. For this reason, Addison figures the workings of false wit through a sort of mimetic personation: "some carry the Notion of Wit so far, as to ascribe it even to external Mimicry; and to look upon a Man as an ingenious Person, that can resemble the Tone, Posture, or Face of another" (1.265).[32] The falsity of wit, from this perspective, has less to do with its unnaturalness than with the presumption of a naturalness that pursues resemblance to exorbitant lengths and imitates externals at the expense of essence. In his own *History*, Weaver suggests that recent pantomimes are false for the same reason as Addison's "external Mimicry," in that their grotesque dancers offer "distorted and ridiculous *Actions*" in the place of "regulated Gesture" (*History*, 56).[33] These dancers not only mimic other persons, but metamorphose other things into that which they are not – a colonnade into a bed of tulips, a mechanic's shop into an ostrich or serpent, or a chair into a magical chest. What Weaver recognizes in such equivocal turns is a disparity between his ambitious theory of stage dancing and its actual practice at Lincoln's Inn Fields and Drury Lane: while pantomime had the potential to function as a universal language, it was prone to the same idiosyncrasy, ostentation, and imposture as verbal language. Far from representing nature as it really exists, eighteenth-century pantomime was more often perceived to represent nature as motions, like words, made it appear to exist. When Weaver complains of the distortions of contemporary harlequinades, he joins contemporary language reformers in proscribing any and all obstacles to the works of nature, whether they be conceits and conundrums or, as he puts it, "Grin and Grimace" (56). In so doing, he reinforces a formal affinity between the "dumb Wit" of pantomime and the luxuriant, illogical, and mixed metaphors, forced similes, and trifling jibes and quibbles that had come to characterize and constitute the rhetoric of false wit.

## Metaphor and metamorphosis

That the harlequinades of the 1720s, 1730s, and 1740s fell short of Weaver's mimetic ideal is not evidence of their incompatibility with Augustan poetics. Quite the opposite, the very fact that pantomime had difficulty realizing "the natural Propensity of Imitation" brought it closer into relation with a literary scene that was subject to similar pitfalls and contradictions, in that the rhetoric that made both arts witty frequently also made them false. According to D. Judson Milburn, rhetoric presented a discursive paradox to writers of the late seventeenth and early eighteenth centuries, who were obliged to make use of its ornamental devices while taking heed of its "inherent knack for extravagance."[34] Unlike the language reformers of the New Science, many of whom advocated no ornamentation at all, contemporary literati recognized the moral and artistic validity of ornament as well as the need for moderation and regularity. If, in the context of wit, rhetoric was often seen as a means to the rational perception and truthful representation of nature, it was just as often proscribed for the misuses and abuses of language to which it was particularly susceptible.

In Book II of *An Essay Concerning Human Understanding* (1690), for example, Locke provisionally explains that wit has its origin in the pleasing "assemblage of *Ideas*, and putting those together with quickness and variety."[35] He immediately warns, however, that the "resemblance or congruity" upon which wit relies sometimes causes readers to be "misled by Similitude" (2.11.2.156). In Book III Locke goes on to link the "assemblage of *Ideas*" with the imperfection and abuse of language:

> Since Wit and Fancy finds easier entertainment in the World, than dry Truth and real Knowledge, *figurative Speeches*, and allusion in Language, will hardly be admitted, as *an* imperfection or *abuse* of it. I confess, in Discourses, where we seek rather Pleasure and Delight, than Information and Improvement, such Ornaments as are borrowed from them, can scarce pass for Faults. But yet, if we would speak of Things as they are, we must allow, that all the Art of Rhetorick, besides Order and Clearness, all the artificial and figurative application of Words Eloquence hath invented, are for nothing else than to insinuate wrong *Ideas*, move the Passions, and thereby mislead the Judgment; and so indeed are perfect cheat. (3.10.34.508)

Locke's careful juxtaposition of terms – fancy and knowledge, delight and improvement, "wrong *Ideas*" and "Things as they are" – suggests that rhetorical wit and "dry Truth" are necessarily incompatible since all forms of linguistic figuration are in some sense false. The former stands in the way of mimetic meaning and makes all manifestations of the latter "less clear and distinct in their signification" (3.10.1.490). The proscriptions of Locke's *Essay* apply to polite language what those of the Royal Society had applied to scientific language, acknowledging at once the secular temptations of rhetoric and the natural virtues of a language that brings words and things into accord. The *Essay* implies that the arts of rhetoric delude the critical judgement, impose upon the senses, and distract from the intended purpose of discourse, and should therefore be limited to works of pleasure instead of the more significant works of nature.[36]

Locke's apprehensions about the pervasiveness and popularity of wit are refined upon by numerous commentators during the period, who try to work out the epistemological implications of wit's problematic association with the imagination, and the imagination's inevitable tendency towards falsehood. Corbyn Morris summons Locke's conclusion that "WIT *consists in something that is not perfectly conformable to Truth, and good Reason*" in order to explain why it is not: "—For the *Direction* of WIT is absolutely different from the *Direction* of TRUTH and GOOD REASON; It being the Aim of WIT to strike the *Imagination*; of TRUTH and GOOD REASON, to convince the *Judgement*: From thence they can never be perfectly coincident."[37] As a cognitive faculty, wit was often conflated with the functions of the imagination, which both inspired and facilitated poetic creation through the discovery of unexpected relationships. Where judgement was understood to discriminate between things, wit and imagination were believed to make all things the same, even if this strained logic and caused language to defy truth, reason, and the pattern of nature. The "definitive motions" of Augustan wit thus involved an articulation of similarities that, as Roger D. Lund observes, "might finally prove illusory, arbitrary, or false."[38] Presupposing this, poets and critics commended wit's imaginative possibilities at the same time as they cautioned against its glaring improprieties. In *The Polite Gentleman* (1700), a wide-ranging study of "the Several Kinds of Wit," Henry Barker notes that "the Ornaments that Men make use of to imbellish their Discourse, let them be of what nature they will, should be regarded only, but as so many Charms which draw us to a stricter and nearer Consideration of those Things, either to know them, or make them useful."[39] Employing communication as his essential criterion, Barker attempts to establish an appropriate relationship between means and ends, and between the ornaments of rhetoric and the objects of discourse, by arguing that an application to "Matter" produces certain knowledge, while a too-great devotion to "Manner" only disguises knowledge, in "making it appear what it is not" (97). "False eloquence" and "over-strained Expressions" subsume mimetic truth in the inscrutable fictions of fancy, and result in species of wit that represent artificial rather than natural likeness. For Barker, as for Morris and Locke, elaborate tropes, figures, and similitudes thus "pervert the Order of Nature" and "almost intirely darken and eclipse" discourse, not because they are aesthetically flawed but, more importantly, because they are fundamentally untrue (53).

False wit is therefore false. But the compelling tautology of Augustan definitions of wit skirts around the purported truth of this falsity. In his important translation of René Rapin, Thomas Rymer remarks that nature must "guide" the use of ornamental "figures and metaphors" and that "all the images that poetry employs in expressing itself are false unless they be natural."[40] In a similarly circular fashion, Matthew Prior stages an imaginary dialogue in which Montaigne qualifies Locke's standard attack on false similitudes by claiming that the discovery of rhetorical deceit reinforces the truth of language: "If your Simile be proper and good, it is at once a full proof, and a lively Illustration of Your matter, and where it does not hold, the very disproportion gives You Occasion to reconsider it, and You set it in all its lights, if it be only to find at least how unlike it is."[41] Several decades later, Allan Ramsay prevaricates over the writer's distrust of but dependence on images of "POETICAL TRUTH," arguing that what commonly passes "by the name of *allegories, metaphors,* or *similies*" are always "to be condemned as false, whenever they present any idea to the imagination that is absurd, mean, or unsuitable."[42] That true wit was true could thus be taken as an assumption. But what precisely put the *lie* in certain "simi*lies*" was harder for the Augustans to determine.

In his *History*, Weaver proscribes pantomime in terms that are analogous in being equally tautological: "*Serious Dancing*" is true because it boasts characters that are "Natural," while "*Grotesque Dancing*" is false because it features "only such Characters as are quite out of Nature; as *Harlequin, Scaramouch, Pierrot, &c.*" (56). Weaver associates the "distorted and ridiculous *Actions*" of these characters with the verbal dynamism that theorists of wit identified as an impediment to *vraisemblance* – verisimilitude between objects and their metaphorical representation. He adds, however, that his conception of "*Serious*" and "*Grotesque*" is "differing in some Measure with the common Acceptation among Persons of our Profession," implying that the difficulty of conveying precisely which dances are grounded in nature, and which deviate from it, has as much to do with conflicting attitudes towards style as with relative truth and falsity (55). Weaver's theory of imitative dance was intended to replace the then-prevailing style of "Baroque" dancing, a sophisticated and ornate form that found beauty in artificial elegance rather than mimesis. In English *belle lettres*, the reaction against rhetorical wit, as against "silent *Rhetorick*," was likewise concerned with a shift in critical taste, one that was usually documented through a self-conscious rejection of "baroque" aesthetics and poetics.[43] In his loose adaptation of Bouhours, *The Arts of Logick and Rhetorick* (1728), John Oldmixon describes "*Metaphors*," "*Equivocals*," and "*Hyperboles*" as "a Sort of Wit which is in no danger of prevailing in so knowing an Age as this" (17). He cites, in particular, the "metaphysical" conceits of Abraham Cowley as an exemplar of wit that has fallen out of favour:

> About forty Years ago, *Cowley*'s Mistress was cry'd up by half Wits and half Criticks, as the Perfection of gallant Poetry; and yet almost all the Thoughts in those Love-Verses are false, because they are unnatural, Full of Affection and Point, and aiming rather to shew the Author's Wit, and even Learning, than his Tenderness and Passion, by which only could he reach and move his Mistress's Heart. (36)

Oldmixon offers several passages from "Eccho" which suggest, in his opinion, that the poet "was half so much griev'd about his Mistress's Cruelty, as he was pleas'd with his own Fancy":

> By Repercussion Beams ingender Fire,
>   Shapes by Reflection Shapes beget;
> The Voice itself, when stopp'd, does back retire,

And a new Voice is made by it.
Thus Things by Opposition
The Gainers grow. My barren Love alone
Does from her stony Breast rebound,
Producing neither Image, Fire, nor Sound. (37)

Being too highly wrought to be thoroughly sincere, Cowley's "Love-Verses" make love only in an obscure and roundabout way. Once again, the Augustan proscription of wit has recourse to tautology: the intricate poetry of *The Mistress* (1647) is false because it is unnatural, and it is unnatural because of its open avowal of language as artifice. However, Oldmixon's historicization of wit makes the question of why the true became false a matter of perception rather than knowledge – an intuitive sense of when and where rhetoric was carried too far. In the absence of any clear measure of truth and falsity, it was generally easier for poets and critics to proscribe than vividly to describe the rhetorical excesses and defects of wit.

For this reason, George Granville's satire, "Concerning Unnatural Flights in Poetry" (1701), identifies overly amplified metaphors with outright lies and the falsity of wit with the false sublime:

But Poetry in Fiction takes delight,
And mounting up in Figures out of Sight,
Leaves Truth behind in her audacious flight;
Fables and Metaphors that always lie,
And rash Hyperboles, that soar so high,
And every Ornament of Verse, must die.[44]

Because of its emphasis on rhapsody, elevation, and grandeur of expression, the sublime was inevitably prone to extravagance through too great a quality of figures or too great a quantity of figures. As a result, commentators frequently draw a distinction between the true sublime, which strongly affects the mind and transports the soul, and the superficially sublime style, which is embodied in bombast, fustian, or mere ornament for ornament's sake. In *A Dissertation Concerning Meteors of Stile, or False Sublimity* (1711), Samuel Werenfels cautions that "if some Parts in a sublime Discourse are to have the Ornament of Words, we shou'd be careful that the Ornament shew it self as little as possible."[45] What Werenfels terms "Meteors of Stile" are the most readily separable stylistic elements, and their separability is what marks their falseness: in calling attention to their own ostentatious rhetoric and gaudy wit, "Meteors" impinge upon the larger meaning of a work. The inordinate use of ornamental figures consequently results in language that aspires to elevated sentiments but realizes only empty pathos. Though "Meteors of Stile" have their origin in the Longinian sublime, Werenfels concludes that "the abuse of it has diverted it into bad Sense" (187). Shaftesbury echoes this conclusion in his *Soliloquy, or Advice to an Author* (1711, 1714), complaining that "what commonly passes for sublime, is formed by the variety of figures, the multiplicity of metaphors, and by quitting as much as possible the natural and easy way of expression for that which is most unlike to humanity or ordinary use" (109). Shaftesbury's attitude is sanctioned by Longinus himself, whose ancient treatise associates the indiscriminate piling of figure upon figure with unnatural writing. In his popular 1739 translation of the *Peri Hupsous*, William Smith warns that "a too frequent and elaborate Application of Figures carries with it a great Suspicion of Artifice, Deceit, and Fraud."[46] Yet Smith has Longinus make the important proviso that it is not figures themselves but the abuse of figures that leads to the false sublime, thus allowing him to discuss the valuable uses of periphrasis, hyperbole, metaphor, amplification, hyperbaton, digression, and other "Artifices of Rhetoric," while acknowledging that they may, nonetheless, "be carried to excess" (77).

In his own upside-down parody of *On the Sublime*, Pope has Scriblerus make the same proviso, for the opposite purpose: it is not the synecdoche, aposiopesis, paronomasia, antithesis, pleonasm, or circumbendibus themselves but the abuse of such figures that leads "the gentle down-hill way to the Bathos; the bottom, the end, the central point, the *non plus ultra*, of true Modern Poesy!"[47] The *Peri Bathous* (1728) compiles and classifies excerpts of what Scriblerus calls the "*anti-natural* way" (192) of writing, so as to compose an ironic rhetorical *ars* (and inverted *Essay on Criticism*) out of the poetry of contemporary poetasters. The collected *works* of the bathos realize the "Artifice, Deceit, and Fraud" that Longinus discovers in the false sublime, and in turn contribute to an "Art of Sinking in Poetry." At the same time, the collected *words* of the bathos embody the discursive power of language to trick the critical judgement and transform the perceived nature of things. Thus Leonard Welsted, in the pastoral "Acon and Lavinia" (1724), employs paronomasia to convert the firmament into clothing for a coy nymph: "—Behold the Virgin lye / Naked and only *cover'd* by the *Sky*" (209). Nathaniel Lee strains a hackneyed metaphor in *Sophonisba* (1676), to reduce armies on the point of engaging to gamblers just about to wager: "Yon' armies are the *Cards* which both must play; / At least come off a *Saver* if you may: / Throw *boldly* at the *Sum* the Gods have *set*; / These on your side will all their fortunes *bet*" (221). And in his notoriously bad epic poem, *Prince Arthur* (1695), Richard Blackmore compares the fate of fallen Briton warriors to the apotheosis of dogs killed in the bull-baiting ring:

> Great Numbers dy'd where the chas'd *Saxon* flew,
> And with his Sword cut his wide Passage thro'
> So when a generous Bull for Clowns Delight,
> Stands with his Line restrain'd, prepar'd for Fight.
> Hearing the Youths loud Clamours, and the Rage,
> Of barking Mastives eager to engage.
> He snuffs the Air, and paws the trembling Ground,
> Views all the Ring, and proudly walks it round.
> Defiance lowring on his brinded Brows,
> Around disdainful Looks, the grisly Warriour throws.
> His haughty Head inclin'd with easie Scorn,
> Th'invading Foe high in the Air is born,
> Tost from the Combatant's victorious Horn.
> Rais'd to the Clouds, the sprawling Mastives fly,
> And add new Monsters to th'affrighted Sky.[48]

The extended metaphor does several things at once: it humbles the dignity and valour of Arthur's knights by likening them to "sprawling Mastives"; it elevates these "sprawling Mastives" by associating them with celestial bodies; and it complicates the significance of Arthur's heroic defence of the Britons against the usurping Saxons, by relating it to the clownish amusement of bull-baiting. The diminishing vehicle of Blackmore's original tenor becomes itself the tenor to a magnifying vehicle: warriors are like dogs that, in turn, are like stars, thus making warriors like dog-stars. The dizzying circumlocution of this figure tests the limits of language and points to the difficulty of communication and the exorbitancy of rhetorical wit, which, as Pope's citations from *Prince Arthur* show, often fails to do what it is expected to do. Pope lays it down as an ironic principle that writers "say nothing in the usual way, but (if possible) in the direct contrary" (205). Blackmore unwittingly adheres to this principle by using words to metamorphose things into that which they manifestly are not. When, in the same poem, Blackmore compares the passing of a powerful ocean storm to the smoothing of a "ruffl'd Bed" (10), and when he has the heavenly host celebrate creation with "rare Fireworks" (45) borrowed from the Lord Mayor's Day festivities, he deludes the critical sense through metaphors that brazenly resist mimeticism. The "*anti-natural* way" of writing makes wit an end in itself, rather than a rhetorical means to the truth of nature. It represents what appears to be the falsity of nature and, in the process, exposes what Augustan poets and critics saw as the most problematic aspect of rhetorical wit: because of its dependence upon the apprehension of likeness or similitude, wit was inclined to various kinds of deception.

The *Peri Bathous* groups these deceptions under the rubric of *catachresis*, a traditional rhetorical term for the misuse or misapplication of language, especially figurative language, which becomes catachrestic when it wrests words from their native signification and stretches them to exaggerated lengths.[49] "Nothing so much conduces to the Bathos," writes Pope, "as the CATACHRESIS," a master of which device will say:

> Mow the Beard,
> Shave the Grass,
> Pin the Plank,
> Nail my Sleeve. (205)

The application of words to things they do not properly denote labours meaning to such an extent that it undermines the communicativeness of language. It is not so much that words cease *to mean*, but that catachrestic rhetoric shifts the literal and semantic foundation upon which words usually come to mean. Harlequin is transformed into the mythological phoenix and words become pantomimic through the motions of figures that vary, confound, or reverse what they ostensibly seek to represent. Pope has Scriblerus describe the effect of linguistic tricks and transformations through an elaborate metaphor of his own, one drawn significantly from the "Reigning Diversions of the Town": catachresis results in "the same kind of pleasure to the mind, as to the eye when we behold Harlequin trimming himself with a hatchet, hewing down a tree with a rasor, making his tea in a cauldron, and brewing his ale in a tea-pot, to the incredible satisfaction of the British spectator" (206). Just as Weaver expresses the "ridiculous senseless *Motions*" of contemporary pantomime through the figure of false wit (*Essay*, 138–39), Pope expresses the unnatural deceits of catachresis by way of the figure of "*Grotesque Dancing.*" In such a way, Pope establishes a formal relationship between poetics and pantomime, by using the popular features of the latter to account for the dubious attractions of the former. Nothing seems more plain to Scriblerus, than that the world has "long been weary of *natural things*":

> How much the contrary are form'd to please, is evident from the universal applause daily given to the admirable entertainments of Harlequin and Magicians on our stage. When an audience behold a coach turn'd into a wheelbarrow, a conjurer into an old woman, or a man's head where his heels should be; how are they struck with transport and delight. (192)

In late seventeenth- and early eighteenth-century poetics, the term "transport" was generally used to describe the overwhelming mental and emotional impact of the sublime. In the *Peri Bathous*, however, the term exemplifies the imposition of the trivial sublime, of catachrestic rhetoric, and of false wit, all of which "delight" the mind by deceiving it. The incongruous application of "transport" to the antics of Harlequin makes contemporary pantomime sublime in order to make contemporary poetry bathetic – nothing more than amusement. Like many commentators of the period, Pope associates the commercialization of literature with the commercialization of leisure, identifying the defects and excesses of "modern" writing with the desires of the pleasure-seeking public. Yet in exploiting one of the "Reigning Diversions" as a visual image through which to expose the duplicitous nature of verbal wit, Pope cannot help but also gesture towards the entertainment value of devices that brazenly deceive, exemplifying the design of art rather than the pattern of nature. Pope's "Art of Sinking" and Weaver's *Essay, Lectures*, and *History* are thus reciprocal in their critical commentary on a cultural shift that has seen both poetics and pantomime dance away from mimesis and towards catachresis – from the "natural Propensity of Imitation" to the "*anti-natural.*"

## Pantomimic poetics

Weaver's censure of the English fondness for "*Trick* and *Show*" and his anxiety about the consequences of "pantomimic poetics" is typical of the kind of commentary directed at "*Grotesque Dancing*" during the early stages of its development. And notwithstanding the usual distortions of his satiric perspective, Pope's account of the various "turns" in the "admirable entertainments of Harlequin" is strikingly consistent with extant records of performance. The shared vocabulary of debates over pantomime and poetics makes it clear that the respective threats of false wit and "dumb Wit" were perceived to be the same. The pantomimes of the early eighteenth century can be divided into three distinct types: those that, like *The Loves of Mars and Venus*, featured only a "serious" part which represented a traditional or mythological story through dancing and gesture alone; those that, like *Harlequin Doctor Faustus* and *The Necromancer*, eschewed the "serious" and represented only a "comic" part through the "grotesque" actions of *commedia* characters; and those that, like *Apollo and Daphne: or, Harlequin's Metamorphoses* and *Perseus and Andromeda: or, The Spaniard Outwitted*, consisted of alternate scenes of "serious" and "comic" material. Although the first type was modelled closely on ancient *mimi* and *pantomimi*, and was therefore considered by apologists to be a legitimate – and genuinely "neoclassical" – art, comic and serio-comic pantomimes were performed more regularly and were far more popular than those of the solely serious type, likely because they afforded greater opportunities for spectacle.[50] Scholars have thus stressed the eclecticism of the genre, variously describing it as a "queer hodge-podge," a "smorgasbord," an "exciting hybrid form," and the "quintessential Georgian entertainment."[51] Despite the hopeful claims of apologists that pantomime might civilize diverse audiences, the raison d'être of the genre tended to comprise its surprising stage-effects – effects that coordinated the theatre's dramatic and mechanical arts in such a way as to create and then exploit a gap between expectation and actuality. Most conspicuous among these were the tricks and transformations that disguised or changed the material reality of things and often seemed to make metaphors literal, not only comparing like with unlike, but converting like *into* unlike. In the audaciously unnatural world of the pantomimes of the 1720s, 1730s, and 1740s, a palace or temple might metamorphose into a cottage or hut; a fine lady might take the shape of a joint-stool or laurel tree; a man's legs might be sawed off and replaced with others of different colours, forms, and sizes; and Harlequin himself might be hatched out of an egg, as he was in Rich's performance of *The Rape of Proserpine*.

Appreciative audiences tended to look upon pantomime's transformative capacity as its chief beauty: that which set it apart from the more modest stage-effects of regular drama as well as the simpler sleight-of-hand tricks of showmen like Isaac Fawkes. Contemporary reviews frequently express admiration for the dexterity of the performers and the delightful novelty of their performances. For example, the Swiss tourist Cesar de Saussure describes John Rich's 1740 production of *Orpheus and Eurydice* as "altogether the most surprising and charming spectacle you can imagine."[52] In a similar way, the anonymous editor of *An Exact Description of the Two Fam'd Entertainments of Harlequin Doctor Faustus . . . and The Necromancer* (1724) explains in his preface that

> The Entertainment of *Doctor Faustus* has at both Houses met with such prodigious Success, that it's grown the Subject of almost all Companies, both in Town and Country; and indeed 'tis a Diversion so very uncommon and surprising, that the Representation of it must certainly be a Satisfaction to every one that is not eaten up with Spleen and Ill-nature. (n.p.)

As the editor suggests, pantomime's popularity was such that it generated a good deal of discourse about how and why it affected audiences. For some commentators, pantomime appealed to the general public because of the way in which the genre consciously shunned the polite middle-class and aristocratic characters who inhabited most main-piece plays of the period, in favour of characters with whom the wider audience could identify. For other "ill-natured" critics, however, this represented a debasement of the stage and a condescension to "vulgar" pleasures. In his doggerel satire on the Faustus pantomimes, *The Dancing Devils: or, The Roaring Dragon* (1724), Ned Ward lays bare the class implications of performances

> Fit only for the Approbation
> Of Mortals in the lowest Station,
> Wherein a huge Sham-Dragon flies,
> And dancing Dev'ls in Crouds arise,
> The Stage where Poets should delight us,
> Is then, become a Hell to fright us.
> Nor does this Pile, which heretofore
> Was justly deem'd a Theatre,
> Deserve, from *Harlequin*'s uncouth
> Designs, a better Name than *Booth*.[53]

According to Ward, Harlequin's "dumb Wit" is responsible for transforming more than just the material reality of things; it also threatened to transform the once-dignified English stage into little more than a fairground amusement. Because pantomime seemed to appeal to the senses at the expense of the mind, it dangerously democratized the theatre and made it accessible even to those of "the lowest Station." As a contributor to *The Weekly Oracle* (1737) puts it:

> In *Pantomimes* no Attention was required; they are no Objects of the Understanding; Reason is not upon her Stretch to carry on the Chain of Incidents which are in a good Play: The Eye Only is necessary to behold *Harlequin* and *Columbine*; and if they, who are captivated with these Entertainments, see *Punch* turned into a Wheelbarrow, the Surprize arising from them is Reward enough for their Money.[54]

To the theatre managers who took in this money, and who were routinely attacked for promoting "irrational" entertainments, the issue was simply a matter of supply and demand: pantomimes were allowable because they were agreeable to the taste of the town. Cibber therefore excuses himself for his role in mounting "the decorated Nonsense and Absurdities of Pantomimical Trumpery" at Drury Lane, by placing the blame squarely on the "Multitude": "If People are permitted to buy it, without blushing, the Theatrical Merchant seems to have an equal Right to the Liberty of selling it, without Reproach" (50–51). Adopting a slightly different approach, Rich defends Lincoln's Inn Fields pantomimes on the grounds that they make accessible to the broad public the kinds of entertainments that were becoming popular among the elite. In his dedication to *The Rape of Proserpine*, Rich claims that his pantomimes adapt the genteel music and venerable fables of Italian opera "to the Taste of an *English* Audience," supplementing them with the "various Embellishments of Machinery, Painting, Dances, as well as Poetry it self" that he believes are necessary in any "general Diversion."[55] Pantomime was able to function as a "general Diversion" because, as apologists and satirists alike agree, it *diverted* – because it "turned aside" from the natural course of things – and thus most reviews highlight the genre's inversion or conversion of physical paradigms. After having allowed that "there is something witty and ingenious in the Plot and Contrivance of such Entertainments," an account in *The Weekly Journal* No. 232 (April 6, 1723) of the Lincoln's Inn Fields production of *Jupiter and Europa: or, The Intrigues of Harlequin* (1723) praises the devices by which Jupiter is transformed into a bull "in Sight of the Audience," maintaining that though the "common People" may take it "for Inchantment," even "men of the best Taste and Judgment cannot forbear being pleased at being so agreeably deceiv'd."[56] The pleasure of pantomime, from this perspective, involves a supra-suspension of disbelief that takes for granted the genre's readiness to flout credibility and transcend nature, and the audience's willingness to be imposed upon by Harlequin's false wit and persuaded by his "silent *Rhetorick*." Pantomime literally and figuratively turned the world topsy-turvy, and audiences of all kinds seem to have derived considerable, if vicarious, satisfaction from this metamorphosis of the natural order.[57]

*Perseus and Andromeda: or, The Spaniard Outwitted* may once again serve as a case in point. From surviving accounts, it seems clear that the pantomime was one of the most popular of the period: it was produced sixty times in its first season at Lincoln's Inn Fields, and more than twenty times a year for several subsequent seasons. It also seems clear that the reason for the pantomime's popularity had less to do with its dramatic coherence than with its fabulous effects and its ubiquitous scenes of transformation. A version of the same myth had recently been mounted at Drury Lane, and Rich's production of *Perseus and Andromeda* represents an attempt to reclaim audiences through a blatant appeal to "show" over "sense."[58] The pantomime typically interweaves two plots: the "serious" follows the adventures of Perseus as he vanquishes Medusa and the Gorgons, rescues the Ethiopian princess Andromeda from a monster rising "from the Flood," and consequently takes the princess as his wife; the "comic" follows the antics of Harlequin, as he dupes Don Spaniard, the father of Colombine, and plays a series of pranks on the foppish Petit Maitre. To a certain degree, the "serious" and "comic" plots are ironic foils to one another: Harlequin's farcical efforts to win Colombine reflect the heroic labours of Perseus to win Andromeda. But the plots themselves are loosely structured and episodic, and there is little logical continuity between one extravagant scene and the next. The serious plot opens in the Gardens of King Cepheus, where the royal family pathetically laments the approach of Medusa and appeals to the gods, and specifically to the semi-divine Perseus, to deliver them from the monster who threatens to turn their entire realm into "breathless Statues."[59] The scene then shifts to a wood, where "*Mercury* rises as from Hell" to assist in arming Perseus with a sword forged by Vulcan, a pair of winged sandals, the diamond shield of Pallas, and a magic helmet from Pluto (4–7). At this point, "the COMIC PART begins" with the transformation of a chair, upon which Harlequin is perched to hang himself, into a magician who encourages Harlequin's frustrated designs on Colombine and gives him the sword that will magically facilitate these designs.[60] Subsequent "serious" and "comic" scenes do little more than provide the heroes with opportunity after opportunity to make use of their newly acquired "Magic Powers." In quick succession, Perseus beheads Medusa, evades the other Gorgons by making himself invisible, and then flies away, leaving several "frightful and fantastic Monsters" to emerge out of the bloody scene (12); Harlequin turns himself into a "DOG," seeks out his rival, "holds up one Leg and pisses on the *Petit Maitre*" (9–10); Perseus returns and conquers the sea monster, claims Andromeda as his reward, and joins the princess in the Palace of Venus, which promptly "ascends" to solemnize their marriage (16); and, after considerable mischief, Harlequin transforms an arbour into a raised cupola and himself into a "Statue of MERCURY" sitting atop the cupola (13).[61] When he is seized and summarily hung, Harlequin falls from the gibbet in pieces, reconstitutes himself, and embraces Colombine, to the wonder of both Don Spaniard and the English audience (19). The "GRAND DANCE" that concludes the entertainment, and seems to have united "serious" and "comic" plots, suggests a harmony of form and content: it expresses the joy of Perseus and Andromeda, Harlequin and Colombine, through the rhetoric of motion, gesture, and attitude, and the materiality of the stage (*Perseus*, 17; *Tricks of Harlequin*, 20).

In an effort to "read meaning" into this and other pantomimes of the period, O'Brien "reconstructs" the plot of *Perseus and Andromeda*, hoping to prove that, despite its knock-about farce, it "is not innocent of ideology or politics" (19). Focussing on the ways in which the feats of a Perseus or a Harlequin might be seen to undermine hegemonic authority, O'Brien claims that lower- and middle-class audiences would necessarily have been gratified by "the various kinds of wish-fulfillments" that pantomimes typically offered (28). He argues that *Perseus and Andromeda* consistently brings into question "the state's power," especially when it threatens to make Harlequin a victim of the criminal justice system (25). And he treats the plot's relation to the state as "a point around which vectors of deference and resistance gather" (24). The problem with O'Brien's generous reading, however, is that the *wit* of the "outwitting" relies mainly upon stage-effects that contribute only superficially to the development or happy resolution of the pantomime's plots. The tricks and transformations of *Perseus and Andromeda* are more or less discrete, and often seem incorporated for their own sake rather than because they are strictly necessary or didactically useful. Moreover, the conventionality and predictability of the classical and *commedia* plots ironically direct attention to the extraordinary formal features of the performance instead of the familiar content of the stories. Audiences knew that Perseus would undergo several trials before marrying Andromeda, but they were surprized by the entry of "Several *Cyclops*," a "Train of Warlike Nymphs," and a "Company of Infernals," all of whom dance while furnishing the hero for battle (5–6). They were certain that Harlequin would defeat his rival for Colombine, but they did not expect him to rise out of a writing table to replace a love letter written by the Petit Maitre with one of his own (14). That managers continued to mount such performances and that audiences continued to delight in their unnatural deceits are indicative of what many commentators viewed as the vitiated state of contemporary entertainment. According to a 1723 letter in *The Weekly Journal*, pantomime entertainments feature "some Transformation in Scenery, but we cannot tell to what End; for we see no Intrigue carrying on, nor no Plot design'd; but those Things are shewn only for the sake of shewing them."[62] This criticism is echoed by a contributor to *British Journal* No. 234 (March 18, 1727), who complains that pantomimes cause him and other spectators to "stare ourselves out of our Sense" because "there is neither Moral nor Fable in any of their *Raree-Shows*."[63] And in a series of papers in *The Prompter* (January 20–30, 1736), Aaron Hill and William Popple argue that audiences are attracted to pantomime out of mere "bodily curiosity," and that such curiosity inclined them "to covet the sight of feats of activity from whence no instruction can be derived." As an example of such "feats," they offer a paradoxical encomium to Rich's famously infamous skills in the role of Harlequin: "To him is due the discovery of the wonderful extent of human genius and ability by convincing us that our species is the most perfect in the Creation, for we now plainly see that Man, mere Man, can personate a dog, a cat, a monkey, a bear, &c. to such a degree of similitude as to deceive the sight."[64] Not every pantomime was able, or willing, to make meaning out of motion; in many cases motion alone seems to have been enough to please audiences. Glossing over the genre's more "local pleasures," O'Brien reproduces the arguments of Weaver and other apologists, treating pantomime as a representative art that shares the same mimetic standards as poetics and that consequently deals with the same social, intellectual, and political issues as works in more traditional "literary" genres. Yet this concentration on the "ideology" of eighteenth-century pantomime causes O'Brien to neglect the other side of mimesis – the fact that pantomime, like poetics, could, and usually did, deviate from the strict representation of nature and defy the kinds of idealized standards laid out by Weaver. The theatrical parallel of wit's "external Mimicry," pantomime involved a cursory kind of imitation that celebrated physical resemblance while suppressing more substantive differences between Harlequin and the things he pretends to represent. If apologists for pantomime emphasize the genre's ancient and mimetic basis, critics of the genre follow Locke, Pope, and Addison in satirizing the misrepresentations of nature characteristic of witty metaphors or metamorphoses. As the seeming similitudes of Rich's performances suggest, pantomime may indeed have exemplified "dumb Wit," but this wit was as false as "*Anagrams, Acrosticks, Conceits, Conundrums, and Puns.*"

The fact that Rich's Harlequin is able to deceive without ever speaking a word seems to bear out the standard anti-theatricalist claim that the stage's materiality nullified the power of language to communicate to audiences. At the same time, it also points to the irony of most accounts of early eighteenth-century pantomime, in that any attempt to render Harlequin's "Wit corporeal" by way of verbal wit could not help but expose its very absurdity. Once excised from its original context in spectacular performance, corporeal wit became an irreconcilable oxymoron. As such, the best way to proscribe pantomime was simply to describe it, since the tricks and transformations of Harlequin resisted translation into meaningful words. This explains why many of the more effective satires on the harlequinades of the 1720s, 1730s, and 1740s take the form of parody or burlesque.[65] In *The British Stage: or, The Exploits of Harlequin* (1724), the mock performance of several "whimsical humorous Scenes" provides an opportunity for some of the most notorious devices of contemporary pantomime to become the most vocal. As the facetious preface explains: "the famous Dr. *Faustus*, the *Dragon*, and the *Windmill*" are "made by the Author to speak in this Performance, to attone for those Characters which are Dumb in the Original Entertainments."[66] So "Mr *Dragon*" brags that "Besides my singing, I've constantly spit Fire, flew about the Air, mounted a Giant on my Back, and squirted a Dancing-Master at every Fizzle." Likewise, "Mr. *Windmill*" boasts that "I have been dancing like a Jack in the Lanthorn all the time," and that "it was so exceeding dext'rous, that all People were amaz'd" (3–4). In addition to a singing dragon and a dancing windmill, the performance also features haggling devils, a bawdy owl, ghosts, fiends, shades, and duelling puppets. Harlequin is presented as himself the author of this farce, and his intrusive commentary indicates that his facility for magic is simultaneously his dramatic art. He informs "Mr. *Owl*" that "you must submit to be transformed," but invites "Mr. *Dragon* and Mr. *Windmill*" to "retain your natural Shapes, to add to our Entertainment" (5). Over the course of the entertainment, the owl is changed from "a Bird of Prey" into "a fine Gentleman," a motley-dressed Don Quixote is "whirl'd round" by the windmill, the dragon descends, "opens his Tail, and evacuates a Dancing-master," and the dancing-master makes a series of "Capers on his Head," only to be transformed into a bird, a baboon, and a bear. Harlequin himself pushes Punch and his "Brother Puppets" about in a wheelbarrow and "at length oversets them," and he cuts off a false wooden leg before "his right Leg appears." Throughout, an "Ass," who conventionally represents the "Judgment of this Town," enthusiastically exclaims: "Wonder of Wonders!" "Surprising!" "These are wonderful Tricks!" "Here's Wit in Perfection!" "These are such prodigious Transformations!" and "I'm diverted, amaz'd, pleas'd, and astonish'd!" When all of the characters in the farce appear on stage to join in a dance, the Ass unwittingly identifies the formal conceit of the satire: "Ha—ha— Entertainment upon Entertainment" (22). In combining the tricks and transformations of multiple pantomimes into one performance, *The British Stage* parodically exaggerates the *im*propriety of thoughts and motions that was characteristic of the genre.

Fielding uses a similar technique in *Tumble-Down Dick: or, Phaeton in the Suds* (1736), a parody of pantomime that takes as its occasion the rehearsal of the aptly named Machine's new pantomimic entertainment, a representation of the Phaeton myth, "Interlarded with Burlesque, Grotesque, Comick Interludes, call'd, Harlequin A Pick-Pocket." This on-stage divertissement is diverted by the off-stage commentary of Machine himself, who remarks upon the action in progress, explains his pantomimic poetics, and intrusively engages in dialogue with Fustian and the critic Sneerwell.[67] Machine's commentary makes it clear that he is a wilful and pragmatic caterer to the public's appetite for unnatural entertainments. When the stage is being prepared for Harlequin's escape from prison, Machine invokes the well-known puffs for Fawkes's fairground theatre in order that there be "no Bungling in the Tricks; for a Trick is no Trick, if not perform'd with great Dexterity."[68] The dexterity is shortly revealed to be Harlequin's own, when the "Genius of *Gin*" rises out of a tub to grant him transformative powers:

> Take, *Harlequin*, this Magick Wand,
> All things shall yield to thy Command:
> Whether you wou'd appear Incog,
> In Shape of Monkey, Cat, or Dog;
> Your Mistress to a Butter-Churn;
> Or else, what no Magician can,
> Into a Wheel-barrow turn a Man. (341)

Although such devices were commonly perceived to delude the critical judgement and impose upon the senses, Machine is happy to purvey them since he recognizes, along with Cibber and Rich, that "Pantomime *Miracles take with the Age*" and that "*nothing but* Harlequin-*Feats will go down*" (351).[69] Harlequin is consequently made to turn a Justice of the Peace into a "Periwig-Block," Neptune descends dressed like a Gravesend "Waterman," and "two or three Girls carrying Farthing Candles" are transformed into stars. When Fustian protests the ludicrousness of this transformation, Machine responds:

> Dear Sir, don't be angry. Why will you not allow me the same Latitude that is allow'd to all other Composers of Entertainments? Does not a Dragon descend from Hell in *Doctor Faustus*? And People go up to Hell in *Pluto and Proserpine*? Does not a Squib represent a Thunderbolt in the Rape of *Proserpine*? And what are all the Suns, Sir, that have ever shone upon the Stage, but Candles? And if they represent the Sun, I think they may very well represent the Stars. (344–45)

Machine's argument from authority, and from the practice of popular pantomime artists, slyly justifies his own entertainment while revealing the excess and irrationality of most others. By putting into words the silent actions and antics of the Faustus and Proserpine pantomimes, Machine, like Scriblerus, inadvertently punishes wicked *dancers* out of their own *motions*, if not their own *mouths*. Where *Peri Bathous* cites contemporary poetry to its disadvantage, parodies such as *The British Stage* and *Tumble-*

*Down Dick* reproduce the devices of contemporary pantomimes in order to draw attention to the way in which Harlequin's false wit misrepresents the truth of nature. Even while Fustian complains of "*anti-natural*" representations wherein the Sun is introduced in "the Character of a Watchman" or a "Dog in a *Harlequin*'s Dress" skips across the stage, Machine is able to respond plausibly that "the chief Beauty of an Entertainment, Sir, is to be unnatural" (348).

Perhaps the best-known parody of unnatural entertainments is James Miller's *Harlequin-Horace: or, The Art of Modern Poetry* (1731), a satire on the general decay of English literature and culture that takes as its test case the contemporary vogue for pantomime. Putting into words the silent action of *Perseus and Andromeda*, *The Rape of Proserpine*, and *Jupiter and Europa*, among others, Miller cites popular pantomimes to their disadvantage by demonstrating the way in which they "shun with Care the Rule prescrib'd of old / That Things too strange, should not be shewn, but told":

> The Feats of *Faustus*, and the Pranks of *Jove*
> Chang'd to a *Bull*, to carry off his Love;
> The *swimming Monster*, and the *flying Steed*,
> *Medusa*'s Cavern, and her Serpent-breed,
> *Domes* voluntar'ly rising from the Ground,
> And *Yahoo Rich* transform'd into a *Hound*,
> All acted, with a Show of Truth deceive,
> Which if related we should ne'er believe;
> Glorious Free-thinking reigns to that degree,
> We credit nothing now, but what we *see*.[70]

As in debates over verbal wit, the relative truth or falsity of "dumb Wit" is ascertained "at Sight." Where eighteenth-century readers visualize the surprising analogies of witty language, eighteenth-century spectators "*see*" the epistemological effects of wit in the astonishing turns of pantomime artists. Like Ralph, Weaver, and Pope all do, Miller identifies a formal relationship between pantomime and poetics, using the antics of Harlequin as a figure for the perversions of order and nature peculiar to the false wit of modern poesy. Expanding upon the standard view that a foolish taste in amusements is symptomatic of a broader kind of folly, Miller argues that the pervasiveness of bathetic poetry encourages, and is encouraged by, irrational diversions.[71] Thus, his mock dedication lauds Rich as "the great Patron of the Art we here treat of" (b1v), mainly because he chooses to exhibit himself to the public in the "Guise" of some "such like Animal" (b1r):

> All the delectable Representations you have entertain'd us with, have been put together in absolute Conformity to the Rules we have laid down; nay verily, but from *those* are the Rules themselves extracted, in likewise as *Aristotle* compil'd his *Art of Antient Poetry* from the Writings of that then renown'd Ballad-maker *Homer*. (b1v)

The studied ambivalence of this praise intimates both that contemporary poetics are based upon the rules of pantomime and that contemporary pantomime relies upon the rules of poetry. As such, Miller conversely uses the trivial sublime, catachrestic rhetoric, and false wit as figures for the unnatural deceits of "*Grotesque Dancing*":

> A Thousands jarring Things together yoke,
> The *Dog*, the *Dome*, the *Temple*, and the *Joke*,
> Consult no Order, but for ever steer
> From grave to gay, from florid to severe. (2–3)[72]

In *Harlequin-Horace*, pantomime and poetics are mutual metaphors for one another, in that they mutually defy truth and nature. Miller brings the two together in an ironic *ars poetica* whose precepts are exactly the reverse of those of the ancients, since they are derived from the specious authority of modern performers – whether authors like "*Welsted*," "*Philips*," and "*Tibbald*" (9) or entertainers like "*Heydigger*" (29), "*Hurlothrumbo*" (10), and "*R—h*" (37). In thus turning Horace to Harlequin, "with his Head where his Heels should be," Miller caters to "the *present Taste*" by making modern poetry pantomimic and the harlequinades of the 1720s, 1730s, and 1740s catachrestic (b3v). Miller's ironic observations may equally apply to the absurd metaphors in *Prince Arthur* and the extravagant scenes of transformation in *Perseus and Andromeda* – to "jarring Things" yoked together as well as "The *Dog*, the *Dome*, the *Temple*, and the *Joke*." The commercial logic that governs the poem advises authors, like entertainers, to "gratify the Town in all you write" and "do any thing for Bread, or—Fame" (2). The Grub Street speaker thus recommends, for instance, that modern poetasters "Take then no Pains, resemblance to pursue, / Give us but something very strange, and new, / 'Twill entertain the more—that 'tis not true" (18). His examples of fallacious novelty include descriptions of the Earl of Dorset as "vain-glorious," Lord Chesterfield as neither "witty, nor polite," and the Duke of Argyll as "unable to speak, or fight" (19), each of which contradict history, good sense, and decorum. Yet examples might also include "*Shipwrecks*, and *Monsters*, *Conjurors*, and *Gods*" (5), since these devices are treated alongside the poem's discussion of "thund'ring" tropes (20), "*pompous*" figures (47), "surprizing" similitudes (8), and other "great Productions of *Profundity*" (5). In some cases, *Harlequin-Horace* goes so far as to become zeugmatic, as when the art of poetry and the arts of pantomime are conflated into a single copious passage:

> With Truth and Likelihood we all are griev'd,
> And take most Pleasure, when we're most deceiv'd.
> Now write obscure, and let your Words move slow,
> Then with full Light, and rapid Ardor glow;
> In one Scene make your *Hero* cant, and whine,
> Then roar out *Liberty* in every Line;
> Vary one Thing a thousand pleasant Ways,
> Shew *Whales* in *Woods*, and *Dragons* in the *Seas*. (5–6)

Miller's actual perspective is generally the opposite of that of his speaker; the would-be poet or pantomimist is therefore sincerely encouraged to adapt his style to his subject, to maintain a regular method, to elevate "sense" over "sound" and "show," and, most importantly, to represent the truth of nature. But in a poetic world "to *Change* inclined," language becomes spectacle because modernity and mimesis are irreconcilable (16). After all, both the modern poet and pantomimist

> ... hate a Piece where Truth and Nature meet,
> Scorn what is real, but enjoy deceit;
> And always give the most Applause to those,
> Who on our very Senses most impose. (18)

The elaborate frontispiece to the first edition of *Harlequin-Horace* renders, in fittingly visual and graphic terms, what Miller sees as the main problem with pantomimic poetics: it necessarily appeals to audiences who "enjoy deceit" (Figure 7). The frontispiece combines several of the more notorious episodes in the Lincoln's Inn Fields production of *Perseus and Andromeda*, including Harlequin's transformation of himself into a statue of Mercury sitting atop a cupola, and his metamorphosis into a dog that urinates on his rival for Colombine. In a surprising transformation of his own, however, Miller changes the Petit Maitre into Orpheus, and thus has Rich, as Harlequin, as a dog "piss" on his own principal rival – the mythological representative of music and poetry. Compare this treatment of Orpheus with the frontispiece to Jacob Tonson's collaborative edition of *The Odes and Satyrs of Horace* (1715), which featured translations by "the most EMINENT HANDS," including Dryden, Congreve, Prior, Otway, Temple, Buckingham, and Roscommon (Figure 8). Orpheus is seen sitting in a similar posture to that in Miller's frontispiece, with leg outstretched and lyre in hand, but in a situation much more appropriate to the dignity of a

*Serpentes avibus geminentur, Tigribus agni*

Figure 7  Frontispiece to James Miller's *Harlequin-Horace: or, The Art of Modern Poetry* (1731)

volume devoted to one of the greatest poets of the original Augustan Age, and boasting some of the pantheon of English Augustan poets. The legendary bard is surrounded by rocks and trees and animals, all of which are said, in *Ode* 1.12, to be charmed by his harmonious strains.

Figure 8 Frontispiece to *The Odes and Satyrs of Horace* (1715)

And quavering at his heels is a white swan that, in *Ode* 2.20, comes to symbolize the pure presence of poetry and the immortality of the poet. Like the ironic precepts of *Harlequin-Horace*, Miller's treatment of Orpheus is exactly the reverse of that of the ancients. In contrast to Tonson's frontispiece, the pissing spaniel that appears at the heels of this Orpheus symbolizes the degenerate and ephemeral nature of pantomimic art, and the corresponding debasement of poetical art that inevitably occurs when Horace turns Harlequin.[73] It is no longer the song of Orpheus, but the "dumb Wit" of Harlequin that, according to Miller, "ne'er can fail to charm a crowded House" (21). The spectators in the theatre boxes view the scene with sheepish but certain interest. In the upper galleries, a group of women watch the spectacle and applaud, and in the lower boxes one woman modestly lifts her fan and turns away from the scene, while another continues to observe Harlequin's antics over her own raised fan.[74] For all of its lack of restraint, pantomime was, the frontispiece confirms, undeniably popular. And it was popular for the same reason as the ornamental devices proscribed as false wit – precisely because of its refusal to stay within the bounds of truth and nature. What Miller says of pantomime's patrons might just as well be said of those eighteenth-century readers avid for linguistic tricks and transformations: "that the Pleasures and Diversions which the present Race of Mortals are most fond of, are such as do the most effectually impose both on their Senses and Understandings; and that the utmost satisfaction they receive, is from being visibly play'd the Fool with" (b3r).

## The region of false wit: a two-part afterpiece

### *The serious*

Theatre historians have generally treated debates concerning pantomime in terms of a broad cultural anxiety about the intrusion of the merely entertaining on the once edifying stage and about the effect on audiences of what one critic describes as "poison'd Sweet-meats, after Feasts."[75] Although pantomimes were in theory supplementary to the tragedies or comedies that they followed, in practice they often dominated or overwhelmed them by placing emphasis on spectacular effects and by consciously avoiding or distracting from the thematic purpose of the main-piece. Thus, when outlining the "evil consequences resulting from pantomime," *Prompter* No. 128 (January 30, 1736) elaborates on how the afterpiece "wipes away all the impressions made by the play and leaves the mind of the auditor unbenefited" (150). But as the "pantomimic poetics" described in this chapter should suggest, the harle-quinades of the 1720s, 1730s, and 1740s also played an active role in ongoing debates over the use and abuse of verbal language, not least because apologist and satirist alike centre their arguments around the ambiguous status of the genre's rhetoric and wit. Pantomime had a similar effect on main-piece drama as luxuriant, illogical, and mixed metaphors, forced similes, and trifling jibes and quibbles were believed to have on discourse. Though rhetorical wit was originally meant as a help to discourse, it had increasingly come to interpolate itself between the purpose and ultimate effects of language. So, when Werenfels proscribes against "Meteors of Stile," he warns that he and other writers must "observe a Mean in our Ornaments, lest we divert a Reader from the Passions we intend to excite in him, to admire the Delicacys of the Stile, and other Mechanical Graces" (215–16). Indeed, to all such commentators, trained in the habits of neoclassical criticism, the popular devices of contemporary poetics and pantomime were equally seen to disturb meaningful communication, to transgress mimetic decorum, and to deviate from truth, reason, and the pattern of nature. When Briton warriors are compared to "sprawling Mastives" and Harlequin is changed into a pissing spaniel, language and spectacle coalesce through the capacity of wit to transform the material reality of words and things. The result is a distinctly modern kind of mimeticism, which repre-sents nature in such a way as to divert from it.

## The comic

Yet as even the staunchest commentators were obliged to acknowledge, this diversion from nature was inherently pleasurable. Ironic discussions of the popularity of Harlequin's "delectable Representations" strikingly resemble more earnest analyses of the "pleasantry of Wit," which, Locke argues, is "so acceptable to all People" because "its Beauty appears at first sight, and there is no labour of thought, to examine what Truth there is in it" (2.11.2.156). For Locke, rhetorical wit is so far removed from the truth of nature that it cannot even be evaluated according to rational standards. But truth, as he nonetheless recognizes, is beside the point, since "Wit and Fancy finds easier entertainment in the World," since the "Arts of Fallacy" continue to thrive, and since "Men find pleasure to be Deceived" (3.10.34.508). The rhetoric of Locke's own language anticipates that of Miller and other commentators who grudgingly draw attention to the satisfaction audiences derive from being deceived by Harlequin's tricks and transformations. And this helps to account for the enduring, if unwitting, attraction of linguistic devices that impertinently distract from discourse: readers enjoyed the "false Wit" of pantomimic poetics in the same way and for the same reason that spectators of the 1720s, 1730s, and 1740s delighted in the "Wit corporeal" of catachrestic harlequinades. English writers during the period recognized the possibilities of a panto-mimic poetics and they exploited these possibilities not because they facilitated the representation of truth, reason, and the pattern of nature, but rather because they pandered to the public's desire for fallacy, non-sense, and the design of art. It is not therefore surprising that the allegorical dream vision with which Addison concludes his "History of false Wit" curiously anticipates the form and content of what would become English pantomime:

> Methoughts I was transported into a Country that was filled with Prodigies and Enchantments, Governed by the Goddess of FALSEHOOD, and entitled the *Region of false Wit*. There was nothing in the Fields, the Woods, and the Rivers, that appeared natural. Several of the Trees blossom'd in Leaf-Gold, some of them produced Bone-Lace, and some of them precious Stones. The Fountains bubbled in an Opera Tune, and were filled with Stags, Wild-Boars, and Mermaids, that lived among the Waters, at the same time that Dolphins and several kinds of Fish played upon the Banks, or took their Pastime in the Meadows. (1.271)

In literalizing witty metaphors into Ovidian metamorphoses, the "*Region of false Wit*" is meant to unsettle readers so as to reform their taste for highly ornamental language.[76] But these same readers were soon made avid spectators of pantomimic entertainments that likewise granted physical shape to extravagant tropes, figures, and similitudes. Given pantomime's relationship to "the *English Wit* and *Ability*," Addison's upside-down images of grotesque abstraction could well be seen to have given birth to the swimming monsters and flying steeds that became fashionable at Lincoln's Inn Fields and Drury Lane. By the same token, however, pantomime might be seen to have revived or sustained an interest in what Addison confidently dismisses as "antiquated Modes of Wit that have been long exploded out of the Common-wealth of Letters" (1.245). The popularity of pantomime in many ways contextualizes the Augustan reaction against false wit, in that it identifies a source of aesthetic pleasure in the public's eagerness to be duped by apparent sameness in difference.[77] To focus, as both theatre and literary historians tend to do, primarily on the "threats" or "challenges" posed by popular genres and pervasive devices, or to bring "dumb Wit" and verbal wit, "silent *Rhetorick*" and the *ars rhetorica*, pantomime and poetics insistently into confrontation, is to overlook what their mingling on the stage or page offered entertainers and authors who wished alternately to divert and instruct their audience. If, as John Sitter summarily claims, Augustan wit is "Nature in ambiguity dressed," this ambiguity could manifest itself in words or in checkered bodysuit, mask, cape, and cap – the material accouterments of falsity in flux.[78] For in a dynamic culture under the sway of Harlequin's magical slapstick, false wit, like corporeal wit, allures the eye only to unbend the mind.

# CHAPTER 3

# "Fasten'd by the eyes": popular wonder, print culture, and the exhibition of monstrosity

From the highest to the lowest, this people seem fond of sights and monsters . . . By their fondness of sights, one would be apt to imagine, that instead of desiring to see things as they should be, they are rather solicitous of seeing them as they ought not to be. A cat with four legs is disregarded, though never so useful; but if it has but two, and is consequently incapable of catching mice, it is reckoned inestimable, and every man of taste is ready to raise the auction. A man, though in his person faultless as an aerial genius, might starve; but if stuck over with hideous warts like a porcupine, his fortune is made for ever, and he may propagate the breed with impunity and applause.

– Goldsmith, *The Citizen of the World* (1762)

But what so ever shall diminish from, or exceed the just proportions of Nature, shall be rejected, as False, and pass for extravagance, as Dwarfs and Gyants, for Monsters.

– Granville, "Concerning Unnatural Flights in Poetry" (1701)

Although *The Touch-Stone* (1728) intends to be reasonably comprehensive in its survey of the "Reigning Diversions of the Town," James Ralph has A. Primcock concede the unlikelihood of gratifying the tastes of all readers *and* pleasure seekers: "I make no Doubt, but several of my Readers will look upon my Method of handling this Topick as too circumstantial and prolix, while others will think me too concise, and perhaps very defective, in omitting what they call a publick Amusement" (235). Among the amusements that are conspicuous by their absence from *The Touch-Stone*, Primcock is made to draw particular attention to public exhibitions and shows featuring what contemporaries variously classified as "prodigies," "wonders," and "monsters." He expresses regret that he cannot do justice to *"Mary of Godliman,"* the illiterate wife of a poor clothier, who was believed to have given birth to seventeen and a half rabbits in 1726, and who "engross'd all Conversation for six Months" (236).[1] He alludes to "the *Cow with five Legs*" and "the *Hare that beats a Drum*," each of which joined a vast menagerie of animal oddities and performing beasts on display throughout Augustan London.[2] And he praises in passing the skill of Matthew Buchinger (1674–1740), the twenty-nine-inch-tall *"High-german Artist, born without Hands or Feet,"* who danced the hornpipe; played at skittles and cup-and-balls; was adept at a half-dozen musical instruments; executed card and conjuring tricks; was an accomplished carafologist, calligrapher, and micrographist; and drew landscapes, coats of arms, and portraits, including a detailed self-portrait (Figure 9), all by way of "two fin-like excrescences" growing from his shoulders (236). The "Little Man of Nuremberg" demonstrated his accomplishments at several European courts, before travelling from Hanover to England in 1714 as part of the retinue of the future King George I. Despite his aversion to exhibiting himself to public view, and despite his lack of hands and feet, Buchinger was able to support both himself and his large family (he was married four times and fathered fourteen children) during the 1720s and early 1730s as one of London's most remarkable "sights."[3]

Such sights had long been a feature of life and leisure in the city. At least since the Elizabethan era, enterprising showmen had exhibited human and animal "curiosities" in the marketplace and at the great London fairs, hoping to make a profit from what were perceived as aberrations and anomalies in the course of nature.[4] The decadence of the court of Charles II and the impetus of the New Science seem, however, to have brought about a resurgence of interest in three-breasted women, scaly boys, "Wild *Hairy*" men, hermaphrodites, learned pigs, conjoined twins, and giants and dwarves. During the late seventeenth and early eighteenth centuries, the swathe leading from Fleet Street and the Strand, up through Charing Cross, and into Leicester Square, Soho, and Piccadilly was daily thronged with paying spectators who crowded inn-yards, taverns, coffee-houses, and itinerant booths in order to gawk at monstrosities of all shapes, sorts, and sizes. What began merely as a vulgar fashion for monsters became, according to several critics, a widespread "relish," an infectious "disease," "an almost universal craze," affecting sightseers from virtually every class, vocation, and social background – from monarch to merchant to mob.[5] Visible errors in the natural order easily attracted a popular mind that remained steeped in superstition and desirous of crude spectacle and shock. At the same time, what might be called "ontological transgressions," errors in the material essence of being, appealed to natural philosophers, scholars, and wits who used the monstrous as a basis for theories of natural history, conceptions of personal identity, and attacks on the apparent corruption and perceived decay of English literature and culture.[6]

Figure 9  Broadside ad for Matthew Buchinger, "being Drawn and Written by
Himself," issued April 29, 1724. The knot of the periwig is inscribed with the Lord's
Prayer in miniature letters, while the curls contain seven Psalms

The taste for monsters, in turn, reproduced itself in published texts ranging from "wonder books," broadside ballads, and miscellaneous town "rambles" to studies in embryology, comparative anatomy, and teratology, pseudo-scientific question-and-answer sheets, and satires such as *A Tale of a Tub* (1704–10) and *The Dunciad* (1728–43), which characteristically figure the massive proliferation of these and other texts as "monstrous."[7] As J. Paul Hunter observes, "the worlds of print and exhibition reinforced one another."[8] The ubiquity of monsters in the marketplace helped to stimulate a vigorous print trade, and the pervasiveness of literature devoted to various kinds of monstrosity encouraged the curious to go and see the real thing.[9] Taking this for granted, Primcock readily acknowledges the popularity of London's monsters, each of which, he claims, "will find their Admirers, who would demand a formal ESSAY in their Favour, to illustrate their Beauties, and make manifest their Use and Instruction" (236). In the cultural climate of *The Touch-Stone*, as explained in Chapter 1, London's readers are sightseers and London's sightseers are increasingly readers. Ralph conceives of both activities as comparable modes of diversion, and thus he associates readerly habits with the experience of commercialized monstrosity. For Ralph, as for contemporaries like Swift and Pope, those who eagerly consume printed "Nonsense" are subject to the same "relish," "disease," and "craze" as those who frequent public exhibitions and shows. Where some go to Bartholomew Fair and pay their two pence to stare at London's latest monsters, others find their "Pygmies of six Inches" and "Giants of sixty Foot" in the bookstalls of St Paul's or the cluttered shops of booksellers.

## Reading the monstrous

Once it is purchased, both sightseers and readers react to monstrosity with what Ralph regards as a similar kind of blank wonder and mindless speculation. It is without irony that he elides the distinction between monsters on display and, as it were, monsters of the text, when he has Primcock remark that "the Majority of Readers" merely "skim the Surface of a Work" and "are fond of strange Monsters" (XXIII). Although it is difficult to determine precisely how the typical audience responded to seventeenth- and eighteenth-century monster exhibitions, extant accounts usually emphasize the way in which literal and figurative "sights" appealed to the senses at the expense of the mind, lulling the critical faculties with the grotesque or gaudy spectacle of physical abnormality.[10] To Ned Ward, London's fair-goers are a "gazing Multitude," a "True *English* unthinking

Mob," "Ignorant Spectators," and a "Gaping Crowd."[11] For John Dunton, a ramble from Cornhill to Charing Cross to Cheapside offers a variety of "Remarkables" for the "*Bumkin*" to "stare his Eyes and Teeth out upon."[12] In the opinion of Tom Brown, pleasure-seeking Londoners "are equally uncapable both of Attention and Patience, and tho' nothing is more quick than the Effects of Hearing and Seeing, yet they don't allow themselves time either to Hear or See."[13] Thomas D'Urfey describes the "attending Multitudes" at a London "Raree-Show," where each "Speculator" remains "speechless, entranced, and incredulous" after having fixed "the *Telescope of his ocular Vision*" to the "private Aperture or *Hiatus*" wrought near the middle of the travelling showman's box.[14] In *Spectator* No. 50 (April 27, 1711), Joseph Addison explains that when the "four *Indian* Kings" were on display at the Two Crowns and Cushion in King Street, Covent Garden, he "often mixed with the Rabble and followed them a whole Day together, being wonderfully struck with the Sight of every thing that is new or uncommon."[15] Alexander Pope takes his "youthful Virtuoso," Martinus Scriblerus, to "the Western confines of the famous Metropolis of Albion," where he is thrust among the "gazing throng," and where his eyes are "drawn upward" by illustrated canvases promoting a "Man-mimicking Manteger," a dwarf prince from "Monomotapa," and a pair of conjoined "Bohemian Damsels" exhibited under the "opprobrious Name of Monstrosity."[16] And Jonathan Swift, perhaps the most playfully abashed of belletristic sightseers, illustrates his own irrational attraction to monsters by allowing the First Earl of Oxford to catch him staring in the streets:

> Some few Days after, *HARLEY* spies
> The Doctor fasten'd by the Eyes,
> At *Charing-Cross*, among the Rout,
> Where painted Monsters are hung out.[17]

The convenient devices of irony or persona are not enough to disguise the pleasing novelty and curiosity dramatized by such accounts. As both first-hand and fictive accounts suggest, the mental lethargy produced by exhibitions was not limited to the "unthinking mob": men of letters, learning, and taste were just as susceptible to the lure of "painted Monsters" and the irregular charm of actual ones. Notwithstanding his professed antipathy towards popular amusements, Swift was easily and habitually drawn in by them.[18] He writes to Stella of "all the sights," describing visits to the Tower, Bedlam, Gresham College, the "Puppet-Shew," and the "famous moving Picture," about which he comments: "I never saw any thing so pretty. Y see a Sea ten miles wide, a Town on tothr end, & Ships sailing in te Sea, & discharging their Canon. Y see a great Sky with Moon & Stars &c. I'm a fool."[19] Swift's familiar self-deprecation hints at his readiness to be imposed upon by the visual cheats characteristic of many sights and shows. And if the wits of the day were prepared to trust their eyes and suspend their disbelief, then it is no wonder that London's other sightseers flocked to see such dubious spectacles as a "Mail *Child* born with a *Bear* growing on his Back" or a "*Wonderful Child*" whose "Body was quite covered with the Scales of Fishes, having nevertheless a beautiful and comely Neck and Face."[20] This was the perceived problem with exhibiting monsters as commercial diversions: human and animal oddities did not so much divert attention from the more serious concerns of life, as they dulled all attention whatsoever. Far from merely unbending the mind, as did other diversions, monster exhibitions were seen utterly to engross it. Sights and shows brazenly catered to what Dennis Todd describes as "man's native predisposition for thoughtlessness."[21] The materiality of the show – featuring a singular body displayed in a booth – tended to invite a passively physical and sensual response from spectators who "gazed," "stared," and "gaped" at the monsters, but did not always think acutely about the broader implications of their fascination. These implications could be scientific, political, social, cultural, religious, or even literary: How do monsters come into being and what constitutes their "monstrosity"? What is the legal status of the monstrous? Should monsters be degraded as amusements and shown for money? In what ways does the monstrous resemble the "normal"? What role does the divine play in prodigious births? What is the symbolic value of the monstrous? The fact that these kinds of questions were ignored by all but the most ingenious and industrious observers pointed to the more pervasive problems of a culture given over to "thoughtlessness" and captivated by the outward appearance of things, one in which naïve empiricism often gawked itself into wilful credulity or impertinent curiosity.[22] According to John R. Clark, credulity and curiosity are twin types of self-absorption that deviate from "normalcy" by believing too much or too little in objects outside the common forms of nature.[23] During the seventeenth and eighteenth centuries, monstrosity was a measure of these types: where credulous sightseers took for granted the reality of monsters as proof of their blind faith in the unknown or idiosyncratic, curious sightseers took monsters for granted in order to justify their singularly transgressive experiments and research. In both cases, the experience of monstrosity had less to do with the monsters themselves than with the realization of a subjective ideal – a world of riddles and mysteries that could and should not be explained, or a world of material phenomena that would inevitably be explained. For both the credulous and the curious sightseer, that is, the experience of monstrosity involved a devotion to what they had seen but had not as yet understood.[24]

It is therefore less important that some monsters were hoaxes than that all monsters maintained a powerful hold over the eighteenth-century imagination, in large part due to their striking impact upon eighteenth-century eyes. If audiences were duped or dazzled by the exhibitions of monsters-mongers, writers were frequently seduced by the intellectual and aesthetic possibilities of the monstrous. Indeed, the same authors who satirized "gazing," "staring," and "gaping" audiences often structured their works around the thematic spectacle of monstrosity. As his eponymous "Spy" makes his way through the metropolis, Ward returns again and again to the image of the monster, documenting the various ways in which London's denizens violate the bounds of physical and, he implies, moral humanity. While visiting Bartholomew Fair, the Spy and his sophisticated companion are "Jostled into a Booth" where they witness "a Dwarf *Comedy*, Sir-nam'd a *Droll*, which most commonly proves as wonderful a Monster as any's to be seen in the Fair" (237). Among these lesser fairground "Monsters" the Spy singles out a group of street performers who infringe upon the limits of their species in a manner akin to the scaly boy and the child with a bruin back. One tightrope-walker is described as having "waddled along the Rope like a Goose over a Barn Threshold" (234). A sword-dancer is said to have "as much Flesh on her Bones as a *Lincoln-shire Heifer*" (256). And the "poor Pedantic Fooleries" of another set of performers are dismissed as "an abuse to humane Shape," their contortions of proportion being scarcely more diverting than "the Accidental Gestures of one Ape" (258). The audience who applaud these performances are no less grotesque than the monsters who participate in them. Having staked out a place to "over-look the Follies of the Innumerable Throng," the Spy explains that the "Impatient Desires of seeing Merry-*Andrew*'s Grimaces" had led spectators "Ancle-deep into Filth and Nastiness, Crowded as close as a Barrel of Figs, or Candles in a Tallow-Chandler's Basket, Sweating and Melting with the heat of their own Bodies" (229–30). From the perspective of Ward, gawking at monsters thus makes monsters out of gawkers: the show transforms sightseers into sights by causing them to be oblivious to their own bestiality.[25]

For Dunton enquiring about monsters exposes, in a similar way, the monstrous stupidity of most enquirers. In his quintessentially modern periodical, *The Athenian Mercury* (1691–97), Dunton attempts to separate legitimate from illegitimate enquiry by providing a forum for anonymous readers to ask questions and to have them answered by the anonymous members of the so-called Athenian Society.[26] The aim of "Athenianism," as the first number explains, is to democratize knowledge by applying the empirical method to all areas of life and learning:

> 'Tis not without great importunity we have undertaken a Task of this Nature, which at first sight appears to be a Subject chosen out and calculated on purpose for *Objections*; but yet a Consideration of those Advantages a great part of the World may reap by it, has superseded this Difficulty. The Design is briefly, To satisfy all *ingenious and curious Enquirers* into *Speculations*, Divine, Moral, and Natural, *&c.* and to remove those Difficulties and Dissatisfactions, that shame, or fear of appearing ridiculous by asking Questions, may cause several Persons to labour under, who now have opportunities of being *resolv'd in any Question*, without knowing their Informer.[27]

Critics have generally praised Dunton's progressive efforts to educate those who could not educate themselves and to disseminate "news and new things," recent information about religion, history, literature, technology, and natural philosophy, to the public at large. In particular, he is credited with having helped to found "Science for Everyman," by opening up the study of the physical world and its phenomena to readers who knew relatively little about Harvey's discovery of the circulation of the blood, Boyle's invention of the air pump, Newton's experiments in optics, or broader developments in anatomy, chemistry, entomology, oceanography, astronomy, geology, microscopy, medicine, psychology, and, for present purposes, teratology: the study of physiological abnormality or monstrosity.[28] Questions are numerous in *The Athenian Mercury* about the mental capacity of monsters, the possibility of salvation for the monstrous, the relationship between fictional and actual monsters, and the nature and causes of monstrosity. Yet the benevolent expression of concern for the common good which opens the *Mercury* is often at odds with the superior and sarcastic tone of many of the society's answers to what it believes are wrong-headed questions about natural philosophy in general and monstrosity in particular. When, for instance, a reader inquires *"Whether Monsters are endued with a rational Soul?"* the society critiques the vagueness of the question before condescending to answer it:

> The word *Monster* is too general a signification and ought to have been distinguish'd, whether by Monster, the Proposer means a monstrous product from Natural Generation, as when two of a kind, as Man and Woman, two Monkeys, &c. produce something of the same species, yet with less or more Limbs, or a commixture of both Sexes (for I have seen an

Hermaphrodite Monkey) or when two Creatures of different Species generate a third betwixt both, as a Man with some other Creature, or a Dog
with a Fox, &c. But because of the word rational, we must suppose
Humanity concerned in the Generation, and then the Question is limited
to one of these, a Monster in Humanity, or a Monster partly humane, and
partly brute. One answer will serve for both; which is this, As fire is known
by the quality of heat, so a rational Soul is distinguishable by its Actions; if
the Monster can Number, discourse in Questions and Answers, &c. (which
no Creature can be taught but what has the Habit and Act of Ratiocination)
it follows, that such a Monster has a rational Soul, and shall be accountable
in the day of Judgment for its Actions. (1.19–20)

Whether or not this answer is correct or even sufficient is beside the point:
Dunton exploits the ill-framed question in order to suggest a lack of
discrimination in the *Mercury*'s audience and, consequently, the cultural
necessity of the Athenian project. The response is slyly satiric while being
self-congratulatory, granting rationality only to those who "discourse in
questions and answers" in the manner of the Athenian Society itself. Those
who fail to do so, readers who ask the wrong kinds of questions, are no
better than the gawking sightseers at London fairs. Even if, as several critics
have claimed, the Athenians themselves were responsible for writing foolish questions in order to "prime the pump," the effect is essentially the
same: fictional queries as well as authentic ones reveal the dullness of a
mind-set that focuses mainly on the physical features that seemingly make
the monster monstrous. If the Athenians feign this mind-set in the pages of
the *Mercury*, it is only to expose its prevalence in the world at large. Thus, a
querist who asks (or is made to ask) about the rationality of a monster
exhibited in France, "*from the waste upward a perfect Woman, and from the
waste downward perfect Swine*," and another exhibited in England, "*from
the shoulders upward perfect Bear, and from thence downward perfect
Woman*," receives a predictably dismissive answer:

> since the shape is only describ'd to us to judge of their reason, we are as
> much in the dark, as if you had ask'd nothing at all; for the External Form is
> not the certain Index for us to judge by: If so, we shou'd conclude that a
> Mandrake, a Satyr, a Mereman, &c. were endued with rational immortal
> Souls, which no one has ever been so ridiculous to believe. (1.139)

Nonetheless, when belief in fabulous creatures suits the satirical purpose of
the Athenians, they are more than happy to be ridiculous. When another
reader asks about the authenticity of "*Satyres*," "*Centaurs*," and other
hybrid monsters found in Greek and Roman "*Stories*," the society mocks
the gullibility implicit in the question, by taking it at its own worth:

We believe there are a great many false things impos'd upon the World, but 'tis a weak Conclusion to infer from thence that all must be false that we hear. If the Authors of this Age shou'd record the late Calf with its Top-knot, they would take it unkindly (if they could be sensible of it when dead) to have their Relations call'd in Question half a dozen Ages hence, especially if they shou'd descend to Circumstances, as to say it was calv'd in such a Place, carry'd to the *Tower*, and expos'd to many Thousands for Gain. We believe there have been Centaurs, Satyrs, &c. we will give you our reasons, and leave your own Faith at Liberty. (1.454)[29]

Despite the empirical evidence of the famous six-legged calf that was shown around London in the 1690s, the society's "reasons" are strangely drawn from the very "*Stories*" about which the reader is curious. Instead of making the obvious connection and proposing that the fabulous creatures of antiquity are the monstrous births of the present, Dunton cites as evidence Plato's allusion to a mare with the neck, head, and hands of a man, Plutarch's discussion of Sulla's encounter with a satyr, and Pausanias' mention of centaurs "in an Island where he was driven by a Storm." The logic of the explanation is backward: Dunton uses as evidence that which cannot be verified in order to prove that which can.[30] By ironically associating fabulous creatures with the "late Calf with its Top-knot," *The Athenian Mercury* makes the real monster "false" while making fools of the mob that are taken in by the commercial exhibition.[31]

Monsters are exhibited to a similar end in several of the playfully satiric sketches of London life featured in Tom Brown's *Amusements Serious and Comical* (1700). Among others, the "Calf with six Legs and a Topknot" is revived by "a damn'd *Trumpeter*" who exhorts the "Rabble" to come in and see the show (3.15). That the "motly Herd of People" respond to this natural wonder with the same frenzied indifference that they respond to London's other commercial amusements suggests the casualness and hasti-ness of contemporary sightseeing (Figure 10). In the hectic world of the Augustan show-circuit, there is little perceived difference between a mon-ster exhibition and a procession of coaches, the Royal Exchange, a "Bookseller turn'd Quack," St Paul's Cathedral, a "brawling Consort of Fish-women," Bedlam, or "those redoubted Authors that take the Benefit of the Air upon the Rails in *Moorfields*" (3.13–37). The "hurry of objects" that characterizes the metropolis makes it next to impossible to view London amusements with anything but distracted eyes. As a result, caught between the serious and the comical, the six-legged calf produces only "several indigested ideas" in the minds of sightseers (3.21). Questions about monstrosity are ignored, not because they are wrong-headed, but because

Figure 10 Frontispiece to the third volume of *The Works of Mr. Thomas Brown,
Serious and Comical*, 5th edn. (1719–20). The scene represents the distracted response
of Londoners to the "Calf with six Legs and a Topknot" that is trumpeted in the
balcony

they slow down the progress from one show to the next. Yet the very fact that urban monstrosity is necessarily "indigested," and thus open-ended, allows Brown to apply monsters as metaphors for a wide variety of social vices. The traditional "characters" that comprise a great part of Brown's *Works* frequently take advantage of the conceptual ambiguity surrounding the monstrous in order to expose the seeming pretension, hypocrisy, and far-reaching folly of a range of London types. For example, Brown attacks religious dissent by describing the outward manifestation of what he sees as the spiritual dubiety of a Quaker:

> But now there rises up a Monster of another kind; and sure he must have a large share of the *Spirit* to inform that *Quagmire of the Flesh*. His Head is as big as *Gogmagog*'s in *Guildhall*, and his Face not behind the Sign of the *Saracen*'s; only his Eyes are so diminutive, that one would think them retired to behold the *Light within*; for what with his large Beetle Brows which like a Penthouse overshadow them, and the *Agitation of the Spirit*, one would think him groping in the Dark without any at all: His cheeks are like two blown Bladders, and a Trumpeter's seem no more to him than a Puppets: His ruddy carbuncl'd Nose seems as if he suck'd his *Inspiration* from *Bacchus* more than the *Bible*; and we may at best suppose him drunk with the *Spirit*. (3.292)

The exaggerated language of this description, as well as the analogies to, among other London sights, the famous "Giants of Guildhall," matches the exaggerated signs of faith that Brown finds so suspicious. And because the Quaker's large head, little eyes, and carbuncled nose are just as glaring and ostentatious as the "*Agitation of the Spirit*," his physical monstrosity bespeaks his apparent moral monstrosity. The same is true of the ruthless practices of a quibbling lawyer or pettifogger, who frightens the town with his ominous "black Gowns and round Caps," whose words are "sufficient to ruine whole Families," and whom Brown portrays as a "most hideous and dreadful Monster" (3.43).[32] Elsewhere, the monstrous helps to give an ironic allure to the vigorous misogyny that Brown shares with many satirists of the early eighteenth century.[33] In "A Consolatory Letter to Mr. H——," a cuckolded husband is encouraged to be more temperate in his grief, since, after all, cuckoldom is the universal plight of all English men. He is assured that fidelity among English women is as uncommon as a monstrous birth among regular ones:

> I tell you once more, Cuckoldom is no Scandal in our Nation; and if you were the first and ancientest—— in *England*, I could say no more to you. If 'tis the Rarity that makes the Monster, you'll never come within the Number of them. 'Tis only the marry'd Men that are not Cuckolds, that,

properly speaking, are the Monsters here, as in *Guiana*; 'tis not those that
have huge Lips and flat Noses, but those that have otherwise, are really the
deform'd. (4.277)

Brown's mischievous turn transforms the once ordinary into the extraordinary as a way of sending up what he sees as the vanity and lust of most
women. Though the cuckold may wear horns upon his head, he is not as
monstrous, because not as unusual, as the husband whose wife is faithful.
The relative rarity that defines the monster as monstrous also accounts for
its appeal to sightseers weary of humdrum entertainments and readers
exasperated by conventional literary tropes and devices. For if, in the
commercial marketplace, "'tis the Rarity that makes the Monster," then
it is also rarity that fills fairground booths and sells new-fangled books.

   This appeal, however, is paradoxical, in that the rarity of the monstrous
necessarily sets it apart from what was traditionally thought to gratify the
eyes: abstract notions of shapeliness, harmony, symmetry, and order. From
the perspective of most early eighteenth-century aestheticians, philosophers, and "physico-theologians," the universe was regular in all its parts,
and this regularity is what constituted its beauty. The logical corollary of
this "argument from design" is that the *ir*regular was inexorably ugly and
abhorrent.[34] According to Roger Lund, the argument from design was thus
"necessarily a doctrine of exclusion": the Augustans were "hard-wired to
embrace beauty and reject deformity" as the "incomplete or botched
attempts" of an absolute artist.[35] The unconsciousness of attraction and
repulsion made it not just normative, but ideological, in that dogmatic
proponents of providential design had either to ignore the shapeless,
discordant, asymmetrical, and disorderly, or to treat all such deviations
as the inevitable and regrettable by-product of a divinely sanctioned
natural process. In either case, Augustan idealism required a suppression
of what the senses revealed to be true: monsters problematized the argument from design by encouraging first-hand sightseers and second-hand
readers to marvel at the deformed rather than the beautiful.

   In *An Essay Towards the Theory of the Intelligible World* (1708),
Thomas D'Urfey uses the surprising attractions of the monstrous to
explode conceptions of the universe that cannot or will not account
for the resolute materiality of less-than-ideal forms.[36] D'Urfey has his
mock-pedantic narrator, Gabriel John, deliver a *"short Apostrophe to
the Ideal World,"* in which "there is not to be found any thing so
mean and despicable as *Things*, but pure *Essences* only" (143). In
assuming the insufficiency of the "Sensible" world, however, the

apostrophe inadvertently points out the inadequacy of any world which limits itself to impossibly perfect neo-platonic abstractions:

> 'Tis well known how the sensible World is disfigur'd by innumerable Blemishes, and a misshapen Brood of Monsters, that affront all the Laws of Nature, and disgust the judicious Observer. Now in the *Ideal* World, on the contrary, every Species keeps to its just Proportions, and never appears distorted, in any Instance, or otherwise than exactly as it should be. (145)

Like most idealists, D'Urfey's *philosophus gloriosus* locates the ideal world in the clouds: he speaks of discovering "inestimable Rarities" (132), coming to terms with "quintessential Truth" (140), and erecting "Castles upon Aerial and Pensile Foundations" (131). Yet for all of his sublime sentiments, the "*Things*" of experience relentlessly drive Gabriel John back to earth. The "*Metaphysic* Wit" of the *Essay* is frequently undercut by allusions to the bilge and bagatelles of London life – to "Mustard," "*Half-crowning*," "Lord Mayors," "Acrosticks," "Chaffing-Dishes," "Stewed-Prunes," and a "Garret-Window in *Barbican*." When Gabriel John turns his "internal Opticks" towards the essences of urban sights, he is predictably startled out of his philosophical speculation by the sheer physicality, the "Mundane Fabrick," of the sights themselves. In his attempt to find a suitable analogy for the ideal world, Gabriel John fixes upon the "Oak *Dodonean*" or "*British* Pastboard" of the popular "*Raree-show*," and is "Wonder-struck to behold" the "new Universe beautiful and immense," enclosed within "a Scull of no larger Proportions, than might have fitted a good reasonable Giant" (132–38). Likewise, when he discusses the "Perfection" of "*Magick*" in the ideal world, along with its "*wonderful*" and "*astonishing*" effects, he descends bathetically to the imperfect tricks and knockabout farce of fairground theatre: "the learned History of the Renowned Dr. *Faustus*, or of our famous Fryar *Bacon*, together with the merry Waggeries of his Man *Miles*, and the Exploits of *Vander-master* the *German*, and Fryar *Bungy* the *English* Conjurer" (158). During his extended analysis of human nature and the "true Idea of a Man," Gabriel John is diverted into a long digression which conjures the kinds of "surprising Spectacles" regularly exhibited by monster-mongers and habitually gawked at by London audiences. "Speculation," in its etymological sense of "seeing," is made to foreground the visual impact of "*intelligible Centaurs*" as well as "Men-Bulls, Men-Camels, Men-Elephants, Men-Sharks, Men-Cuckows, Men-Foxes, or Men-Asses" (173–79).[37] D'Urfey's satiric reduction of the ideal world thus grounds conceptualization in sensation, essences in things, immaterial notions of beauty in monstrous materiality, or what Gabriel John calls

"Monsters in Nature" (175). In so doing, he exposes the fallacy of using the mind's eye to turn a blind eye to experience. The ironic juxtaposition of things as they "should be" and things as they actually are reveals the ridiculousness of a world without "Blemishes," and the necessity of integrating the "misshapen Brood of Monsters" into the natural laws they seem to affront. If, as D'Urfey's *Essay* implies, monstrosity is indeed "well known," then it must take its place alongside the conventionally beautiful in any theory that attempts to account for the sundry pleasures of nature and art.

One such theory was developed by Addison in his *Spectator* series on the "Pleasures of the Imagination" (Nos. 411–21). Responding, in particular, to the limited aesthetics of Shaftesbury and Francis Hutcheson, both of which were founded on the old dichotomy of the beautiful and the deformed or monstrous, Addison opened up a space for what Ronald Paulson refers to as the "stigmatized or marginalized areas of enjoyment."[38] For Addison, the appeal of objects that seem to contradict norms of shapeliness, harmony, symmetry, and order is paradoxical but undeniable. In his enthusiastic sketches of London diversions, Addison reveals a visceral, and notably visual, pleasure in sights and shows that fall outside of orthodox aesthetics – from the contortionist he describes in *Tatler* No. 108 (December 17, 1709) as "a Monster with a Face between his Feet" (2.45) to the Iroquois Sachems with whom he is "wonderfully struck" in *Spectator* No. 50 (1.211). In order to account for this pleasure, Addison replaces the beautiful–deformed dichotomy with a more inclusive set of categories, which he elaborates in *Spectator* No. 412 (June 23, 1712):

> I shall first consider those Pleasures of the Imagination, which arise from the actual View and Survey of outward Objects: And these, I think, all proceed from the Sight of what is *Great, Uncommon,* or *Beautiful.* There may, indeed, be something so terrible or offensive, that the Horrour or Loathsomeness of an Object may over-bear the Pleasure which results from its *Greatness, Novelty,* or *Beauty;* but still there will be such a Mixture of Delight in the very Disgust it gives us, as any of these three Qualifications are most conspicuous and prevailing. (3.540)

Out of the beautiful and/or deformed, Addison extracts two new aesthetic qualities, one of which delights through its "unbounded Views," and the other through its remarkable strangeness and difference. As illustrated in Chapter 1, Addison is most interested in the "*Uncommon,*" primarily because novelty provides a context in which to articulate the appeal of the otherwise unappealing – objects, such as monsters, that are "terrible" or "offensive." He explains: "Every thing that is *new* or *uncommon* raises a Pleasure in the Imagination, because it fills the Soul with an agreeable Surprise, gratifies its Curiosity, and gives it an Idea of which it was not before possest" (3.541). Novelty fulfils the cultural demand for variety: it diverts the sightseer or reader from the ordinary shape of things, from the tediously expansive or mundanely attractive, and suggests an idiosyncratic way of knowing and being. Indeed, it is this novelty that "improves what is great or beautiful, and makes it afford the Mind a double Entertainment" (3.541–42). A "beautiful and comely" child affects the senses through its propriety of parts, but it amuses and refreshes the mind when it also happens to be covered over in hairy scales. "It is this," continues Addison, "that bestows Charms on a Monster, and makes even the Imperfections of Nature please us" (3.541). The monstrous is therefore pleasing precisely because it is *not* beautiful; both its "Loathsomeness" and its "Delight" are the result of its physical "Imperfections."[39] Like the perfections of the beautiful, the imperfections of the monstrous are constituted visually. Addison explicitly identifies the "Pleasures of the Imagination" with the sense of sight, which supplies the defects of all other senses and furnishes the fancy with its subject matter. As he argues in the first essay of the series: "Our sight is the most perfect and most delightful of all our senses. It fills the mind with the largest variety of ideas, converses with its objects at the greatest distance, and continues the longest in action without being tired or satiated with its proper enjoyments" (3.537). Rather than being ideologically excluded from enjoyment, the deformed or monstrous is acknowledged to have a similar impact on the eyes as a "Prospect of Fields and Meadows," a vivid "Description in Homer," or a "Gaiety or Variety of Colours." At first, this might seem at odds with the argument from design, but Addison's aesthetic triad manages to reconcile the attractions of novel monsters with the divine plan of a "Supreme Author." In *Spectator* No. 413 (June 24, 1712), he echoes Francis Bacon in claiming that God has "annexed a secret pleasure to the idea of anything that is new or uncommon, that he might encourage us in the pursuit after knowledge, and engage us to search into the wonders of his Creation" (3.545). From this perspective, the "secret pleasure" that is derived, for instance, from a "Fairy Child" measuring "a Foot and a half high," a "HERMAPHRODITE" whose "private Parts are equally Masculine and Fæminine," or a "painted Prince" emblazoned with "mysterious Characters," has its origin in a kind of divine pedagogy, which exploits credulity and curiosity to convince audiences to believe in monsters by suggesting ways to put them to good use (B.L. N.Tab. 2026/25,

Nos. 6, 15, 2). Addison's "aesthetics of the novel" views monstrosity as delightful in order to make it instructive as well.

## Sightseeing and Scriblerian satire

For Swift, Pope, and the Scriblerians, monstrosity was not intrinsically useful, but was imaginatively so. Monsters were physically disproportionate and had difficulty fitting into the argument from design, but this made them particularly conducive to the designs of parody and satire and to the "rhetoric of exclusion" that recent critics have identified as essential to the project of "Augustanism."[40] Monsters looked different and their visible difference was made to delineate between polite and hack writing, discerning and impercipient reading, and thinking and gawking in their many manifestations. Like many of their contemporaries living in or visiting London, Swift and Pope could not help but be familiar with monsters and their commercial exhibitions, and this familiarity gives shape (or shapelessness) to a variety of satires which employ deformity as a figure for social impertinence, intellectual corruption, scientific absurdity, the commodification of literature, and the dangers of materialism.[41] Though Swift and, especially, Pope are often thought to have reinforced providential design by putting less-than-ideal creatures firmly in their hierarchical place, their works insistently, if ironically, transgress the Great Chain of Being by focussing the gaze of sightseers and readers on the monstrous.[42] Works written in the Scriblerian mode frequently play upon the popular credulity and curiosity associated with hoaxes like the Mary Toft affair, but the most notable of these explore the material implications of genuine monsters on display. *Gulliver's Travels* (1726) and the "Double Mistress" episode in *The Memoirs of Martinus Scriblerus* (1741), two of the most thorough Scriblerian engagements with monstrosity, are famously structured around verifiable details from the Augustan show-circuit. Although the one is a satiric fantasia disguised as a travelogue, and the other is a burlesque romance interpolated into an intellectual farrago, both Scriblerian fictions are rooted in the historical facts of eighteenth-century monstrosity.

The pair of conjoined "Bohemian Damsels" who capture the eyes of Martinus Scriblerus and distract him from his philosophical studies are modelled upon an actual set of Hungarian twins, Helena and Judith, who were exhibited in London in the summer of 1708 (B.L. N.Tab. 2026/25, No. 77). The twins had been shown all over Europe and had excited the interest of "popular" and "polite" spectators alike. William Burnet saw them at The Hague, and was convinced that there was "no cheat in the thing." Hans Sloane had Burnet's enthusiastic epistolary description of the "wonderful union of two twin sisters" read before the Royal Society on May 12, 1708.[43] When they arrived in London, Helena and Judith were placed on public display and promoted with characteristic hyperbole:

> At Mr. John Pratt's, at the Angel in Cornhill ... are to be seen two Girls, who are one of the greatest Wonders in Nature that ever was seen, being Born with their Backs fastn'd to each other, and the Passages of their Bodies are both one way. These Children are very Handsome and Lusty, and Talk three different Languages; they are going into the 7th year of their of Age. Those who see them, may very well say, they have seen a Miracle, which may pass for the 8th Wonder of the World.[44]

Early eighteenth-century London was glutted with purported wonders, and the twins faced vigorous competition, not least from the other monsters assembled in Mr Randall's composite show. The "Manteger" has its origin in a "Man-mimicking" baboon that was exhibited at "the sign of the George against the steps of *Upper More Fields*," where it was puffed as "a most strange and wonderful Creature, the like never seen before in *England*, it being of Seven several Colours, from the Head downwards resembling a Man, its fore parts clear, and his hinder parts all Hairy" (Ashton, 204). Likewise, Ebn-Hai-Paw-Waw, the "black Prince of Monomotapa," is based on another "royal" dwarf, who was shown "*over-against the* Mews-Gate, *at* Charing Cross," and whose handbill describes him as "a little *Black-Man*, being but 3 Foot high, and 32 Years of Age, strait and proportionable every way, who is distinguish'd by the Name of *Black Prince*, and has been shown before most Kings and Princes in *Christendom*" (B.L. N.Tab. 2026/25, No. 19). Nonetheless, for the period during which they were exhibited, Helena and Judith seem to have been the principal diversion of the town – the sheer novelty of twins joined at the small of the back making their show impossible to miss. Sightseers flocked to the Angel in Cornhill, and readers avidly consumed printed pamphlets and periodicals that discussed the "8th Wonder of the World." From early summer to mid-fall, *The British Apollo* (1708–11) ran a series of letters that questioned how the twins came to be conjoined, whether they had one or two souls, if they might marry without being guilty of incest, whether they could conceive and how they would identify their own children, whether both would be culpable for a crime committed by one, if they would die at the same time, and whether they would rise from the dead as one or two bodies. The periodical itself, subtitled "*Curious Amusements for the INGENIOUS*," embodies the hybrid nature of the exhibition, which signified at once an entertaining spectacle and a contribution to what one querist calls *"the arcanas of nature."*[45] Amateur virtuosi prided themselves on being able to classify deviations from the ordinary forms of nature. Yet in their "ingenious" treatments of monstrosity, scientific concerns often gave way to social and aesthetic ones. James Paris Du Plessis' eyewitness account of Helena and Judith, which he includes in his manuscript collection of "Human Prodigieuses & Monstrous Births" and which was reprinted in *The Philosophical Transactions*, is typical in paying greater attention to the twins' endearing physical attributes and polite accomplishments than to the curious formation of their bodies:

> They were brisk, merry, and well-bred: they could read, write, and sing very prettily: they could speak three different languages, as Hungarian or High Dutch, Low Dutch, and French, and were learning English. They were very handsome, very well shaped in all parts, and [had] beautiful faces.[46]

If the Scriblerians did not actually go and see the conjoined twins themselves, they were at least aware of the paradoxical beauty and monstrosity they were widely publicized to possess.

The "Double Mistress" episode is a romantic elaboration on this paradox, and on the details offered in contemporary bills and accounts. Charles Kerby-Miller explains that the Scriblerians "drew on their knowledge rather than their imagination for the materials with which to fashion this episode" (*Memoirs*, 294). But it is more precise to say that their knowledge of London's sights and shows gives them a way of linking the imaginative world with the material, the monsters of antiquity with modern monstrosity. Set off as it is from the rest of the *Memoirs*, the "Double Mistress" episode is itself something of a monster – a conspicuous digression from the "Life, Works, and Discoveries" of Scriblerus that functions as a refreshing foil to the narrative's profusion of intellectual wit.[47] It is subtitled "A Novel" and is prefaced by a disclaimer which accounts for its novelty:

> The style of this Chapter in the *Original Memoirs* is so singularly different from the rest that it is hard to conceive by whom it was penn'd. But if we consider the particular Regard which our Philosopher had for it, who expressly directed that *not one Word of this Chapter should be alter'd*, it will be natural to suspect that it was written by himself, at the Time when *Love* (ever delighting in *Romances*) had somewhat tinctur'd his Style; and that the Remains of his first and strongest Passion gave him a Partiality to this Memorial of it. (143)

The two chapters which comprise the episode of the "Double Mistress" are thus "novel" in two respects: they represent a stylistic turn in the narrative as well as a substantive change of genre, from Menippean memoir to English prose romance of the kind written by Aphra Behn or Eliza Haywood. The reader is diverted from the development of Scriblerus' mind to the heaving of his heart, yet these contradictory motions coalesce through the unexpectedly pleasing monstrosity of the episode. When he first lays eyes on Lindamira-Indamora, Scriblerus is moved by what is described as an uncontrollable "Passion":

> How great is the power of Love in human breasts! In vain has the Wise man recourse to his Reason, when the insinuating Arrow touches his heart, and the pleasing Poison is diffused through his veins. But then how violent, how transporting must that passion prove, where not only the Fire of Youth, but the unquenchable Curiosity of a Philosopher, pitch'd upon the same object! For how much soever our Martin was enamour'd on her as a beautiful Woman, he was infinitely more ravish'd with her as a charming Monster. What wonder then, if his gentle Spirit, already humaniz'd by a polite Education to receive all soft impressions, and fired by the sight of those beauties so lavishly expos'd to his view, should prove unable to resist at once so pleasing a Passion, and so amiable a Phænomenon? (147)

The startling juxtaposition of youthful fire and unquenchable curiosity, female beauty and monstrous charm, physical love and philosophical allure, effects another union of sorts: Scriblerus' disparate passions are made to run in an "eternal Parallel," just like the Bohemian sisters' "common parts of Generation" (146). Having read too deeply in clichéd romances and too widely in classical teratology, Scriblerus' sexual curiosity is, as it were, "conjoined" with his scientific curiosity. His sixpence gives him an opportunity to fix all of his curiosity on the same object, one of "so unparallel'd a Production" that he desires to remove it from "the common Gaze of the multitude" and thereby secure the "Double Mistress" for his eyes alone (147–48). He goes so far as to claim that "Nature" could have designed the twins "for none but a Philosopher," and he requests that they

> Cease then to display those beauties to the profane Vulgar, which were created to crown the desires of
>     Your Passionate Admirer,
>     MARTINUS SCRIBLERUS. (149)

The misdirected passion of their hero provides the Scriblerians with a context in which to satirize many things, from the foolish enthusiasm of virtuosi and the acquisitiveness of collectors, to the pedantry of the law and the extravagance of the romance tradition. But, first and foremost, the episode satirizes the promiscuous way in which monsters were *shown* and the indiscriminate way in which they were *seen*.[48] Monster-mongers, like John Pratt and Mr Randall, demonstrated a marked disregard for due decorum and hierarchy in displaying legitimate objects of enquiry alongside those that were little more than visually striking. And spectators, like James Paris Du Plessis and Martinus Scriblerus, betray a marked lack of taste in being attracted to the beautiful and monstrous alike. The "Double Mistress" is double both because Lindamira and Indamora are simultaneously one woman and two women, and because they are at once a "darling of Nature" and a "Curiosity of Nature." This thematic duality takes the ironic appeal of monsters to its (il)logical extreme: the Scriblerians transform the disinterested empiricism of an amateur virtuoso into proprietary lust. Lindamira and Helena, Indamora and Judith, are not just gawked at; they are possessed by the eyes of their spectators.

Lemuel Gulliver, like Martinus Scriblerus, is fully susceptible to the appeal of curiosities and monstrosities, and his four voyages into "Several Remote Nations of the World" give him ample material with which to fill book or booth.[49] In Lilliput, Gulliver encounters a race of dwarf-like creatures, whose smallness of stature is proportionate to their political pettiness and moral meanness. In Brobdingnag, he is daunted by a nation of spectacular giants who are themselves avid for sights and shows. On the Island of Luggnagg, Gulliver confronts a grotesque species known as Struldbruggs, who are fated to endure perpetual life without "Perpetuity of Youth." And in Houyhnhnmland, he finds it necessary to distance himself from savage "Yahoos" in order to identify with a breed of rational beasts. The fact that Gulliver perceives each of these deviations from the ordinary forms of life as "monstrous" is suggested by his virtuoso impulse to collect, classify, and exhibit them. When he is stocking his boat in preparation for his departure from Blefuscu, Gulliver makes it a point of taking with him a menagerie of miniature animals: "six Cows and two Bulls alive, with as many Yews and Rams." He desires to take "a Dozen of the Natives" as well, but "this was a thing the Emperor would by no Means permit." When he returns to England, Gulliver acknowledges that he has nevertheless made a "considerable Profit" by "shewing" his monstrous cattle to "many Persons of Quality, and others."[50] In his next voyage, Gulliver is "disgusted" by the sight of what he describes as a "monstrous Breast," but he still manages to give the "curious Reader" a detailed account of its "Bulk, Shape, and Colour" (2.1.130). Later, while observing the "nauseous" lice on a beggar's clothing, he explains: "They were the first I had ever beheld; and I should have been curious enough to dissect one of them, if I had proper Instruments" (2.4.159). In another incident, Gulliver preserves the inch-and-a-half-long stings of several enormous wasps, boasting that he has "since shewn them with some other Curiosities in several Parts of *Europe*." Upon returning once again to England, he donates three of these stings to "*Gresham College*," and keeps the fourth for himself (2.3.155). In each case, Gulliver's activity is motivated by "curiosity," the quality that excites inquisitiveness by endowing novel objects with a value outside of their intrinsic worth or function. At the conclusion of his voyages, Gulliver is thus appropriately besieged by a "Concourse of curious People," who visit him at his house in Redriff to witness his fantastic tales of monstrous creatures (15). Having grown "weary" of these people, Gulliver explains, in the misanthropic letter to his Cousin Sympson, that he will condescend to publish his *Travels*, not out of any "Motive of *publick Good*," but as a way of satisfying at a distance those who wonder at his account or doubt his "Veracity" – indulging curious spectators without actually having to see them (10, 14).

What Gulliver does not immediately realize is that the curious are most interested in seeing him, since his strange whinnying and horse-like gait have made him something of a hybrid monster himself, not unlike the contemporary creature advertised as being born with "the Head, Maine, and Feet of a Horse, and the rest like a Man" (B.L. N.Tab. 2026/25, No. 30). Gulliver is an inveterate sightseer, but during his sixteen years and seven months' travels, he spends as much time being gawked at as gawking. Although in England he might purvey miniature cattle and massive wasp stings, in each of the lands that Gulliver visits it is he who is singled out as monstrous. In an uncharacteristic moment of reflection, he comes to terms with the cultural and empirical relativity that structures his experiences: "Undoubtedly Philosophers are in the Right when they tell us, that nothing is great or little otherwise than by Comparison" (2.1.124). Gulliver's perspective on the monstrous cannot therefore be taken as normative because, for the entirety of his travels, Gulliver is not perceived as normal. "In foreign lands," as Barbara M. Benedict puts it, "Gulliver loses his ontological identity."[51] In Lilliput, Gulliver is looked upon as "the greatest Prodigy that ever appeared in the World," rather than as a human being (2.1.124). In Brobdingnag, by contrast, he is variously degraded as "a small dangerous Animal" (125), a "Toad or a Spider" (127), a "piece of Clock-work" contrived by "some ingenious Artist" (2.3.145), and, quite simply, a "Monster" to be "carried about" (2.2.137). After much dispute, the Brobdingnagian scientists conclude bathetically that, since Gulliver is neither an "abortive Birth" nor a meagre "Dwarf," he can only be classified as a species of "*Lusus Naturæ*" – a literal "Sport of Nature" (2.3.146).

Among the Houyhnhnms, Gulliver is physically associated with the "singular," "ugly," and "deformed" Yahoos, yet his "Glimmerings of Reason" separate him from the savages that are supposed to be of his own kind. Formerly a monster-monger, Gulliver now passes "for a Prodigy" (4.6.385) and is known throughout the land as the "wonderful *Yahoo*" (4.3.350).

The epithets used to classify Gulliver recall those used to describe the miscellaneous prodigies, wonders, and monsters exhibited in Swift's London. As Aline Mackenzie Taylor, Richard Altick, Dennis Todd and others have thoroughly documented, *Gulliver's Travels* employs contemporary sights and shows as the basis for both the form and content of Gulliver's extraordinary encounters with rope-dancing dwarves, prodigiously strong giants, exorbitantly old persons, feral men and women, and clever horses.[52] Aside from the many specific connections between real monsters and these Gulliverian ones, critics have drawn particular attention to the "concrete actuality" which lies behind Gulliver's public exhibition in Brobdingnag.[53] The "Indignity" that the little Gulliver suffers by being "exposed for Money as a public Spectacle" has much in common with the experiences of a number of famous dwarves who were shown as monsters during the late seventeenth and early eighteenth centuries (2.2.137). Gulliver is carried from town to town in much the same manner as John Wormberg, the thirty-one-inch-tall Swiss performer who established a fashion for transporting dwarves in boxes. Wormberg, who was displayed in the mid-1680s at "the Plume of Feathers, over against the King on Horseback," seems to have used his box as a prop in his "little mannikin" show, and he was so closely identified with the box that he was once engraved standing in front of it. As another "*Mannikin*" (or "*Grildrig*") in a box, Gulliver complains of the "Agitation" of his journey, but it is Wormberg who was tragically killed when his enclosed box fell into a river, with him still inside.[54] Once he arrives safely in town, Gulliver is advertised in terms which emphasize sameness in difference: a town crier or "*Grultrud*" is hired "to give Notice through the Town, of a strange Creature to be seen at the Sign of the Green *Eagle*, not so big as a *Splacnuck*, and in every Part of the Body resembling an human Creature" (138). This was a highly conventional way of attracting audiences with the characteristics that set a monster apart, and then titillating them with a similitude in scale or behaviour. The handbill for the "little *Scotch* Man," who was seen at "the lower end of Brookfield Market, near Market House," explains that he measures "but two Foot and six Inches high," and that he "hath been admired by all that hath yet seen him." It goes on, however, to supplement these physical accomplishments with personal ones, highlighting the dwarf's essential humanity and blurring the boundaries between the freakish and the familiar:

> He was marry'd several years, and had Issue, by his Wife, two sons, (one of which is with him now.) He Sings and Dances with his son; and has had the Honour to be shown before several *Persons* of Note at their Houses, as far as they have yet Travelled. He formerly kept a Writing-school; and discourses of the *Scriptures*, and of many eminent Histories, very wisely; and gives great satisfaction to all spectators. (B.L. N.Tab. 2026/25, No. 10)

According to Todd, the pleasure of eighteenth-century monster exhibitions resulted from "the *frisson* that comes with seeing how closely the monstrous verges on the normal, the human, the everyday."[55] Yet an equally important part of their pleasure derived from the sheer spectacle of the monstrous imitating the mundane. Gulliver protests the "Ignominy" of being shown as a monster, but when he is brought to the largest room of the Inn and placed upon a table which he estimates to be "near three Hundred Foot square," he attempts to make up for the littleness of his proportions by demonstrating the accomplishments of a gentleman:

> I walked about on the Table as the Girl commanded; she asked me Questions as far as she knew my Understanding of the Language reached, and I answered them as loud as I could. I turned about several Times to the Company, paid my humble Respects, said they were welcome; and used some other Speeches I had been taught. I took up a Thimble filled with Liquor, which *Glumdalclitch* had given me for a Cup, and drank their Health. I drew out my Hanger, and flourished with it after the Manner of Fencers in *England*. My Nurse gave me Part of a Straw, which I exercised as a Pike, having learned the Art in my Youth. (138–39)

What might be thoroughly ordinary in an normal-sized individual is extraordinary in Gulliver, whose "Hundred diverting Tricks" entertain the company for "eight Hours together." His performance is akin to that of a dwarf who was exhibited "at the *Charing-Cross Coffee-House*" on "the Corner of *Spring-Gardens*":

> [A] Man Six and Forty Years old, One Foot Nine Inches high, yet fathoms Six Foot Five Inches with his Arms. He walks naturally upon his Hands, raising his Body One Foot Four Inches off the Ground: Jumps upon a Table near Three Foot high with one Hand, and leaps off without making Use of any Thing but his Hands, or letting his Body touch the Ground. (B.L. N. Tab 2026/25, No. 3)

This advertisement is expressly directed at "*all* GENTLEMEN, LADIES, and *others, Admirers of* CURIOSITIES." The "Bills" and "public Notices" in

Brobdingnag are not so discriminating: Gulliver is shown to all comers at all times, whether the "rude vulgar Folks," the "unlucky School-Boy" who hurls a hazelnut at his head, or the "neighbouring Gentlemen from an Hundred Miles round."

What all of these spectators have in common is the boisterous inanity of their reactions to Gulliver and their common desire to be diverted from the ordinary course of things by deviations from the ordinary nature of things. In the metropolis, the Lorbrulgrudians respond to the strange "*Splacnuck*," the "*Grildrig*," the "*Relplum Scalcath*," in much the same way as Londoners responded to the various monsters on display in the booths at Charing Cross or Bartholomew Fair: they gaze, stare, and gape. Like so many London dwarves, Gulliver is "shewn ten Times a Day to the Wonder and Satisfaction of all People" (141). But as in other historical examples, this wonder is blank: the Lorbrulgrudians have seen Gulliver, but have not as yet understood him. The same is true of Gulliver's encounters with other fantastic races. When he is discovered on the shores of Lilliput, the miniature men show "a thousand Marks of Wonder and Astonishment" at his bulk (1.1.36). Likewise, when Gulliver arrives on the flying island of Laputa, he is "surrounded by a Crowd of People," most of whom behold him "with all the Marks and Circumstances of Wonder" (3.2.226). Even the rational Houyhnhnms are struck by Gulliver's anomalousness: the first native that he meets looks him full in the face "with manifest Tokens of Wonder" (4.1.336). As the consistency of this trope suggests, Swift is as much concerned with sightseers as with sights – with the marks and tokens of wonder as with the objects of wonder. The complacency of each response to Gulliver allegorizes the mindlessness that Swift identifies with contemporary sightseeing and, by extension, with contemporary reading. In publishing his *Travels*, Gulliver self-consciously diverts the eyes of gawkers from his own monstrosity to the monsters in and of his text. In his final chapter, he provides something of a rationale for doing so:

> Thus, gentle Reader, I have given thee a faithful History of my Travels for Sixteen Years, and above Seven Months, wherein I have not been so studious of Ornament as of Truth. I could perhaps like others have astonished thee with strange improbable Tales; but I rather chose to relate plain Matter of Fact in the simplest Manner and Style; because my principal Design was to inform, and not to amuse thee. (4.12.436)

The irony of this rationale is that Gulliver cannot help but amuse, since his decision to publish necessarily turns sightseers into gazing, staring, and gaping readers, who view the monsters of his narrative with the same superficial eyes with which the Lilliputians, Brobdingnagians, Laputans, and Houyhnhnms view him. And like sightseers, these readers are often made credulous by their very curiosity. As if to insinuate that readers should be suspicious of his own claims to truth, Gulliver acknowledges that many travel-writers "impose the grossest Falsities on the unwary Reader," and that these impositions have given him "a great Disgust against this Part of Reading" (436–37). That such a proviso for "unwary" readers appears in the conclusion to a work substantially about "thought-less" sightseers suggests that the two audiences occupy a similar space in a commercial market replete with monsters. Both sightseers and readers must pay a fee to be amused, both trust to their eyes while being amused, and both are often taken in by the amusement. "[T]hose who had seen me," explains Gulliver, "made such wonderful Reports, that the People were ready to break down the Doors to come in" (2.2.139). In an analogous way, writers may amuse readers by adopting the role and rhetoric of monster-mongers. Swift mischievously exploits this possibility, recogniz-ing, like the Brobdingnagian master-of-the-show, "how profitable" Gulliver is "like to be" (140). Swift's notion of profit, however, is moral rather than mercenary: like other Augustan satirists, he draws readers in by appealing to their susceptibilities as sightseers, and then criticizes them for these susceptibilities. Swift enacts the metaphor of monstrosity in order to produce a work that is both satire and show. *Gulliver's Travels* does not simply borrow material from contemporary monster exhibitions, it *is* a monster exhibition.

This is perhaps why James Ralph has A. Primcock allude to *Gulliver's Travels* when comparing his "Method of Writing" to that of other writers who shamelessly cater to the readerly desire for what he calls "mysterious Nothingness": "I suppose no flying Islands, enchanted Castles, or fancy'd Regions, to amuse them. I bring home no Pygmies of six Inches, or Giants of sixty Foot, to moralize and talk Politicks to them; nor speaking Brutes to preach to them" (XXII–XXIII). In order to emphasize the ironic disparity in cultural outlook between Primcock and such arbiters of taste as Swift and Pope, Ralph has his pseudonymous author misread *Gulliver's Travels* and dismiss its imaginative devices as monstrous "Chimæras." Although Primcock seems to notice the topical and political significance of Gulliver's narrative, he fails to realize that Swift's "Pygmies" and "Giants" facilitate his broader criticism of contemporaries who engage with or read their culture in only a cursory way. Like other "thoughtless" sightseers and "unwary" readers, Primcock is fastened by the eyes: he misses the satire and sees only the show. By thus associating the psychology of monster-viewing with the epistemology of shallow reading, Ralph exposes the superficiality and inattentiveness of a world in which Smithfield entertainments have become the touchstone of taste, not just in diversion but in the high arts as well. If most readers only skim "the Surface of a Work," and these same readers are transfixed by "strange Monsters," then the diversions of book and booth may be formally indistinguishable. Joining Swift, Pope, and the other satirists who mingle among the "rout," Ralph subtly argues that modern writers and monster-mongers supply the same commercial demand. Despite or because of this relationship between eighteenth-century textuality and monstrosity, Ralph leaves out an extended discussion of "*the wonderful Rabbit-woman*," the five-legged cow, and "the Little Man of Nuremberg" since the monstrous is already rampant in his alternately "concise" and "circumstantial" treatment of diversion.

## Monsters and mimesis

The rhetoric of Ralph's disclaimer is, in a sense, parodic in that he has Primcock play on contemporary attitudes towards monstrosity while excusing himself from devoting a "formal ESSAY" to the exhibition of monsters and other "strange sights." Whether in an itinerant booth at Bartholomew Fair or a lecture hall at Gresham College, showman and scientist alike usually conceived of deviations from the ordinary forms of life according to the enduring Aristotelian categories of defect and excess.[56] These deviations were consequently described by setting a norm of nature against physical – and necessarily visual – manifestations of omission or addition, deprivation or superfluity, concision or circumstantiality. What Dunton calls the "External Form" may not have been a "certain Index" of rationality, but it was an accepted criterion of Augustan monstrosity. The reason that so many satirists foreground the visual experience of the monstrous is because monsters continued to be defined during the period primarily in terms of their observable characteristics – characteristics that separated them from the normal and normative bodies of their gawking sightseers. Human and animal curiosities most often took the form of what Benedict regards as "an ontological transgression that is registered empirically."[57] Thus, a 1674 pamphlet prefaces its account of "The Northumberland *Monster*" by explaining that, while numerous reasons have been given for the "Many and Strange" monsters that have been documented through the years, "most that have entred into that discussion have either had Excrescencies or Deficiencies in Nature only, that is, as to their Kind and Species" (B.L. N. Tab. 2026/25, No. 30). This opinion is amply substantiated by the dozens of monsters that have come down from the seventeenth and eighteenth centuries in assorted advertisements, hand-bills, and scientific disquisitions, many of which elide causes by emphasiz-ing outward effects: the actual incarnation of monstrosity in missing or extra limbs, miniature or gargantuan stature, malformed, gratuitous, bes-tial, or hybrid features. Take, for instance, the newspaper advertisement for an oddity exhibited in September 1674, at "Mr. *Croomes*, at the signe of the *Shooe* and *Slap* neer the Hospital-gate in *West-Smithfield*":

> *The Wonder of Nature*, viz. A Girl above Sixteen years of Age, born in *Cheshire*, and not much above Eighteen Inches long, having shed the Teeth seven several times, and not a perfect Bone in any part of her, onely the Head, yet she hath all her Senses to admiration; and Discourses, Reads very well, Sings, Whistles, and all very pleasant to hear. (B.L. N.Tab. 2026/25, No. 34)

The marked "Deficiencies" of this "*Wonder of Nature*," were in competi-tion with the "Excrescencies" of "the most strange and wonderful Person, that Nature hath hitherto been known to bring forth: That is, A Man about Twenty-one years of Age, who hath but one Head, yet two distinct Bodies, both of them Male." This "Miracle of the whole World" could be seen "at the *King*'s-Head, near the *May-pole* in the *Strand*" (B.L. N.Tab. 2026/25, No. 5). The "York Minister by holborn barrs" boasted "the Wonder of the Age," a monster who exemplified "Deficiencies" and "Excrescencies" at the same time, and whose bill gives notice that she has "two Heads, one above the other," but that "she has not Fingers nor Toes, yet can dress and undress, Knit, soe, read, sing and do several sorts of Work" (B.L. N.Tab 2026/25, No. 57). Another bill directs sightseers to "*the Sign of the* Prince and Princess of Orange, *over-against the Opera-House in the* Hay-Market," where they could witness a "CURIOSITY which exceeds every Thing that was ever seen or heard of; being a fresh, lively Country Lad, just come from *Suffolk*, who is cover'd all over his Body with Bristles like a Hedge Hog, as hard as Horn, which shoot off Yearly." Notably, the bill also directs "CURIOUS" readers to the pages of *The Philosophical Transactions*, where the "learned Part of Mankind," including Hans Sloane and other members of the Royal Society, provide a "full and particular Account of this surprising Lad" (B.L. N.Tab 2026/25, No. 33). Another early fellow of the Royal Society, Samuel Pepys, records seeing a "great Boy and Girle" at a monster exhibition in Charing Cross in 1668. Pepys describes the brother and sister as being "of most prodigious bigness for their age," concluding that their inordinate size and weight is precisely what makes them "very monstrous."[58] Henry Barker reports to the Royal Society in 1751 on the fifteen-year-old Hopkin Hopkins, who is a "very extraordinary and surprising subject" because he is only two feet seven inches in height and a mere thirteen pounds in weight – prodigiously small for his age.[59] Surveying the nascent field of teratology, a correspondent in *The Philosophical Transactions* for the year 1740 provides an extensive empirical account of, on the one hand, "Monsters that are double," such as a chicken with a "second Rump fixed to its Breast" and a frog which, "besides its four Paws, has a Fifth," and, on the other hand, "imperfect Monsters," such as a sheep with "no Nose" and a premature child born "without Head or Arms" (Figure 11). The monstrosity of the first group is constituted by "superfluous Members," while that of the second group results from "an odd Conformity, as to the Whole, or as to some of the Members."[60]

At both the popular and the learned end of the market the monster was thus a perceptible expression of "too little" or "too much": "Deficiencies" and "Excrescencies" were presented, in the idiom of showmen and the argot of scientists, as nature's glaring mistakes. By the eighteenth century discourses of monstrosity had assimilated the rationalizing impulses of the New Science and monsters had shifted from the "embodiment of wonder" to the "embodiment of error."[61] In Book II of *The Advancement of Learning* (1605), Francis Bacon made it a point of including the "Heteroclites or Irregulars of nature" in his tripartite scheme of "*HISTORIA NATURÆ*," and the consequence was an expansion of the "natural" to include even works exhibiting "a digression and deflexion from the ordinary course of generations, productions, and motions."[62] A girl born without bones, a dual-bodied man, and an armless and headless child ceased to be viewed as singular symbols of God's wrath or personified Nature's whimsy, but became instead representative examples of disorder which at once proved the prevailing order of secular nature and reinforced the argument from design. What had once been treated as a marvellous portent of divine revelation, or as *lusus naturae*, had been "normalized" into something more objective: a violation of species, a perversion of custom, a breach of regularity, a disparity in proportion.

That these categories were as relevant to art as they were to nature is suggested by Bacon's transposition of monsters and digressions: he uses a term for rhetorical extravagance as a figure for the monstrous, rather than the monstrous as a figure for aesthetic defects and excesses. A number of recent scholars have discussed this reciprocity, noting the degree to which

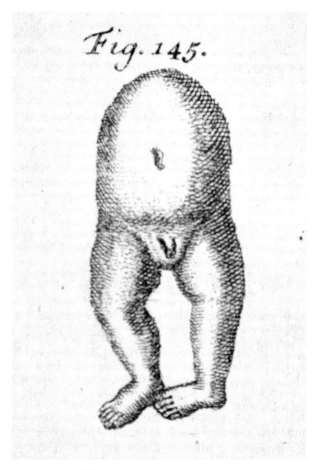

Figure 11 Premature child born without head or arms, documented as one of several
"particular *Monsters*" in *The Philosophical Transactions (From the Year 1732, to the
Year 1744)* (1747)

monstrosity was seen to transgress not only standards in natural philosophy, but literary and cultural standards as well. As Lorraine Daston and
Katherine Park have usefully explained: "Monsters affronted not truth but
taste."[63] At stake were issues of verisimilitude, the appearance of truth
rather than truth itself, and verisimilitude relied upon belletristic conventions of mimesis. It was less important that monsters exhibited too little or
too much nature, than that they were deficient or excessive in their
representation *of* nature and therefore signalled a visible point at which

mimeticism broke down. Contemporary definitions of the word, in its various nominal, adjectival, and adverbial forms, exemplify this through a tendency to conflate the scientific and the aesthetic – monsters in nature with monsters of art. For example, Ephraim Chambers defines "MONSTER" in terms which seem derived as much from the *Essay on Criticism* as from the *Novum Organum*: "a living thing, degenerating from the proper and usual Disposition of Parts, in the Species it belongs to. As when there are too many Members, or too few; or some of 'em are extravagantly out of Proportion."[64] By applying proportionality, a paradigm of neoclassicism, to the natural world, Chambers follows Bacon in seeming to make nature imitate art. His definition points to an ambivalent formal relationship between metaphoric monstrosity and teratological monsters. Other definitions do much the same. In his *New English Dictionary* (1737), Benjamin Norton Defoe explains that a "MONSTER" is "a mishapen living Creature," but that the "MONSTROUS" need only resemble the disproportionate qualities of monstrosity, being "of or like a Monster; prodigious, excessive."[65] In a similar way, Edward Phillips, after having defined a "Monster" as "any thing that is against, or beside the common Course of Nature," adds that in a "figurative Sense" it is said: "*A Monster of Cruelty or Avarice: The giddy Rabble is a Monster with many Heads*, &c."[66] Even Samuel Johnson, in his *Dictionary of the English Language* (1755), manipulates the distinction between literal and figurative monstrosity. He defines "MONSTRO'SITY" solely as an empirical violation: the "state of being monstrous, or out of the common order of the universe." Yet of the four passages he adduces to demonstrate the semantic uses of monstrosity, only one has to do with real physical deformity, while the other three refer metaphorically to human vice and folly:

> This is the *monstruosity* in love, that the will is infinite, and the execution confin'd. *Shakesp. Troil. And Cressida.*

> Such a tacit league is against such routs and shoals of people, as have in their very body and frame of estate a *monstrosity. Bacon.*

> We read of monstrous births, but we often see a greater *monstrosity* in educations: thus, when a father has begot a man, he trains him up into a beast. *South's Sermons.*

> By the same law *monstrosity* could not incapacitate from marriage, witness the case of hermaphrodites. *Arbuthnot and Pope.*[67]

This last passage, drawn from the "Double Mistress" episode of the Scriblerian *Memoirs*, is intended to illustrate the point that monsters in nature play a role in art. Though the passage deals expressly with a literal monster, its context in a digression from a work of imaginative literature gives the male–female hybrid figurative significance. As contemporary definitions confirm, monsters were a visible deviation from the ordinary forms of life, but they also signified a deviation from the accepted forms of art. Indeed, Addison's aesthetic triad might be seen to have its origin in Bacon's taxonomy of nature: where Bacon exhorts scientists to "make a collection or particular natural history of all the monsters and prodigious products of nature, of every novelty, rarity, or abnormality in nature," Addison reminds writers that even the "Imperfections of Nature" have an impact on gawking readers.[68]

This helps to explain why monsters and monstrosity had long been associated with a corrupt taste in literature and culture. Exploiting the metaphoric potential of the monstrous, Horace opened his *Ars Poetica* (c. 18 BC) by drawing an influential analogy between the "wild Design" of a grotesque painter and such anomalous creatures as a winged woman with a horse's neck and the tail of a fish. He compared this image to the "senseless Thought" of a poor poet:

> Believe me, *Sirs*, that Book is like this Piece,
> Where ev'ry Part so strangely disagrees.
> Like *sick Mens Dreams*, there's neither Head nor Tail,
> But strange Confusion, shapeless Monsters all.[69]

Neoclassical critics, whose emphasis was on the expression of nature through reason, harmony, balance, and restraint, frequently invoked Horatian "Monsters" as a way of endorsing mimesis and proscribing all kinds of formal impropriety in writing. According to Judith Hawley, human and animal prodigies represented "grotesque parodies of a neoclassical ideal" and a "potentially dangerous disruption of order," and if this is true then defective or excessive writing was to art what monsters were to nature.[70] In his essay, "Of Idleness," Montaigne jests with the "restless" and "roving" character of his own style by likening its "thousand Extravagancies" to "so many *Chimæra*'s and fantastick Monsters . . . without Order or Design." He overtly links his "Fancy" to the vain and ridiculous "Phantasms" described in "*Hor. De Arte Poetica*":

> ———*velut ægri somnia, vanæ*
> *Finguntur species*———[71]

Other critics were more earnest about the discursive threat of such "Phantasms." In *The Arte of English Poesie* (1589) George Puttenham warns that the representation of things contrary to "their very truth" produces "*Chimeres* & monsters in mans imaginations, & not only in his imaginations, but also in all his ordinarie actions and life which ensues."[72] William Drummond makes a similar appeal to "Nature" against the rhetorical extravagance of "metaphysical" wit, claiming that John Donne's verse "is no more *Poesy* than a Monster is a Man," and that his sonnets and elegies "breed Admiration at the First, but have ever some strange Loathsomeness in them at last."[73] Drummond's master, Ben Jonson, binds the audience of *Bartholomew Fair* (1614) in a mock obligation, having a Scrivener advise them that, despite its setting, the dramatic representation will not be spoiled by "a servant-monster i' the fair," since the playwright "is loth to make Nature afraid in his plays."[74] In his essay "Concerning Humour in Comedy" (1695), William Congreve claims along similar lines that farces comprised of figures that "are not in Nature" merely dramatize "Monsters and Births of Mischance."[75] And in his own adaptation of the Horatian metaphor, George Granville, Lord Lansdowne, lays out the rules of mimetic poetics in order to ask rhetorically:

> Who, driven with ungovernable fire,
> Or void of Art, beyond these bounds aspire,
> Gygantic forms, and monstrous Births alone
> Produce, which Nature shockt, disdains to own [?][76]

From a neoclassical perspective, the traditional notion of writing as the imaginative child of the brain was complemented by a denigration of all species of bad writing as abortive or "monstrous Births."[77] Poems that did not match their style to their subject, plays that favoured elaborate stage effects and bombast to dramatic sense, and prose pieces that digressed from rules of narrative decorum were commonly envisaged as a kind of equivocal generation or aberrant degeneration – as prodigies of the pen.

By the late seventeenth and early eighteenth centuries, however, these prodigies had become increasingly and self-consciously commercial: bad writing is no longer compared to a nightmare world of monstrous abstraction but to the very material world of Augustan London, with its economics of supply and demand and its busy marketplace for monsters of both book and booth. This was less a change in perception than a change in emphasis – from the monsters themselves to their mode and method of presentation. So, when John Dryden reflects in 1695 on the opening lines of the *Ars Poetica*, he explains that Horace describes "unnatural" art through the now familiar image of "a very monster in a Bartholomew Fair, for the mob to gape at for their two-pence." Not only does Dryden draw attention to the gradual secularization and commodification of the monstrous, but he revitalizes the hackneyed metaphor by applying it to the emerging class of so-called hackney writers who hastily produce "shapeless Monsters" in order to "get their living." In so doing, Dryden links the commercial production of literature with the commercial exhibition of monstrosity, both of which cater to what he calls a "bastard-pleasure" that is "taken in at the eyes of the vulgar gazers," whether they be superficial readers or mindless sightseers.[78]

## The monstrosity of print culture

In many ways, Dryden anticipates the unprecedented expansion of print culture during the eighteenth century, as well as the metaphorical and material consequences of this expansion in the complex phenomenon eventually designated "Grub Street."[79] For in the same year that Dryden satirized literary "scribblers" as fairground showmen, a period of relative freedom of the press was initiated by the lapse of the Licensing Act, which had somewhat erratically permitted printing only by government author- ity. Though certain restrictions were still in place, there was a tangible sense of release, as writers of all kinds and capacities suddenly found themselves within a print market that made it possible to earn some manner of living by writing alone. The impact of this "publishing revolution" extended beyond the literate public since, as John Brewer explains, even those who could not read or write lived to an unprecedented degree in a "culture of print."[80] The increasing demand for printed material inevitably produced supply, while the increasing supply multiplied demand by making print an omnipresent part of everyday life. As the market grew, so too did the number of writers willing (if not always best able) to fill the pages bound for press – authors, as Richard Savage derisively puts it, ready "to be lett."

The literary activities of Savage's eponymous author, Iscariot Hackney, are illustrative of a print culture that had developed enough to support a new rank of professional writers but not enough to prevent exploitation. Hackney is a political hireling, writing on either side for pay; he publishes "Obscenity and Profaneness, under the Names of *Pope* and *Swift*"; he is a composer of birthday odes and encomia that turn paradoxical for praising "in the wrong Place"; he plays the "*Plutarch*" to notorious criminals, writing hyperbolic "Lives" to preserve their "Memory"; he is a purveyor of false wit, dealing in "Clenches, Puns, Quibbles, Gibes, Conundrums, and carry Whitchits"; he has familiarized himself with "every Branch of Learning" by the help of "Indexes" and "Technical Dictionaries"; he produces spurious "Second Parts" to other authors' works and claps his own pamphlets with "a new Title-Page to the Sale of every half Hundred"; he has written librettos for operas, panegyrics on pantomimes, puffs for obscene books and plays, and libels on the living and dead alike. "In short," as Hackney himself concludes, he is "a perfect Town Author."[81] The irony of this portrait is that Hackney's dubious talents make him eminently employable since, as J.V. Guerinot explains, "it was the hack writer's job, sometimes with scissors and paste, and sometimes with a flair for the libellous and no scruples about pandering to prurience, to furnish the books to order."[82] In the "modern" literary marketplace, writers might produce books for extrinsic, casual, or pecuniary reasons, not out of any love of literature or commitment to learning. Hackney's own publisher identifies him as one of that class of authors who take up writing "for want of Money" and whose "dirty Tricks" are the consequence of "their Poverty" (A2r–A3r). Writers were paid to please the public and the quantity of this pleasure was deemed as important as the relative quality of pleasure. With such a mercenary principle as a basis for writing, the division between eighteenth-century culture and commerce virtually collapsed, leading to what many commentators viewed as a commoditization of literature and a grotesque celebration of corrupt publishing practices that catered, like sights and shows, to "man's native predisposition for thoughtlessness." Hackney is revealed to spend an inordinate amount of time amongst the freaks at "*Charing-Cross*," and his success as "an author to be lett" is prognosticated by the fact that when his mother was pregnant with him she "dreamt that she was delivered of a Monster" (1–2).[83] Hackney, in turn, delivers his own monstrosities, bringing them forth in printed form in the same topographical locale where monstrous births were exhibited as visual spectacles to gazing, staring, and gaping sightseers. In what Hackney refers to as a "free-thinking Age," it is thus not only bad writing that is figured as monstrous, but bad printing as well. As Savage seems to argue, Grub Street transforms prodigies of the pen into prodigies of the press.

The proliferation of print was initially met with a considerable amount of optimism, since printing seemed the readiest means to cultivate the individual reason and, in turn, generate public awareness and consensus.[84] Early proponents looked upon the printed book as an epitome of the "book of nature," units of type standing analogically for the constituent parts of a physical reality that was coming under increasingly close scrutiny.[85]

Printing quickly became implicated in the standardization and dissemination of knowledge, particularly knowledge about the natural world. Yet as Adrian Johns has demonstrated, the development of a "print culture" and the concomitant process of "knowledge-making" were far from easy or straightforward.[86] Though printing was broadly endorsed as a reliable method of verifying and fixing knowledge, the medium was subject to just as many errors – to say nothing of *errata* – as was nature. If there were so-called digressions in the course of nature, so too were there "Heteroclites or Irregulars of *the book.*"

Like fairground monsters, who charmed spectators with their perceptible violations of ontological limits, printed texts were often seen to transgress the bounds of Augustan decorum by overstepping formal categories and reifying literature into a popular commodity whose saleability was of far greater importance than its intellectual value.[87] Summarizing for an absent friend some of the leading London attractions of June 1708, Swift associates the "sight of two girls joined together at the back" with "a long lampoon publicly printed," wryly concluding that both a newsmonger's account of the Hungarian twins and a satire on "all the young people of quality" who frequent St James's Park "are effects of our liberty of the press."[88] In *A Tale of a Tub*, Swift elaborates on the form that this "liberty" has come to take by making his archetypal Grub Street hack compare the commercial publishing practices of "*Modern Authors*" with the devious marketing strategies of contemporary showmen:

> I do utterly disapprove and declare against that pernicious Custom, of making the Preface a Bill of Fare to the Book. For I have always lookt upon it as a high Point of Indiscretion in *Monster-mongers* and other *Retailers of strange Sights*; to hang out a fair large Picture over the Door, drawn after the Life, with a most eloquent Description underneath: this hath saved me many a Three-pence, for my Curiosity was fully satisfied, and I never offered to go in, tho' often invited by the urging and attending Orator, with his last *moving* and *standing* Piece of Rhetorick; *Sir, Upon my Word, we are just going to begin.* (85)

What constitutes the monstrosity of the modern publishing industry is its tendency either to impose upon the credulity or exploit the curiosity of modern audiences, drawing sightseers and readers in by their willingness to believe or their desire to know more: the novelties of unofficial news, gossip about social elites, the who's, what's, where's, when's, and why's of topical satire. The authenticity of this knowledge is irrelevant to its consumption since, the hack maintains, "Mankind is now disposed" to receive "much greater Advantage by being *Diverted* than *Instructed*" (81). *A Tale of a Tub* is itself one of "those Productions designed for the Pleasure and Delight of Mortal Man" (40), a work whose substance, structure, and style alike reproduce what Swift saw as some of the worst features of the print trade: its propensity to swell volumes with extraneous material, whether digressions or preliminaries like the *Tale*'s ironic dedications, preface, introduction, and list of "Treatises wrote by the same Author"; its related emphasis on the quantity of writing as opposed to the quality; its hasty publication of works that are obviously imperfect, having, for example, gaps or flaws in the manuscript marked by printed lacunae; and, most of all, its brazen commercialism. "I am also happy," writes the hack, "that Fate has flung me into so blessed an Age for the mutual Felicity of *Booksellers* and *Authors*, whom I may safely affirm to be at this Day the two only satisfied Parties in *England*" (117). The hack's own *Tale* is able to achieve "Preferment and Sanction in *Print*" not because it is coherent or meaningful, but because of what he calls the "Liberty and Encouragement of the Press" (136), which subsumes rather than establishes authority even as it saturates society with paper and ink.[89] Whether or not he has anything substantial to say, the hack writes merely because *he can*:

> In my Disposure of Employments of the Brain, I have thought fit to make *Invention* the *Master*, and to give *Method* and *Reason*, the Office of its *Lacquays*. The Cause of this Distribution was, from observing it my peculiar Case, to be often under a Temptation of being *Witty*, upon Occasions, where I could be neither *Wise* nor *Sound*, nor anything to the Matter in hand. And I am too much a Servant of the *Modern* Way, to neglect any such Opportunities, whatever Pains or Improprieties I may be at, to introduce them. (136)

In the economy of "*GRUB-STREET*," units of type provide an opportunity to deviate from the common forms of nature, generating "textual monsters" that engage by their novelty rather than their contribution to natural knowledge. By making "*Invention* the *Master*," and therefore parodying the effects of the modern literary economy, *A Tale of a Tub* criticizes the freedom of the press while paradoxically giving the reading public just what it wants: a "flim-flam," an "idle discourse," a "cock-and-bull story," a tale of nonsense.

Instead of deriving its authority from the sublime "book of nature," modern printing was authorized by the market. As a result, for every instructive or edifying text that was published there were many party pamphlets, broadsides, scandalous "true histories," personal and political libels, salacious criminal "lives," weekly journals, periodical "post-boys,"

"*Trips, Spies, Amusements,*" and other species of what Pope broadly dismisses in *The Dunciad Variorum* as "momentary monsters" that "rise and fall" ([A] 1.81). According to Scriblerus, *The Dunciad* takes the ephemerality of print as its subject and the dangerous "Liberty of the Press" as its occasion. He observes that the author

> lived in those days, when (after providence had permitted the Invention of Printing as a scourge for the Sins of the learned) Paper also became so cheap, and printers so numerous, that a deluge of authors cover'd the land: Whereby not only the peace of the honest unwriting subject was daily molested, but unmerciful demands were made of his applause, yea of his money, by such as would neither earn the one, or deserve the other. ([A] 48)

Far from being an instrument of knowledge, *The Dunciad* represents printing as an agent of misinformation, of "Chaos, Night and Dullness" (48). Outlining the material consequences of the expiration of the Licensing Act, Pope has Scriblerus identify print as a source of social and intellectual evil, as well as the force that threatens to drown classical standards and the humanist tradition in flashy but necessarily fleeting innovations. *The Dunciad* ranges its satire against the commercially driven scribblers who wrote trash in the hopes of earning treasure, portraying the demographic of Grub Street in such a way as to expose what the Scriblerians saw as its vicious bohemianism:

> Where wave the tatter'd ensigns of Rag-Fair,
> A yawning ruin hangs and nods in air;
> Keen, hollow winds howl thro' the bleak recess,
> Emblem of Music caus'd by Emptiness:
> Here in one bed two shiv'ring sisters lye,
> The cave of Poverty and Poetry.
> This, the Great Mother dearer held than all
> The clubs of Quidnunc's, or her own Guildhall.
> Here stood her Opium, here nurs'd her Owls,
> And destin'd here th'imperial seat of Fools.
> Hence springs each weekly Muse, the living boast
> Of Curl's chaste press, and Lintot's rubric post,
> Hence hymning Tyburn's elegiac lay,
> Hence the soft sing-song on Celia's day,
> Sepulchral lyes our holy walls to grace,
> And New-year Odes, and all the Grubstreet race.     ([A] 1.27–42)[90]

Pope's satiric twinning of "Poverty" and "Poetry" provides sharp insight into the psychology of eighteenth-century hack writers: their motivations, their literary ends and means, their situation in life, and its corresponding

pathos. For Pope, hack writers are an exemplar of literary and cultural
iniquity because they do for English *belle lettres* what prostitutes were
believed to do for sex: they sold their services, and their principles,
cheap. "What matters is not what they write," argues Anne Hall Bailey,
"it is only important that they write."[91] Because they wrote for a living,
professional hacks had to be especially sensitive to the requirements of
booksellers who, in their turn, were sensitive to capricious public taste.
This is why Swift associates the London publishing industry with the
activities of "*Monster-mongers*" and "other *Retailers of strange Sights*," and
why Pope opens his "Progress of Dullness" by invoking not Juno or Jove or
any one of the classical muses, but the "Smithfield Muses," glossing
"*Smithfield*" as "the place where Bartholomew Fair was kept," and suggesting that the literature produced in Grub Street has its counterpart in the
popular "Shews, Machines, and Dramatical Entertainments" of "the
Rabble" ([A] 1.2n.). For all of the humanizing possibilities of print, critics
like Swift and Pope insisted that the ubiquity of "Grub Street" ensured that
dullness would remain endemic thanks to a literary marketplace committed to giving the public the kind of printed entertainment it was
believed to want. The period during which printing first became recognized as a unifying and rationalizing force was thus the same period during
which Augustan satire first began to identify Grub Street writers, printers,
and booksellers as the main cause of literary and cultural decline.[92]

### Monsters and the matter of modernity

However, the expansion of print culture and the development of Augustan
satire also happened to coincide with the "universal craze" for monsters. It
is not then surprising that *A Tale of a Tub* and *The Dunciad*, perhaps the
period's greatest satires on the pernicious effects of print, frequently
employ metaphors of monstrosity to describe a world in which hacks
and dunces shamelessly invite readers to gaze, stare, and gape at their
commercial texts.[93] What is more surprising is the way in which these
satires embody monstrosity in their printed form as well as content, and
their recognition that the actual experience of eighteenth-century monsters
was ultimately material rather than metaphorical. Swift's *Tale* conjures
contemporary exhibitions and shows through allusions to "*Stage-
Itinerants*," "transitory Gazers," a "reasonable Quantity of Gyants," and a
pair of "*Bulls*" with wings and "*Fishes Tails*," which are said to rival the
famous hybrid monster in Horace (71). In Pope's *Dunciad*, the Horatian
metaphor gives birth to "Maggots half-form'd," "Tibbald's monster-

breeding breast," a "jumbled race" of "Farce and Epic," and "a monster of a fowl! / Something betwixt a H * * * and Owl" ([A] 1.59, 106, 68, 243–44). At the same time, these metaphorical monsters are made literal by the very textuality of the satires, each of which parody London's popular monsters through the "Deficiencies" and "Excrescencies" of their printed format. *A Tale of a Tub* is rendered monstrous by the dizzying copia of its "*Prefaces, Epistles, Advertisements,*" and other "*Apparatus*'s,*" by the narrative aporia resulting from its missing or endlessly deferred sections, by the sheer exuberance of its digressions and its "Digression Upon Digressions," and by the fragmentation caused by its rows of asterisked ellipses, a typographical mark typically signifying the interruption or loss of text.[94] Likewise, the 1729 *Dunciad* exhibits monstrosity in the throng of dunces whose names are replaced by blanks or dashes, in its exemplification of "Prose swell'd to verse" and "verse loit'ring into prose," and in the fulsome pomp of its "*Proeme, Prolegomena, Testimonia Scriptorum, Index,* and Notes *Variorum.*"[95] For Swift and Pope, "textual monstrosity" is constituted by the defect and excess that they believe distinguishes the growth of printing in England and the concomitant "*Modern* Way" in writing. This critical concern is manifested textually through printed imperfections that produce an abundance of possible meanings and printed profusion that multiplies meaningless vacuity. The result is a distinctly modern text that embodies error in the same way that modern monsters affront "not truth, but taste."

The *Tale*'s numerous "Chasms," manuscript hiatuses, and its printed acknowledgement that "*hic multa desiderantur*" (here there is much wanting) are thus a textual equivalent of exhibitions featuring monsters that represent "too little," like the eighteen-inch dwarf and the sheep without a nose. Indeed, the footnote that accompanies the first of the notably "*pretended*" defects asserts that the "*Hiatus in MS*" is less likely a gap in logic or a hole in the original text, than a deliberate attempt on the part of the Grub Street hack "*to amuse his Reader (whereof he is frequently very fond)*" (40) (Figure 12). In a similar way, the seemingly superfluous apparatus and gratuitous notes that humble the verse of the Variorum *Dunciad* are formally akin to shows featuring monsters that represent "too much," like the chicken with two rumps and the man with two breasts and bellies, four arms, hands, legs, and feet. Scriblerus suggests as much when he markets his apparatus to "the eye of the most curious," precisely the kind of spectator most inclined to gaze, stare, and gape at the monstrous diversions of the "Smithfield Muses" ([A] 23). In a world deluged by print and obsessed with monsters, textual monstrosity connects the

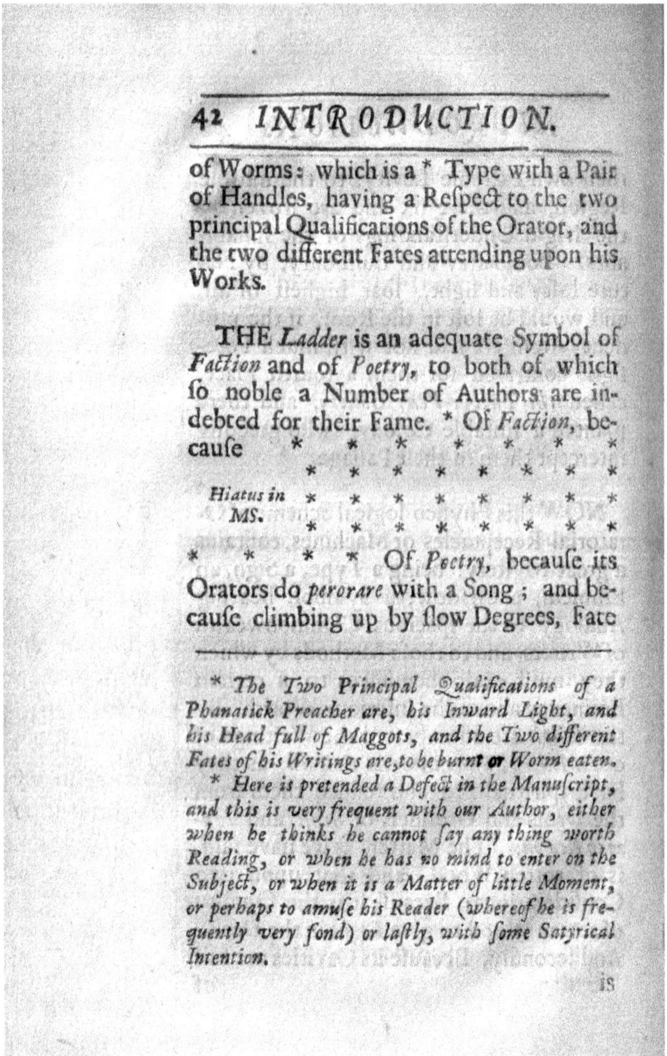

**42** *INTRODUCTION.*

of Worms: which is a * Type with a Pair of Handles, having a Respect to the two principal Qualifications of the Orator, and the two different Fates attending upon his Works.

THE *Ladder* is an adequate Symbol of *Faction* and of *Poetry*, to both of which so noble a Number of Authors are indebted for their Fame. * Of *Faction*, because * * * * * * * *
* * * * * * * *
*Hiatus in* * * * * * * * *
*MS.*
* * * * * * * *
* * * * Of *Poetry*, because its Orators do *perorare* with a Song ; and because climbing up by slow Degrees, Fate

---

* *The Two Principal Qualifications of a Phanatick Preacher are, his Inward Light, and his Head full of Maggots, and the Two different Fates of his Writings are, to be burnt or Worm eaten.*
* *Here is pretended a Defect in the Manuscript, and this is very frequent with our Author, either when he thinks he cannot say any thing worth Reading, or when he has no mind to enter on the Subject, or when it is a Matter of little Moment, or perhaps to amuse his Reader (whereof he is frequently very fond) or lastly, with some Satyrical Intention.*

is

Figure 12  Pretended *"Defect"* in the fifth edition of Jonathan Swift's *A Tale of a Tub*
(1710), p. 42

rhetoric of modern writers with monster-mongers, and the response of modern readers with sightseers. Swift and Pope make their own texts monstrous in order simultaneously to exhibit and expose what they see as the "thoughtlessness" of a culture in which Grub Street and Bartholomew Fair purvey similar sorts of pleasure. According to Benedict, eighteenth-century monsters possessed the power to "objectify satire," illustrating a critical point through awful images of deficiency or excrescence.[96] In *A Tale of a Tub* and *The Dunciad Variorum*, satire objectifies monstrosity, transforming a long tradition of metaphorical monsters into the "freaks" of the text – "*Modern*" books whose constituent parts are "extravagantly out of Proportion."

Augustan monstrosity is thus linked to the expansion of print culture through the materiality of textuality, which directs attention to the relative defects and excesses of "*Modern*" publishing. Monstrosity and textuality converge in literary works that focus readers on the physical and visual features of the printed book, and in printed handbills and advertisements that attract sightseers with the idiosyncrasies of their typography and layout. The ballyhoo of Swift's "*Monster-monger*" is ineffective because it appeals solely to the ears of spectators; his "*moving* and *standing* Piece of Rhetorick" must therefore be accompanied by a "fair large Picture" to entice those who wish to see "*strange Sights.*" In order to avoid this problem, contemporary ads for monster exhibitions endeavour to gratify the *eyes* of sightseeing readers by combining verbal expression with typography that foregrounds the visual impression made, for example, by "ONE of the greatest Curiosities in Nature, of a BOY and GIRL, WITH two distinct Heads and Necks, and but one Body, three Arms, and three Legs, and Feet, and 1 Foot with six Toes" (B.L. N.Tab. 2026/25, No. 42). Because the monstrosity has already been "*expos'd* to Publick *view*," its handbill makes much of the startling effect the show has previously had on "Sir *Hans Sloane*" and other "Curious Gentlemen," reinforcing this through the striking impact of its *mise-en-page*. Beyond the spurious and disproportionately large royal coat of arms, intended to authorize the show by simulating "His Majesty's Permission," the bill employs at least five different sizes of type, and font styles ranging from standard roman-face to upper- and lower-case caps to italics that highlight not just conventional proper nouns, but also verbs that have to do with the actual experience of the monstrous: "*seen,*" "*expos'd,*" and "*shewn*" (Figure 13). Given that "External Form" defines what makes the monster monstrous, the handbill communicates the curiosity of the "BOY and GIRL," both by describing the oddity of their appearance and reproducing this oddity in the

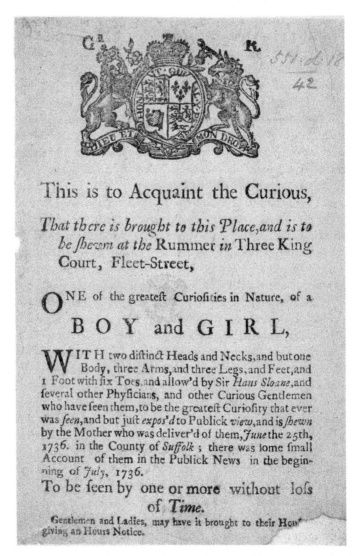

Figure 13 Typographically exuberant handbill for "ONE of the greatest Curiosities in Nature" (c. 1736)

whimsical presentation of its printed text. The advertisement teases sight-seers and readers with the prospect of perceiving the show in the graphic structure of the page, giving them the opportunity to gawk at monsters in and of the text.

Like the advertisement for "ONE of the greatest Curiosities in Nature," the commercial literature of the late seventeenth and early eighteenth centuries frequently fastens the eyes of sightseeing readers on "External Form," making an issue of textuality as such by way of typographical devices that emphasize their own material embodiment on the printed page, and obtrusive paratext that complicates the distinction between a work and its surrounding apparatus of title pages, prefatory matter, annotations, appendices, and printer's paraphernalia.[97] In both book and booth, the medium of print encouraged an awareness of words as tangible things with a material existence, set in ink, laid out on a page, and perceived visually. The "rambunctious materiality" that Janine Barchas and other recent critics have seen as fundamental to the meaning of the period's literature was also essential to its marketability, in that visible deviations from the conventional uses of printing provided for a similar kind of thrill and produced a similar sort of wonder as the deviations shown for money at the London fairgrounds.[98] Writers at the popular end of the market pandered to the public taste for monsters in printed form as well as thematic content. And they did so by making print conspicuous by its self-consciously exaggerated absence *and* presence. John Dunton's pervasive interest in the physical characteristics of the monstrous was matched, for instance, by his fascination with the novelties of the printer's fount and grammar. In a single folio half-sheet issue of *The Athenian Mercury*, curious readers could encounter everything from 𝔊𝔬𝔱𝔥𝔦𝔠 𝔱𝔶𝔭𝔢, oversized initial capitals, and marginal index hands or "manicules" (☞) to the ubiquitous symbol for "etcetera" (&c.), en-dashes (–), em-dashes (—), and even longer elliptical dashes (———). As his own printer and one of the most innovative publishers of the day, Dunton understood that the dissemination of "news and new things" began at the eyes. If *The Athenian Mercury* aimed to democratize knowledge, it had to put it into a format that would make it perceptible and therefore accessible to those who could not hope to comprehend its often esoteric subject matter. Dunton's tactic was to reduce questions about the rationality of monsters, the generation of hybrid creatures, and the existence of "*Satyres*" and "*Centaurs*" to physical marks on the printed page, appealing to that which "all *ingenious and curious Enquirers into Speculations*" have in common: the capacity to see. Thus, when one sceptical querist asks "*what good was ever yet done by your* Athenian Mercury?" Dunton makes a case for the valuable materiality of his periodical:

> [W]e must not be silent here, lest it shou'd be taken *pro confesso*, that we have done no good at all by our *Scribbling* above this Twelve month.

Not therefore to insist on the mighty *benefits*, which (if they are not very ungrateful) the Stationers, Printers, Hawkers, Coffee-Houses, &c. (very profitable Members of the Commonwealth) must own they have receiv'd by our *Mercury*, nor to boast of its merits in helping to carry on the *War against* France, by advancing the Royal Revenue some thousands *per An.* (pence we mean) by the *Penny Post*, (a finer and honester Project than all the *French Horsleaches* ever yet thought of for raising *money*.) And lastly, to say nothing how helpful we have been to the *Pastry-Cooks*, &c. we think we may in earnest, and without *vanity* pretend that our Paper has been of some real *use* both to the *publick*, and in many particular cases of high moment.[99]

Dunton argues by negatives, *not* emphasizing the commercial benefits of his project so as to boast of its service in raising "a kind of *Learned Ferment* in the Nation." Yet his playfully understated insistence that its value rests mainly on its status as object anticipates the kind of satire that was eventually directed at "Grub Street," even while contending for the kind of writing that was produced by so-called hacks during the period. The italicization of "*Learned Ferment*" suggests that the "profit" of the period-ical – both its financial success and its contribution to natural knowledge – depends as much upon its typography as on its questions and answers. *The Athenian Mercury* may be no better than the paper on which it is printed, paper that is sold and circulated and inevitably recycled as wrapping for baked goods, but it exploits its material condition in order to divert and instruct an implied audience of sightseeing readers.

The same is true of Dunton's narrative rendering of his "Athenian" project, *A Voyage Round the World* (1691), which depends for its effects as much upon its flashy paratext as on the "Rare Adventures" of its shifting and digressive narrators.[100] Dunton organizes his rambling survey of the sights and shows of 1690s London around what he identifies as the public's "pure love to *novelty*" (3.30). From the outset, he explains that his work will be very different from that of his topographical forebears, and he reiterates throughout his three volumes the newness of the narrative. "What think ye," the narrator asks:

Of the admirable and surprizing Novelty of both Matter and Method; representing *a Book made, as it were, out of nothing*, and yet containing *every thing*; ... the Grandeur of the City described in a method wholly new (of which more anon) and all the Rarities therein described; the Stateliness of its Palaces, the Magnificence of its Churches, and the honesty of its Booksellers, which singular Subject richly merits a Volume as big as all *Tostatus* together: But alas! is here for want of room, wedg'd up into one or two single Chapters, though neither the last Book, nor this, nor their own, nor all the Shops nor Walls in *London* or the World (*that's a bold word*) are either strong enough, or large enough or weighty enough to contain it. (2.8–9)

According to Dunton, the copiousness of his *Voyage* is wholly appropriate to the variety of "the *famous and gallant* City of LONDON" (1.98). He thus sets up an opposition between "*nothing*" and "*every thing*," only to resolve it through what he represents as a reciprocity between his "Matter" and newfangled "Method." That readers are overwhelmed by his digressive account of London and "*don't know what to make on't*" is merely proof of the efficacy of a style that wittily conveys its subject: they will, after all, be overwhelmed by the actual city as well (2.1). Dunton makes this strategy explicit in Volume III when, having become lost on a ramble from the Royal Exchange to Westminster, his narrator asserts: "my Subject is *Rambling*, and therefore is it that I suffer the least sudden Thought or extravagant Fancy to lead me *ten, twenty, nay sometimes an hundred Pages out of my way*" (3.2). By measuring his topographical progress in pages rather than footsteps, Dunton makes "rambling" a literal metaphor for the literary experience of the city, his narrator's digressions reproducing the activity of sightseers as they set out in search of "*Rarity, Novelty,* and *Diversion*" (2.31).

However, even before Dunton's readers are introduced to the "precious Commodities" trafficked at Cornhill, the performing freaks at Charing Cross, or the "*honourable*" booksellers in Cheapside, they are confronted with fifty-two pages of preliminaries that function as a *reductio ad absurdum* of modern print conventions, deferring or displacing the narrative they seek to familiarize. The first volume alone is preceded by an allegorical frontispiece with an accompanying "Poetical Explanation," a title page comprised of various typefaces, styles, and sizes (Figure 14), a series of "Panegyric Verses" in praise of "*the Ensuing Design*," the art of "Rambling," and the purported "AUTHOR of this BOOK," an assortment of anagrams playing on the author's name (e.g. "*Hid unto None*"), a pair of proleptic epitaphs, a pindaric ode, a lengthy "Introduction," an "Impartial Character of a Rambler," and even an epigram dedicated "To the READER Instead of the *ERRATA*": "The Author *hath his Faults, the* Printer *too,* / *All* Men *whilst here do err, and so do* You" (1.B6v). The preliminaries go on for so long and for so many pages that the narrator is eventually obliged to apologize for his remissness: "Methinks we have been a tedious while in *London* without seeing any of the *Rary shows* in't——'Twould be enough to make my old acquaintance believe I cam[e] hither for nothing at all, if I

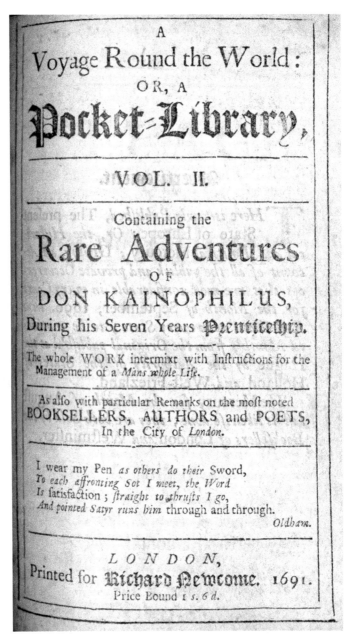

A

Voyage Round the World:

OR, A

𝕻𝖔𝖈𝖐𝖊𝖙=𝕷𝖎𝖇𝖗𝖆𝖗𝖞,

VOL. II.

Containing the

Rare Adventures

OF

DON KAINOPHILUS,

During his Seven Years 𝕻𝖗𝖊𝖓𝖙𝖎𝖈𝖊𝖘𝖍𝖎𝖕.

The whole WORK intermixt with Instructions for the Management of a *Mans whole Life.*

As also with particular Remarks on the most noted BOOKSELLERS, AUTHORS and POETS, In the City of *London.*

I wear my Pen *as others do their* Sword,
*To each affronting Sot I meet, the Word*
*Is* satisfaction ; *straight to thrusts I go,*
*And pointed Satyr runs him* through and through.
                                                *Oldham.*

LONDON,

Printed for 𝕽𝖎𝖈𝖍𝖆𝖗𝖉 𝕹𝖊𝖜𝖈𝖔𝖒𝖊. 1691.

Price Bound 1 *s.* 6 *d.*

Figure 14  Title page to John Dunton's *A Voyage Round the World: or, A Pocket Library* (1691)

don't tell 'em what I saw with these *own Eyes o' mine*, at that very time" (1.128). Yet if Dunton's narrative digresses away from "the famous *Metropolis of England*," his text nonetheless represents the sensory experience of London in the graphic effects of its *mise-en-page*. What Dunton's readers see is not necessarily what the narrator *tells* them, but what the printer *shows* them. Dunton lays bare the materiality of his text by disturbing the conventional ordering of books and using print in unusual ways. When he decides to dedicate a chapter to the worthiness of London booksellers, he demonstrates the many resources of the printer's shop even while distracting readers with the resources themselves. His text is studded with asterisks, dots, dashes, braces, manicules, and single- and double-daggers, many of which seem used for their own sake, rather than because they fulfil a necessary narrative function. Dunton sets off and enlarges certain words and phrases, and vacillates between fonts and typefaces. In so doing, he dupes readers into gazing, staring, and gaping at curiosities in a book intended to epitomize the entire "*visible and intellectual World*" (1.4).

Because it is visually inconsistent, constantly changing its literal and figurative character, the typography of the *Voyage* is made to stand out from its linguistic context on the printed page. Dunton has his narrator describe his own shop, the Black Raven in the Poultry, but then elide his identity while giving an elliptical "character" of its proprietor: "Mr. ———" (2.71). He points towards the cultural and economic importance of booksellers who purvey popular works on one another's behalf, by exaggeratedly printing "Conger," a contemporary term for such a collective, on a line of its own (2.77).[101] He disclaims responsibility for treating "every Man, Woman, and Sucking-child, Stationer, Bookseller, Binder, Stitcher and *Hawker*" through "all *Cheapside, Paul's Church-yard, Little Britain* and *Duck-lane*," joking in one of numerous footnotes that the representation of any one might account for the whole class: "† I say they are as much design'd for *this* Man as *that* Man, and *that* Man as *this* Man, and disprove it if you can" (2.79). Elsewhere in the *Voyage*, Dunton stresses the singularity of his observations by calling them "𝕽𝖆𝖗𝖊" and printing the word in Gothic type (1.B1r); he asserts that the employment of London booksellers is "so liberal and ingenious" that he cannot help but look upon it as "an ART rather than a TRADE" (2.A2r); and he teasingly informs his readers of the age of his narrator, who has "now turn'd of .... score" (2.24). At a narrative level, each of these conspicuous disruptions in the text block the reader's access to the story and signal a perceptible point at which mimeticism breaks down. But at a visual level, the disruptions offer readers the "Novelties" that might otherwise be neglected. The *Voyage* need not survey the "*Rary shows*" of London because, in its disproportionate use of print, it becomes a show in itself: an exhibition of textual monstrosity. By diverting attention from what he calls "the great Book of Nature" (3.A1r), and towards the nature of the book, Dunton expands upon the fallibility that is thematized in the preliminaries, suggesting that errors of the press and errors in nature are analogically related. Dunton's *Voyage* displays monstrous terata in the form of printed errata that are assimilated into his narrative description of London. Just as Dunton's "*Bumkin*" might "stare his Eyes and Teeth out upon" the variety of "Remarkables" being shown between Cornhill and Charing Cross and Cheapside, so too are his readers given the opportunity to fasten their eyes upon the material defects and excesses of his text.

In Dunton's "Athenian" works, as in the ad for the curious "BOY and GIRL," the tools of printing are transformed into rhetorical tools which facilitate the transmission of meaning via textual matter. Reflecting upon Dunton's influence on subsequent authors, the publisher who reprints Volume I of *A Voyage Round the World* in 1762 sarcastically claims that "the art of writing" is now one by which "*Modern*" readers are "to understand that of printing and publishing."[102] For a satirist like Swift, this perceived aesthetic reciprocity between writing and printing threatened to reify knowledge by reducing the mental to the physical, the linguistic to the bibliographical, thematic content to material format. In *A Tale of a Tub*, the "principal Productions of *Grub-street*" are degraded to "immense Bales of Paper" (23), and, in trying to account for these productions, the hack finds himself "sunk in the Abyss of Things" (21). Being prevailed upon to compile "a compleat and laborious Dissertation" on the collected works of his Grub Street brethren, the hack promises, first and foremost, to describe in detail their "beautiful Externals for the Gratification of superficial Readers" (42). It is these readers, he implies, who command the literary market, and it is the striking textual surfaces of contemporary works that best characterize the "*Modern* Way" of writing (136). Swift designs his *Tale* as an exemplification of modernity, baiting his readers with printerly devices that appeal to the eyes before the mind. The hack is thus made to remark in his preface that "whatever word or Sentence is Printed in a different Character, shall be judged to contain something extraordinary either of *Wit* or *Sublime*" (29). The very sight-seers who are "fasten'd by the Eyes" in Swift's "Imitation of the Seventh Epistle of the First Book of Horace" (1713) find their counterparts in the readers pandered to in the *Tale* and later portrayed in *On Poetry: A Rapsody* (1733):

> In modern Wit all printed Trash, is
> Set off with num'rous *Breaks*————and Dashes—
>     To Statesmen wou'd you give a Wipe,
> You print it in *Italick Type*.
> When Letters are in vulgar Shapes,
> 'Tis ten to one the Wit escapes;
> But when in *Capitals* exprest,
> The dullest Reader smoaks a Jest.[103]

That the poem employs the devices that it satirizes, and that it concludes abruptly with a series of dashes and asterisks and a final "* * * * * *Cætera desiderantur* * * * * *," points both to the pervasiveness and the unavoidability of textual monstrosity in Augustan London. At the same time, it suggests that, in the hermeneutics of "modern Wit," it is vision rather than judgement that enables interpretation. By publishing texts that are visually dazzling, satirists implicate themselves and their readers in the economy of monster-mongers and sightseers, and thereby expose a print market where audiences are required *to see*, but not necessarily *to understand*.

## Teratological textuality

Sightseeing readers become aware of the monstrosity of "*Modern*" print when there is too little or too much of it. And monster-mongering writers make them aware by refusing to let print function referentially, especially when dealing with the sights and shows of London. When Ned Ward's "London Spy" decides to abandon his "seven Year's search after Knowledge," and to indulge instead an "Itching Inclination" to visit the metropolis, he condemns his old intellectual companions, "with a Fig for St. *Au[gu]stin[e]* and his Doctrines, a Fart for *Virgil* and his Elegancy, and a T——d for *Descartes* and his Philosophy" (1–2). The ellipsis in Ward's text interrupts with a visual device the verbal composition of the Spy's curse. But at the same time it challenges readers to solve the problem of Cartesian dualism by filling in the blanks and using their minds to confront the body at its most corporeal. Such satiric ellipses are even more common in the *Works* of Tom Brown, who employs the device ubiquitously in his popular surveys of contemporary amusement.[104] Perambulating through the "Meridian of London," Brown's narrator takes stock of everything from the "C—p—ration" of the Magistracy (3.30), the "corrupt" "M—b–rs of P————" (3.30), and the "*L——d M——r*" himself (3.318), to the epic poems of

"Sir *R*—— *B*——*re*" (3.317), the subtle distinction between a "Gamester" and a cheating "Sh————" (3.31), and the antics of "Dr. ——," who is seen preaching in a tub near Covent Garden (3.74). He meets a "*Manteau-maker*" who insists on being called "*Madam Theodosia Br*————" (3.80), a successful prostitute who dreads eternal damnation less than "Justice————" (3.297), and "Mr. *S*————," who is rumoured to have fathered the child of a popular actress (3.40). Before long, Brown's narrator has found occasion to reduce the better part of the "City of *L*——" (3.30–31) to an ellipsis. Substituting dashes for letters in the names of aristocrats or city officials like "L—ds D—S— and H————" or "Sir *H*————" makes sense as a rather transparent method of avoiding political conflict. But Brown's needless suppression of, for example, a frolicking "Merry A——" (3.30), suggests that he (or his publisher) just as often prints dashes for their own sake, baiting credulous readers to gloss over the gaps and curious readers to stare at them much too long. Like the "Calf with six Legs and a Topknot," the omissions and elisions in Brown's *Amusements Serious and Comical* encourage blank wonder and mindless speculation. In Thomas D'Urfey's *Essay Towards the Theory of the Intelligible World*, omission and elision are made issues in themselves through a textual lacuna that is marked typographically by a page of sporadic dashes (Figure 15). D'Urfey's narrator, Gabriel John, calls attention to the defect in his text through the title of the section in which it is printed: "*The Method of making a* Chasm, *or* Hiatus, *judiciously; the great Reach of Thought required for the Contrivance thereof, together with the Difference between the* French *Academies and the* English" (162). When the "Hiatus" actually appears, the narrator places the responsibility for the lost text squarely on the publishing industry, but saves readers the trouble of having to read *between* the lines by giving them the chance to focus *on* the lines. As Gabriel John is made to explain in the margin to the "text" of the lacunae:

> The Author very well understands that a good sizable *Hiatus* discovers a very great Genius, there being no Wit in the World more Ideal, and consequently more refined, than what is display'd in those elaborate Pages, that have ne're a Syllable written on them. Yet this Vacuity, now under your Consideration, was not designed, or compiled, upon that inducement, but full sore against the Author's Will, who has been forced to suppress a Multitude of his choicest things, in Compliance with Mr. Stationer; a Person of so scrupulous intellectuals, as to refuse to print Thing which, he said, he could not understand. (163)

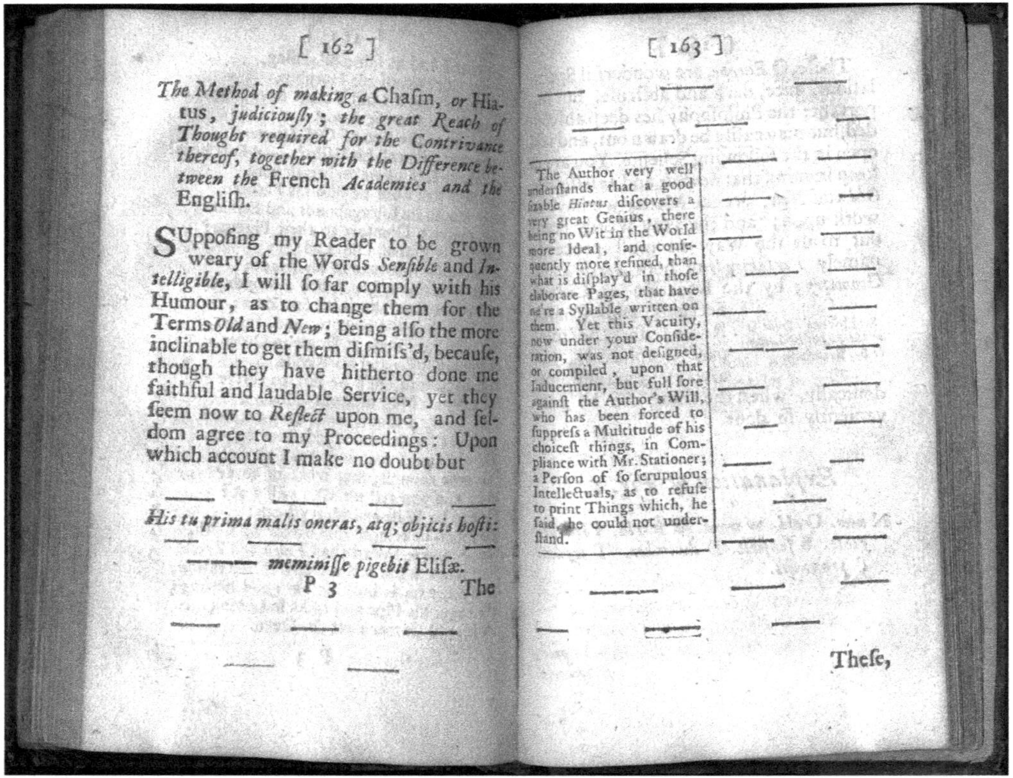

*The Method of making a* Chasm, *or Hiatus, judiciously; the great Reach of Thought required for the Contrivance thereof, together with the Difference between the French Academies and the English.*

SUppofing my Reader to be grown weary of the Words *Senfible* and *Intelligible*, I will fo far comply with his Humour, as to change them for the Terms *Old* and *New*; being alfo the more inclinable to get them difmifs'd, becaufe, though they have hitherto done me faithful and laudable Service, yet they feem now to *Reflect* upon me, and feldom agree to my Proceedings: Upon which account I make no doubt but

*His tu prima malis oneras, atq; objicis hofti:*
—— *meminiffe pigebit Elifæ.*

P 3    The

The Author very well underftands that a good inable *Hiatus* difcovers a very great Genius, there being no Wit in the World fore Ideal, and confequently more refined, than what is difplay'd in thofe elaborate Pages, that have n't a Syllable written on them. Yet this Vacuity, now under your Confideration, was not defigned, or compiled upon that Inducement, but full fore againft the Author's Will, who has been forced to fupprefs a Multitude of his choiceft things, in Compliance with Mr. Stationer; a Perfon of fo fcrupulous Intellectuals, as to refufe to print Things which, he faid, he could not underftand.

Thefe,

Figure 15  A "good sizable *Hiatus*" in Thomas D'Urfey's *An Essay Towards the Theory of the Intelligible World* (1708), pp. 162–63

Being, after all, wordless, the "Hiatus" is similarly incomprehensible; but this is precisely what makes it attractive to readers who are also sightseers, and to writers who wish to divert them. The joke of the "Hiatus" depends upon the paradox that "*Modern*" texts begin to mean only when words begin to fail: the less the text says, the more it reveals. This revelation qualifies the meaning of the rest of the *Essay*, which is replete with paratext that the narrator acknowledges to be "not much to the Purpose" (213). D'Urfey includes a title page with incomplete publishing information ("Printed in the Year One Thousand Seven Hundred, &c."), a "TABLE of the CONTENTS" with facetious and even misleading section titles, a "Tedious Advertisement," "TESTIMONIA de *Mundo Intelligibili*," several stanzas extracted from *Hudibras*, a preliminary section "*Of Prefaces*," an actual "PREFACE" on page 193, a "POSTSCRIPT" beginning six pages later, and a page of obligatory "ERRATA," the whole being interspersed with doggerel verse, popular songs, and miscellanea. The *Essay* is thus characterized both by a defect of text which means too much to be understood, and an excess of text that is the admitted equivalent of "Subtilising upon a fine nothing" (5). D'Urfey's narrator accounts for the fact that an inordinate quantity of his text is comprised of paratext by claiming that, in the interests of gratifying the taste of the town, as well as "Mr. Stationer," he has suppressed much of the best of his material: "'Tis with Tears in my Eye, and great Anguish of Mind, that I am going to mention how many Witty Things I have *Judiciously* blotted out; how many Dainty Thoughts and Curious Strokes, I have either cramp'd, or quite erased, tho' it went grievously against my Will" (213). Among these purportedly "Witty Things," the *Essay* loses all that the "TABLE" had designed between Section XL and Section LI, including a satire on "Criticks," a summary of "How the D— appear'd to *H——*," and what would have been a thematically relevant discussion "Of Monsters." Nonetheless, by omitting some integral parts of his *Essay*, and adding other extraneous parts, Gabriel John is made to replace the monsters formerly *in* his text with the monstrosity *of* his text, which, unlike the "*Ideal* World," does not keep to "just Proportions." With its glaring "Hiatus" and its "Tedious" apparatus, the *Essay* is just as "misshapen" as the "Brood of Monsters" that its narrator tries to avoid or repress. Where D'Urfey uses the surprising attractions of the monstrous to explode the "argument from design," the printed format of his *Essay* provides a material argument against design.

According to Andrew Curran and Patrick Graille, eighteenth-century monsters represent an "anatomical corroboration of the breakdown of objective truth."[105] In the works of popular writers like Dunton, Ward, Brown, and D'Urfey, monsters function as a *textual* corroboration of the breakdown of objective *representation*. Printed ellipses and exaggerated paratext bring an abrupt stop to the flow of paragraphs, sentences, and words on the page, and thus come to intrude as visible obstructions to orderly reading and, as Swift and Pope maintain, perceptible proof of the corruption of English literature and culture. But insofar as these obstructions fasten the eyes of readers on instances of textual "Deficiency" and "Excrescence," they startlingly communicate the kind of imaginative pleasure that Addison identifies in the "sight" of anything that is "*new* or *uncommon.*" For Addison, it is novelty "that bestows Charms on a Monster, and makes even the Imperfections of Nature please us" (*Spectator*, 3.541). Anticipating this aesthetic philosophy, monster-mongers promoted their shows in such a way as to draw sightseers in with the spectacle of deviations from the ordinary forms of life and the prospect of new knowledge. The handbill for the "Monstrous Child," whose body is "covered all over with Scales like unto a Fish," boasts that "the like whereof was never seen in the World" (B.L. N. Tab. 2026/25, No. 75). Another bill gives notice that "there is lately come to this *Famous City of London*, the Rarity of the world, *viz.* A *M*an of the Least Stature that has been seen in the memory of any; being but two Foot and seven Inches in Heighth" (No. 58). An ad for an exhibition featuring a woman "having Three Breasts; and each of them affording Milk at one time," as well as her three-breasted daughter, informs the public that they will be shown "during the time of *Bartholomew Fair*" and that the women are "Wonderful to all that ever did, or shall behold them" (No. 32). And a bill for a sight "to be seen" at "the *Sun* in *Queen-street* in *Cheapside*" describes "a Wonderful and Strange *English Man*, who is Seven foot, Four Inches and an half in hight," but whose most marketable quality is that he "hath not, as yet, been shown in Publick" (No. 62).

The popular print market was not that different from the market for monsters, in that commercial writers tended quite consciously to cater to the public desire for novelty, offering readers not only accounts of the "Imperfections of Nature," but registering these imperfections textually. Dunton expresses considerable optimism that the "novelty of the Humour" will help to sell his *Voyage Round the World*, as it has his *Athenian Mercury* (3.32). Ward similarly claims that his *London Spy* will likely appeal to those "who are always ranging after Novelty" (344). Brown explains, in the preface to his *Amusements Serious and Comical*, that he has "a great Mind to be in Print," but that, above all, he "would fain to be an Original" (3.3). And D'Urfey expects that he will please his readers "in so extraordinary a manner" through what he sees as the "ridiculous Singularity" of his *Essay* (190–92). Even James Ralph promises that his survey of the "Reigning Diversions of the Town" will be engaging to readers because it is "introduc'd after a Method entirely new," one that he explicitly associates with "the Charms of the most beautiful Irregularities" (XVI–XVII). Since the monsters on display in London inn-yards, coffeehouses, and itinerant booths generally had the right parts, but in the wrong number and proportion, the actual "Method" of these writers involved using the conventional features of print in an unconventional way, and redeeming what could be dismissed as the accidentals of printing as a means of unbending the minds of pleasure-seeking readers. And since the novelty, curiosity, and rarity of monster exhibitions was always experienced visually, these writers gave their readers something to gaze, stare, and gape at: the missing arms or asterisks, extra breasts or swollen prolegomena discovered at what Ralph calls "the Surface of a Work."

At the "Surface" of *The Touch-Stone*, readers are diverted by an overly copious title page, with two titles, reference to some two-dozen amusements, and two epigraphs, an "EPISTLE DEDICATORY. To the Right Notable – – – – PAYNE, Esq.," a tongue-in-cheek "PREFACE: or, INTRODUCTION," a detailed summary of the work's "CONTENTS," an interpolated dramatic dialogue between "*Lady* PLYANT" and "*Beau* MODISH," and hundreds of elliptical dashes and asterisks intended, as Ralph declares, to "imploy idle People" (XXIV).[106] He writes:

> I am sensible most People love to meet with such Gaps, in order to fill them up. If every Thing was set down plain, and at full Length in any Work; no Words to be guess'd at, or no Obscurity in the Sense, it would be thought only proper for the perusal of a School-boy, and argue an Author's Assurance, in his giving no fair Play to a Reader's Penetration. (XXIII–XXIV)

In order therefore to engage his readers' penetration, Primcock invites them to analyse the failed attempt to introduce "*English* Operas at L—n's Inn F—ds Theatre" (14), and to interrogate London's principal operatic performers and impresarios, including "H—l," "S—no," "B—ni," "A—o," "F—na," and "C—z—ni" (30–40). He points out the disposition of certain actors for certain theatrical roles, encouraging readers to "consider W——ks as a Heroe, B———th as a fine Gentleman, M—ls as a Lover, C———er an old General, D—y N—is a Tyrant, O—ld a Prude, P———er

a Cocquet, and *B———ker* an Empress" (79). Primcock is made to praise
"Mr. *H———ger*" as one who has always graciously condescended "to act
any Part in Life, which could amuse this Nation in a polite Way" (27–28),
and to criticize, conversely, the "insipid Arguments of *L—w*" against the
nation's amusements. And when in the midst of a discussion of the
oratorical uses of dance, he digresses into an obscure and absurd project
for the improvement of church service:

> Nor would it be amiss, were all our Pu—ts made of a commodious
> Largeness, and then our Par—ns might have Space sufficient to shew us,
> that we must be content with a Sort of a rough, hobbling *Courant*, to
> get to H—n; or, that if we don't take special Care, we may slide in a
> fine easy Minuet-Step (before we are aware) to the D—l: In short, one
> might * * * * * * and so * * * * * and thus * * * * * and * * * * * * and
> then * * * * * * but more of this * * * * * another Time * * * * * as my
> Project thrives in its Infancy. (113)

That each of these ellipses are either easy or impossible to fill in allows
Ralph to divert the credulous and the curious at one and the same time.
The credulous may suspend their disbelief and embrace the asterisks as a
textual enigma, while the curious may strain their faculties to substitute
simple letters for dashes. In either case, Ralph encourages readers to gawk
at the supposed "errors" in his text in the same way as sightseers wondered
at the aberrations and anomalies shown for money in the marketplace and
at the great London fairs. If, as Ralph has Primcock assert, "the Majority of
Readers" merely "skim the Surface of a Work," then his printed defects and
excesses, what he refers to as his "Blanks" and "Gaps" and his "trifling
Superfluity," will appeal to even the most superficial of gawkers. Although
*The Touch-Stone* omits from its copious survey of the "Reigning Diversions
of the Town" "*Mary of Godliman,*" "the *Cow with five Legs,*" and the
"*High-german Artist, born without Hands or Feet,*" it nevertheless diverts
with the "prodigies," "wonders," and "strange Monsters" of its text.

CHAPTER 4

# "Pleasantry for thy entertainment": novelistic discourse and the rhetoric of diversion

The *Town* has been in a Humour to encourage any thing offer'd with an Intent to please.
– *See and Seem Blind: or, A Critical Dissertation on the Publick Diversions* (1732)

The present Age seems pretty well agreed in an Opinion, that the utmost Scope and End of Reading is Amusement only; and such, indeed, are now the fashionable Books, that a Reader can propose no more than mere Entertainment, and it is sometimes very well for him if he finds even this in his Studies.
– Fielding, *The Covent-Garden Journal* No. 10 (February 4, 1752)

Part of the reason that James Ralph places such an emphasis on the linguistic and textual novelty of his survey of the "Reigning Diversions of the Town" is that he is convinced that it is only the unfamiliar, the unusual, and the hitherto unknown that will sell to a contemporary audience with what he repeatedly describes as "a prodigious Tendency to every thing mighty new" (194). This audience was drawn to Fawkes's legerdemain, Rich's harlequinades, and the freak shows at Charing Cross not because of their intrinsic value, but because of their ability to provide entertainment that, as an advertisement for Pinchbeck's "GRAND THEATRE *of the* MUSES" puts it, "surprizes and highly delights all that ever see and hear it."[1] As the previous three chapters have illustrated, the long-standing conception of England as a nation constitutionally inconstant and addicted to "newfangledness" affected amusement as much as it did politics and religion.[2] But what had been perceived during the sixteenth and seventeenth centuries as a cultural threat to the monarchy or established church was exploited during the eighteenth century as a commercial opportunity by authors and entertainers who sought to divert audiences through various kinds of literary and leisurely novelties. In an increasingly secular, urban, and radically individualistic context, the native "Tendency" towards the new and uncommon extended into matters of taste, transforming traditional leisure activities and literary genres into a range of amusements that Ralph identifies as being "new, or out of the Way" (62). Indeed, as the old holiday pastimes of the Renaissance are modernized into the new commercial diversions of Augustan London, novelty becomes an important touchstone of marketability.

Throughout the seven essays that comprise *The Touch-Stone* (1728), Ralph has A. Primcock endorse novelty as the characteristic feature – both the means and hopeful end – of any "Diversion truly *English*" (198). And as Chapter 1 has shown, he simultaneously encourages his pleasure-seeking readers to look for novelty in his survey of the "Reigning Diversions," making it a point of "interspersing" his "Historical, Critical, Political, Philosophical, and Theological Essays" with "some very new Remarks" (48) and "some Hints very New (yet undeniably very useful and solid)" (96). More often than not, these novelties take the form of self-conscious digressions into material that Primcock claims he had not at first intended to discuss. Towards the end of his essay "Of MASQUERADES," Ralph has Primcock ramble into a series of digressions on several diversions that he acknowledges to be foreign to his "Province" (194). He begins by satirizing the "*Ridotto*" as "a tolerable pretty Jumble of MUSICK, DANCING, GAMING, &c.," and at best "a bare-fac'd MASQUERADE, where People are admitted disguis'd without a Vizard, and hide their Hearts by their natural Faces" (192). He goes on to employ the figure of paralepsis in disclaiming responsibility for treating what he calls "private" entertainments, describing their peculiar "Nature" while seeming to pass over them:

> Since I am got into this Road of Amusements, many of my Readers will be desirous, that I should not pass by Drawing-rooms, Assemblies and Visiting-days, without calling in: But as these *Entertainments* are at most of a private Nature, and confin'd to particular Sets of People; to touch upon them would be taking me out of my Way. (193)

Primcock goes even further out of his way when concluding his sixth essay with a digression on "R——n" and an attack on those who attend "C——h meerly as a Diversion": "as they have turn'd the most serious Part of Life into a trifling *Amusement*, none of the public *Entertainments* is frequented with so little Prospect of Improvement, or Design to be instructed" (193–94). In other essays, Primcock gives trifling amusements fuller treatment than would appear to be their due. In "ESSAY VII," he argues that the history of bear-baiting is too long and profound to be written about in brief: "I have been as concise as possible on this Head; but in an Affair of this Consequence, Obscurity is more to be avoided than Prolixity: Therefore I shall at once proceed to consider the Diversions of our *Bear-garden*, upon a Parallel with those of the *Antique Circus*, as succinctly as a necessary Perspicuity will admit of" (210). When resolving to "shut up" his "last ESSAY upon our publick Diversions," he yields yet again to "Prolixity," not wanting to disoblige "five Parts in Six of the numerous Inhabitants of this *Metropolis*" by neglecting "to make honourable Mention of our *Publick Auctions*, which of late Years are become one of the principal Amusements of all Ranks, from the Duke and Dutchess to the Pick-pocket and Street-walker" (232). In each instance, Primcock digresses because he feels obliged "to gratify" the "Generality of Readers," and thus he promises, in his "PREFACE: or, INTRODUCTION," that *The Touch-Stone* will "vary from the common Method of proceeding" (x). If *The Touch-Stone*'s essays endorse novelty as the characteristic feature of contemporary diversion, the digressive style of the essays seems to suggest that novelty is also the feature most characteristic of popular animadversions upon "Diversion truly *English*." As an impartial and studious observer of all the most "noted Entertainments," Primcock realizes that the newness of any subject necessarily diminishes the moment it has first been experienced. He must therefore look for a method of keeping up the novelty and variety of his survey, even while acknowledging the limits of his generic scope and the possibility that his digressive treatment of such diverse matter as music, poetry, dancing, choruses, audiences, masquerades, and the "*modern* Bear-Garden" might prove tedious to English readers who are invariably also pleasure seekers.

## Digression and the problem of satiety

Primcock's matter is best understood by his singular method, which is to digress from subject to subject, breaking up his respective essays on the "Reigning Diversions of the Town" so as to prevent readers from growing too familiar with any one diversion by fixing upon it for too long. Digression is the source of *the new* in discourse, and it is the epitome of the several kinds of disruptive devices so pervasive in the literature of late seventeenth- and early eighteenth-century England. Being derived from the Latin root *digressio*, which translates the Greek *parecbasis*, the term *digression* means the act of "turning aside from a path or track," either from a "rule," a "standard," or a "subject in discourse or writing" (*O.E.D.* 1–2). As itself a classifiable figure of rhetoric, digression is, first, the most exaggerated and conspicuous form of catachresis, in that it abuses language by seeming to stray not only from narrative or thematic content, but also from the mimetic lines by which experience was supposed to be organized.[3] In *The Polite Gentleman* (1700), Henry Barker explains that "the Impression made on the Senses by Things that seem Pleasant" always "wears off" unless the "Brains" of readers are "delicately agitated" by an occasional witty "Turn of Expression" (102–04). He nonetheless equates digressive wit with other species of false wit, banishing from "true" discourse any "vain Imbellishments which disfigure it," such as "useless Digressions," "strain'd Figures," "forc'd Comparisons," and "all those Frothy Speeches full of nothing but Words, and little to the Purpose" (99–100). Second, digression contributes to the "monstrosity of textuality" by occupying inordinate amounts of space on the printed page and producing an excess of matter usually perceived by satirists to be deficient in relevant meaning.[4] In the "Digression in Praise of Digressions" in *A Tale of a Tub* (1704–10), Swift has his Grub Street hack argue that "the Society of Writers would quickly be reduced to a very inconsiderable Number, if Men were put upon making Books, with the fatal Confinement of delivering nothing beyond what is to the Purpose" (95). Yet even as Swift questions the legitimacy of contemporary publishing practices, he has the hack joke that "the great *Modern* Improvement of *Digressions*" runs "Parallel" with the "*debauched Appetite*" of the English for "various Compounds" such as "*Soups* and *Ollio*'s, *Fricassées* and *Ragousts*" and the related "Fashion of jumbling fifty Things together in a Dish" (95). In both linguistic and textual terms, then, digression registers traditional English attitudes towards novelty, threatening to carry readers out of the way and to overwhelm discourse with material that self-conscious writers acknowledge to be pleasant, but beside the point.

As he attempts to analyse the various types of English dance, Primcock remarks that he is "oblig'd, by several material and unavoidable Hints, to stretch this Subject to its utmost Extent." However, he confesses that this thoroughness will likely divert his readers from diversion: "were I to enter into a formal Detail of the Beauties of DANCING . . . new Matter would, every Moment, flow in so copiously, that I should never know when to make an End" (114). Ends are at odds with the relative means of London diversion, which Primcock's rhetoric and diction – for instance, his use of the adverb "copiously" – reveal to be endlessly versatile and varied. *Copia*, perhaps the fundamental Renaissance mode of composition, aimed at achieving a maximum variety in writing or speaking, while avoiding a redundancy of style or subject. In *The Touch-Stone*, Ralph exploits the idea of copiousness in an effort to bring subject and style into accord, promoting novelty and introducing fresh objects of interest through the digressiveness of his writing. Although Ralph has Primcock assure his readers that he fully intends "to proceed methodically," time and again he finds himself in a position where he cannot well avoid "making a small Excursion" to recommend, for example, "some new Movements absolutely essential to the most material Points of private, as well as publick Life" (87). As he develops his argument regarding the "dumb Wit" of modern pantomime artists, Primcock asks apology for what he deems a necessary "*Side-Step towards* TUMBLERS, POSTURE-MASTERS, *and* ROPE DANCERS" (86).⁵ When outlining the reasons why he will not be able to discuss the monster exhibitions of Southwark or Bartholomew Fair, he points out reflexively that were he to "enter into a curious Detail of every particular Amusement to be met with in these *Fairs*," he would "swell this pigmy Volume to an enormous Bulk" (231). And while panegyrizing the "Diversions of our COCK PITS," Primcock digresses to concede the futility of trying to do full justice to the dizzying "Variety" of London amusements:

> I am so elevated with this Subject, that when once I am fairly enter'd, I could talk of it without ceasing; and, perhaps, in my Fury be transported to say something not over much to the Purpose: But such a World of Matter crowds this ESSAY, that I am oblig'd to proceed in examining the Merits of another *Entertainment*. (223)

As Chapters 1–3 have shown, there was something about the subject of diversion that gave frequent occasion to digressive wit, and Primcock's rhetorical "elevation" is typical of contemporary attempts to describe entertainment in an entertaining way. Yet his concession that he is overwhelmed by his subject, and his concern that readers will be "transported" from his purpose, also echoes the perspective of commentators who worry that the English public will be sated rather than productively stimulated by the "Reigning Diversions of the Town."

Just as Ralph celebrates the aesthetic appeal of "Novelty, Beauty and Grandeur" (212), invoking *Spectator* No. 412 (June 23, 1712) in order to contextualize the kind of "Refreshment" that he views as essential to all "usual and ordinary Entertainments," so too is Primcock made to express an anxiety that *The Touch-Stone* will be subject to the "Satiety" that Addison and other critics represent as the bathos of pleasure (3.541). Too much diversion, these critics warn, is just as dull and wearisome as too little, in that satiety can make even pleasure unpleasant through overabundance. The pseudonymous author of *The Danger of Masquerades and Raree-Shows* (1718), for example, blames the unchecked proliferation of "Masquerades, Opera's, Assemblies, Balls, Puppet-shows, Bear-gardens, Cock-fights, Wrestling, Posture-masters, Cudgel-playing, Foot-ball, Rope-dancing, Merry-making, and several other irrational Entertainments" for having destroyed the taste of pleasure seekers by glutting the metropolis with diversion after diversion: "*Nature* puts a stop to the Growth of all other Productions, and feeds them only that they may *Subsist*, not that they may increase to a *Gigantick Size*." "The keenest Appetite," he observes, "may be Cloy'd" (B3v). In a similar vein, one of the correspondents in Charles Gildon's *The Post-Man Robb'd of his Mail* (1719) protests that there is little "Charm" in "the Pursuits of a busy Life, or a Life of Pleasure," which he portrays as being "perpetually the same Things over and over again, with very little Variation" (229). Even more vociferous is the author of *The Tricks of the Town Laid Open* (1747), who complains that London amusements "are all but wretched Counterfeits and Impostures, and will hardly endure the Test of Fruition." "[T]hey may be something grateful to us at first," he admits, "but after we have repeated 'em once, or twice, they grow flat and dull, and at last loathsome" (15–16). Celebrating, on the one hand, traditional rural recreations that he maintains "do not cloy or satiate their Possessors" and "are not spent and wasted by Fruition" (16), the author vigorously attacks, on the other hand, the enervating effects of the itinerary of urban amusements:

> all the Pleasures of this Town may be run through in the narrow Compass of two or three short Days, and when that's done, you do but run the same foolish Round, tread the same Stage over and over again; and what can be more ungrateful to an ingenious Man, than to have his Senses perpetually grated and imposed upon by the dull Repetition of the same Thing? (17)

Summarizing his opinion of London pleasures, and implicating himself in the first person among its pleasure seekers, the author rhapsodizes: "We are here like so many Bees in a Garden, humming and roving about from one Flower to another, foolishly endeavouring to keep up our Course of Pleasure, by a continued Succession and Circle of Varieties" (16).[6] Though the conception of a "Circle of *Varieties*" might seem at odds with the idea of a "dull Repetition," the end-point of a circle is also the beginning, and so pleasure seekers are bound to repeat the "same Thing" over and over again. The author's main problem with the busy round of London pleasures is that it can sometimes begin to feel endless. Being wasted by fruition, the diversion from the ordinary course of things will eventually be absorbed by it unless it can rejuvenate and make itself new again.

In the same way, too much digression can become overwhelming, subjecting readers of animadversions upon diversion to a rhetorical satiety that bores them even while attempting to unbend their weary minds. If *The Touch-Stone* identifies reading as among the newest and most pervasive of the "Reigning Diversions of the Town," it also explores the pitfalls of reading for pleasure in a commercial context where the public is alternately attracted and distracted by competing leisure activities and novel objects of interest. *The Touch-Stone* self-consciously problematizes satiety in its strained effort to accommodate as much diversion and digression as is possible in a survey of 237 octavo pages. Ralph has Primcock confine both himself and his survey to what he describes as "the Circle of the Town-Diversions" (87), but even within this limited urban scope he is left with far too much to talk about and far too many pleasure-seeking readers to divert. By the time he arrives at what he believes will be the final subject of his final essay, Primcock concedes the impossibility of proceeding in a straightforward manner and of satisfying all readers and pleasure seekers:

> I fear most of my Readers will seem shock'd, when after this copious List of Town Diversions I must confess, that I have not touch'd upon the most material Part of all, which gives the greatest Delight to the Majority of Audiences, or Assemblies of every Kind: And without which, the most perfect *Entertainment* is look'd upon as the most ridiculous and insipid: But I hope their Surprize will readily abate, when I set full in their View the Beauty of a Crowd: — A Crowd! —— which never fails to give Harmony to flat OPERAS Spirit, to dull Plays, and Life, to heavy Dances. Nothing could be added more *apropos* to the Nature and Design of these ESSAYS: For even with those who would be esteem'd the principal Judges of all publick Amusements, a Crowd is generally the Touch-stone of Merit. (234)

Ralph titles his work *The Touch-Stone* because it reduces to a single exuberant survey the entire semantic field of *diversion*. Yet for all the rhetorical art of his discursive diversions, he realizes that it is ultimately the support of "Audiences" that will forestall the "flatness," "dullness," and "heaviness" of a work about cultural diversion. Because of the emphasis that Ralph places on novelty and variety in diversion, he ensures that some readers will not enjoy his survey and that others will find the overabundance of his "copious List of Town Diversions" distasteful. "I have, in these ESSAYS, furnish'd out a Magnificent Banquet, to which the whole Town is invited," he explains, "Every Man will either barely commend the Dish he likes, and find fault with all the rest; or if his singular Palate is not touch'd with some particular Kickshaw, damn the whole Treat" (235). While *The Touch-Stone* is representative of the form and content of contemporary animadversions upon diversion, it is also exemplary of the genre's limitations, in that it describes the difficulty of providing leisure for literature as well as the paradoxes of stimulating audiences without fully sating them.

## The novel as a mode of entertainment

Even while questioning the efficacy of *The Touch-Stone* as an "unbending" amusement, Ralph's disclaimer ironically anticipates the form and content of the literary genre that would eventually supersede his "Magnificent Banquet" and become, in the following decades, the genre most affected by the fashion for novelty, most prone to digression and subject to satiety, and most often associated with reading for pleasure: the novel. Despite his interest in "every thing mighty new," Ralph has surprisingly little to say about the eponymous novel, alluding at one point to the "many valuable Volumes of Romances, Memoirs, Novels, and Ballads" produced on the subject of "*Knight-Errantry*" (22), and casually referring, at another point, to "the artificial, natural, and political Mysteries in *Gulliver's Travels*" (236). Novel reading, however, was increasingly one of the many leisure activities available for purchase by a public who might choose to read, but might also choose to be deceived by the "dumb Wit" of Harlequin, to gawk at the "*High-german Artist, born without Hands or Feet,*" or to indulge anything else in Ralph's "Circle of the Town-Diversions." Over the course of the late seventeenth and early eighteenth centuries, the novel itself gradually became one of the most popular of these diversions, and by the late eighteenth century it had effectively replaced the theatre as England's "national Diversion" and the literary-cultural context in which entertainment was most ardently debated.[7] It was able to do so because, as this chapter will suggest, it assimilated the material conventions of England's other diversions into the "telling" and "showing" of its narrative, a narrative structured less by high-minded "authors" than by a demographic that William B. Warner identifies as "entertainers and media workers."[8] Warner and other recent critics have convincingly argued that the novel did not at first emerge as a literary genre per se, but as an innovative "mode of entertainment" that took stock of the changing market for diversion and advanced the freedom of readers to consume only that which brought pleasure commensurate with the time spent and the money laid out. When Henry Fielding famously has the narrator of *Tom Jones* (1749) describe himself as the "Master of an Ordinary," and his opening chapter as a "*Bill of Fare to the Feast*," he alludes subtly to the damning of Ralph's "whole Treat" while foregrounding what Warner sees as the "entertainment function" of the developing novel:

> An Author ought to consider himself, not as a Gentleman who gives a private eleemosynary Treat, but rather as one who keeps a public Ordinary, at which all Persons are welcome for their Money . . . Men who pay for what they eat, will insist on gratifying their Palates, however nice and whimsical these may prove; and if every Thing is not agreeable to their Taste, will challenge a Right to censure, to abuse, and to d—n their Dinner without Controul. (1.1.31)

As yet another new form of commercialized leisure, the early English novel, like the popular entertainments surveyed in *The Touch-Stone*, sought to appeal to the public taste for the strange and uncommon, for farce, spectacle, and sex, and for sound and show over sense.[9] As such, much of the fiction associated with the teleological "rise" of the novel self-consciously acknowledges its status as commodity and rationalizes its value in terms of its novelty, its capacity for entertainment, and its difference and distance from the ordinary course of things – from politics and study and business and from all earnest labour and employment.

For example, in the preface to *The Reform'd Coquet, or Memoirs of Amoranda* (1724), Mary Davys concedes that her "Pen is at the service of the Publick," before going on to express a conventional desire that her novel will give readers "an hour or two of agreeable Amusement."[10] In a similar way, William Congreve explains of *Incognita: or, Love and Duty Reconcil'd* (1692) that the novella "has been some Diversion to me to Write it," and that he ultimately hopes it will "prove such" to those who have "an hour to throw away in Reading of it."[11] The fictional "Editor" of Defoe's *Moll Flanders* (1721) grudgingly acknowledges the "Brightness" of the "criminal Part" of his picaresque narrative, but expresses optimism that "the infinite variety of this Book" will appeal to "the Gust and Palate of the Reader."[12] Delarivière Manley offers her *roman à clef, The Secret History of Queen Zarah and the Zarazians* (1705), as a diverting alternative to French romances, arguing in her introduction "to the Reader" that the latter have "for a long time been the diversion and amusement of the whole world," but that in recent years "little histories of this kind have taken place of romances, whose prodigious number of volumes were sufficient to tire and satiate such whose heads were most filled with those notions." "These little pieces," she archly adds, "are much more agreeable to the brisk and impetuous humour of the English, who have naturally no taste for long-winded performances, for they have no sooner begun a book but they desire to see the end of it."[13] The rhetoric and diction of each of these novelistic paratexts coalesces in obvious ways with the contemporary discourse over diversion. Early novelists emphasize that reading has itself become a popular amusement. They thematize leisure and reflect upon the uses and abuses of time. They describe the novelty and variety of the genre they promote as a "new Species of Writing."[14] Most importantly, they acknowledge the threat of satiety and the difficulty that their long narratives will have in competing for cultural ascendance with other newfangled entertainments in the crowded marketplace. For this reason, Aphra Behn opens *Oroonoko; or, The Royal Slave* (1688) with the surprising admission that she will "omit, for Brevity's sake, a thousand little Accidents of his Life, which, however pleasant to us, where History was scarce, and Adventures very rare; yet might prove tedious and heavy to my Reader, in a World where he finds Diversions for every Minute, new and strange."[15] Even Fielding warns that "common Readers" might not be able to sustain themselves through the "long Journey" of a novel. With this in mind, he proposes that the "*Divisions*" or chapter breaks in his first extended work of fiction, *Joseph Andrews* (1742), should be looked upon as an "Inn or Resting Place," where the reader "may stop and take a Glass, or any other Refreshment, as it pleases him." "A Volume without any such Places of Rest," he observes, "fatigues the Spirit when entered upon."[16] What Fielding and other early novelists paradoxically question is the ability of the new "mode of entertainment" *to entertain*. If the very act of reading a novel was supposed to offer relief from the dullness and repetition of everyday life, how did novelists ensure that their own narratives did not become dull and repetitive? What specifically made novelistic discourse pleasurable, and through what means did novelists like Fielding compete with commercial entertainers?

Fielding had an ambivalent relationship to commercial entertainment, a topic to which he returned again and again over the course of his varied career as satirist, playwright, journalist, and, eventually, comic novelist.[17] In what appears to be his first publication, a six-penny pamphlet in hudibrastic verse entitled *The Masquerade* (1728), Fielding describes in detail one of the notorious assemblies at the King's Opera House in the Haymarket, invoking the Muse's aid for "some Simile [to] indite" the startling "Oddness of the Sight":

> As in a Madman's frantick Skull,
> When pale-fac'd *Luna* is at full,
> In wild Confusion huddled lies
> A Heap of Incoherencies.[18]

Better known than this poem are Fielding's theatrical burlesques of the 1730s, which are often populated by characters who "emblematically" represent the so-called "*Pleasures of the Town*," including masquerade, opera, pantomime, popular oratory, Punch-and-Judy acts, and, notably, the novel. In *The Author's Farce* (1730), Fielding has the impecunious Luckless condescend to the debased taste of the public by mounting a "Puppet-Show in a Playhouse" that parodies the kind of "catch-all" entertainments being offered around London from Pinkethman's Booth and "FAWKES'*s Theatre*" to Lincoln's Inn Fields and Drury Lane. Jack Pudding's "puff" for the performance mimics the copia and commercial hyperbole associated with the promotion of amusement during the period:

> This is to give notice to all gentlemen, ladies, and others, that at the playhouse opposite to the Opera in the Haymarket this evening will be performed the whole puppet show called *The Pleasures of the Town*, in which will be the whole court of Dullness, with abundance of singing and dancing and several other entertainments; also the comical and diverting humours of Somebody and Nobody, Punch and his wife Joan; to be performed by living figures, some of them six foot high, beginning exactly at seven o'clock. God save the King! [*Drum beats.*][19]

When Luckless is challenged with the indignity and irrationality of his play, he explains his dramatic strategy in terms that allow Fielding to satirize the crass commercialism of London's most successful entrepreneurs, showmen, and impresarios: "since every one has not Time or Opportunity to visit all the Diversions of the Town, I have brought most of them together in one" (3.2., p. 258). Through the periodical numbers of *The Champion* (1739–40) and *The Covent-Garden Journal* (1752), Fielding delivers ironic panegyrics on some of the same "*Entertainmatic* Authors," treating the popular performances of Orator John Henley, William Pinkethman, Colley Cibber, and John Rich as metaphors for what he dubs "the Grand Pantomimes on the Stage of Life."[20] When Fielding became Justice of the Peace for Middlesex and Westminster in 1748, he was forced to confront more seriously the social and political problems resulting from what he viewed as "*too frequent and expensive Diversions.*" In his polemical *Enquiry into the Causes of the Late Increase of Robbers* (1751), Fielding cites the itinerary of London plays, operas, routs, riots, masquerades, oratorios, ridottos, hurricanes, and pleasure-gardens as evidence that "the Places of Pleasure are almost become numberless," warning that this expansion of diversion across topographical and temporal boundaries came at the inevitable "Cost of the Public" (82–84). "Vanity and

Voluptuousness," he maintains, are "the two great Motives to Luxury" (78), and "Luxury" leads dangerously to a "Loss of Time and Neglect of Business" (80).

Yet for all of this, Fielding was no enemy of diversion. Like many of his contemporaries, he was well aware that in an increasingly secular, urban, and radically individualistic consumer society, *regulated* diversion served an important cultural function by providing temporary relief from "Business" in its various manifestations. And thus even in his otherwise sober *Enquiry*, Fielding draws upon no less an authority than Seneca to prove that occasional diversion "is the necessary Temperament of Labour": "'Some Remission must be given to our Minds, which will spring up the better, and more brisk from Rest'" (81). Like the apologists discussed in Chapter 1, Fielding understood that the "*Pleasures of the Town*" could be conducive to a more productive exercise of body and mind – "unbending" in order to bend the physical and mental faculties more effectively on their return to the straight and narrow. As such, Fielding recommends not "the Extirpation of Diversion," but only "the Retrenchment" (83).

An important part of this process of "Retrenchment" for Fielding involved adapting the cultural function of diversion to the digressive rhetoric of his fiction. Fielding's inclusion of "Mrs. Novel" as one of the "*Pleasures of the Town*" in Act III of *The Author's Farce* points to his apprehension regarding the market both for amusement and for the popular prose fiction exemplified by the scandal memoirs and amatory novels of Eliza Haywood. At the same time, Mrs Novel is represented as being fertile and undeniably attractive, and the eventual marriage between her and Signor Opera seems to suggest the possibility of a productive union between different modes of entertainment within the new genre of the novel. When Fielding began his novel-writing career, he did so with a sophisticated awareness of the history and development of English fiction *and* English amusement, and he writes this genealogy into his characteristically reflexive novels. The preface to *Joseph Andrews* opens with an acknowledgment by Fielding of his work's novelty and its controversial status *as entertainment*, as well as with an attempt to discriminate his original performance from that of literary and leisurely competitors:

> As it is possible the mere *English* Reader may have a different Idea of Romance with the Author of these little Volumes; and may consequently expect a kind of Entertainment, not to be found, nor which was even intended, in the following Pages; it may not be improper to premise a few Words concerning this kind of Writing, which I do not remember to have seen hitherto attempted in our Language. (3)

In the opening chapter of *Tom Jones*, Fielding expands further upon the kind of diversion offered by the novel, classifying the new genre as a "mental Entertainment" and distinguishing his prose fiction from the "common and vulgar" works "with which the Stalls abound" (1.1.32–33). His narrator's preliminary "Bill of Fare" explains that his work will offer readers a provision of "HUMAN NATURE," boasting, like advertisements for eighteenth-century sights and shows, of the "prodigious Variety" of his entertainment. "Having premised thus much," he assures the reader at the close of his introductory essay, "we will now detain those, who like our Bill of Fare, no longer from their Diet, and shall proceed directly to serve up the first Course of our History, for their Entertainment" (34). Fielding's digressive "Bills of Fare," which contextualize the themes of the narrative and guide the reading experience, have necessarily been lauded as a seminal moment in the "elevation" of the novel as a "self-conscious" literary genre.[21] But what has rarely been recognized is that many of his self-conscious devices were conventional among those who wrote about diversion. It is entirely likely, for example, that Fielding borrowed the conceit of the novel as "public Ordinary" from his partner, collaborator, and friend, James Ralph, whose description of *The Touch-Stone* as a "Magnificent Banquet" and whose analysis of the "singular Palate" of readers seems to have influenced the appeal to the "Palates" of readers in *Tom Jones*.[22] Other literary genres assimilated one or another diversion into their discursive format, but it was the large scale of the novel that gave writers the widest scope to patronize the psychology of readers, as well as their taste in amusement. Although Fielding baits these readers to evaluate what he calls his "Heroic, Historical, Prosaic Poem" (4.1.152) through the high cultural authority of the classical epic, this chapter will argue that his relationship with his audience is legitimized primarily through the popular market authority of the "*Pleasures of the Town.*" In *Tom Jones*, Fielding engages his readers and staves off satiety by adopting the same strategy that Luckless employs to secure London pleasure seekers, doing for prose fiction what the puppet-play in *The Author's Farce* had done for theatre: "since every one has not Time or Opportunity to visit all the Diversions of the Town," his novel brings most of them "together in one."

## Plotting diversion in Fielding's *Tom Jones*

In partial justification of the "Bills of Fare" with which he introduces every book of *Tom Jones*, Fielding has his intrusive narrator joke that he will "not disdain to borrow Wit or Wisdom from any Man who is capable of lending

[him] either" (1.1.32). Referring, in this case, to those anonymous "Victuallers" who give preface to "every Course" of their "Entertainment," the narrator elsewhere invokes the assistance of some of the better-known contributors to London's nascent leisure industry, including Barton Booth, Robert Wilks, Colley Cibber, John Essex, Isaac Fawkes, Catherine "Kitty" Clive, "Cheshire" Samuel Johnson, George Frideric Handel, Johann Jakob Heidegger, William Mills, John Rich, Charles Macklin, John Broughton, and David Garrick. According to the survey of amusement that Fielding incorporates into *Tom Jones*, the "lower sort" of people might be "captivated" by the spectacle of the annual Lord Mayor's pageant (4.1.153), or might take "exquisite Delight" in "one of those Punches in the Guts" customary at "*Broughton's* Amphitheatre" (13.5.702). Town wits might occupy their time at Will's or Button's, "toasting the Charms of a Woman" or "giving their Opinion of a Play" (13.5.700–01), while ladies of fashion might be "relieved" by the music of the "Opera" or the card tables at a "Drum" (17.6.897). The public at large might visit one of the metropolitan theatres to be entertained by "the Tricks of Harlequin" (5.1.214), the conspicuous nonsense of "*Hurlothrumbo*" (4.1.151), or "the judicious Action of a *Garrick*, of a *Cibber*, or a *Clive*" (9.1.493). Or, quite simply, they might take their diversion in the closet, reading commentary about it all in periodicals such as "the Spectator" (9.1.487) or surveys such as *The Touch-Stone*.

Like many English novels of the eighteenth century, *Tom Jones* exuberantly *plots* diversion through extended narrative episodes in which characters partake of social amusements that give them the opportunity both to exercise their taste and judgement and to confront their fallibility in a disinterested environment. These "minor interpolations," as J. Paul Hunter calls them, interrupt the main thrust of the plot and have thus been frequently dismissed as narrative "defects" or digressions.[23] Yet insofar as they reflect upon the effects of diversion on a pleasure-seeking public, the episodes are thematically and formally relevant to Fielding's "mental Entertainment." Regardless of the gravity of their particular circumstances, Tom, Sophia, Partridge, and the rest of their acquaintances routinely take time out to forget their troubles and unbend their minds. In *Tatler* No. 89 (November 3, 1709), Richard Steele warns that "what we take for Diversion, which is a kind of forgetting our selves, is but a mean Way of Entertainment, in Comparison of that which is considering, knowing, and enjoying our selves" (2.60). In Fielding's novelistic rendering of the forms and function of contemporary diversion, characters come to know themselves precisely by enjoying and temporarily forgetting themselves. What these characters take for diversion is any activity that distracts them from the conflicts and distresses that are the essence of the novel.

As the banished Jones makes his way to London, he agrees to pause for a few hours on the road so that his travel companion, Partridge, may see his favourite "of all the Pastimes upon Earth": "A Puppet-show!" (12.5.637). The puppet theatre had long been an attraction of the London fairs, but by the opening decades of the eighteenth century it had precociously assumed a position among the more fashionable diversions of the town. As early as 1709 Martin Powell was delighting audiences at Bath, Bristol, and Oxford with his puppet performances of *The Creation of the World*, which diversified its entertainment by featuring a jig, a rope-dancer, a ghost, a lover hanging himself, and a dance between Punch and Joan in Noah's Ark. In 1710 Powell removed his show to London, setting up first in St Martin's Lane and eventually establishing in 1711 his popular "Punch's Theatre" in the Little Piazza at Covent Garden – this "being a Place both warmer and fitter," as a notice in *The Daily Courant* explained, "to receive Persons of Quality, &c."[24] In such company, Punch's chest puffed to the size of his traditionally bloated belly and his head swelled in proportion to his enormous nose. During the period of its operation (1711–14), Punch's Theatre was hyperbolically acknowledged to be London's third playhouse, and Powell was said to have "gather'd such Wealth as is ten times sufficient to buy all the Poets in *England*."[25] A correspondent in *Spectator* No. 14 (March 16, 1711) ironically celebrated Mr Powell's "Skill in Motions," contending that "[t]he Opera at the *Hay-Market*, and that under the little *Piazza* in *Covent-Garden*" are "at present the Two leading Diversions of the Town" (1.63). Powell's success encouraged other ambitious entertainers to pull at strings and to try their hands at puppetry. In the late 1730s, Charlotte Charke and a showman named Yeates drew diverse audiences to their own miniature theatre above the old tennis court in James Street. Their performances featured puppet adaptations of contemporary ballad operas such as *The Lover His Own Rival* (1736) and *The Harlot's Progress* (1733), as well as of Fielding's *The Mock-Doctor* (1732), *The Old Debauchees* (1732), and *The Covent-Garden Tragedy* (1732), in which a hunchbacked Punch appeared as the proprietress of a brothel, "being the first time in petticoats." According to Martin Battestin, Fielding himself seems also to have appeared "in petticoats" as "Madame de la Nash," who ran a fashionable West End puppet theatre in Panton Street. An advertisement for the theatre in *The General Advertiser* (March 30, 1748) announced "that Excellent old Entertainment, call'd a PUPPET-SHEW," singling out for particular approbation "*the Comical Humours of* PUNCH *and his Wife* JOAN, With all the Original Jokes, F—rts, Songs, Battles, Kickings, &c."[26]

In an age often recognized for its decorum and distinguished by its refined wit, the low-brow "PUPPET-SHEW" enjoyed an unprecedented vogue, becoming, in the words of historian George Speaight, "the talk of the town."[27] Fielding parodies the incongruity between the popularity of Punch and the tediously "sentimental" approach of many contemporary dramatists through his characterization of a hypocritical showman who wrongheadedly seeks to reform the puppet theatre. Jones is initially willing to entertain Partridge's request that they "tarry and see" a performance that he expects will divert them with the "*Comical Humours of* PUNCH." But the "Master of the said Show," who claims that his "Figures" have "given great Satisfaction to all the Quality in every Town in *England*," requires his audience to do more than idly pass their time (12.5.637). As he soberly explains to the travellers, his show diverts only to instruct:

> He said, "The present Age was not improved in any Thing so much as in their Puppet-shows; which, by the throwing out *Punch* and his Wife *Joan*, and such idle Trumpery, were at last brought to be a rational Entertainment. I remember," said he, "when I first took to the Business, there was a great deal of low Stuff that did very well to make Folks laugh; but was never calculated to improve the Morals of young People, which certainly ought to be principally aimed at in every Puppet-show: For why may not good and instructive Lessons be conveyed this Way, as well as any other." (639)

Because he conceives of puppetry as primarily a didactic art, the puppet-show-man celebrates the recent innovation of life-sized marionettes whose approximation of real actors playing real people made them more conducive to "the great Force of Example" (640). He therefore boasts of the verisimilitude of his little wooden actors: "My Figures are as big as the Life, and they represent the Life in every particular; and I question not but People rise from my little *Drama* as much improved as they do from the great."[28] The obvious problem with this perspective is that his drama is not "the Life," but a diversion from it. When the puppet show is finally staged it transforms what had once been enjoyed as a "turning aside" from the ordinary course of things into the ordinary course itself – an entertainment pitched to have a direct impact on the audience:

> The Puppet-show was performed with great Regularity and Decency. It was called the fine and serious Part of the *Provok'd Husband*; and it was indeed a very grave and solemn Entertainment, without any low Wit or Humour, or

Jests; or, to do it no more than Justice, without any thing which could
provoke a Laugh. The Audience were all highly pleased. (638)

The pleasure-seeking Jones is considerably less pleased, and he criticizes the
"Dancer of Strings" for misunderstanding the essential purpose of enter-
tainment. "'I would by no Means degrade the Ingenuity of your
Profession,'" he protests, "'but I should have been glad to have seen my
old Acquaintance Master *Punch* for all that; and so far from improving, I
think, by leaving out him and his merry Wife *Joan*, you have spoiled your
Puppet-show'" (639). With the omission of the vigorous low comedy of
Vanbrugh's *A Journey to London*, the puppet performance of Cibber's *The
Provoked Husband* (1728) eliminates those parts of the play best suited to
the medium of the puppet stage, while retaining the dull and sentimental
parts. As Jones points out, the puppet-show-man purveys diversion devoid
of diversion, producing not, as he seems to think, a puppet profound but
rather a wooden bathos. In "triumphantly descanting" upon "the good
Morals inculcated by his Exhibitions," he is exposed for being too serious
about his play (642).²⁹

    In the novel's next significant episode of amusement, it is Jones who
takes his play too seriously. When he arrives in London, destitute of both
love and money, he chooses nonetheless to participate in what was con-
sidered to be among the most morally and materially extravagant of the
"Reigning Diversions of the Town": the masquerade. In *The Touch-Stone*,
Ralph offers a brief account of the development of the "Midnight
Masque," explaining that "MASQUERADES have for some Years past made
a vast Noise in this Kingdom, to the unspeakable Delight of most fine
Gentlemen and Ladies; and with equal Dissatisfaction to many of his
Majesty's well-meaning Subjects" (169). Masked balls had been held in
England from as early as the Tudor period, but as Ralph has Primcock
observe, their cultural prominence in the early decades of the eighteenth
century was entirely owing to the influence of "Mr. H——r," whom he
credits for having "firmly establish'd that Amusement by his exquisite *Gou*,
in what is polite and diverting" (174). J.J. Heidegger was particularly adept
at reading public taste, and when he took over as manager of the King's
Opera House in 1713 the Haymarket became the recognized home of the
masquerade, while Heidegger himself came to be viewed sarcastically as
"*Surintendant des Plaisirs d'Angleterre*."³⁰ Taking advantage of the diversion's notoriety during the period, Fielding introduces "*Heydegger*" into his
novel as both "the great *Arbiter Deliciarum*" and "the great High-Priest of
Pleasure," who presides over the "Temple" where Jones and Nightingale

experience what his narrator describes as "*the whole Humours of a Masquerade*" (13.7.712).

The pleasure of Heidegger's assembly was grounded in its gratuitous appeal to the senses. With its lavish combination of fine music, elegant dancing, sumptuous food, expensive lighting, and elaborate costume, the masquerade encouraged a sensory overload that voluptuaries found delightful and conservative critics deemed distasteful and dangerous. The author of *The Danger of Masquerades and Raree-Shows*, for instance, warns that "*Wit* has been visibly upon the Decay ever since the Nation seem'd inclin'd to prefer *Haymarket* to *Drury Lane*: And the Pleasures of Sense, to the Beauties of the Mind" (12). Like those satirists who attacked contemporary pantomime for its "Wit corporeal," the author views the characteristic elements of Haymarket masquerades as being analogous to the devices of false wit, and he self-consciously employs a strained simile to exemplify rhetorically the ill effects of the diversion:

> Now as no Distemper comes to a head on a suddain, so this grand Enemy to *Liberal Sciences* call'd a *Masquerade* was usher'd into the Nation by little irrational Entertainments, wich all look'd the same way, and took their rise from the Populace, Stupidity, and want of Reflexion. For as *Nits* by assembling together in corners do grow into Lice, so *Puppet-Shows, Raree-Shows, Balls, Assemblies*, and *Opera's* by a quick growth become a *Masquerade*. (10)

If for some commentators the masquerade thus represented a "residuum" for bad sights and shows, for others it was rather an epitome of entertainment that combined the spectacular features of many of London's "Reigning Diversions," and that catered to the public's desire for liberty in leisure.[31] A contributor to *The Weekly Journal* on February 15, 1718, celebrates the "noble Manner" in which "the ingenious Mr. Headaker" has "contriv'd" his masquerades, before giving an ecstatic account of a recent ball held in the Long Room at the King's Theatre:

> The Room is exceeding large, beautifully adorn'd, and illuminated with 500 Wax Lights; on the Sides are divers Beaufetts, over which is written the several Wines therein contain'd, as Canary, Burgundy, Champaign, Rhenish, &c. each more excellent in its kind; of which all are at Liberty to drink what they please, with large Services of all Sorts of Sweetmeats. There are also two Sorts of Musick; at due Distance from each other, perform'd by very good Hands. By the vast Variety of Dresses (many of them very rich) you would fancy it a Congress of the principal Persons of all the Nations in the World, as Turks, Italians, Indians, Polanders, Spaniards, Venetians, &c. There is absolute Freedom of Speech, without the least Offence given

thereby; while all appear better bred than to offer any Thing profane, rude, or immodest; but Wit incessantly flashes about in Repartee, Honour, and good Humour and all Kinds of Pleasantry.[32]

While this commentator emphasizes the propriety of the occasion, where "the Generality of Masqueraders behave themselves agreeable to their several Habits," his description hints that the appeal of Heidegger's masquerade had at least as much to do with the opportunity it afforded revellers to break with strict social decorum and to explore "absolute Freedom." The presumed anonymity of the event produced a temporary oblivion of the everyday and an imaginative setting in which participants could step outside of themselves to take on what Susanna Centlivre calls "a borrow'd Shape."[33] Fielding's narrator acknowledges that "the Lights, the Music, and the Company" at the Haymarket Opera House are "pretty strong Antidotes against the Spleen" (713). But when Jones and Nightingale attire themselves for the event, it is their masquerade costumes that allow them to forget temporarily their respective crises. Jones is no longer a bereft bastard and unrequited lover, but is rather the fortunate paramour of the "Queen of the Fairies." Nightingale ceases to be star-crossed in his affair with Nancy, becoming instead the hunter who beats about for various "Game." Jones initially marvels at the way in which "his Lady" speaks to other "Masks" with "the same Freedom of Acquaintance as if they had been bare-faced" (716). Before long, however, he too is attempting to "say something smart" to masked women of different "Stature, Shape, or Air" (713). When he eventually removes his mask at the end of the evening, he finds himself in the kind of situation that moralists warned would result from a diversion designed expressly to delude: he mistakes an amorous woman for an honest one, and succumbs almost unwittingly to a "downright Assignation" (716–17).[34]

According to Terry Castle, the masquerade episode in fiction "engenders a set of *liaisons dangereuses* by throwing characters into proximity who would never meet if an exhaustive sociological decorum was truly the goal: the high and the low, the virtuous and the vicious, the attached and the unattached." "And by the same token," she adds, "the episode may bring about, for a time at least, the alienation of characters who *should* be together."[35] In Fielding's novel, the masquerade in Book XIII establishes, "for a time at least," an extraordinary relationship between Jones and Lady Bellaston that muddles the hero's romantic pursuit of Miss Western. Though Tom might long for his Sophia, "Gallantry to the Ladies was among his Principles of Honour; and he held it as much incumbent on him to accept a Challenge to Love, as if it had been a Challenge to Fight" (715). Yet even after the music has faded, the dancing has stopped, and the costumes have all been returned, Jones continues to participate in his *liaison dangereuse* and to "meet his Lady," despite the fact that she should no longer be so in the normative world outside of the Haymarket. In the weeks following the "*whole Humours of a Masquerade*," Jones literally and figuratively comes to inhabit his diversion. As a result of the obligations that Lady Bellaston has "heaped upon him," he becomes "one of the best-dress'd Men about Town" and, in stark contrast to his earlier "Want of a Shilling," he is "raised to a State of Affluence, beyond what he had ever known" (13.9.724). As Jones thus perpetuates his play, he demonstrates his "Imperfections" and frustrates the progress of his own history, in that his protracted dalliance with Lady Bellaston prolongs his separation from the true queen of his heart. Within the delusory sphere of the masquerade, the "Queen of the Fairies" endeavours to "spoil as much Sport" as she is able, but without the masquerade it is disport itself which threatens to spoil the resolution of the novel.

The novel's most lengthy episode of amusement occurs ironically near the height of the hero's distress, just when resolution for Jones is beginning to seem unlikely. Although grieving his exile from Mr Allworthy, bemoaning his vicious past, and despairing an imminent match between Blifil and Sophia, Jones surprisingly joins his London companions in taking in a dramatic performance of *Hamlet* at Drury Lane. Each week, thousands of patrons attended performances at London's numerous playhouses, hoping temporarily to escape reality by immersing themselves in a fictive world created by poets and quickened by actors. And like the performances themselves, these patrons were notoriously mixed, both in terms of their social station and their perceived ability to appreciate what they were watching.[36] In a mid-century pamphlet entitled *A Treatise on the Passions, So Far as They Regard the Stage* (c. 1747), Samuel Foote claims that "[u]pon the least favourable Calculation, the Number of those called Play-Followers, cannot be rated at less than twelve thousand in this Metropolis." Of this number, Foote estimates that no more than "the four and twentieth Part of these" possess "a Capacity of determining on the Excellence, or Imperfections of a Performance, or a Performer."[37] As Foote nonetheless acknowledges, what most "Spectators" had in common was a desire to be diverted and to have their emotions moved by the performance of a "Mr. *Q—N*" or a "Mr. *G—K*," and thus he analyses the effects of the passions on "the Organs of our Bodies" in order to enable audiences "to judge how far the Imitation of those Passions on the Stage be natural" (8).

In the Drury Lane episode, Fielding does the inverse: he dramatizes the effects of naturalistic acting on the passions through Partridge's naïvely animated response to David Garrick's performance as the tragic Prince of Denmark.[38] When watching Hamlet's exchange with the ghost of his slain father, Partridge falls into "so violent a Trembling, that his Knees knocked against each other" (16.5.853). His immersion in the play is so deep that he unintentionally assumes a physical and emotional role in the performance: "during the whole Speech of the Ghost, he sat with his Eyes fixed partly on the Ghost, and partly on *Hamlet*, and with his Mouth open; the same Passions which succeeded each other in *Hamlet*, succeeding likewise in him" (854). If the source of dramatic pleasure is to be found in the suspension of disbelief, the barber's reaction to Garrick's Hamlet exaggerates this pleasure by literalizing it: he does not simply suspend his disbelief, he actually believes. In being "struck dumb" with "Fear" and "Sorrow," Partridge exceeds even the sarcastic expectations of Jones: "'You enjoy the Play more than I conceived possible'" (854–55).

But Partridge's response to *Hamlet* also increases the enjoyment of the other playgoers. The garrulity and absurdity of his commentary diverts not only Jones and Mrs Miller, but all those audience members sitting in the middle gallery who, the narrator admits, "were more attentive to what he said, than to any Thing that passed on the Stage" (857). As his burlesque comedies and rehearsal plays of the 1730s illustrate, Fielding is just as interested in what is happening off-stage as on-stage, and his perennial fascination with the nature of audience response informs both the rhetoric of his fiction and the meta-theatricality of this episode.[39] As Partridge disrupts and even displaces the content of the play, he comes to function as a kind of entr'acte divertissement, parodying through his remarks the dramatic impact of the commercial entertainments that had interpolated themselves onto the London stage during the eighteenth century. "Profitable art was welcomed in theatrical houses," writes Shirley Strum Kenny, but "so was profitable claptrap."[40] A diverting evening at Drury Lane, for instance, might open with an overture played by the theatre's orchestra and close with an afterpiece farce, burletta, or pantomime. In between these entertainments would be performed the main-piece, generally a five-act tragedy or comedy. Yet between each of the acts would be added even lighter fare: an instrumental solo, a grotesque dance, or such speciality acts as conjuring tricks, juggling, dwarf tossing, mechanical automata, and ladder-dancing. To the chagrin of many commentators, eighteenth-century drama was itself diverted by diversions. "I cannot therefore, I confess, with any patience see a *Harlequin*, or *Scaramouch* usurp that *Stage*, where I have been so often delighted with the Distresses of OTHELLO and JAFFIER," complains the author of *A Letter to My Lord* ******* *On The Present Diversions of the Town* (1725). "Where I have seen *Nature* in its greatest Beauties," he continues, "I cannot without resentment see these *Fopperies* of a *Smithfield Booth*" (17). However, as Chapters 1 and 2 have shown, these "fopperies" were introduced by commercially minded theatre mangers expressly to allay the "Distresses" of their mixed audiences. Divertissements were calculated to relieve spectators intermittently from the lofty sentiments and moral seriousness that characterized the drama of the period. Colley Cibber, who was often held responsible both for the "sentimental" turn in English drama and for the institutionalization of "new-fangled Foppery" on the English stage, argues in his *Apology* (1740) that theatrical divertissements had become necessary thanks to "the deprav'd Taste of the Multitude" (50). Defending his controversial role as co-manager of Drury Lane, Cibber explains that the mounting of what he calls "auxiliary Entertainments" compensated for main-piece plays that London audiences had begun to find boring, and that they therefore "supply'd the Defects of weak Action" (280). "Satiety," he warns, would have been the "natural Consequence" of allowing "the same Stock of Plays" to be performed, and he contends that it was only by diversifying theatrical entertainment that he was able to gratify the taste of the town (162). "If I am ask'd (after condemning these Fooleries, myself) how I came to assent, or continue my Share of Expence to them? I have no better Excuse for my Error, than confessing it. I did it against my Conscience! and had not virtue enough to starve by opposing a Multitude" (279–80).

Like a musical interlude, ladder-dancing, or a pantomimic farce, Partridge is a pleasure extraneous to the drama itself, but one which seems to enhance the theatrical experience by providing intermittent refreshment and, as the narrator observes, "much Laughter" (853). And like Cibber's "auxiliary Entertainments," Partridge is largely responsible for drawing in and retaining audiences at Drury Lane: "For as *Jones* had really that Taste for Humour which many affect, he expected to enjoy much Entertainment in the Criticisms of *Partridge*; from whom he expected the simple Dictates of Nature, unimproved indeed, but likewise unadulterated by Art" (852). Each time that Partridge intrudes upon the performance of *Hamlet* to remark "'Lud have Mercy upon such Fool-Hardiness!'" or "'Bless me! What's become of the Spirit?'" or, more profoundly, "'I know it is only a Play,'" he breaks the dramatic frame and, in so doing, exemplifies extra-dramatic diversion. When Partridge is befuddled by *The Mousetrap*, the dumb show designed by Hamlet to "catch the conscience of the King," his effort to enter "into the Spirit" of the play-within-a-play contextualizes the function of Fielding's play-within-a-novel by mediating illusion and holding reality at arm's length (856).[41] Partridge's performance dramatizes wrongheaded response. When he later interrupts the psychological climax of the play with the inane comment, "'I never saw in my Life a worse Grave-digger,'" the barber destroys the pathos of the scene and unwittingly exposes the dramatic consequences of the format of the "whole show" (856). Even his concluding remark serves as a sort of comedic afterpiece tacked incongruously to the end of a tragedy. When Jones questions him which of the players he "'had liked best,'" Partridge replies "'The King without Doubt,'" thereby establishing a humorous disparity between his inadvertent appreciation of Garrick during the play and his retrospective fondness for declamatory words spoken distinctly, "half as loud again as the other" (856–57). Fielding implies that the most entertaining player at Drury Lane is Partridge himself, since it is his antics rather than Garrick's powerful performance that dominate the episode. After all, observes the narrator, "little more worth remembering occurred during the Play" (856). The "Adventure at the Playhouse" draws abruptly to a close when Mrs Fitzpatrick engages Jones with news that might be "of great Service to himself." But before drawing a curtain over the scene and returning to the main action of the plot, the narrator edifyingly informs readers that the excursion to Drury Lane has "afforded great Mirth" to his principal actors or characters (857).

### Interest and audience response

By having his characters partake of unbending amusements at critical moments in the narrative, Fielding makes a case for the usefulness of diversion. And the fact that episodes of amusement play a significant thematic role in a novel that is itself being newly conceived of as a "mode of entertainment" suggests the degree to which *Tom Jones* seeks new ways to engage the reading public. In Book VIII, Fielding goes so far as to allow his readers *to read* his hero reading. After recovering from his head injury, and prior to setting out for Gloucester, Jones requests Benjamin, later revealed as Partridge, to procure him a book:

> "A Book!" cries *Benjamin*; "what Book would you have? *Latin* or *English*? I have some curious Books in both Languages. Such as *Erasmi Colloquia, Ovid de Tristibus, Gradus ad Parnassum*; and in *English* I have several of the best Books, tho' some of them are a little torn; but I have a great Part of *Stowe's* Chronicle; the sixth Volume of *Pope's Homer*; the third Volume of

the Spectator; the second volume of *Echard's Roman* History; the Craftsman; *Robinson Crusoe; Thomas a Kempis*; and two volumes of *Tom Brown's* Works." (8.5.421–22)

Benjamin's library traces the democratization of reading and the popularization of literature through the early Renaissance and into the eighteenth century. He begins with works of esoteric and scholarly appeal: Erasmus' *Colloquies* (1516), which was originally used in England as a Latin grammar, and *An Approach to Parnassus* (1686), which contained the lexicon of Latin synonyms and quotations. He proceeds to works that were fundamental in shaping notions of "Englishness": Stowe's *Chronicles of England* (1580), one of the earliest examples of English historiography, and Pope's translation of the *Iliad* (1715–20), which was reputed for helping to make Homer "speak good English." As periodicals aimed at shaping the social and political economy of the English, *The Spectator* and *The Craftsman* aided in the diffusion of the vernacular during the eighteenth century. And as one of the most successful works of early prose fiction, *Robinson Crusoe* (1719) extended readership down the social scale to allow those who had taught themselves to read for pragmatic purposes – clerks, tradespeople, servants – the opportunity to read for the sole purpose of pleasure. That several of the English volumes are "a little torn," and presumably well-thumbed, suggests that they have routinely served this purpose. What Benjamin's library embodies, then, is the cultural transition from reading as an earnest responsibility to reading as an agreeable pastime and diversion. It is therefore telling that Tom Jones chooses to divert himself with scattered volumes from the *Works* of Tom Brown, who prefaces his *Amusements Serious and Comical* (1700) with a plea for pleasantry: "I know not what Success these Papers will find in the World; but if any amuse themselves in criticizing upon them, or reading them, my Design is answered" (3.2).

The design of Fielding's "mental Entertainment" is fundamentally the same. Fielding's novel classification presupposes some kind of interaction between the methods of an entertainer and the minds of the entertained, who must be held mutually, supported or sustained, occupied, stimulated, and amused – who must, one way or another, be made to take an interest in the narrative as it develops over six volumes and eighteen books.[42] In *Tom Jones*, Fielding takes to its rhetorical extreme his friend James Ralph's observation that the English audience "may be justly look'd upon as the *Primum Mobile* of all Diversions," by whose "Smiles, or Frowns" an entertainer will "flourish or languish" (136–37). Like the diversion-mongers surveyed in *The Touch-Stone*, Fielding's narrator markets his

entertainment to the perceived needs and wants of the public, explaining
early on that though he is "the Founder of a new Province of Writing," and
is thus "at Liberty" to demand obedience to his generic "Laws," he intends
rather to promote "the Ease and Advantage" of his peculiar readers:

> For I do not, like some *jure divino* Tyrant, imagine that they are my Slaves or
> my Commodity. I am, indeed, set over them for their own Good only, and
> was created for their Use, and not they for mine. Nor do I doubt, while I
> make their Interest the great Rule of my Writings, they will unanimously
> concur in supporting my Dignity, and in rendering me all the Honour I
> shall deserve or desire. (2.1.77–78)

Punning on the multiple meanings of the word "interest," Fielding has his
narrator adopt the basic commercial principle of entertainers like Fawkes,
Rich, and Pinchbeck: in order to secure social and financial success, he
must engage his audience of readers by giving them a stake in the novel and
finding new ways to unbend their individual minds. That his tactic was
successful is attested by the fact that the novel sold remarkably well,
running through four authorized editions – and 10,000 copies – within a
single year.[43]

Beginning with the commercial model of a "well-meaning Host" and his
paying "Customers," the narrator goes on to explore a range of different
models for the relationship between an "Author" and his "Readers,"
placing particular emphasis on the surprising freedom granted each reader
to respond as he or she wishes to the "prodigious Variety" of the author's
"Provision" (1.1.32).[44] Sometimes the author is the keeper of a public
ordinary, but at other times he is an arbiter of literary taste, a travel
companion, an interlocutor in a long conversation, or a one-man
"Chorus" obliged on occasion to make a "short Appearance" on the
metaphorical "Stage" to offer commentary on the action:

> It is in Reality for my own Sake, that while I am discovering the Rocks on
> which Innocence and Goodness often split, I may not be misunderstood to
> recommend the very Means to my worthy Readers, by which I intend to
> shew them they will be undone. And this, as I could not prevail on any of my
> Actors to speak, I myself was obliged to declare. (3.7.141–42)

In *Tom Jones*, Fielding reinvigorates the clichéd metaphor of the "world-as-
stage" by turning his gaze from the actors to "the Audience at this great
Drama." In the introductory chapter to Book VII, the narrator questions
the traditional rationale behind the "Similitude of Life to the Theatre,"
pointing out the limitations of any view that neglects the vital experience of
those in attendance at this theatre: "as Nature often exhibits some of her

best Performances to a very full House; so will the Behaviour of her Spectators no less admit the above-mentioned Comparison than that of her Actors" (7.1.325). As a test-case or "Example," the narrator attempts to predict the varying responses of his readers to the theft of Tom's pocket-book by Black George, categorizing their judgements according to their position in the playhouse and their corresponding social status. The foot-men, servants, and coachmen who sit in "the World's upper Gallery" will vent "every Term of scurrilous Reproach"; the citizens and apprentices in the middle gallery will express "an equal Degree of Abhorrence"; the wits, bullies, and whores in the pit will be "divided" between hissing, applause, and "groaning"; and the gentry in the boxes will respond ambivalently with "their accustomed Politeness," though only because they have been "attending to something else" (326).

Like the Drury Lane episode, where the audience is "more attentive" to Partridge "than to any Thing that passed on the Stage," Fielding's meta-commentary concentrates on the reception rather than the performance of the unfolding drama. Just as Garrick's Hamlet is focalized through the "Criticisms" of Partridge, so too is the narrative of *Tom Jones* mediated by the anticipated responses of an audience of implied readers, who are engaged directly by Fielding's notoriously intrusive narrator. These readers are invited to assume an active role in the novel-in-becoming, being addressed at various points in the narrative as indifferent readers, indolent and lazy readers, stupid readers, gentle readers, enslaved readers, "good-natur'd Readers," female readers, "classical Readers," young readers, cur-ious readers, readers of the lowest class and those of a higher station – all of whom, the narrator acknowledges, "will probably be divided in their Opinions" (12.14.680). In Book x Chapter 1, the narrator remarks upon the difficulty of gauging his audience: "Reader, it is impossible we should know what Sort of Person thou would be: For, perhaps thou may'st be as learned in Human Nature as *Shakespear* himself was, and, perhaps, thou may'st be no wiser than some of his Editors." With this in mind, he proceeds to offer readers "Instructions very necessary to be perused by modern Critics," including an important caution "not too hastily to condemn any of the Incidents in this our History, as impertinent to our main Design, because thou dost not immediately conceive in what Manner such Incident may conduce to that Design" (10.1.523–24). Over the course of the chapter, the reader is addressed as a "good Reptile," a critic, and finally as "my worthy Friend."

Although Fielding's narrator refers, in this instance, to the several interpolated stories in the history of Tom Jones, his digressive meta-commentary is intended to apply equally to his own "impertinent" intrusions into the narrative, which betray a perpetual consciousness of his readers even while complicating their reading experience. "Reader," professes the narrator,

> I think proper, before we proceed any farther together, to acquaint thee, that I intend to digress, through this whole History, as often as I see Occasion: Of which I am myself a better Judge than any pitiful Critic whatever; and here I must desire all those Critics to mind their own Business, and not to intermeddle with Affairs, or Works, which no ways concern them. (1.2.37)

The irony of this digression upon digressions is that Fielding's narrator exhorts the critics to mind their business only so that he may be mindless of his own particular business of story-telling. And the critics, notwithstanding, have minded. Shortly after its initial publication, an irascible reviewer styling himself "Orbilius" censured "Mr. *F*'s late celebrated Performance," attacking the novel in particular for its "Incredibilities" and its apparent "Prolixity." In a 1749 letter to Lady Henrietta Luxborough, William Shenstone admitted more modestly that though *Tom Jones* had afforded him "much Amusement," the digressive wit "ty'd up in Bundles at y$^e$ beginning of every *Book*" convoluted the novel and made it "by no means easy." Even Fielding's first French translator, Pierre Antoine de la Place, observed in 1750 that the digressions and other rhetorical "ornaments" in *Tom Jones* were "out of place," in that they made it impossible for readers to suspend their disbelief. Taking for granted that Fielding's readers wished, first and foremost, to be absorbed by the story of Tom and Sophia, he warned that digressions in a novel have a similar effect on readers as divertissements in a tragedy have on theatrical audiences: "Once heated with the interest that comes from a moving and skillfully-woven plot, they endure impatiently all manner of digressions, of essays, or of moral treatises, and they consider these ornaments, however fine they may be, as just so many obstacles to the pleasure which they are eager to enjoy."[45] These contemporary views were reaffirmed in the twentieth century by no less a critic than R.S. Crane, who offhandedly stated, in "The Concept of Plot" (1952), that Fielding's narrator "perhaps intrudes too much in a purely ornamental way."[46] What several centuries of pseudo-formalist critics have argued is that whatever is not plot per se – from the introductory "Bills of Fare" to the ostentatious figures to the digressive asides – is foreign to the narrative. From this perspective, the intrusions and digressions in *Tom Jones* serve no end outside of themselves: they are "ornamental," rather than "instrumental," because they are inimical to the forward momentum of the fictional narrative.[47] Both rhetorically and spatially on the printed page, Fielding's digressive wit stands in the way of the happy ending sympathetic readers desire for Jones, threatening, like a puppet show, a masquerade, or a dramatic entertainment, to distract their attention from the meaning and resolution of the novel.

Fielding's self-conscious narrator routinely intrudes in order to remark upon the action while it is in progress; and while these intrusions are often small, their impact is not necessarily slight. Take, for instance, the narrator's mock-prurient account of Jones's discovery of a man hiding in Molly's garret:

> Now, whether *Molly* in the Agonies of her Rage, pushed this Rug with her Feet; or, *Jones* might touch it; or whether the Pin or Nail gave way of its own Accord, I am not certain; but as *Molly* pronounced those last Words, which are recorded above, the wicked Rug got loose from its Fastning, and discovered every thing hid behind it; where among other female Utensils appeared—(with Shame I write it, and with Sorrow will it be read)—the Philosopher *Square*, in a Posture (for the Place would not near admit his standing upright) as ridiculous as can possibly be conceived. (5.5.229)

Though the discovery of the hypocritical Square acquits the novel's hero, and is thus a joyous event, the narratorial interpolation of "wicked Rug" and "female Utensils" (with the implication that Square is *used* by Molly), and the assumption that the discovery will be read with "Sorrow," problematizes natural reader response. The diction of the passage runs curiously counter to the narrative significance of the action. In other instances, self-conscious narration seems to negate action altogether. When the landlady at the inn at Upton assaults Jones with a "Broomstick," a burlesque description of the weapon takes the place of a description of its use:

> My Landlady... fell upon him with a certain Weapon, which, tho' it be neither long, nor sharp, nor hard, nor indeed threatens from its Appearance with either Death or Wound, hath been however held in great Dread and Abhorrence by many wise Men; nay, by many brave ones; insomuch that some who have dared to look into the Mouth of a loaded Cannon, have not dared to look into a Mouth where this Weapon was brandished; and rather than run the Hazard of its Execution, have contented themselves with making a most pitiful and sneaking Figure in the Eyes of all their Acquaintance. (9.3.501)

At a narrative level, Jones's pursuit of Sophia is interrupted by "*the Battle of Upton*," while at a rhetorical level the narrator's periphrastic description disrupts the readers engagement with the novel. The narrator is inevitably obliged to ask the reader "to suspend his Curiosity," while he struggles to express himself "in vulgar Phrase" and "in plain *English*" (500–01).

Such linguistic perplexities are frequently a pretext for digressive wit. At a loss for how to represent the "extraordinary Condescension" of Deborah Wilkins, the narrator decides to introduce her "*with a Simile*": "Not otherwise than when a Kite, tremendous Bird, is beheld by the feathered Generation soaring aloft, and hovering over their Heads, the amorous Dove, and every innocent little Bird spread wide the Alarm, and fly trembling to their Hiding-places: he proudly beats the Air, conscious of his Dignity, and meditates intended Mischief." Because this extended simile strays from the linear lines of the story and stretches the limits of language, the narrator himself condescends to gloss his meaning and, as he puts it, "to lend the Reader a little Assistance in this Place": "It is my Intention therefore to signify, that as it is the Nature of a Kite to devour little Birds, so is it the Nature of such Persons as Mrs. *Wilkins*, to insult and tyrannize over little People" (1.6.47). It is the nature of Fielding's narrator to exaggerate the "little," and his digressions seem often to turn on the trivial matters that he ironically celebrates through an incongruous tag from Ovid's *Ars Amatoria*: "*Parva leves capiunt Animos*, 'Small Things affect light Minds'" (4.5.165). A single word is often enough to interrupt the story, as when the narrator delays his account of "*The Disasters which befel* Jones *on his Departure for* Coventry," so as to define the meaning of *impossible*:

> a Word which, in common Conversation, is often used to signify not only improbable, but often what is really very likely, and sometimes, what hath certainly happened: An hyperbolic Violence like that which is so frequently offered to the Words Infinite and Eternal; by the former of which it is usual to express a Distance of half a Yard; and by the latter, a Duration of five Minutes. And thus it is as usual to express a Distance of half a Yard; and by the latter, a Duration of five Minutes. (12.11.661)

Elsewhere, it is the omission of certain words (or letters) which paradoxically provokes the most garrulous authorial commentary. Squire Western's verbal quarrel with Jones consists of little more than an elusive elaboration of terms by the narrator:

> He then bespattered the Youth with Abundance of that Language, which passes between Country Gentlemen who embrace opposite Sides of the Question; with frequent Applications to him to salute that Part which is generally introduced into all Controversies, that arise among the lower Orders of the *English* Gentry, at Horse-races, Cock-matches, and other

public Places. Allusions to this Part are likewise often made for the Sake of
the Jest. And here, I believe, the Wit is generally misunderstood. In Reality,
it lies in desiring another to kiss your A— for having just before threatened
to kick his: For I have observed very accurately, that no one ever desires you
to kick that which belongs to himself, nor offers to kiss this Part in another.
(6.9.302–03)

In *Tom Jones*, little things are expressed in the largest of terms. The narrator
claims of "minute Circumstances" that he is "never prolix on such
Occasions" (17.2.880). But if he is willing to employ a long dash as a
diverting textual cue, he is just as ready to make censored words wordy
through ellipsis and periphrasis.

At the same time, Fielding's narrator travesties large matters by treating
them in terms that undercut their importance and make them appear little.
He frequently expresses an anxiety about his facility with language and his
ability to do justice both to the circumstances of his story and the passions
of his characters. At one point, he decides against trying to describe the
"present Situation" of Sophia's "Mind," out of what he admits to be a
"Despair of Success" (4.14.208). At another point, he abstains from
attempting to "render agreeable to the Reader" the particulars of a conversation between Jones and Lady Bellaston, on the grounds that it consisted of "the same ordinary Occurrences as before" (13.9.722). When, in
Book IV, the narrator prepares to introduce Sophia as the "Heroine" of his
history, he explains that he will follow the rules of decorum in using an
"Elevation of Stile ... proper to raise the Veneration of our Reader"
(4.1.154). Yet the rhetorically amplified portrait that follows concludes
with an anti-climactic concession of its very futility:

> Reader, perhaps thou hast seen the Statue of the *Venus de Medicis*. Perhaps
> too, thou has seen the Gallery of Beauties at *Hampton-Court*. Thou may'st
> remember *each bright* Churchill *of the Gallaxy*, and all the Toasts of the *Kit-
> Cat*. Or, if their Reign was before thy Times, at least thou hast seen their
> Daughters, the no less dazzling Beauties of the present Age; whose Names,
> should we here insert, we apprehend they would fill the whole Volume ...
> Yet is it possible, my Friend, that thou mayest have seen all these without
> being able to form an exact Idea of *Sophia*: for she did not exactly resemble
> any of them. (4.2.155–56)

At the close of this description, the reader is no nearer to a physical
conception of Sophia than at the opening. Here, as elsewhere in the
novel, the narrator's figurative comparisons seem to exist for their own
sake, not because they are apt or advance the novel's plot, develop its
characters, or reinforce its thematic argument. In fact, they more often do

the opposite, diverting readers from the pathos that competing novelists like Richardson and Haywood were trying to elicit through vivid portrayals of romantic encounters. In *Tom Jones*, these encounters are interrupted not only by blocking characters, but also by the ornamental rhetoric of Fielding's narrator. As Sophia and Jones stand "silent and trembling" during a rare moment of amorous tension in Book VI, they are broken in upon both by Squire Western and by a catalogue of ridiculous similes:

> As when two Doves, or two Wood-pigeons, or as when *Strephon* and *Phillis* (for that comes nearest to the Mark) are retired into some pleasant solitary Grove, to enjoy the delightful Conversation of Love; that bashful Boy who cannot speak in Public, and is never a good Companion to more than two at a Time. Here while every Object is serene, should hoarse Thunder burst suddenly through the shattered Clouds, and rumbling roll along the Sky, the frightened Maid starts from the mossy Bank or verdant Turf; the pale Livery of Death succeeds the red Regimentals in which Love had before drest her Cheeks; Fear shakes her whole Frame, and her Lover scarce supports her trembling, tottering Limbs. (6.9.300–01)

While Fielding's narrator tests out different similes, trying to determine which vehicle will be most appropriate to his tenor, he distracts attention away from his pining lovers and emphasizes instead the artificial nature of his narrative – its status as a created thing. According to Ian Watt, Fielding's "diverting asides" inevitably "derogate from the reality of the narrative." His self-conscious digressions produce a "distancing effect" which, in the opinion of Watt, "prevents us from being so fully immersed in the lives of the characters that we lose our alertness to the larger implications of their actions."[48] Yet every time the narrator condescends to speak "in simple Phrase" or "in the vulgar Tongue," and each time he concedes that "we dislike something in the former Simile" (11.6.593) or omits a "learned Dispute" because he doubts that "many of our Readers could understand it" (7.9.358), he breaks the mimetic illusion and startles readers out of the narrative of Tom Jones.

Fielding humorously acknowledges the potential hazards of his "disruptive" approach to fiction, as opposed to the "absorptive" approach of many of his contemporaries, when he brings his reader's neck "*into Danger by a Description.*" In a painstaking attempt to situate Paradise Hall topographically in Somersetshire, the narrator describes daunting cascades and meandering rivers that literalize the threat of digressive wit, suggesting at once the narrator's rhetorical skill and the effects of this skill on a reader who is made vulnerable by every departure from plain narrative: "Reader, take care, I have unadvisedly led thee to the Top of as high a Hill as

Mr. *Allworthy*'s, and how to get thee down without breaking thy Neck, I do not well know" (1.4.42–44). Fielding's digressions frequently function as disclaimers that ironically anticipate critics like de la Place and Crane, identifying in the novel likely "obstacles" to readerly pleasure. The narrator rightly predicts, for instance, that "there may be no Parts in this prodigious Work which will give the Reader less Pleasure in the perusing" than "those initial Essays" that preface each of his eighteen books (5.1.209). And he explains that he has routinely done "great Violence to the Luxuriance of our Genius" by leaving out of his work "many excellent Descriptions," from a conviction that the reader "would be very apt to skip [them] entirely over" (12.3.627). If Fielding is just as aware as his critics of the literal and figurative "*Danger*" of intrusion, obstruction, and interruption, then why does he allow his narrator to digress as often as he sees occasion? For with each digression upon the character of "a certain Weapon" or the "Toasts of the Kit-Cat," the sociology of kissing an "A—" or the semantics of the word "impossible," the progress of the history slows to a halt for readers who wish to know what Jones was assaulted with at Upton or how the hero came to be lost on the road to Coventry. Indeed, when "*the Author himself makes his Appearance on the Stage*," Tom Jones and Fielding's other characters appear to fall through a trap door (3.7.140).

### Diversionary reading and the rhetoric of fiction

The experiences of these characters at the puppet show, the Haymarket masquerade, and the performance of *Hamlet* at Drury Lane, however, provide an important reminder of the kind of entertainment being offered by Fielding's digressive novel. Each of the episodes of amusement in *Tom Jones* problematize mimetic illusion by illustrating the absurdity or impropriety of being drawn in too deeply by a manifest fiction. Moreover, each episode demonstrates the pleasure to be derived from breaking illusion and holding it at a distance. In its very digressiveness, *Tom Jones* represents an engaging alternative to what the narrator dismisses as "the Romances and Novels with which the World abounds" (9.1.488). In contrast to the popular epistolary novels of Richardson and the amatory fiction of Haywood, Fielding's "mental Entertainment" seeks not to absorb readers but to divert them, keeping up their interest through devices that temporarily turn aside from the straight and narrow of narrative and, in so doing, simulate the unbending effects of commercial amusement.[49] Fielding's plotting of amusement in *Tom Jones* models different kinds of audience response in order to suggest that, far from being an "obstacle" to the pleasure novel readers are eager to enjoy, digressions might in fact be a tangible source of enjoyment.

Fielding boldly encourages readers *to enjoy* his narrator's digressions by identifying them with the actual *"Pleasures of the Town."* In the introductory chapter to Book v, Fielding has his narrator invoke the dubious authority of John Rich and "the *English* Pantomime" in a facetious attempt to defend the "several digressive Essays" with which he has interspersed his "History." Comparing the impact of the two-part "Entertainment" on London audiences with the effect on readers of his procuring of "Foils," the narrator explains that his digressions "set off" the rest of his narrative in the same way as *"the Serious"* part of pantomime displays *"the Comic"* to "the better Advantage." "For what demonstrates the Beauty and Excellence of any Thing," he asks, "but its Reverse?" (5.1.212–15). When the narrator elsewhere characterizes the so-called "ornamental Parts" of his work, as opposed to the "instrumental" parts which advance the plot, he uses terms that are remarkably con-sonant with the rhetoric of diversion: so that reading may not be laborious, "we have taken every Occasion of interspersing through the whole sundry Similes, Descriptions, and other kind of poetical Embellishments" designed "to refresh the Mind, whenever those Slumbers which in a long Work are apt to invade the Reader as well as the Writer, shall begin to creep upon him." "Without Interruptions of this Kind," he provocatively adds, "the best Narrative of plain Matter of Fact must overpower every Reader" (4.1.151–52). That this "Interruption" precedes the narrator's aborted description of "our Heroine" suggests that the function of this and other "poetical Embellishments" in his prose narrative is not to "form an exact Idea of *Sophia*," but to give readers a discursive time-out. The narrator's *"short Hint of what we can do in the Sublime"* is intended to do for the comic novel what contemporary apologists were claiming diversion did for the English public at large: provide intermittent refreshment and stave off satiety. Because novel-reading is ultimately a gratuitous activity, the purported "authority" of Fielding's self-conscious narrator is con-tingent on his attentiveness to weary and restless readers who might, at any time, abandon the novel in favour of some other new amusement or leisure "Commodity." As Sandra Sherman observes, "readerly tenacity" is always "at issue" in *Tom Jones*. "In order to merit the reader's deference—his attention—the text must continually serve the reader's interest: It must remain interesting."[50] Since the novel is long and its multiple ironies are complex, readers of *Tom Jones*, like the characters in

*Tom Jones*, require something to relieve them from the arduous pursuit of "PRUDENCE." The rhetoric of Fielding's fiction implies that this something should ideally consist of intrusions, obstructions, and interruptions that paradoxically retain readers by diverting them every now and then from the conventional pleasures of a well-developed story.

In *Tom Jones*, episodes of cultural diversion tend to coincide with instances of discursive diversion. Fielding draws attention to his use of diversionary rhetoric by having his narrator bring content and format expressly into accord: "Our Pen, therefore, shall imitate the Expedition which it describes, and our History shall keep Pace with the Travellers who are its Subject" (11.9.612). In those moments when characters divert themselves from the ordinary course of their lives and adventures, the narrator concomitantly "turns aside" from the ordinary course of "plain Narrative," unbending the minds of readers when they are believed to need it most. The entire excursion to Drury Lane, for example, is a kind of interlude in Fielding's drama of fiction, since it bears little on the development of the plot. While the characters take their leisure at the playhouse, readers are given a brief respite from the increasingly dire situation of the hero, who has just broken off his affair with Lady Bellaston, but who is about to be accused of murdering Fitzpatrick and of having sex with his own mother. The narrator intends, however, not only to "keep Pace" with his characters, but to "imitate" them as well. If these characters are periodically encouraged to "tarry" and to refresh their minds with cultural diversions, then the narrator is likewise obliged to employ discursive diversions as breathing spaces for the critical intellect of readers. The "extraordinary obtrusiveness" of Fielding's narrative brings English pleasure seekers *and* readers together in what he calls mutual "Errands of Pleasure" (13.9.726).[51] And like all such "Errands," the "Pleasure" can only be temporary. When, in Book XVII, the narrator details the "Horrours" of a town excursion, in which Sophia is insulted at an opera by Lady Bellaston and courted aggressively at an assembly by Lord Fellamar, he once again breaks the tension of the episode with a self-consciously digressive account of the London social scene and, in particular, of a frivolous entertainment known as a "Drum":

> Having in this Chapter twice mentioned a Drum, a Word which our Posterity, it is hoped, will not understand in the Sense it is here applied, we shall, notwithstanding our present Haste, stop a Moment to describe the Entertainment here meant, and the rather as we can in a Moment describe it.
> A Drum then is an Assembly of well dressed Persons of both Sexes, most of whom play at Cards, and the rest do nothing at all; while the Mistress of

the House performs the Part of the Landlady at an Inn, and like the Landlady of an Inn prides herself in the Number of her Guests, though she doth not always, like her, get any Thing by it. (17.6.897–98)

As a digression upon a fashionable diversion, this description of a drum has the potential to be doubly entertaining, and thus the narrator is willing to interrupt the action to detail what he satirizes as a "Round of Impertinence" (898). Yet coming late in the narrative, with Jones in prison and Sophia in a "Dejection of Spirits," this final episode of amusement is not as gratifying for the principal characters as the ones that came earlier. The narrator explains that although Sophia was "relieved by the Musick at the one Place, and by the Cards at the other," she could not "enjoy herself" (897). At this point in the novel, the characters are more keen to bend than unbend their minds, and to concentrate their attention on the "Melancholy" circumstances that seem likely to result in "tenderest Sorrow" for Sophia and Jones (898). Out of a concern that pleasure-seeking readers will feel the same way, and acknowledging the "present Haste" of the story, the narrator prudently promises that he will only "stop a Moment" to describe "the Entertainment here meant."

At the beginning of Book xviii, when Fielding's narrator finally declares that he will suppress his digressions, he does so out of a conviction that even diversion can become tedious and boring if carried on for too long:

> [I]f I have now and then, in the Course of this Work, indulged any Pleasantry for thy Entertainment, I shall here lay it down. The Variety of Matter, indeed, which I shall be obliged to cram into this Book, will afford no Room for any of those ludicrous Observations which I have elsewhere made, and which may sometimes, perhaps, have prevented thee from taking a Nap when it was beginning to steal upon thee. In this last Book thou wilt find nothing (or at most very little) of that Nature. All will be plain Narrative only. (18.1.913)

The narrator's return to "plain Narrative" is simultaneous with his characters' abandonment of all "Pleasantry." In Book xviii, the entire dramatis personae congregate in London, not to partake of the "Reigning Diversion of the Town," but to apply themselves in earnest to the resolution of their respective troubles. The fact that the narrator forsakes diversionary rhetoric at the same moment that his characters reject unbending amusements reinforces the reciprocity between the two throughout the novel. As such, even while following "plain Narrative," the narrator makes it clear that any deviation from the straight and narrow has been "indulged" for the sake of his readers – "for *thy* Entertainment." For Henry Fielding, as for many novelists of the eighteenth century, the devices of digressive wit are precisely what qualify the early novel as a viable "mode of entertainment," one which entertains as much through its formal presentation as through the story it recounts, the characters it contrives, and the arguments it espouses. Yet *Tom Jones* is in many respects the best representative of the new kind of entertainment offered by the novel for the same reason that *The Touch-Stone* is, perhaps, the best representative of late seventeenth- and early eighteenth-century surveys of amusement: because of the wide scope of its treatment of the "Reigning Diversions of the Town" and because of the self-consciousness with which it employs diversionary rhetoric to engage the "Interest" of pleasure-seeking readers. Fielding's narrator might stress the importance of the "Variety of Matter" that he must "cram into" his final chapters, but his disclaimer hints that it is the variety of his manner that has kept his readers reading through six volumes and eighteen books. Since everyone has "not Time or Opportunity to visit all the Diversions," *Tom Jones* brings them "together in one," distracting readers from the narrative in order to make it more palatable and pleasing. By plotting diversion and providing intrinsic leisure for literature, Fielding makes a persuasive case for the novel as the newest and most gratifying way for the public to while away its idle hours.

# "The soul of reading": conclusion by way of animadversion

> Having for so long a Space, nicely canvass'd, and maturely consider'd all things premis'd in my Title-Page, I cannot but look upon my self as a Person every way adequate to the Undertaking; and may, without Vanity affirm, that by Genius, Study and Experience, I am sufficiently qualify'd to inspect, criticize, and determine upon the reigning Diversions of the TOWN.
>
> – Ralph, *The Touch-Stone* (1728)

Like its mad-cap model, this book has largely confined itself to the "Reigning Diversions of the Town," the amusements that engrossed the time of English pleasure seekers and the literary works that engaged the attention of English readers by offering a vivid, and conspicuously diverting, account of these amusements. But the rhetoric of diversion was not itself confined to works dealing expressly with operas, ridottos, and masquerades, pantomimes, prize fights, and public auctions, bear-baitings, fair-ground exhibitions, and puppet shows, nor to those seeking to represent such thematic content through their discursive format. Among contemporary poems, plays, periodicals, and prose works, "animadversions upon diversion" necessarily stand out because of the playful self-consciousness with which they employ the devices of digressive wit to stave off boredom and satiety and to unbend the minds of restless readers. Yet as even the most casual student of the late seventeenth and early eighteenth centuries will acknowledge, intrusion, obstruction, and interruption pervade most of the literature and para-literature of the period. Although they might have had little particular interest in what Ralph calls "the Standard *Entertainments* of the present Age" (237), writers in a wide range of genres appropriated these devices because they recognized diversionary rhetoric as a means through which to refresh and thereby retain readers who were invariably also pleasure seekers.

The gradual commercialization of leisure between approximately 1690 and 1760 ensured that the English literary market was very much a reader's market; and the coincidental coming of age of literary self-consciousness ensured that writers would cater to the demands of readers through devices that temporarily "turned aside" from plot and character and argument in order to provide intrinsic leisure for literature. Regardless of what specific point writers wished to make, how they made it depended upon the degree to which they combined diversion with instruction. Explaining his own critical method, by way of clichéd analogy to medicine, Ralph has Primcock summarize:

> *Physick* never operates so well, as when the Patient is in good Humour. Thus with every Medicine they give you an equal Dose of Mirth, to prepare you by proper Motions for its working. A *Merry-Andrew* will whip out your Tooth, as he catches you laughing at his dry Jest; or whilst a Country-fellow is gaping at the Rope-dancer, he may have a Paper of Pills, or a black Potion, thrown down his Throat. (226)

Even while in the midst of more serious or sustained endeavours, writers throughout the period proffer pleasure-seeking, theatre-going, and sight-seeing readers the linguistic and textual parallel of London's "Reigning Diversions." In each instance, diversion brazenly disrupts the readerly experience and moves away from what is typically conceived of as mimesis. But as this study has sought to demonstrate, disruption ironically facilitates the experience of readers by providing the "time-outs" necessary to forestall boredom and prevent the tedium that ensues when reading begins to feel like work. Natural philosophers and scientists document divisions in the plenum of nature through abrupt changes in typography. Comedians break the dramatic frame by having on-stage characters engage the off-stage audience in debate. Clergymen and preachers lighten the gravity of their published sermons by intermittently asking apology for digressions from their scriptural text. Poets with epic pretensions elevate their subject while entertaining readers through obviously exaggerated tropes, figures, and similitudes. Journalists and topographers parody perambulatory pro-gress through the many side-steps in their rambling accounts of urban life. Satirists punctuate their printed texts with dashes and asterisks that pro-vocatively conceal the identities of their victims. Tragedians pursue pathos through metaphors that are as laboured as the heroic conflict between love and duty. Moral philosophers and metaphysicians qualify their theories into quiddities by begging frequent leave "to digress a little." Historians suggest the antiquity of their matter by interspersing 𝕲𝖔𝖙𝖍𝖎𝖈 𝖙𝖞𝖕𝖊 through-out their protracted annals. Party-writers and pamphleteers attempt to add authority to their hack-writing by publishing it with dedications, prefaces, and appendices. Travel writers describe the novelty, rarity, and curiosity of their journeys through the singularity of their rhetoric. Literary critics stray from objectivity, giving their own critical opinions "by way of digression." And, as Chapter 4 has argued, novelists like Henry Fielding avail of these and other devices in the hopes of diverting readers away from competing entertainments and, consequently, persuading them to continue reading. It was the self-consciousness with which Fielding engaged his pleasure-seeking readers that helped elevate the "new Species of Writing" to generic prominence and, eventually, prestige. By the middle of the eighteenth century, the novel had subsumed or supplanted many of the other genres that had already exploited the reciprocity between cultural and discursive diversion. Establishing itself as a legitimate genre only after the most important developments in the commercialization of leisure and the coming of age of literary self-consciousness, the novel represents the end of the rhetoric of diversion – both the formal exemplification of its various persuasive strategies and its historical *non plus ultra*.

### Shandean digression and the *ends* of diversion

If the rhetoric of diversion helps to account for the emergence of the novel in the first half of the eighteenth century as a dominant "mode of entertainment" and as *the* modern literary genre, the development of the novel over the second half of the eighteenth century helps to explain what happens to diversionary rhetoric after the age of Swift, Pope, and Fielding. By the 1750s and 1760s, the novel had assimilated "pantomimic poetics," instances of "teratological textuality," and London's digressive "*circle of Varieties*" into the "telling" and "showing" of its narrative, becoming, in the words of Thomas Keymer, "the chosen medium of Swift's 'freshest moderns.'"[1] Meanwhile, other important changes were taking place in English culture – changes that in many ways diminished the role of material pleasure in literature and brought about an end to the paradigm that I have been analysing. This study cuts off at 1760 and limits itself roughly to the formative period in the commercialization of leisure because, as I explained in the Introduction, I wish to focus on a cultural context in which diversion had yet to be widely accepted or fully institutionalized and, in turn, in which it provoked the most considerable amount of anxiety and the most extensive commentary. According to James Raven, literature had become "a major fashion business" by the middle of the eighteenth century.[2] As the preceding chapters have suggested, this was not least because authors in the first half of the century learned how to cater through their discursive devices to broader fashions in the commercial public sphere. But there are also sound philosophical and aesthetic reasons for leaving the nature and purpose of later eighteenth-century diversion to another study with a different focus.³ The year 1759 saw the publication of several important works that altered in a variety of ways the relationship between individual writers and their audience of individual readers. Adam Smith outlined a rational model of sympathy in the first edition of *The Theory of Moral Sentiments*, an ethical examen that encouraged writers to govern the interior self before attempting to reform the reading public. Alexander Gerard put into print his prize-winning *Essay on Taste*, Edward Young published his influential *Conjectures on Original Composition*, and Edmund Burke added an "Introduction on Taste" to the second edition of *A Philosophical Enquiry into the Origins of Our Ideas of the Sublime and Beautiful* (1st edn. 1757), three treatises that questioned the value of Addisonian novelty as a source of aesthetic pleasure, stressing instead the transcendent emotional potential of the beautiful and subli-mely great.⁴ Finally, the year 1759 also witnessed the publication of three seminal novels of "ideas" that emphasized the sensible and intellectual over the commercial: Voltaire's *Candide: or, Optimism*, Samuel Johnson's *The Prince of Abissinia* ("The History of Rasselas"), and, most significantly, Laurence Sterne's *The Life and Opinions of Tristram Shandy, Gentleman*.

Being that it employs self-consciously most of the linguistic and textual devices that previous chapters have discussed, *Tristram Shandy* (1759–67) is conspicuous by its absence from this study of diversion and digression. After all, Sterne is the eighteenth century's most famous digresser, and his profoundly digressive novel is eloquent in its defence of writing that deviates from what his narrator calls "a tolerable straight line" (6.40.570). Throughout the narrative, Tristram is made to express a conventional anxiety that the digressiveness of his work might render it "trifling in its nature, or tedious in its telling" (1.6.9). Yet he attempts to forestall criticism by representing his "Life and Opinions" as an "entertainment" and con-textualizing his digressive wit in terms that seem to recall the rhetoric of diversion (2.2.96). Like Dunton, Tristram resolves "not to be in a hurry," proposing "to go on leisurely" and digress whenever necessary so as to treat the "many views and prospects" that solicit his "eye" (1.14.41–42). Like Swift, he suggests that digression "brings in variety, and forbids the appetite to fail" (1.22.81). Like D'Urfey, he encourages readers to stare blankly at the "breaks and gaps" in his narrative, acknowledging wryly that his "stars" or "* *" do little to illuminate the "darkest passages" (6.33.558). And like Cibber, he argues that his digressions on "HOBBY-HORSES" serve the same purpose in his narrative as do "a dance, a song, or a concerto between the acts" on the London stage (2.8.120). Finally, like Fielding, Tristram describes the artful management of his narrative as "good cookery," and claims that he has incorporated digressions primarily "for the advantage of the reader" (1.22.81). Although Tristram boasts that he will not confine his writing "to any man's rules that ever lived" (1.4.5), Sterne himself appears to have followed his digressive predecessors in satirizing "a vicious taste . . . of reading straight forwards" (1.20.65).

Nonetheless, I have relegated Shandean digression to a brief coda in this book out of a suspicion that, while Sterne certainly intends to divert his readers, he does so for different reasons and to a different end than do most of the authors discussed in my previous chapters on cultural and discursive diversion. Sterne is in no obvious way interested in diversion as such because, during what he characterizes as "this age of levity" (1.2.2), he does not need to be. By the time he publishes the first two volumes of *Tristram Shandy* in the winter of 1759–60, the new commercial diversions had become a much more acceptable feature of English culture, and the novel had become one of the most pervasive genres of English literature. As Keymer observes, "the fashionable prominence of the 'new species of writing' over the previous twenty years made it unnecessary for Sterne to flag his entitlement with the genre."[5] Sterne was thus able to direct his attention elsewhere. He uses extravagant wit to expose the difficulty of translating genuine emotion into verbal language.[6] He substitutes inadequate words with dashes and asterisks which place a new value on fragmentary discourse and discover sublimity in print.[7] He narrativizes Lockean psychology by foregrounding digressions that are "owing, entirely . . . to the succession of our ideas" (3.18.222). And he employs a literary self-consciousness that is actually about the affective *self*. *Tristram Shandy* is not the end point of the tradition I have been tracing, but the beginning of a distinct tradition that views digression as a device through which to withdraw from the proto-capitalist public sphere and pursue a more rarefied form of pleasure in intellectual play and, especially, fellow-feeling. Sterne's novel heralds a cultural and literary shift in which digressions become "subjective" rather than "objective" phenomena – the formal embodiment of a new private sphere where introspective writers communicate their thoughts and emotions to sympathetic readers.[8] "True *Shandeism*," writes Sterne's narrator, "opens the heart and lungs, and like all those affections which partake of its nature, it forces the blood and other vital fluids of the body to run freely thro' its channels, and makes the wheel of life run long and cheerfully round" (4.32.401). Tristram digresses from a long-deferred (and nearly aborted) account of his own birth in order to relate an anecdote about Uncle Toby's mercy towards a troublesome fly, explaining that the gesture "instantly set my whole frame into one vibration of most pleasurable sensation," and suggesting further that it might do the same for his readers: "☞ This is to serve for parents and governors instead of a whole volume upon the subject" (2.12.130–31). Instead of unbending the minds of individual readers, Shandean digression cultivates their sensibility and gives occasion to "universal good-will" (131). For Sterne, digressive wit is not therefore analogous to the "Reigning Diversions of the Town," but is, as he poignantly puts it, "the life, the soul of reading" (1.22.81).

Sterne resists his predecessors' tendency to reduce digressive wit to a marketable commodity, and his self-conscious asides often parody the commercialism implicit in what I have theorized as the rhetoric of diversion. For instance, in his "chapter upon chapters" he pokes fun at Fielding's chapter on the same topic, distinguishing his narrative technique from that of earlier writers who insist upon the practical purpose of their linguistic and textual disruptions:

> Is not this ten times better than to set out dogmatically with a sententious parade of wisdom, and telling the world a story of a roasted horse—that chapters relieve the mind—that they assist—or impose upon the imagination—and that in a work of this dramatic cast they are as necessary as the shifting of scenes—with fifty other cold conceits, enough to extinguish the fire which roasted him. (4.10.337)

The cold conceits to which Sterne refers are, of course, those that artificially compare digression to diversion and that attempt to vindicate intrusion, obstruction, and interruption through the language of contemporary amusement. Tristram calls his meta-chapter "the best chapter in my whole book," but his tongue-in-cheek assertion that its readers will be "full as well employed, as in picking straws," reveals what Sterne views as the dullness of any writing that conceptualizes itself in terms of "work time" and "leisure time" (338). By the 1760s, the devices associated with the rhetoric of diversion had grown hackneyed and stale, obliging Sterne to explore new ways of gratifying his "gentle" readers and rationalizing his penchant for "bastardly digression" (8.1.655). In his digression in praise of digressions, Sterne conceives of digression not as a diversion or a "turning aside," but as an integral and organic part of his whimsical narrator's story. "[T]ho' my digressions are all fair," writes Tristram, "and that I fly off from what I am about, as far and as often too as any writer in *Great-Britain*; yet I constantly take care to order affairs so, that my main business does not stand still in my absence." This "master-stroke of digressive skill," he adds, is "an excellence seldom looked for, or expected indeed, in a digression" (1.22.80). Sterne's claim that his work is "of a species by itself" (as distinct from the "new species") is sincere in that he emphasizes the inseparability of digression from the straight-and-narrow of discourse, challenging the assumption of his predecessors that the "two contrary motions" are "at variance" (81). *Tristram Shandy* reconciles these motions in order to reflect the inextricable web of thoughts and emotions that vie for attention in day-to-day life:

> I have constructed the main work and the adventitious parts of it with such intersections, and have so complicated and involved the digressive and progressive movements, one wheel within another, that the whole machine, in general, has been kept-a-going;—and, what's more, it shall be kept a-going these forty years, if it pleases the fountain of health to bless me so long with life and good spirits. (81–82)

Tristram's narrative wheels echo the sentimental "wheel of life" that Sterne associates with "True *Shandeism*," and the parallel metaphor illustrates the fundamental difference between Shandean digression and the rhetoric of diversion. In *Tristram Shandy*, digression is not diversion because it can no more be set apart from narrative than can the heart and mind be separated from the "small accidents" that are constitutive of an individual "self" (3.8.196).

Overlooking the mid-century transition from a rhetoric of diversion to a rhetoric of "sentiment" or "selfhood," scholars have anachronistically read the digressiveness of earlier writers through developments that begin to take place only after the commercialization of leisure and the coming of age of literary self-consciousness. Indeed, the regularity with which authors like Swift, Cibber, and Fielding have been identified as a "proto-Shandean" suggests that the massive achievement of Sterne has distorted subsequent interpretations of late seventeenth- and early eighteenth-century English literature.[9] This perhaps helps to explain the critical disposition to "intellectualize" digressive wit, seeing the self, the sublime, or the Shandean in devices that were initially intended to simulate the experience of commercial entertainment. The editor of the 1762 reprint of Dunton's *A Voyage Round the World* attempts to capitalize on the success of *Tristram Shandy*, proclaiming "that *Shandeism* (or something very like it) had an existence in this kingdom long before a late well-known publication," and assuring readers that both works are "chiefly calculated" for "amusement and entertainment." However, he also warns that the nature of entertainment has changed in the seventy or so years between Dunton and Sterne, conceding that *The Life, Travels, and Adventures of Christopher Wagstaff* might not succeed "in an age of more refined taste."[10] In a strained effort to market his reprint to "the polite world" (IV), appealing to audiences who had just been moved by the episode at Le Fever's deathbed in Volume 6 of *Tristram Shandy*, the editor extracts from Dunton's *Voyage* matter conducive to pathos, retitling the author's grave reflections on life and death, for instance, "*An excellent sentimental chapter*" (48) and "*More sentiments, or something like it*" (51).[11] Moreover, the editor explains that he has simplified Dunton's original language, normalized his typography, and "expunged a considerable deal of trifling and insignificant matter" (XII). He even admits that he has "modernized" Dunton's diverting description of a London "*Puppet-shew*" (XIV). The opening chapter of the reprint is actually interpolated "By the Editor," and contains a list of "*definitions and rules, &c.*" intended to gloss some of Dunton's idiosyncratic (and, by now, outmoded) devices (1). A "—— or long *dash*," the editor observes, is "chiefly designed to relieve the breath of the reader" (2). A "parenthesis" is the insertion of sentences "which are nothing at all to the purpose" (2). And "half a dozen lines of *asterisks*, as * * *" denote that "an author's meaning is not be understood" (3). While the editor's glossary provides a belated summary of what I have classified as "diversionary rhetoric," the fact that he feels it necessary to account for the form and function of such disruptive devices insinuates that Sterne is appealing to an audience with a rather different taste than were Dunton and the other authors discussed in this book. In restoring these devices to their original cultural context, in the recreations of a voluptuous society as opposed to the lucubrations of a self-conscious mind, I hope I have restored as well some of the pleasure with which literature in the age of Swift, Pope, and Fielding was first read.

This age can be a difficult sell for modern readers, many of whom are easily exasperated by discursive devices that play the wag with their expectations and refuse to grant them an easy read. After all, in the twenty-first century, as in the eighteenth century, reading is conceived of as a leisure activity that is supposed to provide relief from any kind of work. Yet because they insistently thrust themselves into view and threaten to block access to traditional literary meaning, readers have always had to acknowledge, sometimes grudgingly, the *fact* of devices like false, abusive, or catachrestic wit, textual and typographical play, and, of course, digression. This book has proposed a new way of understanding the *function* of such devices. As soon as readers are made aware that writers disrupt their reading experience only so that it will be more pleasurable and that intrusion, obstruction, and interruption exist mainly *for their sake*, they will be inclined not only to continue reading, but to begin revelling in a body of literature that entertains and engages in the same way as did the "Reigning Diversions of the Town." Filling an ellipsis in most previous treatments of English leisure and literature, *The Rhetoric of Diversion* describes both why writers of the period employed diversionary rhetoric and how readers of any period might enjoy it. It is therefore appropriate that I close this study of amusement with the words with which James Ralph opens his endeavour to make an amusement out of study: "I hope my Animadversions upon all polite Entertainments, will be allow'd more agreeably just, if not deeply Learned" (xvii).

*FINIS.*

# Notes

## "Unbending the mind": introduction by way of diversion

1. J.H. Plumb, *The Commercialisation of Leisure in Eighteenth-Century England* (Reading: University of Reading, 1973), 1. Plumb's influential essay was reprinted in *The Birth of a Consumer Society: The Commercialization of Eighteenth-Century England*, eds. Neil McKendrick, John Brewer, and J.H. Plumb (Bloomington: Indiana University Press, 1982), 265–85. In the Introduction to this volume, Neil McKendrick describes the "*development*" of a consumer society during the late seventeenth and eighteenth centuries, while emphasizing a "sharp break in trend between Stuart England and Georgian England" (5).

2. Lawrence E. Klein, *Shaftesbury and the Culture of Politeness: Moral Discourse and Cultural Politics in Early Eighteenth-Century England* (Cambridge: Cambridge University Press, 1994); Harold Love, *Scribal Publication in Seventeenth-Century England* (Oxford: Clarendon Press, 1993); Brean S. Hammond, *Professional Imaginative Writing in England, 1670–1740: "Hackney for Bread"* (Oxford: Clarendon Press, 1997); J. Paul Hunter, *Before Novels: The Cultural Contexts of Eighteenth-Century English Fiction* (New York: W.W. Norton & Company, 1990); Erin Mackie, *Market à la Mode: Fashion, Commodity, and Gender in* The Tatler *and* The Spectator (Baltimore: Johns Hopkins University Press, 1997); William B. Warner, *Licensing Entertainment: The Elevation of Novel Reading in Britain, 1684–1750* (Berkeley: University of California Press, 1998); John O'Brien, *Harlequin Britain: Pantomime and Entertainment, 1690–1760* (Baltimore: Johns Hopkins University Press, 2004); and Patricia Meyer Spacks, *Boredom: The Literary History of a State of Mind* (Chicago: University of Chicago Press, 1995).

3. John Brewer examines at length the interrelated features of this cultural revolution in *The Pleasures of the Imagination: English Culture in the Eighteenth Century* (London: HarperCollins, 1997).

4. Wayne C. Booth, "The Self-Conscious Narrator in Comic Fiction before *Tristram Shandy*," *PMLA* 67 (1952): 163–85. Although initially an attempt to correct "critical misconceptions" about *Tristram Shandy*, Booth's classic essay

ended up provoking serious scholarly interest in literary self-consciousness through its demonstration of how and why Sterne and his seventeenth- and eighteenth-century precursors employed reflexive and digressive devices "to salvage order out of seeming chaos" (164).

5. Laurence Sterne, *The Life and Opinions of Tristram Shandy, Gentleman, The Text*, 2 vols., ed. Melvyn and Joan New (Gainesville: University of Florida Press, 1978), 1.22.81. For a discussion of the connection between Dunton and Sterne, see René Bosch, *Labyrinth of Digressions: Tristram Shandy as Perceived and Influenced by Sterne's Early Imitators*, trans. Piet Verhoeff (Amsterdam: Rodopi, 2007), esp. 58–61.

6. *The Life, Travels, and Adventures of Christopher Wagstaff, Gentleman, Grandfather to Tristram Shandy*, 2 vols. (London, 1762), 1.x–xiv.

7. See, in particular, the "Third Booke" of George Puttenham's *The Arte of English Poesie* (London, 1589; rpt. Menston: Scolar Press, 1968), 114, 140–41. For a discussion of the "expressive function of rhetorical figures" in the sixteenth and seventeenth centuries, see Brian Vickers, *In Defence of Rhetoric* (Oxford: Clarendon Press, 1988), 294–339. Also see John Lennard, *But I Digress: The Exploitation of Parenthesis in English Printed Verse* (Oxford: Clarendon Press, 1991).

8. See, among other treatments of the "tolerability" of rhetorical disorder in early modern English literature: William C. Carroll, *The Great Feast of Language in* Love's Labour's Lost (Princeton: Princeton University Press, 1976); Eugene Korkowski, "Genre and Satiric Strategy in Burton's *Anatomy of Melancholy*," *Genre* 8 (1975): 74–87; and Anne Cotterill, *Digressive Voices in Early Modern English Literature* (Oxford: Oxford University Press, 2004).

9. For representative examples, see Eugene Korkowski, "*Tristram Shandy*, Digression, and the Menippean Tradition," *Scholia Satyrica* 1 (1975): 3–15; and Christopher Fanning, "Small Particles of Eloquence: Sterne and the Scriblerian Text," *Modern Philology* 100.3 (2003): 360–92.

10. For a systematic discussion of changing attitudes towards language during the period, and especially of the shift from the informal, colloquial, and "oral" rhetoric of the early eighteenth century to the precise, studied, and "written" rhetoric of the late eighteenth century, see Carey McIntosh, *The Evolution of English Prose, 1700–1800: Style, Politeness, and Print Culture* (Cambridge: Cambridge University Press, 1998).

11. Wayne C. Booth, *The Rhetoric of Fiction*, 2nd edn. (Chicago: University of Chicago Press, 1983), 227–28. Most treatments of self-consciousness in eighteenth-century literature either revise or build upon the observations made by Booth. See, for example, Sheldon Sacks, *Fiction and the Shape of Belief: A Study of Henry Fielding, with Glances at Swift, Johnson, and Richardson* (Berkeley: University of California Press, 1966); Robert Alter,

*Partial Magic: The Novel as a Self-Conscious Genre* (Berkeley: University of California Press, 1975); and Thomas Keymer, *Sterne, the Moderns and the Novel* (New York: Oxford University Press, 2002).

12. Christina Lupton, *Knowing Books: The Consciousness of Mediation in Eighteenth-Century Britain* (Philadelphia: University of Pennsylvania Press, 2012), VII. As Lupton points out, this traditional critical approach to self-consciousness is actually Marxist in its assumption that an author who reflects upon representation or the textual production of literature "works against its commercial operation." In contrast, Lupton explores the ways in which "writers elucidating the way literature is made might also conform to a market in entertainment." Reflexive writing, she claims, was among "the most fashionable commodities of all" (13).

13. Garry Sherbert, *Menippean Satire and the Poetics of Wit: Ideologies of Self-Consciousness in Dunton, D'Urfey, and Sterne* (New York: Peter Lang, 1996), 29; Christopher Flint, *The Appearance of Print in Eighteenth-Century Fiction* (Cambridge: Cambridge University Press, 2011), 115–17; and J. Paul Hunter, *Occasional Form: Henry Fielding and the Chains of Circumstance* (Baltimore: Johns Hopkins University Press, 1975), 69.

14. Thomas Brown, *Amusements Serious and Comical, The Works of Mr. Thomas Brown, Serious and Comical*, 4 vols., 5th edn. (London, 1719–20), 3.44; John Dunton, *A Voyage Round the World: or, A Pocket Library* (London, 1691), 1.126, 2.7; Jonathan Swift, *A Tale of a Tub*, A Tale of a Tub *and Other Works*, ed. Marcus Walsh (Cambridge: Cambridge University Press, 2010), 85; Richard Blackmore, *An Essay Upon Wit*, Essays Upon Several Subjects (London, 1716), 201; Thomas D'Urfey (Gabriel John, pseud.), *An Essay Towards the Theory of the Intelligible World. Intuitively Considered. Designed for Forty-Nine Parts. Part III. Consisting of a Preface, a Post-script, and a Little Something Between* (London, 1708), 135, 162; Charles Gildon, *All for the Better; or, The World Turn'd Up-Side Down* (London, 1720), n.p.; Alexander Pope, *Peri Bathous: or, Martinus Scriblerus, His Treatise on the Art of Sinking in Poetry*, The Prose Works of Alexander Pope, vol. 2, ed. Rosemary Cowler (Hamden: Archon Books, 1986), 7.199; Colley Cibber, *An Apology for the Life of Colley Cibber, With An Historical View of the Stage During His Own Time*, ed. B.R.S. Fone (Ann Arbor: University of Michigan Press, 1968), 281; Henry Fielding, *The History of Tom Jones, A Foundling*, ed. Fredson Bowers, intro. Martin C. Battestin (Middletown: Wesleyan University Press, 1975), 1.1.33; James Ralph (A. Primcock, pseud.), *The Touch-Stone: or, Historical, Critical, Political, Philosophical, and Theological Essays on the Reigning Diversions of the Town* (London, 1728, intro. Arthur Freeman; rpt. New York: Garland Publishing Inc., 1973), XXIV.

15. According to the *O.E.D.*, the first recorded use of *diversion* in the nominal sense occurred in 1648, while the use of the word in the verbal sense first occurred in 1600.

16. Samuel Johnson, *A Dictionary of the English Language* (London, 1755; rpt. New York: Arno Press, 1979).

17. Paul Keen, *Literature, Commerce, and the Spectacle of Modernity, 1750–1800* (Cambridge: Cambridge University Press, 2012), 23. Partially anticipating my argument about the late seventeenth and early eighteenth centuries, Keen identifies in the later eighteenth century "literary styles whose form actively embodied and, as a result, made a virtue of the instabilities and discontinuities of polite commercial society" (30).

18. Robert L. Montgomery, *Terms of Response: Language and Audience in Seventeenth and Eighteenth-Century Theory* (Pennsylvania: Pennsylvania State University Press, 1992), 49.

19. Spacks, *Boredom*, 24.

20. Terry Castle, *Masquerade and Civilization: The Carnivalesque in Eighteenth-Century English Culture and Fiction* (Stanford: Stanford University Press, 1986), 1–2.

21. O'Brien, *Harlequin Britain*, esp. 1–29.

22. Dennis Todd, *Imagining Monsters: Miscreations of the Self in Eighteenth-Century England* (Chicago: University of Chicago Press, 1995), esp. 106–78.

23. Barbara M. Benedict, *Curiosity: A Cultural History of Early Modern Inquiry* (Chicago: University of Chicago Press, 2001), esp. 1–23 and 71–117.

24. Julie Park, *The Self and It: Novel Objects in Eighteenth-Century England* (Stanford: Stanford University Press, 2010), esp. XIII–XXIX and 3–47.

25. Brian Cowan, *The Social Life of Coffee: The Emergence of the British Coffeehouse* (New Haven: Yale University Press, 2005), esp. 79–146.

26. For a discussion of the socially hybridized nature of eighteenth-century masquerade, see Dror Wahrman, *The Making of the Modern Self: Identity and Culture in Eighteenth-Century England* (New Haven: Yale University Press, 2004), esp. 157–79. Also see Gillian Russell, *Women, Sociability and Theatre in Georgian London* (Cambridge: Cambridge University Press, 2007), 38–62.

27. Jacques Derrida, "White Mythology: Metaphor in the Text of Philosophy," *New Literary History* 6 (1974): 5–74; Roland Barthes, *The Pleasure of the Text*, trans. Richard Miller (New York: Hill and Wang, 1975); Gérard Genette, *Figures of Literary Discourse*, trans. Alan Sheridan, intro. Marie-Rose Logan (New York: Columbia University Press, 1982), esp. 134–35.

28. The most compelling recent treatment of the history of reading in early modern England is Adrian Johns, *The Nature of the Book: Print and Knowledge in the Making* (Chicago: University of Chicago Press, 1998), esp.

40–48 and 380–443. Also see the essays in *The Practice and Representation of Reading in England*, ed. James Raven, Helen Small, and Naomi Tadmor (Cambridge: Cambridge University Press, 1996); and *Books and Their Readers in Eighteenth-Century England: New Essays*, ed. Isabel Rivers (Harrisburg: Continuum, 2003).

29. See Stephen Cohen's useful overview of the critical pragmatics of "Historical Formalism" in *Shakespeare and Historical Formalism*, ed. Stephen Cohen (Aldershot: Ashgate Publishing, 2007), 1–27. According to Cohen, Historical Formalism invites us "to (re)turn our attention to the 'pleasure of the text,' or literary affect, not as an end in itself but as an essential element of literature's cultural function" (14).

30. See, for example, Austin Dobson, *Eighteenth-Century Vignettes* (London: Chatto & Windus, 1892) and *Side-Walk Studies* (London: Oxford University Press, 1924); Walter Besant, *London in the Eighteenth Century* (London: A. & C. Black, 1902); Ronald Paulson, *Popular and Polite Art in the Age of Hogarth and Fielding* (Notre Dame: University of Notre Dame Press, 1979); and Pat Rogers, *Literature and Popular Culture in Eighteenth-Century England* (Sussex: Harvester Press, 1985).

31. Rogers, *Literature and Popular Culture*, 3.

32. Alexander Pope, *The Dunciad, The Twickenham Edition of the Poems of Alexander Pope*, vol. 5, ed. James Sutherland, 3rd edn. (London: Methuen, 1963), [A] 1.2. Subsequent references to *The Dunciad Variorum* of 1729 will be cited as "[A]," while those to 1743 *The Dunciad in Four Books* will be cited as "[B]."

33. Thomas Creech translates the relevant passage from Horace thus: "*Poets* wou'd *profit*, or *delight* alone, / Or join both *Praise* and *Delight* in one." *To The Pisones, on the Art of Poetry, The Odes, Satyrs, and Epistles of Horace*, 3rd edn., trans. Thomas Creech (London, 1711), 399. Predictably, the translation of the aristocratic Earl of Roscommon is more prescriptive, employing "should" instead of "wou'd": "A Poet should instruct, or please, or both." *The Odes and Satyrs of Horace, that have been done into English by the most Eminent Hands . . . With his* Art of Poetry, *By the Earl of Roscommon* (London, 1715), 197.

34. See, for example, Rogers, *Literature and Popular Culture*; Claude Rawson, *Satire and Sentiment 1660–1830: Stress Points in the English Augustan Tradition* (New Haven: Yale University Press, 1994); *Swift's Travels: Eighteenth-Century Satire and Its Legacy*, eds. Nicholas Hudson and Aaron Santesso (Cambridge: Cambridge University Press, 2008); Hugh Ormsby-Lennon, *Hey Presto! Swift and the Quacks* (Newark: University of Delaware Press, 2011); and Ashley Marshall, *The Practice of Satire in England, 1658–1770* (Baltimore: Johns Hopkins University Press, 2013), esp. 201–05.

35. Bogel observes that "the traditional approach" to satire keeps critics from investigating more subtle forms of "rhetorical activity": "not gestures of referentiality, in this case, but acts of exclusion, efforts of boundary-policing, and introductions of difference and distinction that create—rather than grow out of—an opposition between the satirist and the satiric scene or world." See *The Difference Satire Makes: Rhetoric and Reading from Jonson to Byron* (Ithaca: Cornell University Press, 2001), 12.

36. Neil McKendrick, "The Consumer Revolution in Eighteenth-Century England," *The Birth of a Consumer Society*, 9, 14–15. To a certain degree, the rhetoric of consumerism is distinct from that analysed in this book because the production of leisure required less overhead and fewer commercial networks than did, for instance, retailing. A popular entertainer like "Orator" John Henley or the posture-master Joseph Clark could have an impact on literature and culture with little more than ingenuity and a temporary venue.

37. It is at this point in history when the highest proportion of London's inhabitants were migrants. One estimate suggests that about a sixth of all people born in England would have needed to live some part of their lives in London simply to account for the capital's population growth during the seventeenth and eighteenth centuries. For a general overview of London demography and the process of urbanization, see Roy Porter, *London: A Social History* (Cambridge: Harvard University Press, 1994) and Peter Earle, *A City Full of People: Men and Women of London 1650–1750* (London: Methuen, 1994). Also see the excellent "Old Bailey Proceedings Online," authored and administered by Clive Emsley, Tim Hitchcock, and Robert Shoemaker (www.oldbaileyonline.org).

38. For a discussion of the ways in which the literature of the late seventeenth and eighteenth centuries represents the city, see: William Henry Irving, *John Gay's London, Illustrated from the Poetry of the Time* (Cambridge: Harvard University Press, 1928); Max Byrd, *London Transformed: Images of the City in the Eighteenth Century* (New Haven: Yale University Press, 1978); and the essays in *Imagining Early Modern London: Perceptions and Portrayals of the City from Stow to Strype. 1598–1720*, ed. J.F. Merritt (Cambridge: Cambridge University Press, 2001). For an analysis of how the city influences the rhetorical and generic structures of literature, see Cynthia Wall, *The Literary and Cultural Spaces of Restoration London* (Cambridge: Cambridge University Press, 1999) and Erik Bond, *Reading London: Urban Speculation and Imaginative Government in Eighteenth-Century Literature* (Columbus: Ohio State University Press, 2007).

39. McKendrick, "The Consumer Revolution," 21.

40. See Lorna H. Mui and Hoh-Cheung Mui, *Shops and Shopkeeping in Eighteenth-Century England* (Montreal: McGill-Queen's University Press, 1989), esp. 3–28.

41. Roy Porter, "Material Pleasures in the Consumer Society," *Pleasure in the Eighteenth Century*, ed. Roy Porter and Marie Mulvey Roberts (London: Macmillan Press Ltd., 1996), 19.

42. For a fascinating discussion of London and the "Topography of the Metropolitan Book Trade," see Johns, *The Nature of the Book*, 62–74.

43. For an analysis of the development of a provincial leisure industry, see Peter Borsay, *The English Urban Renaissance: Culture and Society in the Provincial Town 1660–1770* (Oxford: Oxford University Press, 1989).

44. For a treatment of the relationship between the London and provincial book trade, see: G.A. Cranfield, *The Development of the Provincial Newspaper 1700–1760* (Oxford: Clarendon Press, 1962); John Feather, *The Provincial Book Trade in Eighteenth-Century England* (Cambridge: Cambridge University Press, 1985); and John Brewer, "Authors, Publishers and the Making of Literary Culture," *The Pleasures of the Imagination*, 125–66.

45. The best treatment of the symbolic significance of the "Meridian of Grub Street" remains Pat Rogers, *Grub Street: Studies in a Subculture* (London: Methuen, 1972). Also see Johns, "Literary Life," *The Nature of the Book*, 58–186.

46. Jonathan Swift, *A Proposal for Correcting, Improving and Ascertaining the English Tongue, Parodies, Hoaxes, Mock Treatises, Polite Conversation, Directions to Servants and Other Works*, ed. Valerie Rumbold (Cambridge: Cambridge University Press, 2013), 142. Swift obviously refers to the popular genre of armchair guidebooks to London that were ubiquitous during the period – works like Ward's *The London Spy* (1698–1700), Brown's *Amusements Serious and Comical* (1700), and the anonymous *A Trip Through the Town, Containing Observations on the Humours and Manners of the Age* (1735). See Hugh Ormsby-Lennon, "'Trips, Spies, Amusements' and the Apogee of the Public Sphere," *Reading Swift: Papers from the Fourth Münster Symposium on Jonathan Swift*, ed. Hermann J. Real and Helgard Stöver-Leidig (Munich: Wilhelm Fink Verlag, 1998), 177–224.

47. "Introduction," *Walking the Streets of Eighteenth-Century London: John Gay's Trivia*, eds. Clare Brant and Susan Whyman (Oxford: Oxford University Press, 2007), 2.

48. For an extended analysis of the conventions of eighteenth-century London rambles, see Alison O'Byrne, "Walking, Rambling and Promenading in Eighteenth-Century London: A Literary and Cultural History" (Ph.D. Dissertation, University of York, 2003).

49. Benedict, *Curiosity*, 2.

50. Ralph (d. 1762) is mainly known to literary history as a political pamphleteer and an antagonist of Alexander Pope, who satirized him in *The Dunciad Variorum* (1729). But during his own day he was reasonably well regarded as a dramatist, a journalist, a notably impartial historian, and an occasional collaborator of Henry Fielding. When Fielding took over management of the Little Haymarket Theatre, he invited Ralph to be his assistant manager. Ralph owned shares in the theatre and advised Fielding on theatrical production, and, in this capacity, he was influential in setting a programme for the London stage of the 1730s. Ralph was also an ardent apologist for Grub Street. In *Sawney: An Heroic Poem* (London, 1728), he chides Pope for his ridicule of professional writers in the "*Cave of* Poverty *and* Poetry," contending that "Poverty and ill Circumstances represent an Object of Pity and Compassion, to the humane, generous, and friendly Mind," and protesting the assumption that "the want of a Dinner made a Man a Fool, or Riches and good Sence only kept company" (vii). In *The Case of Authors by Profession or Trade* (London, 1758), Ralph goes even further, audaciously suggesting that literary greatness should be determined by sales figures: "instead of censuring an Author for taking Money for his Works, we ought to esteem Those most who get most Money by them: And then *Pope*, and *Voltaire* after *his* Example, would deserve to be considered more, for what they *made* of their *Works*, than for the *Works* themselves" (6). See Helen Sard Hughes, "Fielding's Indebtedness to James Ralph," *Modern Philology* 20.1 (1922): 19–34; and Laird Okie, "James Ralph (d. 1762)," *Oxford Dictionary of National Biography* (Oxford: Oxford University Press, 2004).
51. Mackie is especially interested in the ways in which "both literature and fashion are in part shaped by the discourses of other cultural productions." See *Market à la Mode*, esp. 203–62.
52. Warner, *Licensing Entertainment*, xi.

## 1   "The *predominant* taste of the present age": diversion and the literary market

1. According to Ralph's twentieth-century editor, Arthur Freeman, *The Touch-Stone* "is by no means as zany as its title suggests." It is instead "a rather sober examination of playgoing habits and other forms of entertainment, the Prynne-Collier-Bedford-Law axis, a serious suggestion to revive religious drama for playing on Sundays and holidays, and critiques of audience behaviour, practices of dancing, masquerades, puppet shows, and cockfighting, 'antient' athletic sports, and even the pulpit performance of 'Orator' John Henley" (6). In assigning a solely earnest purpose to a pseudonymous work, Freeman falls short of recognizing that much of what

Ralph has Primcock propose is ironic. Moreover, he neglects the fact that *The Touch-Stone* devotes as much attention to the important cultural functions of diversion as to its perceived dangers. Finally, he fails fully to appreciate the subtlety of Ralph's approach, which reproduces the pleasure of the "Reigning Diversions," even while seeming to proscribe them.

2. Musicologist Lowell Lindgren has recently questioned the traditional attribution of *The Touch-Stone* to James Ralph, arguing, on the grounds of the pseudonymous author's specialist knowledge of contemporary opera, that the work was more likely written by the critic, translator, and professed lover of "Italian music," Robert Samber, who anticipates several of A. Primcock's observations about opera in *Eunuchism Display'd* (1718). The problem with this attribution, however, is that it cannot sufficiently account for Primcock's observations regarding the rest of London's "Reigning Diversions," to say nothing of its so-called Mushroom Amusements (237). Giving inordinate treatment to Essay I, "Of Musick," Lindgren largely ignores *The Touch-Stone*'s six other essays on a wide range of subjects in which Samber seems not to have shown any interest. Ralph, on the other hand, frequently addresses the "copious List of Town Diversions" in his works of the 1730s and 1740s, particularly in the ballad opera *The Fashionable Lady* (1730) and in his contributions to *The Champion* (1739–44). Moreover, Lindgren makes the same mistake that Freeman and other earlier critics made in taking *The Touch-Stone* too seriously, reading the work's hyperbolic recommendations for reform as though they were proposed by Jeremy Collier, instead of by an author lineally descended from "the Family of the Cocks" (x). Lindren goes so far as to look for parallels between the life and career of Robert Samber and that of "A. Primcock," overlooking the obvious irony of the biographical details traced in the "The Preface: or, Introduction." For these reasons, I retain the attribution of *The Touch-Stone* to James Ralph, "a Person of some Taste and some Quality." See Lowell Lindgren, "Another Critic Named Samber, Whose 'Particular Historical Significance Has Gone Almost Entirely Unnoticed,'" *Festa Musicologica*, ed. Thomas J. Mathiesen and Benito V. Rivero (Stuyvesant, NY: Pendragon Press, 1995), 407–34.

3. See Hammond, *Professional Imaginative Writing in England, 1670–1740*, 278–79.

4. For analysis of the commercialization of leisure and its implication in the ideology of England's broader consumer revolution, see the essays in: *The Birth of a Consumer Society; Consumption and the World of Goods*, ed. John Brewer and Roy Porter (London: Routledge, 1993); *The Consumption of Culture 1600–1800: Image, Object, Text*, ed. John Brewer and Ann Bermingham (London: Routledge, 1995); and Porter and Roberts (eds.), *Pleasure in the Eighteenth Century*.

5. For discussion of the relationship between leisure and the changing conceptions of time in pre- and early-industrial Britain, see, in particular: Keith Thomas, "Work and Leisure in Pre-Industrial Society," *Past and Present* 29 (1964): 50–66; and E.P. Thompson, "Time, Work-Discipline, and Industrial Capitalism," *Customs in Common: Studies in Traditional Popular Culture* (New York: The New Press, 1991), 353–403.

6. Christopher R. Miller makes a similar point when discussing Robinson Crusoe's "Strange Surprizing Adventures": "What usually gets overlooked in this phrase is the peculiar role of the 'surprizing': this modifier does not function merely as a synonym for 'strange' but rather names its affective register—the emotional response activated by the extraordinary, the inexplicable, or the sudden" (*Surprise: The Poetics of the Unexpected from Milton to Austen* [Ithaca: Cornell University Press, 2015], 63).

7. See "*The Book of Sports*, with Remarks in Vindication of King Charles the First," *A Collection of Choice, Scarce, and Valuable Tracts*, ed. John Dunton (London, 1721), A3r–A8v. Though Dunton's edition seems to be a reprint of a 1709 edition of *The Book of Sports* (sold by J. Baker), there is obviously considerable irony in the fact that this declaration, formerly published "by Royal Authority," was here put back into print by one of the eighteenth century's most enterprising commercial publishers.

8. Leah S. Marcus, *The Politics of Mirth: Jonson, Herrick, Milton, Marvell, and the Defense of Old Holiday Pastimes* (Chicago: University of Chicago Press, 1986), 3.

9. John Dryden, *Satires of Decimus Junius Juvenalis* and *Aulus Persius Flaccus, The Works of John Dryden*, vol. 4, ed. A.B. Chambers, William Frost, and Vinton Dearing (Berkeley: University of California Press, 1974), 30.

10. Cotterill, *Digressive Voices in Early Modern English Literature*, 247, 251.

11. Joseph Addison, *The Free-holder, The Works of the Right Honourable Joseph Addison, Esq.*, 4 vols. (London, 1721), 4.486–87.

12. O'Brien, *Harlequin Britain*, 101, 217.

13. The idealization of coffeehouse culture in *The Tatler* and *The Spectator* is central to Jürgen Habermas's discussion of the emergence of a "bourgeois public sphere" in post-Restoration England. See *The Structural Transformation of the Public Sphere: An Inquiry into a Category of Bourgeois Society*, trans. Thomas Burger with Frederick Lawrence (Cambridge: MIT Press, 1989), esp. 42–43.

14. Henry Fielding, *An Enquiry into the Causes of the Late Increase of Robbers and Related Writings*, ed. Malvin R. Zirker (Middletown: Wesleyan University Press, 1988), 77.

15. Every pastime advocated in *The Book of Sports* is of a "country kind." James I and Charles I only mention urban entertainments, such as "Bear and Bull-

baitings" and "Playing at *Cards*," to prohibit them. For discussion of the resilience of more traditional pastimes during the eighteenth century, see Robert W. Malcolmson, *Popular Recreations in English Society: 1700–1850* (Cambridge: Cambridge University Press, 1973); and Emma Griffin, *England's Revelry: A History of Popular Sports and Pastimes, 1660–1830* (New York: Oxford University Press, 2005).

16. These entrepreneurs operated primarily in London, and, according to Pat Rogers, they were substantially responsible for turning the city into "an unprecedented gallery of delights" (*Literature and Popular Culture*, 10–11).

17. Brewer, "'The Most Polite Age and the Most Vicious': Attitudes towards Culture as a Commodity, 1660–1800," *The Consumption of Culture 1600–1800*, 346.

18. By the middle of the eighteenth century, according to George Winchester Stone Jr., "the total impact of an evening in the theatre was derived from a varied 'whole show,' consisting of a *Prologue*, a full five act *Mainpiece*, an *Epilogue*, some form of *theatrical dance* (usually narrative and comic), a two-act *Afterpiece*, a good deal of popular *music*, and during the benefit season, a number of *specialty acts*." See the introduction to *The London Stage*, Part IV: 1747–1776, 2 vols. (Carbondale: Southern Illinois University Press, 1962), esp. XXIV. For discussion of the broad theatrical implications of this move to a "whole show," see the essays in *Prologues, Epilogues, Curtain-Raisers, and Afterpieces: The Rest of the Eighteenth-Century London Stage*, ed. Daniel J. Ennis and Judith Bailey Slagle (Newark: University of Delaware Press, 2007).

19. See George Speaight, *The History of the English Puppet Theatre*, 2nd edn. (Carbondale: Southern Illinois University Press, 1990), esp. 92–175.

20. For eighteenth-century bear- and bull-baiting, see William B. Boulton, *The Amusements of Old London*, 2 vols. (London, 1901; rpt. New York: Benjamin Blom, 1969), esp. 1.1–17.

21. Simon During, *Modern Enchantments: The Cultural Power of Secular Magic* (Cambridge: Harvard University Press, 2002), 74–85.

22. *The Daily Post* No. 2302 (February 8, 1727).

23. In an "unabashedly quantitative" essay, Robert D. Hume questions scholarly assumptions about culture as a commodity by demonstrating how few people could actually have afforded a seat at the theatre or a five-shilling book. Although Hume's primary concern is with "elite culture," his analysis of the actual value (and buying power) of money is an important reminder that even the two shillings, one shilling, and sixpence charged by Fawkes would have been prohibitively expensive for a high percentage of the London population in the early eighteenth century. See "The Economics of Culture in London, 1660–1740," *Huntington Library Quarterly* 69.4 (2006): 487–533.

24. *The Daily Post* No. 1361 (February 6, 1724).

25. Brewer, "Attitudes towards Culture as a Commodity, 1660–1800," 346. Also see Peter M. Briggs, "'News from the Little World' A Critical Glance at Eighteenth-Century British Advertising," *Studies in Eighteenth-Century Culture* 23 (1994): 29–45.

26. See Michael Harris, *London Newspapers in the Age of Walpole: A Study in the Origins of the Modern English Press* (Rutherford: Fairleigh Dickinson Press, 1987), esp. 176–77.

27. *The Daily Post* No. 1317 (December 17, 1723).

28. Barbara M. Benedict argues that it was during the eighteenth century that "advertising as announcement glided into advertisement as persuasion." She notes, in particular, that newspaper ads for commercial goods and services took the form of "promotion in print." See "Wants and Goods: Advertisement and Desire in Haywood and Defoe," *Studies in Eighteenth-Century Culture* 33 (2004): 221–53. For an interesting discussion of "advertising rhetoric," see Benedict, "Encounters with the Object: Advertisements, Time, and Literary Discourse in the Early Eighteenth-Century Thing-Poem," *Eighteenth-Century Studies* 40.2 (2007): 193–207.

29. *The Daily Post* No. 1331 (January 2, 1724).

30. *The Weekly Journal: or, Saturday's Post* No. 272 (January 11, 1724). The advertisement alludes to *Jupiter and Europa: or, The Intrigues of Harlequin* and *The Necromancer: or, Harlequin Doctor Faustus*, both of which were mounted in 1723 by John Rich at Lincoln's Inn Fields.

31. *Pasquin* No. 105 (February 4, 1724).

32. *The Daily Courant* No. 2845 (December 5, 1710).

33. C.R. (pseud.), *The Danger of Masquerades and Raree-Shows, or the Complaints of the Stage Against Masquerades, Opera's, Assemblies, Balls, Puppet-shows, Bear-gardens, Cock-fights, Wrestling, Posture-makers, Cudgel-playing, Foot-ball, Rope-dancing, Merry-makings, and several other irrational Entertainments, as being the Ground and Occasion of the late Decay of Wit in the Island of Great-Britain* (London, 1718; rpt. New York: Garland Publishing Inc., 1974), 10.

34. *A Letter to My Lord ******* On The Present Diversions of the Town. With The True Reason of the Decay of our Dramatic Entertainments* (London, 1725; rpt. New York: Garland Publishing Inc., 1974), 10–11.

35. For an account of Pinkethman's fairground ventures, see Sybil Rosenfeld, *The Theatre of the London Fairs in the 18th Century* (Cambridge: Cambridge University Press, 1960), esp. 9–29.

36. *The Fair in an Uproar: or, The Dancing-Doggs. As They Perform in Mr. Pinkeman's New Opera in Bartholomew Fair* (London, [1707]). The only extant copy (according to the ESTC) of this engraved satire on the contemporary lust for novelty in amusement is found in the Newberry Library, Chicago, in one of six scrapbooks of broadsides compiled and

dated by the annalist and book collector Narcissus Luttrell between approximately 1678 and 1730 (Case 6A 159 No. 65). Luttrell dates the broadside August 30, 1707, which means it would have been published just after the close the fair, while Pinkethman's dancing dogs would still have been the talk of the town. The broadside was advertised in *Post Boy* No. 1917 (August 28–30, 1707): "This day is Published, The Fair in an Uproar, or a Prologue to the Dancing-Dogs. With their Figures exactly Engrav'd on Copper-Plates, as they perform in Pinkeman's Opera in Bartholomew Fair."

37. John Downes, *Roscius Anglicanus*, ed. Judith Milhous and Robert D. Hume (London: Society for Theatre Research, 1987), 108.

38. *Fog's Weekly Journal* No. 18 (January 25, 1729).

39. *The Tatler* No. 130 (February 4–7, 1710).

40. *The Daily Advertiser* No. 181 (September 1, 1731). *The Daily Post*, a newspaper that regularly carried puffs for Fawkes's shows, reports on March 29, 1731, that "The famous Mr. Fawkes, who had not his Equal in this or any other Kingdom in Performances by Dexterity of Hand, was buried last Night in a Vault in St. Martin's Church; and we hear died worth about Ten Thousand Pounds."

41. Brewer, "Attitudes towards Culture as a Commodity, 1660–1800," 346. For discussion of the conflict between *utile* and *dulce* in amusements at the popular end of the market, see Lance Bertelsen, "Popular Entertainment and Instruction, Literary and Dramatic: Chapbooks, Advice Books, Almanacs, Ballads, Farces, Pantomimes, Prints and Shows," *The Cambridge History of English Literature, 1660–1780*, ed. John Richetti (Cambridge: Cambridge University Press, 2005), 61–86.

42. John Rich, "Dedication," *The Rape of Proserpine: With the Birth and Adventures of Harlequin* (London, 1727), vi.

43. See Shirley Strum Kenny, "Theatre, Related Arts, and the Profit Motive: An Overview," *British Theatre and the Other Arts, 1660–1800*, ed. Shirley Strum Kenny (Toronto: Associated University Presses, 1984), 15–38.

44. *The Tricks of the Town Laid Open: or, A Companion for Country Gentlemen, Eighteenth-Century Diversions*, ed. Ralph Straus (London: Chapman and Hall, 1927), 47.

45. Edward Muir, *Ritual in Early Modern Europe* (Cambridge: Cambridge University Press, 1997), 56.

46. For representative examples of religious attacks on the pernicious social and spiritual consequences of diversion, see Jeremy Collier's *A Short View of the Immorality and Profaneness of the English Stage* (London, 1698; rpt. Menston: Scolar Press, 1971), Arthur Bedford's *A Serious Remonstrance in Behalf of the Christian Religion* (London, 1719; rpt. New York: Garland Publishing Inc., 1974), and William Law's *The Absolute Unlawfulness of the Stage-*

*Entertainment* (London, 1726). I take the phrase "commerce of everyday life" from *The Commerce of Everyday Life: Selections from* The Tatler *and The* Spectator, ed. Erin Mackie (Boston: Bedford/St Martin's, 1998).

47. See Sarah Jordan, *The Anxieties of Idleness: Idleness in Eighteenth-Century British Literature and Culture* (Lewisburg: Bucknell University Press, 2003), 37–83.

48. Daniel Defoe, *The Complete English Tradesman, In Familiar Letters* (London, 1726), 126.

49. Samuel Richardson, *The Apprentice's Vade Mecum: or, Young Man's Pocket-Companion, Early Works,* ed. Alexander Petit (Cambridge: Cambridge University Press, 2012), 24. The belief that the pursuit of pleasure might turn otherwise good apprentices bad was widespread during the period. See O'Brien's discussion of "Apprentices, Entertainment and the Mass Audience" in *Harlequin Britain*, 138–80.

50. Thomas Keymer usefully observes that "verbs of distraction and disintegration recur with ominous frequency" in Richardson's pamphlet, which offers "a coherent rhetoric of civic antitheatricalism." See *Richardson's* Clarissa *and the Eighteenth-Century Reader* (Cambridge: Cambridge University Press, 1992), 142–50.

51. *The Daily Post* No. 3418 (September 2, 1730).

52. *The Daily Courant* No. 2592 (February 13, 1710).

53. *The Daily Post* No. 1860 (September 10, 1725).

54. Eliza Haywood, *The Female Spectator*, 4 vols. (London, 1744–46), 3.142.

55. It is, perhaps, ironic that some of the most vocal critics of the "Reigning Diversions" were themselves attacked for the idleness, concupiscence, and luxury which their early novels seemed to promote or facilitate. See William B. Warner's discussion of "antinovel discourse" and the controversial novels of Defoe, Richardson, Haywood, and Fielding in *Licensing Entertainment,* esp. 128–75.

56. Brad Pasanek explains that "for much of the eighteenth century the very foundation of thought and sensation was supposed to belong to the circulation of 'animal spirits,'" which came to be "a standard element in most theories of mind." See *Metaphors of Mind: An Eighteenth-Century Dictionary* (Baltimore: Johns Hopkins University Press, 2015), 35–38.

57. See G.S. Rousseau, "Nerves, Spirits, and Fibres: Towards Defining the Origins of Sensibility," *Studies in the Eighteenth Century III,* ed. R.F. Brissenden and J.C. Eade (Canberra: Australian National University Press, 1976), 137–57.

58. Susan James, *Passion and Action: The Emotions in Seventeenth-Century Philosophy* (Oxford: Clarendon Press, 1997), 1.

59. This idea was central to the theories of eighteenth-century medical writers like Dr George Cheyne, who recommended mental and physical diversion – and

particularly exercise – as the best preventative against the spleen. See Carol Houlihan Flynn, "Running Out of Matter: The Body Exercised in Eighteenth-Century Fiction," *The Languages of Psyche: Mind and Body in Enlightenment Thought*, ed. G.S. Rousseau (Berkeley: University of California Press, 1990), 147–85.

60. Charles Cotton, *Games and Gamesters of the Restoration*, intro. Cyril Hughes Hartmann (London: George Routledge and Sons, 1930), xxv.

61. John Dunton, *Athenian Sport: or, Two Thousand Paradoxes Merrily Argued, To Amuse and Divert the Age* (London, 1707), xvi.

62. Joseph Addison and Richard Steele, *The Tatler*, 3 vols., ed. Donald F. Bond (Oxford: Oxford University Press, 1987), 2.175.

63. Joseph Addison and Richard Steele, *The Spectator*, 5 vols., ed. Donald F. Bond (Oxford: Oxford University Press, 1965), 3.541. See Ronald Paulson, *The Beautiful, Novel, and Strange: Aesthetics and Heterodoxy* (Baltimore: Johns Hopkins University Press, 1996), esp. 48–75.

64. According to Warner, *Spectator* No. 411 suggests an aesthetic appropriate to modern "media culture," offering "a critique of leisure activities," while at the same time developing "a rationale for entertainment as a vehicle of enlightenment" (*Licensing Entertainment*, 232–33).

65. Although "diversion," "amusement," and "entertainment" are frequently used figuratively, and although reprints and subsequent editions partially account for the large number of titles, the fact that booksellers believed certain kinds of works worth publishing and reprinting suggests something about the commercial appeal of the diversionary.

66. Anthony Ashley Cooper (3rd Earl of Shaftesbury), *Soliloquy, or Advice to an Author, Characteristics of Men, Manners, Opinions, Times*, ed. Lawrence E. Klein (Cambridge: Cambridge University Press, 1999), 90.

67. Christina Lupton argues that the conventional acknowledgement that a work might be "boring, incoherent, written only for profit, and likely to be used as scrap paper" is "productive of an unusually flat kind of reflexivity" (*Knowing Books*, 23).

68. Edward Ward, *The Fourth Volume of the Writings of the Author of* The London Spy (London, 1709), A1r.

69. Like Ward's *London Spy* (1698–1700), *The London Terræfilius* was first published in periodical form, being issued in six parts from July 1707 to April 1708.

70. Howard William Troyer, *Ned Ward of Grubstreet: A Study of Sub-Literary London in the Eighteenth Century* (Cambridge: Harvard University Press, 1946), 135–41.

71. Charles Gildon, *The Post-Man Robb'd of his Mail: or, The Packet Broke Open* (London, 1719), 1–6.

72. This letter is part of a large packet sent in the post by a correspondent named "Charles Dickson." According to Christopher Flint, "*C.D.*" is a "cryptic allusion to Gildon's authorship," since Gildon's first name was Charles and he was the son of Richard Gildon – the "son of Dick." See "*Post*-Scripts: The Fate of the Page in Charles Gildon's Epistolary Fiction," *The Appearance of Print*, 61–102, esp. 67.

73. In Brown's ironic usage, "Meridian" denotes both the great imaginary circle across the centre of the earth and the point or period of highest development or perfection, after which decline inevitably sets in (*O.E.D.*).

74. Benjamin Boyce, *Tom Brown of Facetious Memory: Grub Street in the Age of Dryden* (Cambridge: Harvard University Press, 1939), 135–36.

75. *Amusements Serious and Comical* is one of many works of the period to invert the convention of satirizing the familiar through an exotic setting, by exoticizing the familiar through the ostensibly impartial perspective of a foreign visitor who is introduced into a contemporary setting. Because descriptions of this setting are usually put in the mouth of the foreigner, authors like Brown are able to satirize the familiar context with cultural distance – and without recourse to allegory or fantasy. That Brown's "*Indian*" companion is also indiscriminately referred to as an "*Oriental*," a "*Moletto*," and an "*Antipodean*" suggests that his actual ethnicity is of less importance than the fact of his being foreign.

76. While the *O.E.D.* defines the verb *perambulate* as the action of walking through or about a territory, it defines the noun *perambulation* as a comprehensive relation or description.

77. In her comprehensive study of the various modes of late seventeenth- and eighteenth-century satire, Ashley Marshall classifies Brown and Ward as authors whose works are "essentially popular and commercial." She notes that their satires are not initially "printed in great books or sold at high prices," and claims on somewhat ambiguous grounds that "they pay little attention to literary quality or philosophical profundity." See *The Practice of Satire in England, 1658–1770*, 136–39.

78. Flint argues that the status of "hackney writers" remained ambiguous through the period because they produced works "tainted by mercenary and material motives" and were named "for an object of both commerce and transport." "As such," he observes, "other writers vilified them for confounding writing with its commodity forms or for making books opportune vehicles for a random mass of consumers." See *The Appearance of Print*, 61–62.

79. Flint, *The Appearance of Print*, 62. For Pope's frequently satiric exploitation of print, see James McLaverty, *Pope, Print, and Meaning* (Oxford: Oxford University Press, 2001).

80. In another instance of reflexive play with the literary market, *The Post-Man Robb'd of his Mail* includes a letter from George Sewell expressing a hope that

the sale of Gildon's recently published *Complete Art of Poetry* "will answer its Worth" (269).

81. Compare Cibber's defence of "unbending" with *Tatler* No. 112, where Steele argues that amusements are not only consistent with a "great Character," but are in some ways vital to greatness, since "little relaxations" vent any "Turbulence of Spirit" that might interfere with more serious employments: "A great Mind has something in it too severe and forbidding, that is not capable of giving it self such little Relaxations, and of condescending to these agreeable Ways of Trifling. Tully, when he celebrates the Friendship of Scipio and Lelius, who were the greatest, as well as the politest, Men of their Age, represents it as a beautiful Passage in their Retirement, that they used to gather up Shells on the Sea-Shore, and amuse themselves with those little unregarded Works of this Nature. The great Agesilaus could be a Companion to his own Children, and was surprised by the Ambassadors of Sparta, as he was riding among them on a Hobby-Horse. Augustus indeed had no Play-Fellows of his own begetting; but is said to have passed many of his Hours with little Moorish Boys at a Game of Marbles, not unlike our modern Taw. There is (methinks) a Pleasure in seeing great Men thus fall into the Rank of Mankind, and entertain themselves with Diversions and Amusements that are agreeable to the very weakest of the Species. I must frankly confess, that it is to me a Beauty in Cato's Character, that he would drink a chearful Bottle with a Friend; and I cannot but own, that I have seen with great Delight one of the most celebrated Authors of the last Age feeding the Ducks in St. James's Park. By Instances of this Nature, the Heroes, the Statesmen, the Philosophers, become, as it were familiar with us, and grow the more amiable, the less they endeavour to appear awful" (2.174–5). Also see Tristram Shandy's well-known apology for hobby-horses, which owes much to Cibber's *Apology*: "have not the wisest men of all ages, not excepting *Solomon* himself,—have they not had their HOBBY-HORSES;—their running horses,— their coins and their cockle-shells, their drums and their trumpets, their fiddles, their pallets,——their maggots and their butterflies?—and long as a man rides his HOBBY-HORSE peaceably and quietly along the King's high-way, and neither compels you or me to get up behind him,——pray, Sir, what have either you or I to do with it?" (1.7.12).

82. In a partial defence of the entertainments he was responsible for mounting at Drury Lane, Cibber explains that "the best Play that ever was writ, may tire by being too often repeated, a Misfortune naturally attending the Obligation, to play every Day." "Satiety is, seldom, enough consider'd, by either Critics, Spectators, or Actors, as the true, not to say just, Cause of declining Audiences, to the most rational Entertainments: And tho' I cannot say, I never saw a good new Play, not attended with due Encouragement, yet to keep a Theatre daily open, without sometimes giving the Publick a bad old

one, is more than, I doubt the Wit of human Writers, or Excellence of Actors, will ever be able to accomplish" (171).

83. Richard Blackmore, *An Essay Upon Wit, Essays Upon Several Subjects* (London, 1716), 213–14.

84. For a witty elaboration on the theme of idleness in digression (or literary "loitering"), see Ross Chambers, *Loiterature* (Lincoln: University of Nebraska Press, 1999), esp. 85–153. For a sharp defence of postmodern reading *as* distraction, see Alan Jacobs, *The Pleasures of Reading in an Age of Distraction* (New York: Oxford University Press, 2011).

85. Henry Grove, *The Regulation of Diversions. Design'd Principally for the Benefit of Young Persons* (London, 1708), 27.

## 2 "Pleas'd at being so agreeably deceiv'd": pantomime and the poetics of dumb wit

1. Eighteenth-century pantomimes were invariably twice-titled, one for each half of the entertainment: e.g. *Jupiter and Europa: or, The Intrigues of Harlequin*. In the introductory chapter to Book 5 of *Tom Jones*, Fielding provides what has become a standard definition of serio-comic pantomime: "This Entertainment consisted of two Parts, which the Inventor distinguished by the Names of *the Serious* and *the Comic*. The *Serious* exhibited a certain Number of Heathen Gods and Heroes, who were certainly the worst and dullest Company into which an Audience was ever introduced; and (which was a Secret known to few) were actually intended so to be, in order to contrast the *Comic* Part of the Entertainment, and to display the Tricks of Harlequin to the better Advantage" (5.1.213–14).

2. For critical analysis of the contribution of John Rich, who performed under the stage name of "Lun," to the development of English pantomime, see Paul Sawyer, "Smorgasbord on the Stage: John Rich and the Development of Eighteenth Century English Pantomime," *The Theatre Annual* 34 (1979): 37–65; Phyllis T. Dircks, "The Eclectic Comic Genius of John Rich in *The Necromancer*," *Theatre Notebook* 49.3 (1995): 165–72; and the essays in *"The Stage's Glory": John Rich, 1692–1761*, ed. Berta Joncus and Jeremy Barlow (Newark: University of Delaware Press, 2011).

3. Ralph takes for granted the etymology of *pantomime*, which is derived from the Greek word for imitator or imitation of all manner of persons and things.

4. John Thurmond, *Apollo and Daphne: or, Harlequin's Metamorphoses* (London, 1726), 30; Lewis Theobald and John Rich, *The Rape of Proserpine* (London, 1727), 8; and Theobald and Rich, *The Tricks of Harlequin: or, The Spaniard Outwitted . . . Being the Comic Part of the Celebrated Entertainment of Perseus and Andromeda* (Derby, 1739), 7–8. *Perseus and Andromeda*, first

produced on January 2, 1730, at Lincoln's Inn Fields, is significant as one of the rare examples of a pantomime with a complete textual record of both its "serious" and its "comic" parts. The two parts were published separately, the "serious" as *Perseus and Andromeda* (London, 1730) and with copper plates by Hogarth. For discussion of the textual and performance history of the pantomime, see Antoni N. Sadlak, "Harlequin Comes to England: The Early Evidence of the *Commedia dell'arte* in England and the Formulation of English Harlequinades and Pantomimes" (Ph.D. Dissertation, Tufts University, 1999), 478–86. Also see the opening chapter of *Harlequin Britain*, where John O'Brien uses *Perseus and Andromeda* to reconstruct what an eighteenth-century pantomime might actually have been like.

5. John Locke, *An Essay Concerning Human Understanding*, ed. Peter H. Nidditch (Oxford: Clarendon Press, 1975), 3.10.1.490; Cooper, *Characteristics*, 108; Alexander Pope, *An Essay on Criticism, The Twickenham Edition of the Poems of Alexander Pope*, vol. 1, ed. E. Audra and Aubrey Williams (London: Methuen, 1961), l. 292; John Oldmixon, *The Arts of Logic and Rhetorick* (London, 1728; rpt. New York: Georg Olms, 1976), 16; Addison and Steele, *The Spectator*, 1.253.

6. Although "mime" and "pantomime" are now used interchangeably to signify any silent, gestural performance, in ancient Rome they were quite distinct. Mime troupes were composed of men and women who performed popular farces featuring stock characters. Pantomimes, on the other hand, involved a male dancer's solo representation of a comprehensive and universal subject. In having Primcock link the antics of modern Harlequins to those of the "old *Mimes*" – rather than the "old *Pantomimes*" – Ralph suggests a disparity between the civilizing performances of the past and those of the present.

7. The classic discussion of the influence of the New Science on English stylistics is Richard Foster Jones, "Science and English Prose Style in the Third Quarter of the Seventeenth Century," *The Seventeenth Century: Studies in the History of English Thought from Bacon to Pope* (Stanford: Stanford University Press, 1951), 75–110. For an argument against the prevailing view that the Royal Society had a significant impact on the style of the period, see Brian Vickers, "The Royal Society and English Prose Style: A Reassessment," *Rhetoric and the Pursuit of Truth: Language Change in the Seventeenth and Eighteenth Centuries* (Los Angeles: William Andrews Clark Memorial Library, 1985), 1–76.

8. See James Knowlson, *Universal Language Schemes in England and France, 1600–1800* (Toronto: University of Toronto Press, 1975).

9. Primcock places particular emphasis on the benefits of pantomime, as universal language, to a commercial trading nation like England: "A Toss of the Head, a Wink of an Eye, or Shrug of the Shoulders, will distinguish

whether you deal in *South-Sea, India*, or *Bank-Stock*; an Arm or Leg will tell whether you are a Buyer or Seller. And as to Numbers, every Child knows, we may reckon to Millions by our Fingers in the readiest Manner of Accompts; and to the greatest Exactness in Arithmetick" (111–12).

10. For example, Johns Wilkins's *Essay Towards a Real Character and a Philosophical Language* (1668) was widely dismissed because it failed to account for the "connotative" aspect of words, their power to invest the immaterial creations of the imagination with material life. That other schemes suffered from similar weaknesses is suggested by Book III of *Gulliver's Travels* (1726), where Swift takes universal languages to their logical extreme in the Lagadon professor who proposes not simply to replace one system of signs with another, but to abolish "all Words whatsoever." See Robert Phiddian, "A Hopeless Project: Gulliver Inside the Language of Science in Book III," *Eighteenth-Century Life* 22 (1998): 50–62.

11. Joseph Glanvill, *Scepsis Scientifica: or, Confest Ignorance, the Way to Science; In an Essay of The Vanity of Dogmatizing* (London, 1665), c4.

12. For further discussion of the role of the passions in theatrical performance, see Joseph R. Roach, *The Player's Passion: Studies in the Science of Acting* (Newark: University of Delaware Press, 1985), esp. 58–115.

13. *An Exact Description of the Two Fam'd Entertainments of Harlequin Doctor Faustus; With the Grand Masque of the Heathen Deities: And the Necromancer, or Harlequin Doctor Faustus. As Now Perform'd, in Grotesque Characters, At Both Theatres. Containing the Particular Tricks, Incidents, Songs, Dances, Alterations, and Additions, Throughout Both Performances* (London, [1724]), 35. *The Necromancer* premiered at Lincoln's Inn Fields on December 12, 1723, roughly a month after the Drury Lane premier of John Thurmond's *Harlequin Doctor Faustus* (November 26, 1723). This edition reprints the pantomimes complete, providing not only the sparse "spoken" part of each performance, but detailed stage directions as well. The editor explains that he has reprinted the pantomimes complete so that readers, like audiences, "may have the Pleasure of seeing, in Print at least, the wonderful Tricks and Powerful Art of the so much talk'd of Faustus, as perform'd at both Theatres" (n.p.). Although Rich's pantomime imitated Thurmond's, it proved much more popular, enjoying ninety-seven performances in its first season as opposed to its rival's thirty-nine.

14. Thomas Davies, *Memoirs of the Life of David Garrick, Esq.*, 2 vols. (London, 1780), 1.368–69.

15. *The Grub Street Journal* No. 384 (May 5, 1737), Ar. For a general discussion of the journal's attitude towards pantomime, see James T. Hillhouse, *The Grub Street Journal* (Durham: Duke University Press, 1928; rpt. New York: Benjamin Blom, 1967), 223ff.

16. Reproduced in *A Register of English Theatrical Documents: 1660–1737*, 2 vols., ed. Judith Milhous and Robert D. Hume (Carbondale: Southern Illinois University Press, 1991), 2.678. The review is of Thurmond's *Harlequin Doctor Faustus*.
17. Cibber, *Apology*, 279–81.
18. In an appendix to *The History of the Mimes and Pantomimes* (London, 1728), which lists all "the Modern Entertainments that have been exhibited on the *English* STAGE," Weaver credits himself with having devised the first English pantomime of the type that became popular with eighteenth-century London audiences: "The first Entertainment that appeared on the *English* Stage, where the Representation of the Story was carried on by Dancing, Action, and Motion only, was performed in Grotesque Characters, after the manner of the Modern *Italians*, such as *Harlequin, Scaramouch*, &c. and was called The Tavern Bilkers. Composed by Mr. Weaver. And first performed in *Drury-Lane* Theatre, 1702" (45). Because a definite record of *Tavern Bilkers* has not been located, Weaver's priority has not always been accepted. What is more certain is that Weaver's *The Loves of Mars and Venus* was the first pantomime to silence Harlequin. For a historical discussion of Weaver's contributions to both the theory and practice of English pantomime, see Emmet L. Avery, "Dancing and Pantomime on the English Stage, 1700–1737," *Studies in Philology* 31 (1934): 417–52; Virginia P. Scott, "The Infancy of English Pantomime: 1716–1723," *Educational Theatre Journal* 24 (1972): 125–34; and, especially, Richard Ralph, *The Life and Works of John Weaver* (New York: Dance Horizons, 1985).
19. John Weaver, *Anatomical and Mechanical Lectures Upon Dancing. Wherein Rules and Institutions for that Art are Laid Down and Demonstrated* (London, 1721), 4.
20. John Weaver, *An Essay Towards a History of Dancing, In Which the Whole Art and Its Various Excellencies Are In Some Measure Explain'd* (London, 1712), 16.
21. In *Spectator* No. 466 (August 25, 1712), Richard Steele endorses Weaver's *Essay*, asserting that "if the Art was under proper Regulations, it would be a mechanick way of implanting insensibly in Minds not capable of receiving it so well by any other Rules, a sense of good Breeding and Virtue" (4.148).
22. John Dryden, "The Author's Apology for Heroic Poetry and Poetic License (1677)," *Essays*, 2 vols., ed. W.P. Ker (Oxford, 1900; rpt. New York: Russell & Russell, 1961), 1.190.
23. Perhaps paradoxically, Weaver goes so far as to define "rhetoric" (traditionally an art of effective oral and written communication) in a lecture upon dancing (an obviously physical art): "RHETORICK is an Art of Eloquence, which arises from an elegant Choice of Words, perswasive, and of such Force, as to express the Passions, as to raise, or allay the Affections of Man" (*Lectures*, 144).

24. See Nancy Taylor, "John Weaver and the Origins of English Pantomime: A Neoclassical Theory and Practice for Uniting Dance and Theatre," *Theatre Survey* 42.2 (2001): 191–214.

25. John Weaver, *The Loves of Mars and Venus: A Dramatick Entertainment of Dancing, Attempted in Imitation of the Ancient Greeks and Romans* (London, 1717), XI, IX. Weaver's preface restates many of the observations made in his *Essay Towards a History of Dancing*.

26. Having their foundation in "dumb Wit," eighteenth-century pantomimes did not readily lend themselves to transcription and publication. As a result, most of our knowledge of the genre comes from contemporary commentary – much of it satiric and thus exaggerated or ironic.

27. While analysing the dramatic impact of Weaver's choreography in *The Loves of Mars and Venus*, Taylor extends her discussion to the ways in which the typography and layout of the text reflects Weaver's "aesthetic priorities": "The emotion depicted is paramount, written in all caps and centered above its descriptive paragraph. It is italicized even within the paragraph and usually is the first word of the description. In this way, Weaver emphasized the passion, the inner life of the character, and, thus, the imitative quality of this new form. Program typography encouraged viewers to 'see' dance movements as genuinely expressive of character's feelings as they developed throughout a coherent story, while Weaver's descriptions helped audiences resist the temptation to sort dance movements into traditional categories" ("John Weaver and the Origins of English Pantomime," 202).

28. Cicero, *De Oratore*, trans. H. Rackham (London: Loeb, 1942), 3.56.213.

29. Henry Fielding, *Pasquin. A Dramatick Satire on the Times, Plays: Volume III, 1734–1742*, ed. Thomas Lockwood (Oxford: Clarendon Press, 2011), 5.1. p. 308; *Letters from a Moor at London to His Friend at Tunis* (London, 1736), 109; Edward Ward, *The Dancing Devils: or, The Roaring Dragon. A Dumb Farce* (London, 1724; rpt. New York: Garland Publishing Inc., 1974), 15.

30. Ralph, *The Life and Works of John Weaver*, 66.

31. Taking for granted that "Nothing is so much admired and so little understood as Wit" (1.244), Addison classifies the various species of false wit, which consists in the "Resemblance and Congruity" of letters, words, and sentences, as a way of discriminating it from true wit, which consists in the "Resemblance and Congruity" of ideas (1.264). Addison deals with pattern poems in *Spectator* No. 58, lipograms, rebuses, and echo poems in No. 59; anagrams, acrostics, chronograms, *bouts rimez*, and double rhymes in No. 60; puns and conundrums in No. 61; and the general nature of true, false, and "mixt" wit in No. 62. In *Spectator* No. 63, Addison recounts a "Night's Dream or Vision," which forms "into one Continued Allegory the several Schemes of

Wit" (1: 270). See Elizabeth Kraft, "Wit and *The Spectator's* Ethics of Desire," *Studies in English Literature* 45.3 (2005): 625–46.

32. Of this passage, Neil Saccamano remarks: "As 'external Mimicry,' false wit is a perverse *metaphora* that carries things too far by explicitly operating at the level of letters or faces instead of meaning; its substitutions are made possible not by some extra-linguistic perception or cognition but by the perception of marks or sounds 'external' to sense though constitutive of representational systems. Hence false wit is not simply artificial or 'conventional,' possessing no relation to nature, since its mimicry foregrounds resemblance and consequently the 'natural' character of language." See "Wit's Breaks," *Body and Text in the Eighteenth Century*, ed. Veronica Kelly and Dorothea Von Mücke (Stanford: Stanford University Press, 1994), 51.

33. It is not surprising that Weaver's treatment of "dumb Wit" recalls Addison's papers on true and false wit, since his earliest discussions of pantomimic dance seem to have appeared in *The Spectator*. The letter from a Shrewsbury dancing-master that comprises most of No. 334 (March 24, 1712) regrets the "low Ebb to which Dancing is now fallen" and exhorts "some ingenious Pen" to "set Dancing in its true Light." As an encouragement to future apologists, the anonymous author boasts: "I who teach to dance have attempted a small Treatise as an Essay towards an History of Dancing; in which I have enquired into its Antiquity, Original, and Use, and shewn what Esteem the Ancients had for it: I have likewise considered the Nature and Perfection of all its several Parts, and how beneficial and delightful it is, both as a Qualification and an Exercise; and endeavour'd to answer all Objections that have been maliciously rais'd against it" (3.237). In the preliminary section of No. 466 (August 25, 1712), the matter of Weaver's treatises is anticipated, and in a manner that is reminiscent of the *Essay, Lectures*, and *History* themselves: "As all Art is an Imitation of Nature, this is an Imitation of Nature in its highest Excellence, and at a Time when she is most agreeable. The Business of Dancing is to display Beauty, and for that Reason all Distortions and Mimickries, as such, are what raise Aversion instead of Pleasure: But Things that are in themselves excellent, are ever attended with Imposture and false Imitation. Thus, as in Poetry there are laborious Fools who write Anagrams and Acrosticks, there are Pretenders in Dancing, who think merely to do what others cannot, is to excel" (4.146). For an account of the reasons why these papers have been attributed to Weaver, see Ralph, *The Life and Works of John Weaver*, 110–15.

34. D. Judson Milburn, *The Age of Wit: 1650–1750* (New York: Macmillan, 1966), 38. Milburn's continues to be the most readable study of eighteenth-century wit. Also see: Martin C. Battestin, *The Providence of Wit: Aspects of Form in Augustan Literature and the Arts* (Oxford: Clarendon Press, 1974); John Sitter,

*Arguments of Augustan Wit* (Cambridge: Cambridge University Press, 1991); and Roger D. Lund, *Ridicule, Religion and the Politics of Wit in Augustan England* (Aldershot: Ashgate Publishing, 2012).

35. In *Spectator* No. 62 (May 11, 1711), Addison quotes Locke's definition, endorsing it as "the best and most philosophical Account that I have ever met with of Wit," adding only that, in order to be true wit, the resemblance or congruity of ideas must give *"Delight* and *Surprize* to the Reader" (1.264). Addison's treatment of Locke is, however, misleading, since he excises from his quotation Locke's regret that wit is only "acceptable to all People" because "there is required no labour of thought, to examine what Truth or Reason there is in it. The Mind without looking any farther, rests satisfied with the agreeableness of the Picture, and the gayety of the Fancy: And it is a kind of an affront to go about to examine it, by the severe Rules of Truth, and good Reason; whereby it appears, that it consists in something, that is not perfectly conformable to them" (2.11.2.156–57). Addison thereby neutralizes Locke's anxiety about wit, shifting the emphasis from the vices of wit to its limited virtues. See John Sitter, "About Wit: Locke, Addison, Prior, and the Order of Things," *Rhetorics of Order / Ordering Rhetorics in English Neoclassical Literature*, ed. J. Douglas Canfield and J. Paul Hunter (Newark: University of Delaware Press, 1989), 137–57.

36. Locke concludes his discussion of the imperfection and abuse of language by setting out "the *ends of Language in our Discourse with others*": "*First, To make known* one Man's Thoughts or *Ideas* to another. *Secondly*, To do it *with* as much ease and *quickness*, as is possible; and *Thirdly*, Thereby *to convey* the *Knowledge* of Things. Language is either abused, or deficient, when it fails in any of these Three" (3.10.23.504).

37. Corbyn Morris, *An Essay Towards Fixing the True Standards of Wit, Humour, Raillery, Satire and Ridicule*, intro. James L. Clifford (London, 1744; rpt. Los Angeles: William Andrews Clark Memorial Library, 1947), xv.

38. Roger D. Lund, "Wit, Judgment, and the Misprisions of Similitude," *Journal of the History of Ideas* 65.1 (2004): 53–74 (72). The present discussion of the inherent falsity of wit owes much to Lund's extended analysis of the unsuccessful attempts of Augustan poets and critics to rehabilitate the similitude and "defend truth with a lie" (57).

39. Henry Barker, *The Polite Gentleman: or, Reflections Upon the Several Kinds of Wit* (London, 1700), 125.

40. René Rapin, "Reflections on Aristotle's Treatise of Poesy," *The Continental Model: Selected French Critical Essays of the Seventeenth Century, in English Translation*, ed. Scott Elledge and Donald Schier, rev. edn. (Ithaca: Cornell University Press, 1970), 292.

41. Matthew Prior, "A Dialogue Between Mr. John Lock and Seigneur de Montaigne," *The Literary Works of Matthew Prior*, 2nd edn., 2 vols., eds. H. Bunker Wright and Monroe K. Spears (Oxford: Clarendon Press, 1959), 1.625.
42. Allan Ramsay, *An Essay on Ridicule* (London, 1753), 56.
43. Blanford Parker argues that English Augustanism constitutes itself by its express opposition to the "conceitful mentality" of baroque or metaphysical poetics. See *The Triumph of Augustan Poetics: English Literary Culture from Butler to Johnson* (Cambridge: Cambridge University Press, 1998), 1–135.
44. George Granville (Lord Lansdowne), "Concerning Unnatural Flights in Poetry," *Augustan Critical Writing*, ed. David Womersley (London: Penguin Books, 1997), ll. 19–24.
45. Samuel Werenfels, *A Dissertation Concerning Meteors of Stile, or False Sublimity*, intro. Edward Tomarken (London, 1711; rpt. Los Angeles: William Andrews Clark Memorial Library, 1980), 215.
46. Longinus, *On the Sublime*, trans. William Smith (London, 1739; rpt. New York: Scholars' Facsimiles and Reprints, 1975), 50.
47. Pope, *Peri Bathous*, 186.
48. Richard Blackmore, *Prince Arthur. An Heroick Poem* (London, 1695), 231–32. Cf. the excerpt from *Prince Arthur* in Pope's *Peri Bathous*, 211. Although Pope satirizes several dozen dunces in his *Art of Sinking in Poetry*, the majority of his representative quotations are drawn from the poems of Blackmore, and the majority of these quotations are drawn from *Prince Arthur*, Blackmore's first and worst epic poem. Typical of his "bibliographical" practice, Pope frequently manipulates Blackmore's verse to make it appear more absurd, and he mischievously cites from "the best, the last, and most correct" edition of the poem (4th ed., 1714), which, being "Enlarged," was also the bulkiest and most profuse.
49. The *O.E.D.* defines *catachresis* as: "Improper use of words; application of a term to a thing which it does not properly denote; abuse or perversion of trope or metaphor." Theorists as diverse as Michel Foucault, Paul Ricoeur, Jacques Derrida, Gayatri Spivak, and Hayden White have adopted catachresis as a figure for the various projects of Deconstruction.
50. For an interesting quantitative analysis of the popularity of early pantomime, see: Paul Sawyer, "The Popularity of Pantomime on the London Stage, 1720–1760," *Restoration and Eighteenth-Century Theatre Research* 5.2 (1990): 1–16. Sawyer determines that, for the period between 1720 and 1733 (the first vogue of English pantomime), the average proceeds for all theatrical programmes was £67, for plays alone, £40, and for plays supplemented by pantomime and other "additional entertainments," £91.
51. Mitchell P. Wells, "Some Notes on the Early Eighteenth-Century Pantomime," *Studies in Philology* 32 (1935): 598; Sawyer, "Smorgasbord on

the Stage," 37ff.; Dircks, "The Eclectic Comic Genius of John Rich," 165; and Richard Bevis, *English Drama: Restoration and Eighteenth Century, 1660–1789* (London: Longman, 1982), 182.

52. Cesar de Saussure, *A Foreign View of the England in the Reigns of George I and George II*, trans. Madame van Muyden (New York: Caliban, 1995), 172.

53. Ward, *The Dancing Devils: or, The Roaring Dragon*, 15.

54. Cited in Emmet L. Avery, "The Defense and Criticism of Pantomimic Entertainments in the Early Eighteenth Century," *English Literary History* 5 (1938): 135.

55. Theobald and Rich, *The Rape of Proserpine*, iii–iv.

56. *The Weekly Journal, or Saturday's Post* (April 6, 1723). Also cited in O'Brien, *Harlequin Britain*, 2.

57. Pantomimes that attempted to stay within the bounds of reason and nature seem to have been less popular than those that employed spectacular transformations as *deus ex machinae*. This partially explains the failure of John Thurmond's *Harlequin Sheppard. A Night Scene in Grotesque Characters* (London, 1724), which gives material rather than magical explanations for Jack Sheppard's notorious escapes from Newgate Prison. Harlequin Sheppard, for instance, uses a "small Nail" to break open the padlock that fixes his chains to the floor; he undoes his manacles with the aid of "Implements" that are smuggled into his cell in a pie; and he picks out the bricks of the Chimney with a "broken Piece of his Chain."

58. The Drury Lane original, Monsieur Roger's *Perseus and Andromeda: or, The Devil Upon Two Sticks* (London, 1729), was already quite spectacular, featuring, among other things, "Humane Figures Metamorphos'd into Stone," a dance of the Gorgons, a "wing'd Horse" which springs from the blood of Medusa and flies away, a bottled genie who brings about "various Incidents of the Comic Entertainments," and a magic wand that makes possible Harlequin's "Intrigue with *Columbine*."

59. Theobald and Rich, *Perseus and Andromeda*, 2.

60. Theobald and Rich, *Tricks of Harlequin*, 1–6. The author of the comic part of *Perseus and Andromeda* is unknown, but it was probably also written by Theobald, in collaboration with Rich.

61. In order to take advantage of every opportunity for stage-effects, Theobald conflates into one continuous narrative Perseus's two most famous feats: his beheading of Medusa and his rescue of Andromeda from the sea monster. In Ovid, the Medusa story is distinct from the story of the sea monster that is sent by the gods to seize Andromeda as punishment for Cassiope's excessive vanity (in believing that her beauty rivalled that of the nymphs).

62. *The Weekly Journal, or, Saturday's Post* No. 267 (December 7, 1723).

63. Cited in O'Brien, *Harlequin Britain*, 90.

64. *The Prompter: A Theatrical Paper (1734–1736)*, eds. William W. Appleton and Kalman A. Burnim (New York: Benjamin Blom, 1966), 145, 150, 147.
65. Parodies offer a significant amount of information about how pantomimes were performed and how they were received. Some of the more compelling examples are: Ward, *The Dancing Devils: or, The Roaring Dragon*; Henry Fielding, *The Author's Farce and the Pleasures of the Town* (London, 1730); James Ralph, *The Fashionable Lady; or, Harlequin's Opera. In the Manner of a Rehearsal* (London, 1730), *Harlequin Student: or, The Fall of Pantomime* (London, 1741), and *The British Frenzy: or, The Mock-Apollo. A Satyr* (London, 1745). See Leo Hughes, "Rival Entertainments: Pantomime, Burlesque, Satire, Sentiment," *A Century of English Farce* (Princeton: Princeton University Press, 1956), 94–129.
66. *The British Stage; or, The Exploits of Harlequin: A Farce* (London, 1724), VII.
67. For an analysis of Fielding's satiric usage of the rehearsal format, see Richard Bevis, "Fielding's Normative Authors: *Tom Jones* and the Rehearsal Play," *Philological Quarterly* 69.1 (1990): 55–70. Also see: Peter Lewis, *Fielding's Burlesque Drama: Its Place in the Tradition* (Edinburgh: University of Edinburgh Press, 1987); and Albert J. Rivero, *The Plays of Henry Fielding: A Critical Study of His Dramatic Career* (Charlottesville: University Press of Virginia, 1989).
68. Henry Fielding, *Tumble-Down Dick: or, Phaeton in the Suds, Plays: Volume III, 1734–1742*, ed. Thomas Lockwood (Oxford: Clarendon Press, 2011), 339.
69. In the mock dedication to *Tumble-Down Dick*, Fielding, under the pseudonym of "Pasquin," panegyrizes Rich: "It is to You, Sir, we owe (if not the Invention) at least the bringing into Fashion, that sort of Writing which you have pleased to distinguish by the Name of *Entertainment*. Your Success herein (whether owing to your Heels or your Head, I will not determine) sufficiently entitles you to all Respect from the inferior Dablers in Things of this Nature" (329).
70. James Miller, *Harlequin-Horace: or, The Art of Modern Poetry* (London, 1731), 25–26. *Harlequin-Horace* completes a trilogy with James Bramston's *The Art of Politicks, in Imitation of Horace's Art of Poetry* (London, 1729) and Walter Harte's *An Essay on Satire* (London, 1730), in which the three major themes of *The Dunciad* are taken up and analysed individually: public life, literature and learning, and the state of contemporary amusement – especially the stage. Miller's poem was the most successful of the three, reaching four editions by 1741.
71. Miller makes this relationship clear in his dedication to William Talbot in the fourth edition of the poem: "The greatest and wisest States have always deem'd it a Point of no small Importance, that the Public Diversions should be properly conducted, as being sensible that Barbarity in Taste is a

sure Forerunner of Barbarity in Manners, and that a Delicacy in Pleasure is one of the greatest Supports to the Social Virtues" (James Miller, *Harlequin-Horace: or, The Art of Modern Poetry*, intro. Antony Coleman, 4th edn. [London, 1741; rpt. Los Angeles: William Andrews Clark Memorial Library, 1976], B3v). The fourth edition of *Harlequin-Horace* was considerably expanded from the first. Along with the dedication to Talbot, the 1741 edition included a new frontispiece engraved by Van der Gucht, a number of local textual additions and emendations, and mock footnotes in the manner of *The Dunciad Variorum* (1729), which substantiate the observations of the poem with concrete examples from the pantomimes *and* poetry of the period.

72. In the fourth edition, a note indexed to these lines explains: "In the farce of *Perseus and Andromeda*, a most obscene Dance was perform'd in a *Temple*, several Persons in the Characters and Habits of Priests and Bishops being present; at the same Time the ingenious Mr. *Lun* [Rich] deported himself very naturally in the Shape of a Dog, till a Dome rising voluntarily from under the Stage, gave him room for another Transformation by standing on the Top of it in the guise of a *Mercury*, to the high Admiration and Delight of a *British* Audience" (ll. 26n).

73. There is additional irony in the fact that the Orpheus myth became a favourite subject for eighteenth-century pantomime. The first of many to represent the myth in mime, Weaver mounted *Orpheus and Eurydice: A Dramatick Entertainment in Dancing* in 1718. According to Richard Ralph, Weaver "appears to have identified with Orpheus," performing the part himself and appending a scholarly discussion of his supposed life and works to the printed text of the pantomime (67). In some sense, then, for Miller to have Harlequin piss on Orpheus is to have him piss on both his greatest apologist and himself.

74. O'Brien asks: "What can this image—which, given its prominence at the beginning of ... one of the period's most trenchant satires of pantomime seemingly intended more to mock pantomime than to advertise it—teach us about the kind of appeal *Perseus and Andromeda* might have had for contemporary spectators?" He draws his answer from the frontispiece motto: "*Serpentes avibus geminentur, Tigribus agni*" / "Serpents will lie down with birds, tigers with lambs," which, he argues, "surely refers to the mixed nature of pantomime itself" (*Harlequin Britain*, 15).

75. *The British Frenzy: or, The Mock-Apollo. A Satyr* (London, 1745), 7.

76. For the Augustans, Ovid was a problematic "ancient" in that his language was too ornate to be considered tasteful. The ambivalent remarks that Samuel Garth prefixes to his collaborative edition of the *Metamorphoses* (1717) is representative of the prevailing view of Ovid in early eighteenth-century England: "I shall not pretend to impose my Opinion on others with the

magisterial Authority of a Critic; but only take the Liberty of discovering my own Taste. I shall endeavour to show our Poet's Redundance of Wit, Justness of Comparisons, Elegance of Descriptions, and peculiar Delicacy in touching every Circumstance relating to the Passions, and Affections; and with the same Impartiality, and Frankness, I shall confess the too frequent Puerilities of his luxuriant Fancy, and the too great Negligence of his sometimes unlabour'd Versification" (*Ovid's Metamorphoses in Fifteen Books. Translated by the most Eminent Hands* [London, 1717], 1). See David Hopkins, "Dryden and Ovid's 'Wit Out of Season,'" *Ovid Renewed: Ovidian Influences on Literature and Art from the Middle Ages to the Twentieth Century*, ed. Charles Martindale (Cambridge: Cambridge University Press, 1988), 167–90.

77. The "*Region of False Wit*" helps to put this into perspective. When Addison's dreamer comes upon a "Party of *Punns*," he explains that this "Set of Merry People" were "engaged at a Diversion, in which the whole Jest was to mistake one Person for another. To give occasion for these ludicrous Mistakes, they were divided into Pairs, every Pair being covered from Head to Foot with the same kind of Dress, though perhaps, there was not the least Resemblance in their Face. By this means an old Man was sometimes mistaken for a Boy, a Woman for an Old Man, and a Black-a-moor for an *European*, which very often produced great Peals of Laughter" (1.272–73).

78. Sitter, *Arguments of Augustan Wit*, 49.

## 3 "Fasten'd by the eyes": popular wonder, print culture, and the exhibition of monstrosity

1. The most thorough account of Mary Toft appears in Dennis Todd's *Imagining Monsters*, where the hoax of "the whole Rabbit-scene" is used as a starting point for an exploration of eighteenth-century beliefs about the power of imagination, the figurative and literal causes of monstrosity, and the problems of personal identity.

2. For discussion of the fashion for menageries and performing animals, see Richard D. Altick, *The Shows of London: A Panoramic History of Exhibitions, 1600–1862* (Cambridge: Belknap Press, 1978), 34–49 and 302–31. For an analysis of how entrepreneurs legitimized such performances by marketing them as a combination of theatre and natural philosophy, see: Marius Kwint, "The Legitimation of the Circus in Late Georgian England," *Past and Present* 174 (2002): 72–115; and Deidre Coleman, "Entertaining Entomology: Insects and Insect Performers in the Eighteenth Century," *Eighteenth-Century Life* 30 (2006): 107–34.

3. See the entry on Buchinger in *A Biographical Dictionary of Actors, Actresses, Musicians, Dancers, Managers and Other Stage Personnel in London, 1660–*

*1800*, ed. Philip H. Highfill, Kalman A. Burnim, and Edward A. Langhans, 16 vols. (Carbondale: Southern Illinois University Press, 1973–93). Also see Ricky Jay, *Learned Pigs and Fireproof Women: Unique, Eccentric, and Amazing Entertainers* (New York: Villard Books, 1987), 45–58.

4. See, for instance, Shakespeare's *The Tempest* (1611), where Trinculo's initial wonder at Caliban, "half a fish and half a monster," is quickly commercialized: "A strange fish! Were I in England now (as once I was) and had but this fish painted, not a holiday fool there but would give a piece of silver. There would this monster make a man; any strange beast there makes a man" (William Shakespeare, *The Tempest*, ed. Virginia Mason Vaughan and Alden T. Vaughan [London: Arden Shakespeare, 1999], 2.2.27–31).

5. Altick, *Shows of London*, 3; Henry Morley, *Memoirs of Bartholomew Fair*, 4th edn. (London: George Routledge and Sons, 1892), 246; and Paul Semonin, "Monsters in the Marketplace: The Exhibition of Human Oddities in Early Modern England," *Freakery: Cultural Spectacles of the Extraordinary Body*, ed. Rosemarie Garland Thomson (New York: New York University Press, 1996), 69. For a thorough discussion of the ubiquity of monsters in early modern culture, see: Lorraine Daston and Katherine Park, "Unnatural Conceptions: The Study of Monsters in Sixteenth- and Seventeenth-Century France and England," *Past and Present* 92 (1981): 20–54.

6. Paul Keen has described the way in which the rhetoric and "discourse of wonder" became a "satirical mode" during the eighteenth century. See *Literature, Commerce, and the Spectacle of Modernity, 1750–1800*, 177. Also see Benedict, *Curiosity*, 2.

7. As is suggested by R.C. Alston's qualitative survey of eighteenth-century "printed ephemera," material relating to monster exhibitions must have comprised a significant part of what the Scriblerians satirize as the "deluge" of print that "cover'd the land." See "The Eighteenth-Century Non-Book: Observations on Printed Ephemera," *Buch und Buchandel in Europa im achtzehnten Jahrhundert*, ed. Giles Barber and Bernhard Fabian (Hamburg: Dr Ernst Hauswedell & Co., 1981), 349–50.

8. Hunter, *Before Novels*, 210. Hunter identifies seventeenth-century wonder literature as an important precursor to the novel, claiming that books of wonder, such as Nathaniel Wanley's *The Wonders of the Little World: or, a General History of Man* (1678) and Nathaniel Crouch's *Memorable Accidents, and Unheard Transactions, Containing an Account of Several Strange Events* (1693), responded ambivalently to the empirical demand to understand the universe by trading *on* "anti-explanatory desires," and trading *in* "oddities, curiosities, and rarities of nature."

9. According to Anita Guerrini, broadsides, pamphlets, and other popular forms of print "forged and maintained" a connection between commercial

exhibition and natural philosophy. See "Advertising Monstrosity: Broadsides and Human Exhibition in Early Eighteenth-Century London," *Ballads and Broadsides in Britain, 1500–1800*, ed. Patricia Fumerton and Anita Guerrini, with Kris McAbee (Burlington: Ashgate Publishing, 2010), 109–27.

10. Dennis Todd regrets that while monster shows may have appealed to all social strata, the bulk of the audience, the lower classes, left no testimony. The records that do survive express the often satiric perspectives peculiar to the upper classes who left them. Moreover, those who did leave records are usually vague in their descriptions of their personal responses to monsters, preferring the objectivity of Baconian science to subjective speculation about the nature and causes of their own fascination. This is particularly the case for members of the Royal Society such as John Evelyn, Robert Hooke, Samuel Pepys, Ralph Thoresby, and Hans Sloane, all of whom viewed their observations as contributions to empirical knowledge. See Todd, *Imagining Monsters*, 153–55.

11. Edward Ward, *The London Spy Compleat, In Eighteen Parts* (London, 1703), 165, 231, 251, 231.

12. Dunton, *A Voyage Round the World*, 2.13.

13. Brown, *Amusements Serious and Comical*, 3.25.

14. D'Urfey, *An Essay Towards the Theory of the Intelligible World*, 132–7. The raree-show was an elaborate miniature scene contained or carried about in a box, and viewed through a peep-hole with slanted mirrors to achieve the effect of camera obscura. During the early eighteenth century, it was among the most popular of the many shows of London, so popular, in fact, that the term "raree-show" eventually came to be applied to any kind of popular exhibition or spectacle.

15. Addison and Steele, *The Spectator*, 1.211. Ironically, the Iroquois Sachems themselves took in the usual sights of London – from the Tower and Bedlam and Gresham College to the Haymarket and Hockley-in-the-Hole and Powell's Puppet Theatre. See Richmond P. Bond, *Queen Anne's American Kings* (Oxford: Clarendon Press, 1952), 6–10.

16. Alexander Pope et al., *Memoirs of the Extraordinary Life, Works, and Discoveries of Martinus Scriblerus*, ed. Charles Kerby-Miller (New Haven, 1950; rpt. New York: Oxford University Press, 1988), 143ff.

17. Jonathan Swift, "Part of the Seventh Epistle of the First Book of Horace Imitated," *Poetical Works*, ed. Herbert Davis (London: Oxford University Press, 1967), ll. 57–60, p. 109.

18. This is something of a commonplace in studies of eighteenth-century monstrosity, many of which use Swift's imaginative exploitation of dwarves, giants, conjoined twins, and the like to prove his own fascination

with monsters. In fact, scholars have frequently drawn upon works such as *A Tale of a Tub* and *Gulliver's Travels* for information about the "roster" of sights available to early eighteenth-century audiences. See, in particular: Aline Mackenzie Taylor, "Sights and Monsters in Gulliver's *Voyage to Brobdingnag*," *Tulane Studies in English* 7 (1957): 29–82; Altick, *Shows of London*, 34–35 and 43–44; Rogers, *Literature and Popular Culture*, 1–39; Todd, *Imagining Monsters*, 140–78; and Benedict, *Curiosity*, 71–117.

19. Jonathan Swift, *Journal to Stella: Letters to Esther Johnson and Rebecca Dingley, 1710–1713*, ed. Abigail Williams (Cambridge: Cambridge University Press, 2013), 87–88 and 519.

20. British Library N.Tab. 2026/25 (superseded shelf-mark: 551.d.18), Nos. 54 and 78. These descriptions are taken from a scrapbook collection of broadsides, handbills, and newspaper advertisements "Relating to Dwarfs, Giants, and Other Monsters and Curiosities Exhibited for Public Inspection." The clippings cover the extraordinary range of monsters exhibited between the reigns of Charles II and George II, although the greater number belong to "freak shows" during the reigns of William and Mary and Anne. The scrapbook was once owned by Hans Sloane, and is generally believed to have been compiled by this future founder of the British Museum. Many of the advertisements in the collection are reprinted by Morley in Chapter XVI of his *Memoirs of Bartholomew Fair*, and by John Ashton in his *Social Life in the Reign of Queen Anne*, New Impression (London: Chatto & Windus, 1919), Chapter XII.

21. Todd, *Imagining Monsters*, 149. In attempting to understand how Mary Toft's claim to have given birth to seventeen and a half rabbits could be widely accepted, Todd explains that our conventional notions of "belief" and "disbelief" may be "too crude" to define precisely the way in which people responded to the incident. The experience of eighteenth-century monstrosity occupied instead what Todd describes as a "hazy psychological realm where distinctions between belief and disbelief are not clear-cut and where degrees of conviction are hard to measure" (42).

22. To a certain degree, periodicals were an exception. Questions regarding monstrosity were predictably taken up in *The Philosophical Transactions*, as well as in Dunton's *The Athenian Gazette: or, Casuistical Mercury, Resolving All the Most Nice and Curious Questions Proposed by the Ingenious (The Athenian Mercury)* and Aaron Hill's imitation of Dunton's project, *The British Apollo, or, Curious Amusements for the Ingenious*. The *Mercury* and *Apollo* endeavoured to popularize science, doing for the masses what *The Philosophical Transactions* had done for the learned public.

23. For an interesting discussion of the paradoxical relationship between credulity and curiosity, see John R. Clark, *Form and Frenzy in Swift's Tale*

*of a Tub* (Ithaca: Cornell University Press, 1970), 17–35. Also see Paul Keen's examination of the role of incredulity in popular exhibition, where it functions as "an interpretive posture which unsettled the tension between naïve credulity (an uncritical desire for 'wonderful knowledge') and misanthropic disavowal." See *Literature, Commerce, and the Spectacle of Modernity, 1750–1800*, 182–201.

24. Benedict revises Clark by analysing the relationship between credulity and curiosity in terms of the enquiring eye – at once "the paramount organ of curious perception" and the distorting lens of naïve but nascent empiricism. See: Barbara M Benedict, "The 'Curious Attitude' in Eighteenth-Century Britain: Observing and Owning," *Eighteenth-Century Life* 14 (1990): 59–98; and *Curiosity*, 30, 92–117.

25. According to Benedict, Ward's Spy "differentiates legitimate and illegitimate curiosity." See *Curiosity*, 93–96.

26. The "Athenian Society" consisted principally of the mathematician and translator, Richard Sault (c. 1660–1702), the polymath, poet, and Church of England clergyman, John Wesley (c. 1662–1735), and Dunton himself, who acted as general editor and saw to it that each contributor responded to the questions they were most qualified to answer. The Oxford Platonist, John Norris (1657–1711), was also an occasional contributor, though he refused to contract himself an official "Member of Athens." Sault usually answered questions relating to mathematics, surveying, astronomy, and physics. Wesley handled most questions on theology, philosophy, history, and literature. Questions concerning courtship, marriage, and social behaviour, as well as those relating to the natural and supernatural world were the domain of no particular Athenian, though the contributions of Dunton are often recognizable by their self-conscious and facetious style. Discussions of monstrosity tend to fall into this category. See Gilbert D. McEwan, *The Oracle of the Coffee House: John Dunton's* Athenian Mercury (San Marino: The Huntington Library, 1972), 23–32.

27. John Dunton et al., *The Athenian Oracle: Being an Entire Collection of All the Valuable Questions and Answers in the Old* Athenian Mercuries, 3 vols. (London, 1703–04), 1.1.

28. The amount that the Athenians wrote about the sciences is second only to the *Philosophical Transactions* during the same period. Although the proportions vary from volume to volume, McEwan claims that about 20 per cent of all questions and answers – a total of 760 – were devoted to science. See McEwan, *The Oracle of the Coffee House*, 113–40.

29. Since there is nothing particularly monstrous about a calf with an ornamental tuft of hair on the crown of its head, the *Mercury* must refer to the well-known six-legged calf that seems always to have been exhibited with

a ribboned and bowed topknot – a conventional method of normalizing the monstrous. If this is not the case, the topknot might be figurative, the "late calf" being a "horned" calf with a simple malformation of the skull.

30. According to McEwan, what contemporary readers see as a lack of discrimination in the *Mercury* appears in "an occasional acceptance of conclusions based upon insufficient or dubious observation" and in "their giving monsters and maggots equal importance with valid scientific data" (116). As demonstrated, however, the Athenians often mingle monsters and maggots in order to expose the lack of discrimination in their audience.

31. Ironically, it was not the monsters they discussed, but the Athenian Society itself that was something of a hoax. Dunton, Sault, and Wesley purported to be the official organ of an Oxbridge collective, a large, exclusive, academic organization devoted to the enlightenment of the reading public. In reality, only one of the three members of the society had any university training, and despite being well read and enthusiastic, none of the Athenians actually mixed in learned circles. This, of course, did not stop them from making the public believe in their authority. Even Swift, as he later regretted, was taken in by their Grub Street philosophy: "An Ode to the Athenian Society" was published under his own name, along with a rather embarrassing letter in praise of the fictional "Society," in the *Supplement to the Fifth Volume of the Athenian Gazette* (1692). See Anne Cline Kelly, *Jonathan Swift and Popular Culture: Myth, Media, and the Man* (New York: Palgrave Macmillan, 2002), 13–18.

32. Brown's extended sketch of the "Monster called *Petty-fogging*" closely resembles Ward's characterization of the pettifogger as "an amphibious monster that partakes of two natures, and those contrary; he's a great lover both of peace and enmity, and has no sooner set people together by the ears, but he is soliciting the Law to make an end of the difference" (146).

33. As Susan Gubar points out, early-eighteenth-century satirists frequently used metaphors of monstrosity to attack the "debased and debasing" activities of most women. In her opinion, "the misogyny of our literary past" is best exemplified by the ubiquity of these "female monsters." See "The Female Monster in Augustan Satire," *Signs: Journal of Women in Culture and Society* 3.2 (1977): 380–94. Also see *Curiosity*, where Benedict expands upon female monstrosity by analysing a parallel trope: "the reciprocal objectification of curiosity and femininity" (118–57).

34. John Dennis succinctly summarizes this doctrine in *The Grounds of Criticism in Poetry* (1704): "The Universe is regular in all its parts and it is to that exact Regularity that it owes its admirable beauty. The Microcosm owes the Beauty and Health both of its Body and Soul to Order, and the Deformity and Distempers of both, to nothing but the want of Order"

(*The Critical Works of John Dennis*, 2 vols., ed. Edward Niles Hooker [Baltimore: Johns Hopkins University Press, 1939], 1.335).

35. Roger Lund, "Laughing at Cripples: Ridicule, Deformity and the Argument from Design," *Eighteenth-Century Studies* 39.1 (2005): 97–8. For analysis of the "deep-seated cultural assumptions that made the deformed and disabled almost automatic figures of fun," see Simon Dickie, *Cruelty and Laughter: Forgotten Comic Literature and the Unsentimental Eighteenth Century* (Chicago: University of Chicago Press, 2011), esp. 45–110 (102). Standard discussions of the Augustan "argument from design" include: Paul Fussell, *The Rhetorical World of Augustan Humanism* (Oxford: Clarendon Press, 1962); Battestin, *The Providence of Wit*; and Margaret Doody, *The Daring Muse: Augustan Poetry Reconsidered* (Cambridge: Cambridge University Press, 1986).

36. Although D'Urfey's *Essay* satirizes all species of overly abstract reasoning, its specific target is its namesake, John Norris' *An Essay Towards the Theory of the Intelligible World* (1701–04). For an account of how D'Urfey parodies Norris' "Subtilizing upon a fine nothing," see Sherbert, *Menippean Satire and the Poetics of Wit*, 75–118.

37. As Sherbert points out, the digression on centaurs is a "simple inversion of idealism." D'Urfey turns from parodying the speculative philosophy of Norris to satirizing the notorious materialism of Hobbes, which is embodied in the man-beast's association with lechery, war, and satire. Though D'Urfey's pairing of idealism and materialism might seem paradoxical, the theories of both Norris and Hobbes elide essential aspects of human nature: Norris optimistically eschews the monstrous while Hobbes cynically ignores the beautiful. Thus, both Norris' *Essay* and Hobbes' *Leviathan* represent, as Sherbert puts it, "a grand deduction" (90).

38. Paulson, *The Beautiful, Novel, and Strange*, 49.

39. Of course, the loathsomeness is permanent while the delight is fleeting, being dependent on an experience of novelty that can only last as long as the new experience itself.

40. See, in particular: Parker, *The Triumph of Augustan Poetics*, 1–95; and Bogel, *The Difference Satire Makes*, 1–83.

41. Part of the satiric usefulness of monstrosity derives from its etymology. Some sources derive the term "monster" from the Latin verb *monstrare* meaning "to show," while others link it to the verb *monere*, "to warn." Seventeenth- and eighteenth-century showmen, being less interested in the origins of words than in their common usage, tended to collapse these derivations in order to stimulate both fascination and horror in their audiences. See Leslie Fiedler, *Freaks: Myths and Images of the Secret Self* (New York: Simon and Schuster, 1978), 20; Rosemarie Garland Thomson, "Introduction: From

Wonder to Error – A Genealogy of Freak Discourse in Modernity," *Freakery*, 3; and Barbara M. Benedict, "European Monsters Through English Eyes: Eighteenth-Century Cultural Icons," *Symbolism* 1 (2000), 84.

42. This view is best illustrated by Pope's *An Essay on Man* (1733–34): "Vast chain of being, which from God began, / Nature's æthereal, human, angel, man, / Beast, bird, fish, insect! what no eye can see, / No glass can reach! from Infinite to thee, / From thee to Nothing!—On superior pow'rs / Were we to press, inferior might on ours: / Or in the full creation leave a void, / Where, one step broken, the great scale's destroy'd: / From Nature's chain whatever link you strike, / Tenth or ten thousandth, breaks the chain alike" (*The Twickenham Edition of the Poems of Alexander Pope*, vol. 3.1, ed. Maynard Mack [London: Methuen, 1950], I.237–46). For an excellent discussion of Pope's satiric exploitation of deformity, see Helen Deutsch, *Resemblance and Disgrace: Alexander Pope and the Deformation of Culture* (Cambridge: Harvard University Press, 1996), esp. 1–10.

43. Burnet's description was reprinted, along with a number of other materials relating to the twins (including an engraved print of them), in *The Philosophical Transactions* 50.39 (London, 1757), 315–22. Because the Scriblerians used Helena and Judith as the basis for Lindamira and Indamora, they have attracted a good deal of critical attention. See, for example: Taylor, "Sights and Monsters," 60–61; Christopher Fox, *Locke and the Scriblerians: Identity and Consciousness in Early Eighteenth-Century Britain* (Berkeley: University of California Press, 1988), 109–17; Todd, *Imagining Monsters*, 126–35, 156; Maja-Lisa von Sneidern, "Joined at the Hip: A Monster, Colonialism, and the Scriblerian Project," *Eighteenth-Century Studies* 30:3 (1997): 213–31; and Judith Hawley, "Margins and Monstrosity: Martinus Scriblerus his 'Double Mistress,'" *Eighteenth-Century Life* 22 (1998): 31–49. Also see Charles Kerby-Miller's discussion of the "Double Mistress" episode in his edition of Pope et al., *Memoirs of Martinus Scriblerus*, 293–307.

44. Reprinted in Ashton, *Social Life in the Reign of Queen Anne*, 210.

45. *The British Apollo: Containing Two Thousand Answers to Curious Questions in Most Arts and Sciences, Serious, Comical, and Humorous*, 3 vols., 3rd edn. (London, 1726), 1.299–301. Other questions, asked and answered in the manner of Dunton's *Athenian Mercury*, appear on pages 308–09, 316, 326–27, 365–66, and 663–64. Since many of these questions figure in the plot "Double Mistress" episode, Charles Kerby-Miller speculates that some may originally have been submitted, and perhaps even responded to, by John Arbuthnot, whose rough manuscript of Chapters XIV and XV of the *Memoirs* was revised substantially by Pope (*Memoirs*, 295–96).

46. *The Philosophical Transactions* 50.39 (1757): 317–18. James Paris Du Plessis was one-time secretary to another amateur virtuoso, Samuel Pepys, from whom he likely acquired a taste for monsters. Over the course of many years, Du Plessis compiled a manuscript collection of freaks, entitled *A Short History of Human Prodigieuses & Monstrous Birth of Dwarfs, Sleepers, Giants, Strong Men, Hermaphrodites, Numerous Births, and Extream Old Age &C.* Completed in 1730, the manuscript is 163 pages long and is most remarkable for its thirty-six painted illustrations of monsters, including Helena and Judith and Matthew Buchinger. Acknowledging himself in the preface to the work to be "quite moneyless," Du Plessis sold the manuscript to Hans Sloane. For information regarding Du Plessis and his fascinating manuscript, see James Aubrey, "Revising the Monstrous: Du Plessis' *Short History of Prodigies* and London Culture in 1730," *Studies in Eighteenth-Century Culture* 23 (1994): 74–91.

47. Kerby-Miller's account of the motivations behind the episode partially anticipates my argument about the rhetorical function of digression: "In addition to its obvious merits as an individual piece, the episode of the Double Mistress contained in this and the succeeding chapter serves a very useful purpose in bringing to the *Memoirs* dramatic action and a change in the style of humour at a time when their need is beginning to be felt by the reader. After the often brilliant but somewhat static wit of the preceding chapters the broad humour and farcical action of Martinus' experience with the *'tender Passion'* come as a refreshing change. And when the last court of appeal has brought the strange romance to a close by dissolving the marriage, the reader returns to Martinus' intellectual adventures with renewed zest" (*Memoirs*, 293ff).

48. Taking the "Double Mistress" episode as exemplary, Judith Hawley summarizes the "problems" that the "Augustans" had with monsters and monster exhibitions: "(i) they are physically disproportioned, not the best part of creation, and thus a disproportionate object of study; (ii) those who collect them betray their lack of discrimination by heaping them together with other oddities; (iii) the scientist lowers himself socially if he takes his researches too seriously; (iv) collectors of curios are over-credulous, and tend to be duped by unscrupulous dealers, 'Nicknacktorians,' as those at the lower end of the market came to be called; and (v) monsters were not only to be found in private collections, but on display at freak shows where the pretence of higher knowledge was debased by the pressures of the commercial market and the physical pressure of the proximity to the mob. Serious scientists, trivial virtuosi, and the vulgar crowd all rubbed shoulders in their eagerness to see the latest sight at Bartholomew Fair or in other dens of popular resort" (Hawley, "Margins and Monstrosity," 43).

49. It appears likely that *Gulliver's Travels* began as an intended contribution to the Martinus Scriblerus project – an account of the various voyages of the Scriblerians' fictional "Prodigy of Science." Chapter XVI of the *Memoirs* offers "*some Hint of his* Travels," and this seems intended to associate Scriblerus with Gulliver: "Thou shalt know then, that in his first Voyage he was carried by a prosperous Storm, to a Discovery of the Remains of the ancient *Pygmæn* Empire." "That in his second, he was happily shipwreck'd on the Land of the *Giants*, now the most humane people in the world." "That in his third Voyage, he discover'd a whole Kingdom of *Philosophers*, who govern by the *Mathematicks*; with those admirable Schemes and Projects he return'd to benefit his own dear Country, but had the misfortune to find them rejected by the envious Ministers of *Queen Anne*, and himself sent treacherously away." "And hence it is, that in his fourth Voyage he discovers a Vein of Melancholy proceeding almost to Disgust of his Species; but above all, a mortal Detestation to the whole flagitious Race of *Ministers*, and a final Resolution not to give in any *Memorial* to the *Secretary of State*, in order to subject the Lands he discover'd to the *Crown of Great Britain*" (165). For a thorough account of the relationship between the Scriblerian *Memoirs* and Swift's masterpiece, see Charles Kerby-Miller's discussion in his edition of the *Memoirs of Martinus Scriblerus*, 315–23. For a dissenting view that questions the influence of a "Scriblerian mode" on eighteenth-century satire, see Ashley Marshall, "The Myth of Scriblerus," *Journal for Eighteenth-Century Studies* 31.1 (2008): 77–99.

50. Jonathan Swift, *Gulliver's Travels*, ed. David Womersley (Cambridge: Cambridge University Press, 2012), 1.8.110–12.

51. Benedict, *Curiosity*, 115.

52. The seminal work is by Taylor, who long ago pointed out that "[t]he details of Gulliver's exhibition may be matched so closely in the extant records of popular shows that the episode itself might well serve as primary evidence for the practices and customs of eighteenth-century showmen and their shows" ("Sights and Monsters," 29–30). Richard Altick refines Taylor's claim, giving the sights and shows of *Gulliver's Travels* a literary function: "Seeking to endow his flights of fantastic invention with verisimilitude and his narrator with credibility, Swift was at pains to provide a base of realistic detail to which every reader in touch with London life at the moment could give his instant assent" (*The Shows of London*, 35). Dennis Todd goes even further, emphasizing what Gulliver's experiences indicate about how audiences responded to monster exhibitions: "In *Gulliver's Travels* Swift is alive to both the possibilities and failures of popular diversions. He himself is willing to tease out the meanings in sights and diversions. But he is just as interested in the failure of these shows to mean

anything—that is, in the refusal of the spectators to overcome their predisposition to gaze thoughtlessly at them" (*Imagining Monsters*, 153).

53. Taylor, "Sights and Monsters," 36.

54. Edward J. Wood, *Giants and Dwarves* (London: Richard Bentley, 1868), 302–04.

55. Todd, *Imagining Monsters*, 157. Todd argues that the identity between monstrous and normal was glossed over by audiences more inclined to gawk than to think: "But this appeal to the audience's intuition of a hidden identity with the monsters was all titillation. For at the same time the exhibitions blurred the boundaries between viewers and monsters, they firmly drew the lines again, comfortably distancing the audience by emphasizing the monster's sheer difference. Displayed in a circumscribed part of the city set aside for the purpose, placed on a stage, shown during holidays, exhibited precisely because of their anomalousness, the monsters were, in the end, not us at all but just freaks in a fair booth. The intuition of identity that attracted the audience in the first place, instead of being allowed to ripen into conscious self-awareness, was diverted into the mindless pleasures of spectacle. And so the economy of monster exhibitions answers perfectly to the dance of attraction and avoidance. What begins as titillation ends as mere entertainment, to the infinite satisfaction of an audience who 'purely come to hear, and stare'" (160).

56. See Barbara Maria Stafford, *Body Criticism: Imaging the Unseen in Enlightenment Art and Medicine* (Cambridge: MIT Press, 1991), 259.

57. Benedict, *Curiosity*, 2.

58. Samuel Pepys, *The Diary of Samuel Pepys*, 11 vols., ed. Robert Latham and William Matthews (Berkeley: University of California Press, 1970–76), 8.326.

59. *The Philosophical Transactions* 47.42 (1753): 278–81.

60. *The Philosophical Transactions* 41.2 (1744): 294–307. Richard Altick claims that "[f]ew of the freaks, human and subhuman, exhibited in London between 1665 and 1800," go unmentioned in the "grave and lively pages" of *The Philosophical Transactions* (37). Judith Hawley quantifies this claim, observing that the first seventy volumes of *The Philosophical Transactions* feature around fifty articles on human or animal monsters (Hawley, "Margins and Monstrosity," 40).

61. See Thomson, "Introduction: From Wonder to Error," 13.

62. Francis Bacon, *The Advancement of Learning, The Major Works*, ed. Brian Vickers (New York: Oxford University Press, 2002), 176.

63. Lorraine Daston and Katherine Park, *Wonders and the Order of Nature: 1150–1750* (New York: Zone Books, 2001), 212–13.

64. Ephraim Chambers, *Cyclopedia: or, An Universal Dictionary of Arts and Sciences*, 2 vols. (London, 1728), 2.573.

65. Benjamin Norton Defoe, *A New English Dictionary, Containing a Large and Almost Compleat Collection of Useful English Words* (London, 1737).

66. Edward Phillips, *The New World of Words: or, Universal English Dictionary*, 6th edn. (London, 1706). The first edition was published in 1671, but the definition of "monster" expanded over subsequent editions.

67. Johnson, *A Dictionary of the English Language*. In contrast, Johnson defines the noun "MO′NSTER" in such a way as to distinguish the literal from the figurative. In one sense, a monster is "Something out of the common order of nature," but in another sense, it is "Something horrible for deformity, wickedness, or mischief." He illustrates the first through a passage from Locke, and the second through Shakespeare and Pope.

68. Francis Bacon, *The Novum Organum*, trans. Michael Silverthorne, ed. Lisa Jardine (Cambridge: Cambridge University Press, 2000), 149. Addison's argument that monsters encourage a "search into the wonders" of the natural world also seems to have its basis in Bacon's claim that monsters "fortify the intellect in the face of the commonplace, and reveal common forms": "He who knows the ways of nature will also more easily recognize the deviations. And conversely he who recognizes the deviations will more accurately describe the ways" (148).

69. Horace, *To The Pisones, on the Art of Poetry, The Odes, Satyrs, and Epistles of Horace*, trans. Thomas Creech, 3rd edn. (London, 1711), 399. The Earl of Roscommon's translation associates the monstrous with the ridiculous: "If in a Picture (*Piso*) you should see / A handsom Woman with a Fish's Tail, / Or a Man's Head upon a Horse's Neck, / Or Limbs of Beasts of the most diff'rent Kinds, / Cover'd with Feathers of all sorts of Birds, / Wou'd you not laugh, and think the Painter mad? / Trust me that Book is as ridiculous, / Whose incoherent Style (like Sick Mens Dreams) / Varies all Shapes, and mixes all Extremes" (*The Odes and Satyrs of Horace*, 186).

70. Hawley, "Margins and Monstrosity," 42. Also see Daston and Park, *Wonders and the Order of Nature*, 210–14.

71. Michael de Montaigne, *Essays of Michael Seigneur de Montaigne*, 4th edn., 3 vols., trans. Charles Cotton (London, 1711), 1.38–40. The first two books of Montaigne's *Essais* appeared in 1580, and the third in 1588. John Florio was the first to translate the complete *Essayes* into English (1603, 1613), but his colourful baroque translation was eventually replaced by Cotton's more literal translation of 1685. Cotton's is the translation used by most writers and readers of the late seventeenth and early eighteenth centuries.

72. Puttenham, *The Arte of English Poesie*, 15.

73. William Drummond, "To His Much Honoured Friend Dr. Arthur Johnston, Physician to the King (c. 1629)," *Literary Criticism of Seventeenth Century England* (New York: Alfred A. Knoph, 1967), 216.

74. Ben Jonson, *Bartholomew Fair*, ed. Maurice Hussey (London: Ernest Benn Ltd., 1964), Induction ll. 123–30. Jonson's Induction uses monstrosity both literally and figuratively, since the "servant-monster" is obviously a reference to an actual monster-character: Caliban. The Scrivener cites the audience's fondness for "Tales, Tempests, and such like Drolleries" as a way of indicting Shakespeare's neglect of dramatic poetics.

75. William Congreve, "Concerning Humour in Comedy," *Critical Essays of the Seventeenth Century*, 3 vols., ed. J.E. Springarn (Bloomington: Indiana University Press, 1957), 3.244.

76. Granville, "Concerning Unnatural Flights in Poetry," ll. 13–16.

77. For a provocative discussion of the relationship between monstrosity and mimesis during the Renaissance, see Marie-Hélène Huet, *Monstrous Imagination* (Cambridge: Harvard University Press, 1993).

78. John Dryden, "A Parallel of Poetry and Painting (1695)," *Essays*, 2 vols., ed. W.P. Ker (Oxford, 1900; rpt. New York: Russell & Russell, 1961), 2.132–33.

79. The scholarship on the expansion of print culture in eighteenth-century England is enormous, but much of it builds upon the important topographic, demographic, and literary-critical work done by Pat Rogers in *Grub Street*. Other standard studies include: Elizabeth L. Eisenstein, *Print Culture and Enlightenment Thought* (Chapel Hill: Hanes Foundation, University of North Carolina, 1986); Mark Rose, *Authors and Owners: The Invention of Copyright* (Cambridge: Harvard University Press, 1993); Hammond, *Professional Imaginative Writing in England, 1670–1740*; Johns, "Literary Life," *The Nature of the Book*, 58–186; and Margaret J.M. Ezell, *Social Authorship and the Advent of Print* (Baltimore: Johns Hopkins University Press, 1999). Also see *Grub St. Stripped Bare* (London: Constable and Company, 1968), where Philip Pinkus engagingly surveys the consequences of the lapse of the Licensing Act, by way of an edited collection of the "scandalous lives & pornographic works of the original Grub St. writers."

80. Brewer, *The Pleasures of the Imagination*, 187.

81. Richard Savage, *An Author to be Lett* (London, 1729, intro. James Sutherland; rpt. Los Angeles: William Andrews Clark Memorial Library, 1960), 11. Although this satire is an extension of Swift's and Pope's war with the hacks and dunces, Savage himself was an acknowledged "author to be lett." The experiences of Iscariot Hackney thus offer an ironic but informative perspective on the activities of the typical Grub Street author.

82. J.V. Guerinot, *Pamphlet Attacks on Alexander Pope, 1711–1744* (London: Methuen, 1969), XL.

83. That monstrous dreams portend the birth of a scribbler was a conventional trope in satiric literature of the period. Better known than the

prognostication of Mrs Hackney is that of the mother of Martinus Scriblerus. "Nor was the Birth of this great man unattended with *Prodigies*," explains the purported editor of the Scriblerian *Memoirs*. "He himself has often told me, that, on the night before he was born, Mrs. Scriblerus dream'd she was brought to bed of a huge *Ink-horn*, out of which issued several large streams of Ink, as it had been a fountain: This dream was by her husband thought to signify, that the child should prove a very voluminous Writer. Likewise a *Crab-tree* that hath been hitherto barren, appeared on a sudden laden with a vast quantity of Crabs: This sign also the old gentleman imagined to be a prognostic of the acuteness of his Wit. A great swarm of *Wasps* play'd round his Cradle without hurting him, but were very troublesome to all in the room besides: This seemed a certain presage of the effects of his Satire. A Dunghill was seen within the space of one night to be covered all over with *Mushrooms*: This some interpreted to promise the infant great fertility of fancy, but no long duration to his works; but the Father was of another opinion ... But what was of all most wonderful, was a thing that seemed a monstrous *Fowl*, which just then dropt through the sky-light, near his wife's apartment. It had a large body, two little disproportioned wings, a prodigious tail, but no head. As its colour was white, he took it at first sight for a Swan, and was concluding his son would be a Poet; but on a nearer view, he perceived it to be speckled with black, in the form of letters; and that it was indeed a Paper kite which had broke its leash by the impetuosity of the wind. His back was armed with the Art Military, his belly was filled with Physick, his wings were the wings of Quarles and Withers, the several Nodes of his voluminous tail were diversify'd with several branches of science; where the Doctor beheld with great joy a knot of Logick, a knot of Metaphysick, a knot of Casuistry, a knot of Polemical Divinity, and a knot of Common Law, with a *Lanthorn of Jacob Behem*" (*Memoirs*, 98–99).

84. See Elizabeth L. Eisenstein, *The Printing Press as an Agent of Change: Communications and Cultural Transformation in Early-Modern Europe*, 2 vols. (Cambridge: Cambridge University Press, 1979), esp. 1.225–302, and Habermas, *The Structural Transformation of the Public Sphere*, 38, 51.

85. Richard W.F. Kroll explains that "the age seems to have delighted in the concreteness of the page impressed by visible marks, ascending atomically from letters to word, to sentences, to entire discourses" (*The Material Word: Literate Culture in the Restoration and Early Eighteenth Century* [Baltimore: Johns Hopkins University Press, 1991], 14).

86. See Johns, *The Nature of the Book*, esp. 1–57.

87. Benedict sees this kind of writing as a consequence of commodity culture's perversion of individual identity: "To many writers, hybrids, giants, and

dwarfs provided metaphors for the commodification of identity wrought by modern consumption, the excessive desire for experience or acquisitions. Like ontological 'monsters' whose bodies violate human limits, yet whose verbal skills prove their humanity, both acquisitive consumers and exploitative writing that oversteps formal categories challenged distinctions between art and nature" (*Curiosity*, 72).

88. Swift to Dean Stearne, June 10, 1708, *The Correspondence of Jonathan Swift*, 5 vols., ed. Harold Williams (Oxford: Clarendon Press, 1963–65), 1.82–83.

89. See Flint, *The Appearance of Print*, 113–26.

90. In the 1743 *Dunciad in Four Books*, Pope moved the "Cave of Poverty and Poetry" from the clothing market near the Tower of London to the vicinity of Bedlam, in Moorfields, where Grub Street was actually located "[c]lose to those walls where Folly holds her throne" (1.29ff).

91. Anne Hall Bailey, "How Much for Just the Muse?: Alexander Pope's *Dunciad*, Book IV and the Literary Market," *Eighteenth Century: Theory and Interpretation* 36.1 (1995), 34. Also see: Marlon B. Ross, "Authority and Authenticity: Scribbling Authors and the Genius of Print in Eighteenth-Century England," *The Construction of Authorship: Textual Appropriation in Law and Literature*, ed. Martha Woodmansee and Peter Jaszi (Durham: Duke University Press, 1994), 231–57; and Shef Rogers, "Pope, Publishing, and Popular Interpretations of *The Dunciad Variorum*," *Philological Quarterly* 74.3 (1995): 279–95.

92. In the opinion of Christopher Flint, the coincidental expansion of print and development of Augustan satire was fortuitous, since it encouraged writers like Swift, Richardson, and Sterne to imitate and exploit the "material practices of the print industry": "Late seventeenth and early eighteenth-century prognostications about the press in England frequently display an almost missionary zeal when recording the impact of print technology on cultural advancement ... But the early part of this period was also one in which the English 'Republic of Letters' witnessed one of the most influential and distinctive literary movements in British history, Augustan satire, whose target was repeatedly a Grub Street world controlled by printers and booksellers such as Edmund Curll – quintessential modernists, whose manipulations of the print industry gave rise to a new and, for many, degraded model of authorship and civil society. Such publishers were often charged with creating the Grub Street hack in order to fulfil an unprecedented market for printed material." See "In Other Words: Eighteenth-Century Authorship and the Ornaments of Print," *Eighteenth-Century Fiction* 14 (2002): 627–72, esp. 628–31.

93. For a discussion of the use of the monstrosity motif in Scriblerian satires on print, particularly *The Dunciad*, see: Roger D. Lund, "Pope's Monsters:

Satire and the Grotesque in *The Dunciad*," *The Scope of the Fantastic –
Culture, Biography, Themes, Children's Literature: Selected Essays from the
First International Conference on the Fantastic in Literature and Film*, ed.
Robert A. Collins and Howard D. Pearce (Westport: Greenwood Press,
1985), 61–78; Todd, *Imagining Monsters*, 179–268; and Richard Nash, *Wild
Enlightenment: The Borders of Human Identity in the Eighteenth Century*
(Charlottesville: University of Virginia Press, 2003), 15–41.

94. For a discussion of the uses of asterisked ellipses during the period, see
Elizabeth Wanning Harries, *The Unfinished Manner: Essays on the Fragment
in the Later Eighteenth Century* (Charlottesville: University Press of Virginia,
1994), 27–32, and Anne C. Henry, "The Re-mark-able Rise of '. . .': Reading
Ellipsis Marks in Literary Texts," *Ma[r]king the Text: The Presentation of
Meaning on the Literary Page*, ed. Joe Bray, Miriam Handley, and Anne C.
Henry (Aldershot: Ashgate Publishing, 2000), 120–42.

95. Pope to Swift, June 28, 1728, *The Correspondence of Alexander Pope*, 5 vols.,
ed. George Sherburn (Oxford: Clarendon Press, 1956), 2.503.

96. Benedict, "European Monsters Through English Eyes," 86.

97. Gérard Genette defines "paratext" as those miscellaneous elements that
"surround" or "extend" a primary text "precisely in order to *present* it."
Paratext is "what enables a text to become a book and to be offered as such to
its readers and, more generally, to the public" (*Paratexts: Thresholds of
Interpretation*, trans. Jane E. Lewin [Cambridge: Cambridge University
Press, 1997], 1–2).

98. Janine Barchas, *Graphic Design, Print Culture, and the Eighteenth-Century
Novel* (Cambridge: Cambridge University Press, 2003), 6. Barchas' opening
chapter, "Expanding the Literary Text," provides a succinct summary of the
theory and practice of modern "textual studies," which takes for granted that
the printed book itself is an expressive form (1–18).

99. *The Athenian Mercury*, vol. 8, no. 1 (July 12, 1692).

100. The complex narrative of *A Voyage Round the World* is controlled by at least
four distinct and ostensibly autobiographical voices: "Don Kainophilus"
(whose name "signifies, by the by, a *Lover of News*"), "Evander," "Philaret,"
and John Dunton himself. Due to its play with personae, its typographical
oddity, and its digressiveness, critics have seen Dunton's *Voyage* as an
important analogue for Swift's *Tale of a Tub*. See: J.M. Stedmond,
"Another Possible Analogue for Swift's *Tale of a Tub*," *Modern Language
Notes* 72 (1957): 12–18; J. Paul Hunter, "The Insistent 'I'," *Novel* 13 (1979): 19–
37; and Robert Adams Day, "Richard Bentley and John Dunton: Brothers
Under the Skin," *Studies in Eighteenth-Century Culture* 16 (1986): 125–38.

101. According to Stephen Parks, Dunton was the first to apply the designation
to "the wholesaling associations developing in the trade" (*John Dunton and*

*the English Book Trade* [New York: Garland Press, 1976], 205–10). Dunton provides a more comprehensive survey of the London book trade in his *Life and Errors* (1705).

102. *The Life, Travels, and Adventures of Christopher Wagstaff, Gentleman, Grandfather to Tristram Shandy*, 1.34

103. Jonathan Swift, *On Poetry: A Rapsody, Poetical Works*, ed. Herbert Davis (London: Oxford University Press, 1967), ll. 93–100, p. 572.

104. So extensive is Brown's use of the device that his twentieth-century editor claims, on dubious grounds, that he was "the first to employ the thin disguise of substituting dashes for the vowels in the names of his victims, concealing his venom under such subterfuges as 'Sir R—ch—d Bl—k—re'" (Thomas Brown, *Amusements Serious and Comical and Other Works*, ed. Arthur L. Hayward [London: George Routledge & Sons, 1927], xiv).

105. Andrew Curran and Patrick Graille, "The Faces of Eighteenth-Century Monstrosity," *Eighteenth-Century Life* 21.2 (1997): 3.

106. The first of Ralph's epigraphs, drawn from the first book and tenth satire of Horace, speaks to themes of this study: "*Ridiculum Acri Fortiùs & meliùs magnas plerumque secat res.*" / "Jesting oft cuts hard knots more forcefully and effectively than gravity." The second of Ralph's epigraphs, drawn from the tenth book and fourth epistle of Martial, speaks to the themes of this chapter: "*Non hic Centauros, non Gorgonas, Harpyiasque Invenies: Hominem pagina nostra sapit.*" / "Not here will you find Centaurs, not Gorgons and Harpies: 'tis of man my page smacks." The irony is that Ralph's "page" exposes man's obsession with monsters.

## 4   "Pleasantry for thy entertainment": novelistic discourse and the rhetoric of diversion

1. *The Daily Journal* No. 2491 (January 1, 1729).

2. For discussion of the anxieties over the traditional English "addiction unto novelties," see Sara Warneke, "A Taste for Newfangledness: The Destructive Potential of Novelty in Early Modern England," *Sixteenth-Century Journal* 26 (1995): 881–96. For analysis of the material and conceptual implications of this addiction, see Marina Bianchi, "Consuming Novelty: Strategies for Producing Novelty in Consumption," *Journal of Medieval and Early Modern Studies* 28.1 (1998): 3–18.

3. For a critical summary of the rhetorical history of digression, see Cotterill, *Digressive Voices*, 1–43. Dedicating her attention primarily to seventeenth-century England, Cotterill explores how digression "helped to focus around speech and eloquence the social and political anxieties of an age, exactly when a variety of historical forces were effecting a gradual long-range shift from oral

to print and market culture" (13). She argues that in Donne, Marvell, Browne, Milton, and Dryden, digression functions as a rhetorical vehicle of self-defence – "underground writing" – which offers a "veiled expression of political doubt and enmity together with an elaboration of hidden and unruly or disturbing parts of the speaker's self" (2). Picking up where Cotterill leaves off, I argue that in the eighteenth century digression helps to focus around rhetoric the respective pleasures of the age – an age of rapid urbanization and commercialization.

4. See Susan Stewart, *On Longing: Narratives of the Miniature, the Gigantic, the Souvenir, the Collection* (Baltimore: Johns Hopkins University Press, 1984), 29–30.

5. The "honourable Mention" that Primcock gives to these performers is consistent with his emphasis on the pleasant deceits of modern pantomimes: "The two first we look upon as humble Creepers in DANCING, as the last are generally High-flyers: They all have their Merits in their different Stations. *Tumbling* and *Postures* require as great Agility and Dexterity, and their various Tricks may appear as pleasing to the Eye as the brave Attempts of *Rope-Dancing*: But this last is more surprising and hazardous, giving the Spectator a sort of painful Pleasure" (109).

6. *The Tricks of the Town Laid Open* was originally printed as a short pamphlet in 1699 under the title *The Country Gentleman's Vade-Mecum*, just a few years after John Dunton's *A Voyage Round the World* (1691) had used virtually the same lines on London's "*circle of Varieties*" to an opposite end. Following three days "*Rambling about* the City and Suburbs" of the metropolis," Dunton's narrator concedes that after "long *feasting my Eyes* with Novelties, I began at last to be even tir'd with Pleasures, and glutted with City Charms." However, instead of advising his readers to abandon London pleasures and retire themselves to the country, as does his anonymous plagiarizer, Dunton has his narrator suggest that they accommodate themselves to the city by diversifying their diversions: "*This is the Nature and common Condition of even the most pleasing, sensible Objects: They first tempt, then please a little, then disappoint, and lastly vex. The Eye that beholds them blasts them quickly, riffles and destroys their Glory, and views them with not more delight at first; than disdain afterwards. Hence, there must be frequent diversions; and other Pleasures must be sought out; and are chosen, not because they are better, but because they are new*" (1.141).

7. In order to win support for a declining theatre, as well as for his digressive *Apology*, Colley Cibber urges readers to see their patronage of plays and players as a patriotic duty: "I would fain flatter my self, that those, who are not too wise, to frequent the Theatre (or have Wit enough to distinguish what sort of Sights there, either do Honour, or Disgrace to it) may think their

national Diversion no contemptible Subject, for a more able Historian, than I
pretend to be" (195).

8. Warner, *Licensing Entertainment*, XII. According to Warner, Fielding's novels
"entertain" readers by conceptualizing their "essential freedom" as "a
pleasurable responsibility." See Warner's chapter on *"Joseph Andrews* as
Performative Entertainment," *Licensing Entertainment*, 231–76.

9. "What did readers seek in novels and what did they find?" queries J. Paul
Hunter, "Pleasure of course, first and foremost: The joy of escape from
drudgery or routine" ("The Novel and Social/Cultural History," *The
Cambridge Companion to the Eighteenth-Century Novel*, ed. John Richetti
[Cambridge: Cambridge University Press, 1996], 22).

10. Mary Davys, *The Reform'd Coquet, Familiar Letters Betwixt a Gentleman and a
Lady*, and *The Accomplish'd Rake*, ed. Martha F. Bowden (Lexington:
University Press of Kentucky, 1999), 5–6.

11. William Congreve, *Incognita* and *The Way of the World*, ed. A. Norman
Jeffares (Columbia: University of South Carolina Press, 1970), 31.

12. Daniel Defoe, *Moll Flanders*, ed. Albert J. Rivero (New York: W.W. Norton
& Company, 2003), 4–5.

13. Delarivière Manley, *The Secret History of Queen Zarah and the Zarazians,
Popular Fiction by Women, 1660–1730: An Anthology*, ed. Paula R. Backscheider
and John R. Richetti (Oxford: Clarendon Press, 1996), 46–47.

14. Francis Coventry, *An Essay on the New Species of Writing Founded by Mr.
Fielding*, intro. Alan Dugald McKillop (London, 1751; rpt. Los Angeles:
William Andrews Clark Memorial Library, 1962), 1. In this essay, Coventry,
himself a novelist, is at pains to differentiate Fielding's fiction from volumes
"commonly known by the Name of Romances, or Novels, Tales, &c. fill'd
with any thing which the wildest Imagination could suggest" (1).

15. Aphra Behn, *Oroonoko; or, The Royal Slave*, ed. Catherine Gallagher with
Simon Stern (Boston: Bedford/St Martin's, 2000), 37–38.

16. Henry Fielding, *The History of the Adventures of Joseph Andrews, and of His
Friend Mr. Abraham Adams*, ed. Martin C. Battestin (Middletown: Wesleyan
University Press, 1967), 2.1.89–90.

17. Jill Campbell provides a useful summary of Fielding's complex attitude
towards diversion, emphasizing in particular the ways in which the
representation of the *"Pleasures of the Town"* in his novels and plays reveals
the role of modern entertainers in the "feminization" of English culture. See,
*Natural Masques: Gender and Identity in Fielding's Plays and Novels* (Stanford:
Stanford University Press, 1995), esp. 1–16.

18. Henry Fielding, "The Masquerade. A Poem," *The Journal of a Voyage to Lisbon,
Shamela, and Occasional Writings*, ed. Martin C. Battestin, Sheridan W. Baker
Jr., and Hugh Amory (Oxford: Clarendon Press, 2008), ll. 61–66, p. 17.

19. Henry Fielding, *The Author's Farce; and the Pleasures of the Town, Plays One: 1728–1731*, ed. Thomas Lockwood (Oxford: Clarendon Press, 2004), 2.7., p. 252.

20. Henry Fielding, *The Champion* (April 22, 1740), *Contributions to* The Champion *and Related Writings*, ed. W.B. Coley (Oxford: Clarendon Press, 2003), 287.

21. See, for example, Keymer, *Sterne, the Moderns, and the Novel*, esp. 36–48.

22. Critics have long noted that Fielding was indebted to James Ralph for his burlesque treatment of the *"Pleasures of the Town"* in *The Author's Farce* and other plays, but what has never been noticed is that the format of *The Touch-Stone* also appears to have influenced the rhetoric of his fiction. See: Hughes, "Fielding's Indebtedness to James Ralph," 19–34; and Martin C. Battestin with Ruthe R. Battestin, *Henry Fielding: A Life* (London: Routledge, 1989), 80–82. Fielding, of course, also plays on a familiar trope in *A Tale of a Tub*, where Swift's Grub Street hack denounces "that pernicious Custom, of making the Preface a Bill of Fare to the Book" (85).

23. Hunter analyses the digressive episodes and lengthy inset autobiographies (e.g. the story of the Man of the Hill) characteristic of Fielding's fiction as necessary "pauses" in the social and spiritual journey of a Joseph Andrews or a Tom Jones. "In their near suspension from the ongoing plot and in their soporific contrasts to Fielding's own method," Hunter explains, "the interpolations are places of rest and refreshment, but they also flesh out the offerings of Fielding's novels to indicate alternative literary possibilities and to alert readers to responses that, while ludicrous, may mirror and parody their own." See *Occasional Form*, 142–65, esp. 160–61.

24. *The Daily Courant* No. 2893 (January 27, 1711).

25. Charles Gildon, *Les Soupirs de la Grand Britaigne: or, The Groans of Great Britain* (London, 1713), 74. Citing an advertisement for Punch's Theatre as an ironic "Argument of fine Taste," Gildon proceeds to attack what he views as the "incredible Folly" exemplified by Powell's success: "It is so much below ridicule, that the bare Recital is a Satyr upon all, who frequent this fantastick and childish Entertainment. Is it not madness for any Man of Sense to expect Encouragement for writing Poetry in *Britain*? The Stage had been debauch'd with Dancers, and Singers, and Tumblers, and Ladder Dancers, Mr. *Clinch* of *Barnet*, Posture-Masters and Eunuchs. But still all these left an Interval to Poetry to appear now and then to the Audience. This has with as much Wonder as Success, excluded it entirely. Well may Foreigners conclude us Barbarians, when such are Entertainments of our Persons of Figure" (74–75).

26. Cited in Martin C. Battestin, "Fielding and 'Master Punch' in Panton Street," *Philological Quarterly* 45 (1966): 193. For a discussion of Fielding's playful exploitation of the medium of the puppet theatre, see Anthony J. Hassall, "Fielding's Puppet Image," *Philological Quarterly* 53.1 (1974): 71–83.

27. Speaight, *The History of the English Puppet Theatre*, 92.
28. The mid eighteenth-century taste for formal realism seems to have affected puppeteers as much as playwrights, and the boast of Fielding's puppet-show-man is not so extravagant when compared with contemporary commentary on the "Genius" of the English puppet theatre. Describing life in England in 1734, the Abbé Prevost reported that "marionettes of human size had been seen for several years performing entire tragedies with great success ... with dress, gestures, walk, and moving lips and eyes, in every way resembling human beings." In 1744, an Italian commentator named Quadrio similarly observed that "the English, with their ingenious skill have to-day developed [puppetry] to perfection." "Without departing from its primary principle," he continued, "they have introduced a type of puppet which is still more worthy of playing spectacles before the eyes of a Court even more cultured than that of France. Figures about four-feet high and finely dressed are made to appear upon a fairly high stage, before which a net has been drawn; a great many threads, handled from somewhere out of sight, control the hands, the feet, the mouth, and even the eyes, so as to give to each figure the natural movement and gestures of a living person." See Speaight, *The History of the English Puppet Theatre*, 161–65.
29. The "Harangue" of the puppeteer is brought to a comic conclusion when the maidservant Grace is discovered on the stage "in Company with the Merry Andrew, and in a Situation not very proper to be described" (640). Grace's naïve defence of her actions reveals what Fielding views as the danger of absorptive novels and plays and the absurdity of conflating representation with "the Life": "'If I am a Wh—e ... my Betters are so as well as I. What was the fine Lady in the Puppet-show just now? I suppose she did not lie all Night out from her Husband for nothing'" (641).
30. See James Bramston's *The Art of Politicks*, where a footnote explains this epithet: "*All Mr.* Heydegger's *Letters come directed to him from abroad,* A Monsieur, Monsieur *Heydegger,* Surintendent des Plaisirs d'Angleterre" (5). "Count" Heidegger was officially Master of the Revels under George II. For an account of the controversy over his promotion of lavish entertainments, see Rogers, *Literature and Popular Culture*, esp. 40–69.
31. See Rogers, *Literature and Popular Culture*, 57.
32. *The Weekly Journal: or, Saturday's Post* No. 62 (February 15, 1718).
33. The phrase appears in Centlivre's poem, *The Masquerade* (1712), cited in John Wilson Bowyer, *The Celebrated Mrs. Centlivre* (Durham: Duke University Press, 1952), 150–52.
34. See, for instance, *Spectator* No. 8 (March 9, 1711), where Addison reprints two letters attacking the lawlessness of the "Midnight Masque." The first letter, written by "one of the Directors of the Society for the Reformation of

Manners," warns that "the whole Design of this libidinous Assembly seems to terminate in Assignations and Intrigues." The next letter, written by a "young Templer," realizes this warning through the author's admission that his recent trip to the masquerade resulted in his being duped by a prostitute dressed as "a Woman of first Quality" and thereby mistaking "a *Cloud* for a *Juno*" (1.35–38).

35. Castle, *Masquerade and Civilization*, 121.

36. See Harry William Pedicord, "The Changing Audience," *The London Theatre World, 1660–1800*, ed. Robert D. Hume (Carbondale: Southern Illinois Press, 1980), 236–52.

37. Samuel Foote, *A Treatise on the Passions, So Far as They Regard the Stage* (London, [1747]), 3. Foote's anonymously published pamphlet sparked a critical controversy by questioning the "Dramatick Genius" of David Garrick, whom he argues is ineffective in conveying "the Passions of Love, Grief, and Horror with equal Force" (15). Fielding's emphasis throughout this episode on Garrick's ability to provoke terror in Partridge is an attempt to defend his close friend as, in the town's opinion, "the best Player who ever was on the Stage" (856).

38. For discussion of eighteenth-century acting and contemporary theories of the passions, see Alan S. Downer, "Nature to Advantage Dressed: Eighteenth-Century Acting," *PMLA* 58 (1943): 1002–37; George Taylor, "'The Just Delineation of the Passions': Theories of Acting in the Age of Garrick," *Essays on the Eighteenth-Century Stage*, ed. Kenneth Richards and Peter Thomson (London: Methuen, 1972), 55–72; and Roach, *The Player's Passion*, esp. 58–92.

39. Critics have often noted that the "anti-mimetic" format of Fielding's most successful plays – which resist pure representation and seem to break illusion for their own sake – contributed in important ways to the intrusive and self-consciously reflexive narrative technique of his novels. See, for instance: Claude Rawson, "Some Considerations on Authorial Intrusion and Dialogue in Fielding's Novels and Plays," *Durham University Journal* 33 (1971): 32–44; Hunter, *Occasional Form*, esp. 48–74; and Bevis, "Fielding's Normative Authors," 55–70.

40. Kenny, "Theatre, Related Arts, and the Profit Motive," 15.

41. William Shakespeare, *Hamlet*, ed. G.R. Hibbard (New York: Oxford University Press, 1987), 2.2.594. See John Allen Stevenson, "Fielding's Mousetrap: Hamlet, Partridge and the '45," *Studies in English Literature* 37.3 (1997): 553–71.

42. As Warner observes, some of the now-obsolete definitions of *entertain* listed in the *Oxford English Dictionary* reflect common eighteenth-century usage: to "hold mutually"; to "hold intertwined"; to "keep (a person, country, etc.) in a certain state or condition"; to "keep (a person) in a certain frame of mind"; to

"maintain, persist in (a course of action, 'attitude,' state of feeling)"; to "keep in repair of efficiency"; to "keep, retain (a person) in one's service"; to "maintain"; to "support"; to "provide sustenance for (a person)"; to "deal with, have communication with (a person)"; to "treat in a (specified) manner"; to "engage, keep occupied the attention, thoughts, or time of (a person)"; to "occupy, fill up, wile away (time)"; and to "receive (a person)." The modern usage of the term was also current in the eighteenth century: "To engage agreeably the attention of (a person); to amuse." See *Licensing Entertainment*, 231–34.

43. See Battestin, *Henry Fielding: A Life*, 440.
44. For discussion of the role of the reader in Fielding's fiction, see: John Preston, *The Created Self: The Reader's Role in Eighteenth-Century Fiction* (London: Heinemann, 1970), esp. 94–113; Nicholas Hudson, "Fielding's Hierarchy of Dialogue: 'Meta-Response' and the Reader in *Tom Jones*," *Philological Quarterly* 68 (1989): 177–94; and Thomas Keymer, "Readers and Stage Coaches in Fielding and Sterne," *Notes and Queries* 41.2 (1994): 209–11.
45. *Henry Fielding: The Critical Heritage*, ed. Ronald Paulson and Thomas Lockwood (London: Routledge, 1969), 187–88, 164, 224. In order to keep his French readers "heated," de la Place actually omitted the introductory essays prefacing each book of *Tom Jones* from his translated edition of 1750. He also suppressed "all the low comic scenes spread in profusion through this history."
46. R.S. Crane, "The Concept of Plot and the Plot of *Tom Jones*," *Critics and Criticism*, abridged edn., ed. R.S. Crane (Chicago: The University of Chicago Press, 1957), 85. A leading proponent of the neo-Aristotelian "Chicago School" of critics, Crane was deeply invested in the idea of "form" as the emotional force behind a literary work and the principle governing its disposition of parts or "structure."
47. For a summary of the strain of criticism that questions the value of the "ornamental" parts of Fielding's narrative, see Robert L. Chibka, "Taking 'The Serious' Seriously: The Introductory Chapters of *Tom Jones*," *Eighteenth-Century: Theory and Interpretation* 31.1 (1990): 23–45.
48. Ian Watt, *The Rise of the Novel: Studies in Defoe, Richardson, and Fielding* (London, 1957; rpt. Harmondsworth: Penguin Books, 1963), 298.
49. Warner argues that Fielding's novels make a case for the advantages of "performative entertainment" over the "absorptive entertainment" provided by novels like Richardson's *Pamela* (1740), which encourage "an overly literal imitative reading." See *Licensing Entertainment*, 235–40.
50. Sandra Sherman, "Reading at Arm's Length: Fielding's Contract with the Reader in *Tom Jones*," *Studies in the Novel* 30.2 (1998): 234–35.
51. The phrase "extraordinary obtrusiveness" is taken from Irvin Ehrenpreis, *Fielding: Tom Jones* (London: Arnold, 1964), 7.

## "The soul of reading": conclusion by way of animadversion

1. Keymer, *Sterne, the Moderns and the Novel*, 7. According to Keymer, the mid-century novel represented "the quintessential mode—subjective, circumstantial, digressive, transgressive—of commercial modern writing" (7–8).

2. James Raven, *Judging New Wealth: Popular Publishing and Responses to Commerce in England, 1750–1800* (Oxford: Clarendon Press, 1992), 63.

3. One such study is Paul Keen's *Literature, Commerce, and the Spectacle of Modernity, 1750–1800*, which analyses the "radically intersubjective nature of commercial modernity" in the second half of the eighteenth century (4). Rather than focussing on conservative resistance to modernity, Keen discusses the "resourcefulness, wit, and theoretical self-consciousness" with which writers in the later period accommodated themselves to changes in the nature of commerce, fashion, and communicative technologies (2). Keen argues that these writers "began to absorb the experience of commerce, not just into their political self-understanding but into their cultural self-understanding in the broadest sense of that phrase" (16).

4. See Paulson, "From Novel to Strange to 'Sublime,'" *The Beautiful, Novel, and Strange*, 198–224.

5. Keymer, *Sterne, the Moderns and the Novel*, 16. In *Knowing Books*, Christina Lupton analyses the coalescence of literary innovation and self-consciousness, and takes up the question of why novelists during the middle decades of the eighteenth century continued to employ intrusive narrative devices even after the genre of the novel ceased to be "new." Echoing Keymer, she explains that "with the exception of *Tristram Shandy*, which can itself be understood as a reflexive reiteration of the process of which it announces the end, relatively few mid-century works advance the history of the novel—or of literary novelty" (2–3).

6. See, for example, Garry Sherbert's discussion of Shandean wit as a parody of literary creativity and an exploration of "moral self-consciousness" in *Menippean Satire and the Poetics of Wit*, 119–90.

7. According to Christopher Fanning, Sterne's manipulation of asterisked ellipses is representative of the "shifting aesthetics" between the satiric mode of *A Tale of a Tub* and *The Dunciad*, and the sentimental mode of *Tristram Shandy*: "Whereas the Scriblerians use textual presence to enact the failure of the mental to free itself from the material, Sterne's period in some ways celebrated this failure as an indication of finer feelings, the inexpressibility of which protected them from the compromising materiality of the text" ("Small Particles of Eloquence," 384). Also see Elizabeth Wanning Harries's discussion of fragmentation and affective aesthetics in *The Unfinished Manner*, esp. 34–55 and 98–121.

8. See Paul Langford, *A Polite and Commercial People: England, 1727–1783* (Oxford: Clarendon Press, 1989), 463–67. René Bosch challenges the standard claim that *Tristram Shandy* participates in a "sentimental revolution" in the middle of the eighteenth century, demonstrating that early readers seem to have regarded Sterne's sentimentalism "as a continuation of the sceptical tradition." See *Labyrinth of Digressions*, 85–90.

9. In his influential essay on "The Self-Conscious Narrator in Comic Fiction before *Tristram Shandy*," Wayne Booth established a trend for damning Sterne's digressive precursors with faint praise, describing such works as "mad books, most of them long since wisely forgotten" (163). Other representative examples of a "proto-Shandean" approach to late seventeenth- and early eighteenth-century literature include: Melvyn New, "The Dunce Revisited: Colley Cibber and *Tristram Shandy*," *The South Atlantic Quarterly* 72 (1973): 547–59; Korkowski, "*Tristram Shandy*, Digression, and the Menippean Tradition," 3–15; and Robert Folkenflik, "*Tristram Shandy* and Eighteenth-Century Narrative," *The Cambridge Companion to Laurence Sterne*, ed. Thomas Keymer (Cambridge: Cambridge University Press, 2009), 49–63. In contrast to scholars who have contextualized Sterne in terms of his "anxiety of influence," Thomas Keymer argues that *Tristram Shandy* is a "contemporary" work of fiction, very much of its own peculiar literary and cultural moment. His discussion offers an important corrective to the long-competing views of the novel as either inheriting the Renaissance tradition of learned wit or anticipating the stream-of-consciousness techniques of twentieth-century modernists like James Joyce and Virginia Woolf. See *Sterne, the Moderns and the Novel*, esp. 1–82.

10. *The Life, Travels, and Adventures of Christopher Wagstaff, Gentleman, Grandfather to Tristram Shandy*, 2 vols. (London, 1762), I.VII, X, XIII.

11. See Bosch, *Labyrinth of Digressions*, 58–90. Bosch describes the adventures of Uncle Toby and Corporal Trim at the deathbed of Lieutenant Le Fever as "the famous beauty by which the recognition of Sterne's pathetic talents was to get its definitive form" (60). Notably, *Christopher Wagstaff* appeared about six months after the publication of the third instalment of *Tristram Shandy* in December 1761.

# Bibliography

## Primary works

Addison, Joseph. *The Free-holder, The Works of the Right Honourable Joseph Addison, Esq.* 4 vols. London, 1721.

Addison, Joseph and Richard Steele. *The Spectator.* 5 vols. Ed. Donald F. Bond. Oxford: Oxford University Press, 1965.

*The Tatler.* 3 vols. Ed. Donald F. Bond. Oxford: Oxford University Press, 1987.

*An Apology for the Life of Mr. T. . . . . . . . . C. . . ., Comedian. Being A Proper Sequel to the Apology for the Life of Mr. Colley Cibber, Comedian.* London, 1740.

Bacon, Francis. *The Advancement of Learning. The Major Works.* Ed. Brian Vickers. New York: Oxford University Press, 2002.

*The Novum Organum.* Trans. Michael Silverthorne. Ed. Lisa Jardine. Cambridge: Cambridge University Press, 2000.

Barker, Henry. *The Polite Gentleman: or, Reflections Upon the Several Kinds of Wit.* London, 1700.

Beford, Arthur. *A Serious Remonstrance in Behalf of the Christian Religion.* London, 1719. Rpt. New York: Garland Publishing Inc., 1974.

Behn, Aphra. *Oroonoko: or, The Royal Slave.* Ed. Catherine Gallagher with Simon Stern. Boston: Bedford/St Martin's, 2000.

Blackmore, Richard. *An Essay Upon Wit, Essays Upon Several Subjects.* London, 1716.

*Prince Arthur. An Heroick Poem.* London, 1695.

Bramston, James. *The Art of Politicks, in Imitation of Horace's Art of Poetry.* London, 1729.

*The British Apollo: Containing Two Thousand Answers to Curious Questions in Most Arts and Sciences, Serious, Comical, and Humorous.* 3rd edn. 3 vols. London, 1726.

*The British Frenzy: or, The Mock-Apollo. A Satyr.* London, 1745.

*The British Stage: or, The Exploits of Harlequin: A Farce.* London, 1724.

Brown, Thomas. *The Works of Mr. Thomas Brown, Serious and Comical.* 5th edn. 4 vols. London, 1719–20.

*Amusements Serious and Comical and Other Works.* Ed. Arthur L. Hayward. London: George Routledge & Sons, 1927.

Bysshe, Edward. *The Art of English Poetry.* London, 1702.

Centlivre, Susanna. *The Masquerade: A Poem*. London, 1713.

Chambers, Ephraim. *Cyclopedia: or, An Universal Dictionary of Arts and Sciences*. 2 vols. London, 1728.

Cibber, Colley. *An Apology for the Life of Colley Cibber, With An Historical View of the Stage During His Own Time*. Ed. B.R.S. Fone. Ann Arbor: University of Michigan Press, 1968.

Cicero. *De Oratore*. Trans. H. Rackham. London: Loeb, 1942.

"A Collection of 77 Advertisements Relating to Dwarves, Giants, and Other Monsters and Curiosities Exhibited for Public Inspection." British Library N.Tab. 2026/25. Superseded shelf-mark: 551.d.18.

*A Collection of Choice, Scarce, and Valuable Tracts*. Ed. John Dunton. London, 1721.

Collier, Jeremy. *A Short View of the Immorality and Profaneness of the English Stage*. London, 1698. Rpt. Menston: Scolar Press, 1971.

*The Commerce of Everyday Life: Selections from* The Tatler *and* The Spectator. Ed. Erin Mackie. Boston: Bedford/St Martin's, 1998.

Congreve, William. *Incognita and The Way of the World*. Ed. A. Norman Jeffares. Columbia: University of South Carolina Press, 1970.

Cooper, Anthony Ashley (3rd Earl of Shaftesbury). *Soliloquy, or Advice to an Author. Characteristics of Men, Manners, Opinions, Times*. Ed. Lawrence E. Klein. Cambridge: Cambridge University Press, 1999.

Cotton, Charles. *The Compleat Gamester. Games and Gamesters of the Restoration*. Intro. Cyril Hughes Hartmann. London: George Routledge and Sons, 1930.

Coventry, Francis. *An Essay on the New Species of Writing Founded by Mr. Fielding*. Intro. Alan Dugald McKillop. London, 1751. Rpt. Los Angeles: William Andrews Clark Memorial Library, 1962.

C.R. (pseud.). *The Danger of Masquerades and Raree-Shows, or the Complaints of the Stage Against Masquerades, Opera's, Assemblies, Balls, Puppet-shows, Bear-gardens, Cock-fights, Wrestling, Posture-makers, Cudgel-playing, Foot-ball, Rope-dancing, Merry-makings, and several other irrational Entertainments, as being the Ground and Occasion of the late Decay of Wit in the Island of Great-Britain*. London, 1718. Rpt. New York: Garland Publishing Inc., 1974.

*Critical Essays of the Seventeenth Century*. 3 vols. Ed. J.E. Springarn. Bloomington: Indiana University Press, 1957.

*The Daily Advertiser*. London, 1730–98.

*The Daily Courant*. London, 1702–35.

*The Daily Journal*. London, 1721–37.

*The Daily Post*. London, 1719–46.

Davies, Thomas. *Memoirs of the Life of David Garrick, Esq.* 2 vols. London, 1780.

Davys, Mary. *The Reform'd Coquet, Familiar Letters Betwixt a Gentleman and a Lady, and The Accomplish'd Rake*. Ed. Martha F. Bowden. Lexington: University Press of Kentucky, 1999.

Defoe, Benjamin Norton. *A New English Dictionary, Containing a Large and Almost Compleat Collection of Useful English Words*. London, 1737.

Defoe, Daniel. *The Complete English Tradesman, In Familiar Letters*. London, 1726.

*Moll Flanders*. Ed. Albert J. Rivero. New York: W.W. Norton & Company, 2003.

Dennis, John. *The Critical Works of John Dennis*. 2 vols. Ed. Edward Niles Hooker. Baltimore: Johns Hopkins University Press, 1939–41.

Dryden, John. *Essays*. 2 vols. Ed. W.P. Ker. Oxford, 1900. Rpt. New York: Russell & Russell, 1961.

*Satires of Decimus Junius Juvenalis and Aulus Persius Flaccus. The Works of John Dryden*. Vol. 4. Ed. A.B. Chambers, William Frost, and Vinton Dearing. Berkeley: University of California Press, 1974.

Dunton, John. *Athenian Sport: or, Two Thousand Paradoxes Merrily Argued, To Amuse and Divert the Age*. London, 1707.

*A Voyage Round the World: or, A Pocket Library. The First of Which Contains the Rare Adventures of Don Kainophilus, from his Cradle to his Fifteenth Year. The Like Discoveries in Such a Method Never Made by Any Rambler Before. The Whole Work Intermixed with Essays, Historical, Moral, and Divine; and All Other Kinds of Learning*. London, 1691.

Dunton, John, *et al. The Athenian Oracle: Being an Entire Collection of All the Valuable Questions and Answers in the Old Athenian Mercuries*. 3 vols. London, 1703–04.

D'Urfey, Thomas (Gabriel John, pseud.). *An Essay Towards the Theory of the Intelligible World. Intuitively Considered. Designed for Forty-Nine Parts. Part III. Consisting of a Preface, a Post-script, and a Little Something Between*. London, [1708].

*An Exact Description of the Two Fam'd Entertainments of Harlequin Doctor Faustus; With the Grand Masque of the Heathen Deities: And the Necromancer, or Harlequin Doctor Faustus. As Now Perform'd, in Grotesque Characters, at both Theatres*. London, [1724].

*The Fair in an Uproar: or, The Dancing-Doggs. As They Perform in Mr. Pinkeman's New Opera in Bartholomew Fair*. London, [1707].

Fielding, Henry. *The Author's Farce; and the Pleasures of the Town. Plays: Volume I, 1728–1731*. Ed. Thomas Lockwood. Oxford: Clarendon Press, 2004.

*Contributions to The Champion and Related Writings*. Ed. W.B. Coley. Oxford: Clarendon Press, 2003.

*An Enquiry into the Causes of the Late Increase of Robbers and Related Writings*. Ed. Malvin R. Zirker. Middletown: Wesleyan University Press, 1988.

*The History of the Adventures of Joseph Andrews, and of His Friend Mr. Abraham Adams*. Ed. Martin C. Battestin. Middletown: Wesleyan University Press, 1967.

*The History of Tom Jones, A Foundling*. Ed. Fredson Bowers. Intro. Martin C. Battestin. Middletown: Wesleyan University Press, 1975.

"The Masquerade. A Poem." *The Journal of a Voyage to Lisbon, Shamela, and Occasional Writings*. Ed. Martin C. Battestin, Sheridan W. Baker Jr., and Hugh Amory. Oxford: Clarendon Press, 2008.

*Pasquin. A Dramatick Satire on the Times. Plays: Volume III, 1734–1742*. Ed. Thomas Lockwood. Oxford: Clarendon Press, 2011.

*Tumble-Down Dick: or, Phaeton in the Suds. Plays: Volume III, 1734–1742.* Ed. Thomas Lockwood. Oxford: Clarendon Press, 2011.

*Fog's Weekly Journal.* London, 1728–37.

Foote, Samuel. *A Treatise on the Passions, So Far as They Regard the Stage.* London, [1747].

Gildon, Charles. *All for the Better; or, The World Turn'd Up-Side Down.* London, 1720.

   *The Post-Man Robb'd of his Mail: or, The Packet Broke Open.* London, 1719.

Glanvill, Joseph. *Scepsis Scientifica: or, Confest Ignorance, the Way to Science; In an Essay of The Vanity of Dogmatizing.* London, 1665.

Granville, George (Lord Lansdowne). "Concerning Unnatural Flights in Poetry." *Augustan Critical Writing.* Ed. David Womersley. London: Penguin Books, 1997.

Grove, Henry. *The Regulation of Diversions. Design'd Principally for the Benefit of Young Persons.* London, 1708.

*The Grub Street Journal.* London, 1730–37.

Haywood, Eliza. *The Female Spectator.* 4 vols. London, 1744–46.

*Henry Fielding: The Critical Heritage.* Ed. Ronald Paulson and Thomas Lockwood. London: Routledge, 1969.

Hill, Aaron and William Popple. *The Prompter: A Theatrical Paper (1734–1736).* Ed. William W. Appleton and Kalman A. Burnim. New York: Benjamin Blom, 1966.

Horace. *The Odes and Satyrs of Horace, that have been done into English by the most Eminent Hands. . . With his Art of Poetry, By the Earl of Roscommon.* London, 1715.

   *To The Pisones, on the Art of Poetry. The Odes, Satyrs, and Epistles of Horace.* 3rd edn. Trans. Thomas Creech. London, 1711.

Johnson, Samuel. *A Dictionary of the English Language.* London, 1755. Rpt. New York: Arno Press, 1979.

Jonson, Ben. *Bartholomew Fair.* Ed. Maurice Hussey. London: Ernest Benn Ltd., 1964.

Law, William. *The Absolute Unlawfulness of the Stage-Entertainment.* London, 1726.

*A Letter to My Lord \*\*\*\*\*\*\* On The Present Diversions of the Town. With The True Reason of the Decay of our Dramatic Entertainments.* London, 1725. Rpt. New York: Garland Publishing Inc., 1974.

*Letters from a Moor at London to His Friend at Tunis.* London, 1736.

*The Life, Travels, and Adventures of Christopher Wagstaff, Gentleman, Grandfather to Tristram Shandy.* 2 vols. London, 1762.

*Literary Criticism of Seventeenth-Century England.* New Work: Alfred A. Knopf, 1967.

Locke, John. *An Essay Concerning Human Understanding.* Ed. Peter H. Nidditch. Oxford: Clarendon Press, 1975.

*The London Daily Post and General Advertiser.* London, 1734–44.

*The London Journal.* London, 1720–44.

*The London Stage: 1660–1800.* 11 vols. Ed. William Van Lennep, Emmett L. Avery, Arthur H. Scouten, George Winchester Stone, and Charles Beecher Hogan. Carbondale: Southern Illinois University Press, 1960–68.

Longinus. *On the Sublime.* Trans. William Smith. London, 1739. Rpt. New York: Scholars' Facsimiles and Reprints, 1975.

Manley, Delarivière. *The Secret History of Queen Zarah and the Zarazians. Popular Fiction by Women, 1660–1730: An Anthology.* Ed. Paula R. Backscheider and John R. Richetti. Oxford: Clarendon Press, 1996.

Miller, James. *Harlequin-Horace: or, The Art of Modern Poetry.* London, 1731.

*Harlequin-Horace: or, The Art of Modern Poetry.* 4th edn. London, 1741. Intro. Antony Coleman. Rpt. Los Angeles: William Andrews Clark Memorial Library, 1976.

*Mist's Weekly Journal.* London, 1725–28.

Montaigne, Michael de. *Essays of Michael Seigneur de Montaigne.* 4th edn. 3 vols. Trans. Charles Cotton. London, 1711.

Morris, Corbyn. *An Essay Towards Fixing the True Standards of Wit, Humour, Raillery, Satire and Ridicule.* London, 1744. Intro. James L. Clifford. Rpt. Los Angeles: William Andrews Clark Memorial Library, 1947.

"Old Bailey Proceedings Online." Ed. Clive Emsley, Tim Hitchcock, and Robert Shoemaker. www.oldbaileyonline.org.

Oldmixon, John. *The Arts of Logic and Rhetorick.* London, 1728. Rpt. New York: Georg Olms, 1976.

*Pamphlet Attacks on Alexander Pope, 1711–1744.* Ed. J.V. Guerinot. London: Methuen, 1969.

*Pasquin.* London, 1722–24.

Pepys, Samuel. *The Diary of Samuel Pepys.* 11 vols. Ed. Robert Latham and William Matthews. Berkeley: University of California Press, 1970–76.

Phillips, Edward. *The New World of Words: or, Universal English Dictionary.* 6th edn. London, 1706.

Pope, Alexander. *The Correspondence of Alexander Pope.* 5 vols. Ed. George Sherburn. Oxford: Clarendon Press, 1956.

*The Dunciad. The Twickenham Edition of the Poems of Alexander Pope.* Vol. 5. Ed. James Sutherland. 3rd edn. London: Methuen, 1963.

*An Essay on Criticism. The Twickenham Edition of the Poems of Alexander Pope.* Vol. 1. Eds. E. Audra and Aubrey Williams. London: Methuen, 1961.

*An Essay on Man. The Twickenham Edition of the Poems of Alexander Pope.* Vol. 3.1. Ed. Maynard Mack. London: Methuen, 1950.

*Peri Bathous: or, Martinus Scriblerus, His Treatise on the Art of Sinking in Poetry. The Prose Works of Alexander Pope.* Vol. 2. Ed. Rosemary Cowler. Hamden: Archon Books, 1986.

*The Prose Works of Alexander Pope.* Vol. 1. Ed. Norman Ault. Oxford, 1936. Rpt. Oxford: Basil Blackwell, 1968.

Pope, Alexander, *et al. Memoirs of the Extraordinary Life, Works, and Discoveries of Martinus Scriblerus*. Ed. Charles Kerby-Miller. New Haven, 1950. Rpt. New York: Oxford University Press, 1988.

*The Post Boy*. London, 1695–1728.

Prior, Matthew. *The Literary Works of Matthew Prior*. 2nd edn. 2 vols. Ed. H. Bunker Wright and Monroe K. Spears. Oxford: Clarendon Press, 1959.

Puttenham, George. *The Arte of English Poesie*. London, 1589. Rpt. Menston: Scolar Press, 1968.

Ralph, James. *The Case of Authors by Profession or Trade*. London, 1758.

Ralph, James (A. Primcock, pseud.). *The Touch-Stone: or, Historical, Critical, Political, Philosophical, and Theological Essays on the Reigning Diversions of the Town*. London, 1728. Intro. Arthur Freeman. Rpt. New York: Garland Publishing Inc., 1973.

Ramsay, Allan. *An Essay on Ridicule*. London, 1753.

Rapin, René. "Reflections on Aristotle's Treatise of Poesy." *The Continental Model: Selected French Critical Essays of the Seventeenth Century, in English Translation*. Ed. Scott Elledge and Donald Schier. Rev. edn. Ithaca: Cornell University Press, 1970.

*A Register of English Theatrical Documents: 1660–1737*. 2 vols. Ed. Judith Milhous and Robert D. Hume. Carbondale: Southern Illinois University Press, 1991.

Richardson, Samuel. *The Apprentice's Vade Mecum: or, Young Man's Pocket-Companion. Early Works*. Ed. Alexander Petit. Cambridge: Cambridge University Press, 2012.

Roger, M. *Perseus and Andromeda: or, The Devil Upon Two Sticks*. London, 1729.

Saussure, Cesar de. *A Foreign View of the England in the Reigns of George I and George II*. Trans. Madame van Muyden. New York: Caliban, 1995.

Savage, Richard. *An Author To Be Lett*. London, 1729. Intro. James Sutherland. Rpt. Los Angeles: William Andrews Clark Memorial Library, 1960.

*See and Seem Blind: or, A Critical Dissertation on the Public Diversions, &c.* London, 1732. Intro. Robert D. Hume. Rpt. Los Angeles: William Andrews Clark Memorial Library, 1986.

Shakespeare, William. *Hamlet*. Ed. G.R. Hibbard. New York: Oxford University Press, 1987.

*The Tempest*. Ed. Virginia Mason Vaughan and Alden T. Vaughan. London: Arden Shakespeare, 1999.

Sterne, Laurence. *The Life and Opinions of Tristram Shandy, Gentleman, The Text*. 2 vols. Ed. Melvyn and Joan New. Gainesville: University of Florida Press, 1978.

Swift, Jonathan. *The Correspondence of Jonathan Swift*. 5 vols. Ed. Harold Williams. Oxford: Clarendon Press, 1963–65.

*Gulliver's Travels*. Ed. David Womersley. Cambridge: Cambridge University Press, 2012.

*Journal to Stella: Letters to Esther Johnson and Rebecca Dingley, 1710–1713*. Ed. Abigail Williams. Cambridge: Cambridge University Press, 2013.

*Poetical Works*. Ed. Herbert Davis. London: Oxford University Press, 1967.

*A Proposal for Correcting, Improving and Ascertaining the English Tongue. Parodies, Hoaxes, Mock Treatises, Polite Conversation, Directions to Servants and Other Works*. Ed. Valerie Rumbold. Cambridge: Cambridge University Press, 2013.

*A Tale of a Tub and Other Works*. Ed. Marcus Walsh. Cambridge: Cambridge University Press, 2010.

*The Tatler*. London, 1709–11.

Theobald, Lewis and John Rich. *Perseus and Andromeda*. London, 1730.

*The Rape of Proserpine: With the Birth and Adventures of Harlequin*. London, 1727.

*The Tricks of Harlequin: or, The Spaniard Outwitted . . . Being the Comic Part of the Celebrated Entertainment of Perseus and Andromeda*. Derby, 1739.

Thurmond, John. *Apollo and Daphne: or, Harlequin's Metamorphoses*. London, 1726.

*Harlequin Sheppard. A Night Scene in Grotesque Characters*. London, 1724.

*The Tricks of the Town Laid Open: or, A Companion for Country Gentlemen. Eighteenth-Century Diversions: Tricks of the Town*. Ed. Ralph Straus. London: Chapman and Hall, 1927.

*A Trip Through the Town. Containing Observations on the Humour and Manners of the Age. Eighteenth-Century Diversions: Tricks of the Town*. Ed. Ralph Straus. London: Chapman and Hall, 1927.

Ward, Edward. *The Dancing Devils: or, The Roaring Dragon. A Dumb Farce*. London, 1724. Rpt. New York: Garland Publishing Inc., 1974.

*The London Spy Compleat, In Eighteen Parts*. London, 1703.

*The London Terræfilius: or, The Satyrical Reformer. The Fourth Volume of the Writings of the Author of the London-Spy. Prose and Verse*. London, 1709.

Weaver, John. *Anatomical and Mechanical Lectures Upon Dancing. Wherein Rules and Institutions for that Art are Laid Down and Demonstrated*. London, 1721.

*An Essay Towards a History of Dancing, In Which the Whole Art and Its Various Excellencies Are In Some Measure Explain'd*. London, 1712.

*The History of the Mimes and Pantomimes*. London, 1728.

*The Loves of Mars and Venus: A Dramatick Entertainment of Dancing, Attempted in Imitation of the Ancient Greeks and Romans*. London, 1717.

*The Weekly Journal or Saturday's Post*. London, 1716–25.

Werenfels, Samuel. *A Dissertation Concerning Meteors of Stile, or False Sublimity*. Intro. Edward Tomarken. London, 1711. Rpt. Los Angeles: William Andrews Clark Memorial Library, 1980.

## Secondary works

Alston, R.C. "The Eighteenth-Century Non-Book: Observations on Printed Ephemera." *Buch und Buchandel in Europa im achtzehnten Jahrhundert*. Ed. Giles Barber and Bernhard Fabian. Hamburg: Dr Ernst Hauswedell & Co., 1981. 343–60.

Alter, Robert. *Partial Magic: The Novel as a Self-Conscious Genre.* Berkeley: University of California Press, 1975.

Altick, Richard D. *The Shows of London: A Panoramic History of Exhibitions, 1600–1862.* Cambridge: The Belknap Press, 1978.

Aubrey, James. "Revising the Monstrous: Du Plessis' *Short History of Prodigies* and London Culture in 1730." *Studies in Eighteenth-Century Culture* 23 (1994): 74–91.

Avery, Emmet L. "Dancing and Pantomime on the English Stage, 1700–1737." *Studies in Philology* 31 (1934): 417–52.

"The Defense and Criticism of Pantomimic Entertainments in the Early Eighteenth Century." *English Literary History* 5 (1938): 127–45.

Bailey, Anne Hall. "How Much for Just the Muse?: Alexander Pope's *Dunciad*, Book IV and the Literary Market." *Eighteenth Century: Theory and Interpretation* 36.1 (1995): 24–37.

Barchas, Janine. *Graphic Design, Print Culture, and the Eighteenth-Century Novel.* Cambridge: Cambridge University Press, 2003.

Barthes, Roland. *The Pleasure of the Text.* Trans. Richard Miller. New York: Hill and Wang, 1975.

Battestin, Martin C. "Fielding and 'Master Punch' in Panton Street." *Philological Quarterly* 45 (1966): 191–208.

*The Providence of Wit: Aspects of Form in Augustan Literature and the Arts.* Oxford: Clarendon Press, 1974.

Battestin, Martin C. and Ruthe R. Battestin. *Henry Fielding: A Life.* London: Routledge, 1989.

Benedict, Barbara M. *Curiosity: A Cultural History of Early Modern Inquiry.* Chicago: University of Chicago Press, 2001.

"The 'Curious Attitude' in Eighteenth-Century Britain: Observing and Owning." *Eighteenth-Century Life* 14 (1990): 59–98.

"Encounters with the Object: Advertisements, Time, and Literary Discourse in the Early Eighteenth-Century Thing-Poem." *Eighteenth-Century Studies* 40.2 (2007): 193–207.

"European Monsters through English Eyes: Eighteenth-Century Cultural Icons." *Symbolism* 1 (2000): 81–119.

"Wants and Goods: Advertisement and Desire in Haywood and Defoe." *Studies in Eighteenth-Century Culture* 33 (2004): 221–53.

Bertelsen, Lance. "Popular Entertainment and Instruction, Literary and Dramatic: Chapbooks, Advice Books, Almanacs, Ballads, Farces, Pantomimes, Prints and Shows." *The Cambridge History of English Literature, 1660–1780.* Ed. John Richetti. Cambridge: Cambridge University Press, 2005.

Besant, Walter. *London in the Eighteenth Century.* London: A. & C. Black, 1902.

Bevis, Richard. *English Drama: Restoration and Eighteenth Century, 1660–1789.* London: Longman, 1982.

"Fielding's Normative Authors: *Tom Jones* and the Rehearsal Play." *Philological Quarterly* 69.1 (1990): 55–70.

Bianchi, Marina. "Consuming Novelty: Strategies for Producing Novelty in Consumption." *Journal of Medieval and Early Modern Studies* 28.1 (1998): 3–18.

Bogel, Frederic V. *The Difference Satire Makes: Rhetoric and Reading from Jonson to Byron*. Ithaca: Cornell University Press, 2001.

Bond, Erik. *Reading London: Urban Speculation and Imaginative Government in Eighteenth-Century Literature*. Columbus: Ohio State University Press, 2007.

Bond, Richmond P. *Queen Anne's American Kings*. Oxford: Clarendon Press, 1952.

Booth, Wayne C. *The Rhetoric of Fiction*. 2nd edn. Chicago: University of Chicago Press, 1983.

"The Self-Conscious Narrator in Comic Fiction before *Tristram Shandy*." *PMLA* 67 (1952): 163–85.

Borsay, Peter. *The English Urban Renaissance: Culture and Society in the Provincial Town 1660–1770*. Oxford: Oxford University Press, 1989.

Bosch, René. *Labyrinth of Digressions: Tristram Shandy as Perceived and Influenced by Sterne's Early Imitators*. Trans. Piet Verhoeff. Amsterdam: Rodopi, 2007.

Boulton, William B. *The Amusements of Old London*. 2 vols. London, 1901. Rpt. New York: Benjamin Blom, 1969.

Bowyer, John Wilson. *The Celebrated Mrs. Centlivre*. Durham: Duke University Press, 1952.

Boyce, Benjamin. *Tom Brown of Facetious Memory: Grub Street in the Age of Dryden*. Cambridge: Harvard University Press, 1939.

Brant, Clare and Susan Whyman, eds. *Walking the Streets of Eighteenth-Century London: John Gay's* Trivia. Oxford: Oxford University Press, 2007.

Brewer, John. "'The Most Polite Age and the Most Vicious': Attitudes towards Culture as a Commodity, 1660–1800." *The Consumption of Culture 1600–1800: Image, Object, Text*. Ed. Ann Bermingham and John Brewer. London: Routledge, 1995. 341–61.

*The Pleasures of the Imagination: English Culture in the Eighteenth Century*. London: HarperCollins, 1997.

Brewer, John and Ann Bermingham, eds. *The Consumption of Culture 1600–1800: Image, Object, Text*. London: Routledge, 1995.

Brewer, John and Roy Porter, eds. *Consumption and the World of Goods*. London: Routledge, 1993.

Briggs, Peter M. "'News from the Little World': A Critical Glance at Eighteenth-Century British Advertising." *Studies in Eighteenth-Century Culture* 23 (1994): 29–45.

Brown, Laura. *Fables of Modernity: Literature and Culture in the English Eighteenth Century*. Ithaca: Cornell University Press, 2001.

Byrd, Max. *London Transformed: Images of the City in the Eighteenth Century*. New Haven: Yale University Press, 1978.

Campbell, Jill. *Natural Masques: Gender and Identity in Fielding's Plays and Novels*. Stanford: Stanford University Press, 1995.

Carroll, William C. *The Great Feast of Language in* Love's Labour's Lost. Princeton: Princeton University Press, 1976.

Castle, Terry. *Masquerade and Civilization: The Carnivalesque in Eighteenth-Century English Culture and Fiction*. Stanford: Stanford University Press, 1986.

Chambers, Ross. *Loiterature*. Lincoln: University of Nebraska Press, 1999.

Chibka, Robert L. "Taking 'The Serious' Seriously: The Introductory Chapters of *Tom Jones*." *Eighteenth Century: Theory and Interpretation* 31.1 (1990): 23–45.

Clark, John R. *Form and Frenzy in Swift's* Tale of a Tub. Ithaca: Cornell University Press, 1970.

Cohen, Stephen. "Historical Formalism." *Shakespeare and Historical Formalism*. Ed. Stephen Cohen. Aldershot: Ashgate Publishing, 2007. 1–27.

Coleman, Deidre. "Entertaining Entomology: Insects and Insect Performers in the Eighteenth Century." *Eighteenth-Century Life* 30 (2006): 107–34.

Cotterill, Anne. *Digressive Voices in Early Modern English Literature*. Oxford: Oxford University Press, 2004.

Cowan, Brian. *The Social Life of Coffee: The Emergence of the British Coffeehouse*. New Haven: Yale University Press, 2005.

Crane, R.S. "The Concept of Plot and the Plot of *Tom Jones*." *Critics and Criticism*. Abridged edn. Ed. R.S. Crane. Chicago: University of Chicago Press, 1957. 62–93.

Cranfield, G.A. *The Development of the Provincial Newspaper 1700–1760*. Oxford: Clarendon Press, 1962.

Curran, Andrew and Patrick Graille. "The Faces of Eighteenth-Century Monstrosity." *Eighteenth-Century Life* 21.2 (1997): 1–15.

Daston, Lorraine and Katherine Park. "Unnatural Conceptions: The Study of Monsters in Sixteenth- and Seventeenth-Century France and England." *Past and Present* 92 (1981): 20–54.

*Wonders and the Order of Nature: 1150–1750*. New York: Zone Books, 2001.

Day, Robert Adams. "Richard Bentley and John Dunton: Brothers under the Skin." *Studies in Eighteenth-Century Culture* 16 (1986): 125–38.

Derrida, Jacques. "White Mythology: Metaphor in the Text of Philosophy." *New Literary History* 6 (1974): 5–74.

Deutsch, Helen. *Resemblance and Disgrace: Alexander Pope and the Deformation of Culture*. Cambridge: Harvard University Press, 1996.

Dickie, Simon. *Cruelty and Laughter: Forgotten Comic Literature and the Unsentimental Eighteenth Century*. Chicago: University of Chicago Press, 2011.

Dircks, Phyllis T. "The Eclectic Comic Genius of John Rich in *The Necromancer*." *Theatre Notebook* 49.3 (1995): 165–72.

Dobson, Austin. *Eighteenth-Century Vignettes*. London: Chatto & Windus, 1892.

*Side-Walk Studies*. London: Oxford University Press, 1924.

Domingo, Darryl P. "'The Natural Propensity of Imitation': or, Pantomimic Poetics and the Rhetoric of Augustan Wit." *Journal for Early Modern Cultural Studies* 9.2 (2009): 51–95.

"Unbending the Mind: or, Commercialized Leisure and the Rhetoric of Eighteenth-Century Diversion." *Eighteenth-Century Studies* 45.2 (2012): 207–36.

Doody, Margaret. *The Daring Muse: Augustan Poetry Reconsidered.* Cambridge: Cambridge University Press, 1986.

Downer, Alan S. "Nature to Advantage Dressed: Eighteenth-Century Acting." *PMLA* 58 (1943): 1002–37.

During, Simon. *Modern Enchantments: The Cultural Power of Secular Magic.* Cambridge: Harvard University Press, 2002.

Earle, Peter. *A City Full of People: Men and Women of London 1650–1750.* London: Methuen, 1994.

Ehrenpreis, Irvin. *Fielding: Tom Jones.* London: Arnold, 1964.

Eisenstein, Elizabeth L. *Print Culture and Enlightenment Thought.* Chapel Hill: Hanes Foundation, University of North Carolina, 1986.

   *The Printing Press as an Agent of Change: Communications and Cultural Transformation in Early-Modern Europe.* 2 vols. Cambridge: Cambridge University Press, 1979.

Ennis, Daniel J. and Judith Bailey Slagle, eds. *Prologues, Epilogues, Curtain-Raisers, and Afterpieces: The Rest of the Eighteenth-Century London Stage.* Newark: University of Delaware Press, 2007.

Ezell, Margaret J.M. *Social Authorship and the Advent of Print.* Baltimore: Johns Hopkins University Press, 1999.

Fanning, Christopher. "The Scriblerian Sublime." *Studies in English Literature* 45.3 (2005): 647–67.

   "Small Particles of Eloquence: Sterne and the Scriblerian Text." *Modern Philology* 100.3 (2003): 360–92.

Feather, John. *The Provincial Book Trade in Eighteenth-Century England.* Cambridge: Cambridge University Press, 1985.

Fiedler, Leslie. *Freaks: Myths and Images of the Secret Self.* New York: Simon & Schuster, 1978.

Flint, Christopher. *The Appearance of Print in Eighteenth-Century Fiction.* Cambridge: Cambridge University Press, 2011.

   "In Other Words: Eighteenth-Century Authorship and the Ornaments of Print." *Eighteenth-Century Fiction* 14 (2002): 627–72.

Flynn, Carol Houlihan. "Running Out of Matter: The Body Exercised in Eighteenth-Century Fiction." *The Languages of Psyche: Mind and Body in Enlightenment Thought.* Ed. G.S. Rousseau. Berkeley: University of California Press, 1990.

Fox, Christopher. *Locke and the Scriblerians: Identity and Consciousness in Early Eighteenth-Century Britain.* Berkeley: University of California Press, 1988.

Fussell, Paul. *The Rhetorical World of Augustan Humanism.* Oxford: Clarendon Press, 1962.

Genette, Gérard. *Figures of Literary Discourse.* Trans. Alan Sheridan. Intro. Marie-Rose Logan. New York: Columbia University Press, 1982.

   *Paratexts: Thresholds of Interpretation.* Trans. Jane E. Lewin. Cambridge: Cambridge University Press, 1997.

Griffin, Emma. *England's Revelry: A History of Popular Sports and Pastimes, 1660–1830.* New York: Oxford University Press, 2005.

Gubar, Susan. "The Female Monster in Augustan Satire." *Signs: Journal of Women in Culture and Society* 3.2 (1977): 380–94.

Guerrini, Anita. "Advertising Monstrosity: Broadsides and Human Exhibition in Early Eighteenth-Century London." *Ballads and Broadsides in Britain, 1500–1800*. Ed. Patricia Fumerton and Anita Guerrini, with Kris McAbee. Burlington: Ashgate Publishing, 2010. 109–27.

Habermas, Jürgen. *The Structural Transformation of the Public Sphere: An Inquiry into a Category of Bourgeois Society*. Trans. Thomas Burger with Frederick Lawrence. Cambridge: MIT Press, 1989.

Hammond, Brean S. *Professional Imaginative Writing in England, 1670–1740: "Hackney for Bread."* Oxford: Clarendon Press, 1997.

Harries, Elizabeth Wanning. *The Unfinished Manner: Essays on the Fragment in the Later Eighteenth Century*. Charlottesville: University Press of Virginia, 1994.

Harris, Michael. *London Newspapers in the Age of Walpole: A Study in the Origins of the Modern English Press*. Rutherford: Fairleigh Dickinson Press, 1987.

Hassall, Anthony J. "Fielding's Puppet Image." *Philological Quarterly* 53.1 (1974): 71–83.

Hawley, Judith. "Margins and Monstrosity: Martinus Scriblerus His 'Double Mistress.'" *Eighteenth-Century Life* 22 (1998): 31–49.

Henry, Anne C. "The Re-mark-able Rise of '. . .': Reading Ellipsis Marks in Literary Texts." *Ma[r]king the Text: The Presentation of Meaning on the Literary Page*. Ed. Joe Bray, Miriam Handley, and Anne C. Henry. Aldershot: Ashgate Publishing, 2000. 120–42.

Highfill, Philip H., Kalman A. Burnim, and Edward A. Langhans, eds. *A Biographical Dictionary of Actors, Actresses, Musicians, Dancers, Managers and Other Stage Personnel in London, 1660–1800*. 16 vols. Carbondale: Southern Illinois University Press, 1973–93.

Hillhouse, James T. *The Grub Street Journal*. Durham: Duke University Press, 1928. Rpt. New York: Benjamin Blom, 1967.

Hopkins, David. "Dryden and Ovid's 'Wit Out of Season.'" *Ovid Renewed: Ovidian Influences on Literature and Art from the Middle Ages to the Twentieth Century*. Ed. Charles Martindale. Cambridge: Cambridge University Press, 1988. 167–90.

Howe, Tonya. "'All Deformed Shapes': Figuring the Posture-Master as Popular Performer in Early Eighteenth-Century England." *Journal for Early Modern Cultural Studies* 12.4 (2012): 26–47.

Hudson, Nicholas. "Fielding's Hierarchy of Dialogue: 'Meta-Response' and the Reader in *Tom Jones*." *Philological Quarterly* 68 (1989): 177–94.

Hudson, Nicholas and Aaron Santesso, eds. *Swift's Travels: Eighteenth-Century Satire and Its Legacy*. Cambridge: Cambridge University Press, 2008.

Huet, Marie-Hélène. *Monstrous Imagination*. Cambridge: Harvard University Press, 1993.

Hughes, Helen Sard. "Fielding's Indebtedness to James Ralph." *Modern Philology* 20.1 (1922): 19–34.

Hughes, Leo. "Rival Entertainments: Pantomime, Burlesque, Satire, Sentiment." *A Century of English Farce.* Princeton: Princeton University Press, 1956.

Hume, Robert D. "The Economics of Culture in London, 1660–1740." *Huntington Library Quarterly* 69.4 (2006): 487–533.

Hunter, J. Paul. *Before Novels: The Cultural Contexts of Eighteenth-Century English Fiction.* New York: W.W. Norton & Company, 1990.

"The Insistent I." *Novel* 13 (1979): 19–37.

"The Novel and Social/Cultural History." *The Cambridge Companion to the Eighteenth-Century Novel.* Ed. John Richetti. Cambridge: Cambridge University Press, 1996. 9–40.

*Occasional Form: Henry Fielding and the Chains of Circumstance.* Baltimore: Johns Hopkins University Press, 1975.

Irving, William Henry. *John Gay's London, Illustrated from the Poetry of the Time.* Cambridge: Harvard University Press, 1928.

Jacobs, Alan. *The Pleasures of Reading in an Age of Distraction.* New York: Oxford University Press, 2011.

James, Susan. *Passion and Action: The Emotions in Seventeenth-Century Philosophy.* Oxford: Clarendon Press, 1997.

Jay, Ricky. *Learned Pigs and Fireproof Women: Unique, Eccentric, and Amazing Entertainers.* New York: Villard Books, 1987.

Johns, Adrian. *The Nature of the Book: Print and Knowledge in the Making.* Chicago: University of Chicago Press, 1998.

Joncus, Berta and Jeremy Barlow, eds. *"The Stage's Glory": John Rich, 1692–1761.* Newark: University of Delaware Press, 2011.

Jones, Richard Foster. "Science and English Prose Style in the Third Quarter of the Seventeenth Century." *The Seventeenth Century: Studies in the History of English Thought from Bacon to Pope.* Stanford: Stanford University Press, 1951. 75–110.

Jordan, Sarah. *The Anxieties of Idleness: Idleness in Eighteenth-Century British Literature and Culture.* Lewisburg: Bucknell University Press, 2003.

Kareem, Sarah Tindal. *Eighteenth-Century Fiction and the Reinvention of Wonder.* Oxford: Oxford University Press, 2014.

Keen, Paul. *Literature, Commerce, and the Spectacle of Modernity, 1750–1800.* Cambridge: Cambridge University Press, 2012.

Kelly, Anne Cline. *Jonathan Swift and Popular Culture: Myth, Media, and the Man.* New York: Palgrave Macmillan, 2002.

Kenny, Shirley Strum. "Theatre, Related Arts, and the Profit Motive: An Overview." *British Theatre and the Other Arts, 1660–1800.* Ed. Shirley Strum Kenny. Toronto: Associated University Presses, 1984.

Keymer, Thomas. "Readers and Stage Coaches in Fielding and Sterne." *Notes and Queries* 41.2 (1994): 209–11.

*Richardson's* Clarissa *and the Eighteenth-Century Reader.* Cambridge: Cambridge University Press, 1992.

*Sterne, the Moderns and the Novel.* New York: Oxford University Press, 2002.

Klein, Lawrence E. *Shaftesbury and the Culture of Politeness: Moral Discourse and Cultural Politics in Early Eighteenth-Century England.* Cambridge: Cambridge University Press, 1994.

Knowlson, James. *Universal Language Schemes in England and France, 1600–1800.* Toronto: University of Toronto Press, 1975.

Koehler, Margaret. *Poetry of Attention in the Eighteenth Century.* New York: Palgrave Macmillan, 2012.

Korkowski, Eugene. "Genre and Satiric Strategy in Burton's *Anatomy of Melancholy.*" *Genre* 8 (1975): 74–87.

"*Tristram Shandy*, Digression, and the Menippean Tradition." *Scholia Satyrica* 1 (1975): 3–15.

Kraft, Elizabeth. "Wit and *The Spectator*'s Ethics of Desire." *Studies in English Literature* 45.3 (2005): 625–46.

Kroll, Richard W.F. *The Material Word: Literate Culture in the Restoration and Early Eighteenth Century.* Baltimore: Johns Hopkins University Press, 1991.

Kwint, Marius. "The Legitimation of the Circus in Late Georgian England." *Past and Present* 174 (2002): 72–115.

Langford, Paul. *A Polite and Commercial People: England, 1727–1783.* Oxford: Clarendon Press, 1989.

Lennard, John. *But I Digress: The Exploitation of Parenthesis in English Printed Verse.* Oxford: Clarendon Press, 1991.

Lewis, Peter. *Fielding's Burlesque Drama: Its Place in the Tradition.* Edinburgh: University of Edinburgh Press, 1987.

Lindgren, Lowell. "Another Critic Named Samber, Whose 'Particular Historical Significance Has Gone Almost Entirely Unnoticed.'" *Festa Musicologica.* Ed. Thomas J. Mathiesen and Benito V. Rivero. Stuyvesant, NY: Pendragon Press, 1995.

Love, Harold. *Scribal Publication in Seventeenth-Century England.* Oxford: Clarendon Press, 1993.

Lund, Roger D. "Laughing at Cripples: Ridicule, Deformity and the Argument from Design." *Eighteenth-Century Studies* 39.1 (2005): 91–114.

"Pope's Monsters: Satire and the Grotesque in *The Dunciad.*" *The Scope of the Fantastic – Culture, Biography, Themes, Children's Literature: Selected Essays from the First International Conference on the Fantastic in Literature and Film.* Ed. Robert A. Collins and Howard D. Pearce. Westport: Greenwood Press, 1985. 61–78.

*Ridicule, Religion and the Politics of Wit in Augustan England.* Burlington: Ashgate Publishing, 2012.

"Wit, Judgment, and the Misprisions of Similitude." *Journal of the History of Ideas* 65.1 (2004): 53–74.

Lupton, Christina. *Knowing Books: The Consciousness of Mediation in Eighteenth-Century Britain.* Philadelphia: University of Pennsylvania Press, 2012.

Mackie, Erin. *Market á la Mode: Fashion, Commodity, and Gender in* The Tatler *and* The Spectator. Baltimore: Johns Hopkins University Press, 1997.

Malcolmson, Robert W. *Popular Recreations in English Society: 1700–1850*. Cambridge: Cambridge University Press, 1973.

Marcus, Leah S. *The Politics of Mirth: Jonson, Herrick, Milton, Marvell, and the Defense of Old Holiday Pastimes*. Chicago: University of Chicago Press, 1986.

Marshall, Ashley. "The Myth of Scriblerus." *Journal for Eighteenth-Century Studies* 31.1 (2008): 77–99.

    *The Practice of Satire in England, 1658–1770*. Baltimore: Johns Hopkins University Press, 2013.

McEwan, Gilbert D. *The Oracle of the Coffee House: John Dunton's Athenian Mercury*. San Marino: The Huntington Library, 1972.

McIntosh, Carey. *The Evolution of English Prose, 1700–1800: Style, Politeness, and Print Culture*. Cambridge: Cambridge University Press, 1998.

McKendrick, Neil, John Brewer, and J.H. Plumb, eds. *The Birth of a Consumer Society: The Commercialization of Eighteenth-Century England*. Bloomington: Indiana University Press, 1982.

McLaverty, James. *Pope, Print, and Meaning*. Oxford: Oxford University Press, 2001.

Merritt, J.F., ed. *Imagining Early Modern London: Perceptions and Portrayals of the City From Stow to Strype. 1598–1720*. Cambridge: Cambridge University Press, 2001.

Milburn, D. Judson. *The Age of Wit: 1650–1750*. New York: Macmillan, 1966.

Miller, Christopher R. *Surprise: The Poetics of the Unexpected from Milton to Austen*. Ithaca: Cornell University Press, 2015.

Montgomery, Robert L. *Terms of Response: Language and Audience in Seventeenth- and Eighteenth-Century Theory*. Pennsylvania: Pennsylvania State University Press, 1992.

Morley, Henry. *Memoirs of Bartholomew Fair*. 4th edn. London: George Routledge and Sons, 1892.

Mui, Lorna H. and Hoh-Cheung Mui. *Shops and Shopkeeping in Eighteenth-Century England*. Montreal: McGill-Queen's University Press, 1989.

Muir, Edward. *Ritual in Early Modern Europe*. Cambridge: Cambridge University Press, 1997.

Nash, Richard. *Wild Enlightenment: The Borders of Human Identity in the Eighteenth Century*. Charlottesville: University of Virginia Press, 2003.

O'Brien, John. *Harlequin Britain: Pantomime and Entertainment, 1690–1760*. Baltimore: Johns Hopkins University Press, 2004.

O'Byrne, Alison. "Walking, Rambling and Promenading in Eighteenth-Century London: A Literary and Cultural History." Ph.D. Dissertation. University of York, 2003.

Okie, Laird. "James Ralph (d. 1762)." *Oxford Dictionary of National Biography*. Oxford: Oxford University Press, 2004.

Ormsby-Lennon, Hugh. *Hey Presto! Swift and the Quacks*. Newark: University of Delaware Press, 2011.

    "'Trips, Spies, Amusements' and the Apogee of the Public Sphere." *Reading Swift: Papers from the Fourth Münster Symposium on Jonathan Swift*. Ed. Hermann J. Real and Helgard Stöver-Leidig. Munich: Wilhelm Fink Verlag, 1998. 177–224.

*The Oxford English Dictionary.* 2nd edn. 20 vols. New York: Oxford University Press, 1989.

Park, Julie. *The Self and It: Novel Objects in Eighteenth-Century England.* Stanford: Stanford University Press, 2010.

Parker, Blanford. *The Triumph of Augustan Poetics: English Literary Culture from Butler to Johnson.* Cambridge: Cambridge University Press, 1998.

Parks, Stephen. *John Dunton and the English Book Trade.* New York: Garland Press, 1976.

Pasanek, Brad. *Metaphors of Mind: An Eighteenth-Century Dictionary.* Baltimore: Johns Hopkins University Press, 2015.

Paulson, Ronald. *The Beautiful, Novel, and Strange: Aesthetics and Heterodoxy.* Baltimore: Johns Hopkins University Press, 1996.

   *Popular and Polite Art in the Age of Hogarth and Fielding.* Notre Dame: University of Notre Dame Press, 1979.

Pedicord, Harry William. "The Changing Audience." *The London Theatre World, 1660–1800.* Ed. Robert D. Hume. Carbondale: Southern Illinois University Press, 1980. 236–52.

Phiddian, Robert. "A Hopeless Project: Gulliver Inside the Language of Science in Book III." *Eighteenth-Century Life* 22 (1998): 50–62.

Phillips, Natalie. "Narrating Distraction: Problems of Focus in Eighteenth-Century Fiction, 1750–1820." Ph.D. Dissertation. Stanford University, 2010.

Pinkus, Philip. *Grub St. Stripped Bare.* London: Constable and Company, 1968.

Plumb, J.H. *The Commercialisation of Leisure in Eighteenth-Century England.* Reading: University of Reading, 1973.

Porter, Roy. *London: A Social History.* Cambridge: Harvard University Press, 1994.

   "Material Pleasures in the Consumer Society." *Pleasure in the Eighteenth Century.* Ed. Roy Porter and Marie Mulvey Roberts. London: Macmillan Press Ltd., 1996. 19–35.

Porter, Roy and Marie Mulvey Roberts, eds. *Pleasure in the Eighteenth Century.* London: Macmillan Press Ltd., 1996.

Preston, John. *The Created Self: The Reader's Role in Eighteenth-Century Fiction.* London: Heinemann, 1970.

Ralph, Richard. *The Life and Works of John Weaver.* New York: Dance Horizons, 1985.

Raven, James and Helen Small, Naomi Tadmor, eds. *The Practice and Representation of Reading in England.* Cambridge: Cambridge University Press, 1996.

Rawson, Claude. *Satire and Sentiment 1660–1830: Stress Points in the English Augustan Tradition.* New Haven: Yale University Press, 1994.

   "Some Considerations on Authorial Intrusion and Dialogue in Fielding's Novels and Plays." *Durham University Journal* 33 (1971): 32–44.

Rivero, Albert J. *The Plays of Henry Fielding: A Critical Study of His Dramatic Career.* Charlottesville: University Press of Virginia, 1989.

Rivers, Isabel, ed. *Books and Their Readers in Eighteenth-Century England: New Essays.* Harrisburg: Continuum International Publishing, 2003.

Roach, Joseph R. *The Player's Passion: Studies in the Science of Acting.* Newark: University of Delaware Press, 1985.

Rogers, Pat. *Grub Street: Studies in a Subculture.* London: Methuen, 1972.

*Literature and Popular Culture in Eighteenth-Century England.* Sussex: Harvester Press, 1985.

Rogers, Shef. "Pope, Publishing, and Popular Interpretations of *The Dunciad Variorum.*" *Philological Quarterly* 74.3 (1995): 279–95.

Rose, Mark. *Authors and Owners: The Invention of Copyright.* Cambridge: Harvard University Press, 1993.

Rosenfeld, Sybil. *The Theatre of the London Fairs in the 18th Century.* Cambridge: Cambridge University Press, 1960.

Ross, Marlon B. "Authority and Authenticity: Scribbling Authors and the Genius of Print in Eighteenth-Century England." *The Construction of Authorship: Textual Appropriation in Law and Literature.* Ed. Martha Woodmansee and Peter Jaszi. Durham: Duke University Press, 1994. 231–57.

Rousseau, G.S. "Nerves, Spirits, and Fibres: Towards Defining the Origins of Sensibility." *Studies in the Eighteenth Century III.* Ed. R.F. Brissenden and J. C. Eade. Canberra: Australian National University Press, 1976.

Russell, Gillian. *Women, Sociability and Theatre in Georgian London.* Cambridge: Cambridge University Press, 2007.

Saccamano, Neil. "Wits Breaks." *Body and Text in the Eighteenth Century.* Ed. Veronica Kelly and Dorothea E. Von Mücke. Stanford: Stanford University Press, 1994. 45–67.

Sacks, Sheldon. *Fiction and the Shape of Belief: A Study of Henry Fielding, with Glances at Swift, Johnson, and Richardson.* Berkeley: University of California Press, 1966.

Sadlak, Antoni N. "Harlequin Comes to England: The Early Evidence of the *Commedia dell'arte* in England and the Formulation of English Harlequinades and Pantomimes." Ph.D. Dissertation. Tufts University, 1999.

Sawyer, Paul. "The Popularity of Pantomime on the London Stage, 1720–1760." *Restoration and Eighteenth-Century Theatre Research* 5.2 (1990): 1–16.

"Smorgasbord on the Stage: John Rich and the Development of Eighteenth Century English Pantomime." *The Theatre Annual* 34 (1979): 37–65.

Scott, Virginia P. "The Infancy of English Pantomime: 1716–1723." *Educational Theatre Journal* 24 (1972): 125–34.

Semonin, Paul. "Monsters in the Marketplace: The Exhibition of Human Oddities in Early Modern England." *Freakery: Cultural Spectacles of the Extraordinary Body.* Ed. Rosemarie Garland Thomson. New York: New York University Press, 1996.

Sherbert, Garry. *Menippean Satire and the Poetics of Wit: Ideologies of Self-Consciousness in Dunton, D'Urfey, and Sterne.* New York: Peter Lang, 1996.

Sherman, Sandra. "Reading at Arm's Length: Fielding's Contract with the Reader in *Tom Jones.*" *Studies in the Novel* 30.2 (1998): 232–45.

Sitter, John. "About Wit: Locke, Addison, Prior, and the Order of Things." *Rhetorics of Order/Ordering Rhetorics in English Neoclassical Literature.* Ed.

J. Douglas Canfield and J. Paul Hunter. Newark: University of Delaware Press, 1989. 137–57.

*Arguments of Augustan Wit.* Cambridge: Cambridge University Press, 1991.

Spacks, Patricia Meyer. *Boredom: The Literary History of a State of Mind.* Chicago: University of Chicago Press, 1995.

Speaight, George. *The History of the English Puppet Theatre.* 2nd edn. Carbondale: Southern Illinois University Press, 1990.

Stafford, Barbara Maria. *Body Criticism: Imaging the Unseen in Enlightenment Art and Medicine.* Cambridge: MIT Press, 1991.

Stedmond, J.M. "Another Possible Analogue for Swift's *Tale of a Tub*." *Modern Language Notes* 72 (1957): 12–18.

Stevenson, John Allen. "Fielding's Mousetrap: Hamlet, Partridge, and the '45." *Studies in English Literature* 37.3 (1997): 553–71.

Stewart, Susan. *On Longing: Narratives of the Miniature, the Gigantic, the Souvenir, the Collection.* Baltimore: Johns Hopkins University Press, 1984.

Taylor, Aline Mackenzie. "Sights and Monsters in Gulliver's *Voyage to Brobdingnag*." *Tulane Studies in English* 7 (1957): 29–82.

Taylor, George. "'The Just Delineation of the Passions': Theories of Acting in the Age of Garrick." *Essays on the Eighteenth-Century Stage.* Ed. Kenneth Richards and Peter Thomson. London: Methuen, 1972. 55–72.

Taylor, Nancy. "John Weaver and the Origins of English Pantomime: A Neoclassical Theory and Practice for Uniting Dance and Theatre." *Theatre Survey* 42.2 (2001): 191–214.

Thomas, Keith. "Work and Leisure in Pre-Industrial Society." *Past & Present* 29 (1964): 50–66.

Thompson, E.P. *Customs in Common: Studies in Traditional Popular Culture.* New York: The New Press, 1991.

Thomson, Rosemarie Garland. "Introduction: From Wonder to Error – A Genealogy of Freak Discourse in Modernity." *Freakery: Cultural Spectacles of the Extraordinary Body.* Ed. Rosemarie Garland Thomson. New York: New York University Press, 1996. 1–22.

Todd, Dennis. *Imagining Monsters: Miscreations of the Self in Eighteenth-Century England.* Chicago: University of Chicago Press, 1995.

Troyer, Howard William. *Ned Ward of Grubstreet: A Study of Sub-Literary London in the Eighteenth Century.* Cambridge: Harvard University Press, 1946.

Vickers, Brian. *In Defence of Rhetoric.* Oxford: Clarendon Press, 1988.

"The Royal Society and English Prose Style: A Reassessment." *Rhetoric and the Pursuit of Truth: Language Change in the Seventeenth and Eighteenth Centuries.* Los Angeles: William Andrews Clark Memorial Library, 1985. 1–76.

von Sneidern, Maja-Lisa. "Joined at the Hip: A Monster, Colonialism, and the Scriblerian Project." *Eighteenth-Century Studies* 30.3 (1997): 213–31.

Wahrman, Dror. *The Making of the Modern Self: Identity and Culture in Eighteenth-Century England.* New Haven: Yale University Press, 2004.

Walker, R.B. "Advertising in London Newspapers, 1650–1750." *Business History* 15.2 (1973): 112–30.

Wall, Cynthia. *The Literary and Cultural Spaces of Restoration London*. Cambridge: Cambridge University Press, 1999.

*The Prose of Things: Transformations of Description in the Eighteenth Century*. Chicago: University of Chicago Press, 2006.

Warneke, Sara. "A Taste for Newfangledness: The Destructive Potential of Novelty in Early Modern England." *Sixteenth-Century Journal* 26 (1995): 881–96.

Warner, William B. *Licensing Entertainment: The Elevation of Novel Reading in Britain, 1684–1750*. Berkeley: University of California Press, 1998.

Watt, Ian. *The Rise of the Novel: Studies in Defoe, Richardson, and Fielding*. London, 1957. Rpt. Harmondsworth: Penguin Books, 1963.

Wells, Mitchell P. "Some Notes on the Early Eighteenth-Century Pantomime." *Studies in Philology* 32 (1935): 598–607.

Wood, Edward J. *Giants and Dwarves*. London: Richard Bentley, 1868.

# Index

Italicized page numbers refer to illustrations.

Addison, Joseph, 22, 64, 120, 153, 251n.77, 262n.68
  and aesthetics, 56–57, 136–38, 153
  *The Free-holder*, 35, 57
  on novelty, 58, 126, 136–38, 175
  on pleasures of the imagination, 56–57,
    136–38, 175
  *The Spectator*, 35, 44, 56–57, 58, 84, 95, 126,
    136–38, 175, 182, 191, 192, 201, 232n.13,
    237n.64, 244n.31, 245n.33, 246n.35, 271n.34
  *The Tatler*, 35, 44, 136, 232n.13
  on wit, 84, 95, 110, 120, 244n.31, 245n.33,
    246n.35, 251n.77
advertising, 19, 234n.30, 270n.25
  through handbills, 12, 22, 139, 144, 145, 149, 163,
    *164*, 175
  and monstrosities, 22, 143, 144, 145, 149, 163, 175
  newspaper, 12, 22, 42–44, 45, 52, 178, 192,
    235n.40, 254n.20
  and print culture, 41–44, 163–64, 234n.28
  rhetoric in, 42–44
  *See also* Fawkes, Isaac; Pinchbeck,
    Christopher; Pinkethman, William; Powell,
    Martin
aesthetics, 2, 4, 7, 22, 35, 64, 86, 98, 99, 120, 170,
    217, 237n.64, 244n.27, 274n.7
  and beauty, 134, 136, 182, 217
  and imagination, 56–57, 58, 136–38, 175
  of monstrosities, 128, 134–38, 140, 150–53, 175
  and novelty, 10, 20, 137, 182, 217
  *See also* Addison, Joseph; neoclassicism
Allestree, Richard, 54
Alston, R.C., 252n.7
Altick, Richard, 144, 260n.52, 261n.60
amusements. *See* diversion; entertainment;
    pastimes
animadversion
  definitions of, 58
  upon diversion, 21, 23, 58, 59, 63, 75, 76, 79,
    180, 184, 185, 214, 222

animal spirits, 53, 54, 236n.56
  *See also* "unbending the mind"
Anne, Queen, 254n.20, 260n.49
*An Approach to Parnassus*, 201
Arbuthnot, John, 152, 258n.45
argument from design, 134, 137, 138, 150, 174
Aristotle, 90, 114, 148
asterisks. *See* ellipses; typography
Athenian Society, 128–31, 255n.26, 256n.30
  *See also* Dunton, John
attention, 3, 9, 19, 20, 25, 32, 34, 52, 54, 55, 58–59,
    60, 63, 67, 70, 83, 85, 106, 126, 127, 163, 170,
    205, 208, 210, 212, 214, 227n.29, 273n.42
  *See also* animadversion; boredom; distraction
audience, 41, 43, 49, 52, 56, 60, 62, 63, 103, 130,
    166, 171, 184, 185, 190, 193, 194, 198, 199, 203,
    204, 209, 217, 221
  and interest, 55, 199, 202
  and monstrosities, 23, 125, 128, 135, 137, 144,
    147, 256n.30, 257n.41, 260n.52, 261n.55,
    263n.74
  and novelty, 39, 55, 157, 178
  as object of diversion, 3, 25, 40, 42, 45, 47, 55,
    57, 64, 66, 67, 75, 76, 77, 79, 121, 178, 193,
    197, 198, 201, 230n.1
  and taste, 44, 47, 199, 221
  and theatre, 9, 22, 57, 86, 87, 88, 90, 91, 93, 94,
    105, 106, 107, 108–10, 115, 118, 119, 121, 199,
    202, 203, 210, 215
  *See also* attention
Augustans
  and monstrosities, 134, 138, 148, 154, 160, 163,
    171, 259n.48
  and poetics, 96, 247n.43, 250n.76
  and response to popular literature, 13–15
  and satire, 13–15, 30, 138, 147, 160, 265n.92
  and wit, 22, 83–104, 120, 121, 246n.38
  *See also* neoclassicism; *individual authors*
automata. *See* mechanical entertainments

295

Bacon, Francis, 135, 137, 152
  *The Advancement of Learning*, 150
  *Novum Organum*, 152, 153, 262n.68
Bailey, Anne Hall, 160
Barchas, Janine, 165, 266n.98
Barker, Henry, 150
  *The Polite Gentleman*, 98, 181
Barthes, Roland, 12
*bathos*, 101–4, 112, 113, 135, 143, 182, 194
Battestin, Martin, 192
bear-baiting, 27, 28, 30, 38, 40, 55, 58, 64, 179, 180, 183, 214, 232n.15
Bedford, Arthur, 28, 49, 50, 230n.1
Bedlam, 18, 68, 126, 131, 253n.15, 265n.90
Behn, Aphra, 141
  *Oroonoko*, 187
Benedict, Barbara M., 10, 23, 143, 148, 163, 234n.28, 255n.24, 256n.33, 264n.87
Besant, Walter, 13
Blackmore, Richard, 6
  *An Essay Upon Wit*, 76, 77
  *Prince Arthur*, 101, 102, 114, 247n.48
Bogel, Frederic V., 15, 228n.35
booksellers, 18, 27, 65, 68, 72, 125, 131, 158, 160, 166, 167, 169, 237n.65, 265n.92
*The Book of Sports*, 32–34, 37, 232n.7
Booth, Barton, 191
Booth, Wayne, 3, 5, 223n.4, 275n.9
boredom, 3, 25, 55, 56, 75, 214
  as impetus for disruption, 8, 215
  as perceived cultural threat, 66
  *See also* attention
Bosch, René, 275n.8
Boyce, Benjamin, 67
Bramston, James
  *The Art of Politicks*, 249n.70
Brant, Clare, 19
Brewer, John, 39, 40, 47, 155, 223n.3
*The British Journal*, 109
*The British Stage*, 81, 111, 112
Broughton, John, 191
Brown, Thomas, 21, 23, 175, 238n.77, 267n.104
  *Amusements Serious and Comical*, 6, 66–71, 126, 131–34, 172, 175, 201, 229n.46, 238n.73, 256n.32
  *The Works of Mr. Thomas Brown, Serious and Comical*, 72, 73, 132, 133, 171, 201
Browne, Thomas, 4, 268n.3
Buchinger, Matthew, 123, 124, 251n.3, 259n.46
bull-baiting, 18, 64, 102, 232n.15, 233n.20
Burke, Edmund, 217
burlesque, 110, 111, 138, 188, 198
Burnet, William, 138, 258n.43
Burton, Robert
  *Anatomy of Melancholy*, 4

Bysshe, Edward
  *The Art of English Poetry*, 26

Campbell, Jill, 269n.17
carnivalesque, 12, 31, 32, 33, 37
  *See also* Castle, Terry; masquerade
Castle, Terry, 8, 9, 11, 196
catachresis, 3, 12, 22, 23, 103–4, 114, 120, 180, 221, 247n.49
Centlivre, Susanna, 271n.33
Chambers, Ephraim, 152
*The Champion. See* Fielding, Henry
Charing Cross, 123, 126, 139, 145, 146, 149, 156, 167, 170
Charke, Charlotte, 11, 192
Charles I, 33, 232n.15
Charles II, 123, 254n.20
Cheyne, George, 236n.59
Cibber, Colley, 16, 21, 39, 73–75, 188, 191
  *Apology*, 6, 89, 106, 199, 239n.81, 268n.7
  *The Provoked Husband*, 194
Cicero, 4, 90, 92
Clark, John R., 127, 255n.23
Clark, Joseph, 20, 37, 38, 228n.36
Clive, Catherine, 191
coffeehouses, 2, 3, 9, 11, 18, 22, 27, 39, 62, 68, 73, 123, 145, 166, 176, 232n.13
Collier, Jeremy, 3, 28, 49, 230n.1, 231n.2
*commedia dell'arte*, 45, 81, 104, 109
  *See also* Harlequin
commercialization, 10, 18, 188, 268n.3
  of curiosities, 10, 123, 154
  of diversion, 218
  of leisure, 2, 3, 15, 21, 31, 32, 37, 54, 80, 186, 191, 214, 216, 220, 231n.4
  of literature, 165, 225n.12
  of literature and leisure, 4, 8, 13, 30, 44, 59, 79, 104, 184
  of monstrosity, 125, 148
  of spectacle and amusement, 7, 15, 187, 199
  *See also* consumer revolution
commodification of literature, 138, 156, 157, 186
Congreve, William, 115
  "Concerning Humour in Comedy," 154
  *Incognita*, 186
conjoined twins, 123, 138–40, 157, 253n.18, 258n.43, 259n.46
consumer revolution, 15, 49, 228n.36, 231n.4
  *See also* McKendrick, Neil; Plumb, J.H
Cooper, Anthony Ashley (3rd Earl of Shaftesbury), 63, 84, 136
  *Soliloquy*, 101
copiousness, 4, 28, 48, 58, 60, 75, 115, 161, 167, 176, 177, 181, 188
Cotterill, Anne, 34, 267n.3

Cotton, Charles, 4, 262n.71
  *The Compleat Gamester*, 54
*The Country Gentleman's Vade-Mecum. See*
  *The Tricks of the Town Laid Open*
Covent Garden, 10, 13, 17, 37, 39, 55, 126, 172, 192
*The Covent-Garden Journal. See* Fielding, Henry
Coventry, Francis, 269n.14
Cowan, Brian, 11
Cowley, Abraham, 99, 100
Cox, James, 11
*The Craftsman*, 201
Crane, R.S., 204, 209, 273n.46
credulity. *See* curiosity
Crouch, Nathaniel, 252n.8
cultural revolution in England, 3, 21
curiosity, 9, 10, 27, 56, 65, 74, 109, 126, 137, 141,
  143, 149, 157, 206, 255n.24
  and credulity, 40, 127, 128, 137, 138, 147, 157,
    177, 255n.24
  *See also* monstrosities; novelty
Curll, Edmund, 265n.92
Curran, Andrew, 175

*The Daily Courant*, 42, 44, 52, 192
*The Daily Journal*, 44
*The Daily Post*, 40, *41*, 42, 44, 235n.40
dance, 6, 32, 33, 39, 40, 52, 86, 93, 109, 179, 184,
  188, 192, 194, 195, 198, 218, 230n.1, 233n.18,
  270n.25
  and audience, 9, 57, 91, 107
  grotesque, 23, 40, 95, 99, 103, 104, 114, 198
  history and theory of, 65, 89–96, 99, 177, 181,
    243n.18, 244n.27, 245n.33
  and novelty, 42, 43, 44, 45, *46*, 55, 123, 128, 145,
    235n.36
  and pantomime, 9, 65, 82, 83, 84, 86, 87, 89,
    90, 91, 92, 94, 99, 104, 108, 111, 112, 241n.6,
    243n.18, 245n.33, 248n.58, 250n.72, 268n.5
  rope, 14, 28, 45, 144, 182, 183, 192, 215, 268n.5
  *See also* pantomime; Weaver, John
*The Danger of Masquerades and Raree-Shows*, 44,
  182, 195
Daston, Lorraine, 151
Davies, Thomas, 87
Davys, Mary, 186
Defoe, Benjamin Norton, 152
Defoe, Daniel, 53, 236n.55
  *The Complete English Tradesman*, 50, 77
  *Robinson Crusoe*, 201
  *Moll Flanders*, 186
de la Place, Pierre Antoine, 204, 209, 273n.45
Dennis, John, 256n.34
Derrida, Jacques, 12, 247n.49
digression, 3, 4, 5, 6, 7, 12, 19, 30, 34, 57, 58, 69, 70,
  74, 75, 77, 78, 80, 150, 153, 154, 157, 167, 180,

204, 209, 216, 218, 221, 224n.4, 240n.84,
  257n.37
  and amusements, 21, 23, 60, 62, 67, 70, 75, 77,
    80, 179, 182
  apologetics for, 6, 20, 63, 67, 70, 73, 74, 75, 76,
    204, 210, 215, 217, 218, 219
  appropriateness of, 76, 79, 101, 184, 212
  criticism of, 5, 75, 76, 181
  defined, 180
  effects of, 7, 8, 12, 14, 20, 24, 25, 74, 161, 167,
    204, 208, 210, 214, 217, 259n.47, 267n.3
  and leisure, 8, 75
  and the novel, 185, 191, 210, 216–20, 270n.23
  and novelty, 140, 179, 180, 181, 182
  and pleasure, 8, 20, 79, 204, 209, 210, 268n.3
  as related to diversion, 2, 14, 18, 19, 20, 21, 23,
    25, 30, 51, 62, 75, 78, 135, 179, 182, 184, 191,
    212, 217, 219, 220
  and rhetoric, 70, 101, 180, 189, 217, 259n.47
  and satiety, 24, 184, 185, 214
  *See also* wit, digressive
discursive revolution, 3, 21
disruption, 5
  and amusement, 78
  criticism of, 75
  cultural, 49, 54, 153
  linguistic, 5, 22, 75, 78, 219
  narrative, 3, 62, 198, 205, 208, 215
  textual, 5, 7, 8, 22, 24, 59, 60, 73, 75, 78, 169,
    180, 219, 221
  *See also* digression
distraction, 6, 7, 34, 35, 40, 49, 50, 58, 60, 66, 73,
  97, 118, 120, 132, 138, 169, 184, 192, 205, 208,
  236n.50, 240n.84
  motives behind, 8, 14, 62, 64, 213
  *See also* attention; disruption; diversion
diversion
  and commercial economy, 3, 8, 15, 17, 23, 32,
    34, 37, 39, 40, 42, 45, 47, 48, 49, 50, 53, 54, 55,
    59, 63, 73, 75, 79, 179, 218
  and copiousness, 19, 31, 36, 37, 42, 55, 181
  definitions of, 7, 30, 226n.15
  and digression, 2, 7, 18, 19, 20, 21, 23, 24, 62, 75,
    76, 78, 79, 179, 180, 182, 184, 189, 191, 212,
    217, 219, 220
  and effects upon literary practices, 3, 6, 7, 8, 13,
    14, 21, 22, 23, 24, 59, 214
  "innocent," 28, 30, 50, 53, 56, 66
  and knowledge, 49, 215
  and labouring classes, 33
  and leisure, 2, 31, 32, 33, 47, 74, 213
  and the novel, 24, 25, 201, 210, 211–13, 216, 218,
    219, 220, 221, 269n.17
  and novelty, 10, 20, 105, 139, 167, 176, 178, 179,
    180, 184

diversion (cont.)
  and pleasure, 15, 28, 31, 36, 50, 55, 56, 57, 58, 66, 67, 77, 118, 119, 184, 239n.81, 268n.6
  prescriptive attitudes towards, 24, 27, 28, 44, 50, 51, 57, 78, 182, 188
  problems ascribed to, 36, 37, 44, 48, 49, 50, 51, 52, 53, 54, 75, 76, 127, 182, 188, 195, 196, 231n.1
  purpose and usefulness of, 7, 8, 13, 15, 24, 30, 31, 32, 33, 35, 36, 37, 47, 50, 53, 54, 55, 59, 62, 63, 191, 200, 210, 231n.1, 236n.59
  relationship between cultural and discursive, 7, 13, 14, 18, 20, 21, 22, 23, 24, 58, 63, 70, 75, 76, 77, 79, 125, 148, 184, 190, 191, 201, 211, 216, 218
  *See also* animadversion; entertainment
Dobson, Austin, 13
*Donaldson vs. Beckett* (1774), 3
Donne, John, 154, 268n.3
Don Saltero's, 3, 55
Downes, John, 45
Drummond, William, 154
Drury Lane, 14, 25, 75, 81, 86, 89, 94, 96, 106, 120, 188, 195, 197, 198, 199, 200, 203, 209, 211, 239n.82, 243n.18, 248n.58
  competition with Lincoln's Inn Fields, 242n.13
  management of, 39, 73, 199
Dryden, John, 90, 115, 154, 155, 268n.3
  *A Discourse Concerning the Original and Progress of Satire*, 34, 35, 37
Dunton, John, 3, 14, 175, 232n.7, 255n.26, 256n.31, 266n.101
  *The Athenian Mercury*, 128–31, 148, 165–66, 254n.22, 255n.28, 256n.30, 258n.45
  *Athenian Sport*, 54
  *Life and Errors*, 267n.101
  *A Voyage Round the World*, 3, 5, 6, 19–20, 126, 166–70, *168*, 175, 220, 221, 266n.100, 268n.6
  *See also The Life, Travels, and Adventures of Christopher Wagstaff*
Du Plessis, James Paris, 140
D'Urfey, Thomas, 23
  *An Essay Towards the Theory of the Intelligible World*, 6, 126, 134–36, 172–75, *173*, 176, 257n.36
During, Simon, 40
dwarves, 22, 122, 123, 126, 128, 139, 142, 143, 144, 145, 146, 161, 198, 253n.18, 254n.20, 259n.46, 265n.87
  *See also* Buchinger, Matthew; monstrosities

Echard, Laurence, 201
ellipses, 22, 24, 60, 61, 161, 171, 172, 175, 177, 207, 267n.104, 274n.7
English Short-Title Catalogue (ESTC), 59, 234n.36

entertainment, 2, 7, 8, 9, 18, 30, 31, 34, 39, 51, 59, 60, 89, 94, 105, 106, 107, 109, 111, 112, 113, 119, 134, 148, 160, 179, 182, 191, 194, 195, 199, 220, 221, 230n.1, 237n.64, 261n.55
  and advertising, 41, 44, 178
  and concerns of authors, 2, 4, 62, 64, 72, 82, 97, 185
  and the novel, 6, 24, 190, 194–201, 209, 211, 212, 213, 216, 217, 221, 273n.49
  and novelty, 52, 55, 56, 67, 91, 137, 180, 185, 186, 187, 189
  relationship between entertainers and authors, 14, 30, 187
  and variety, 37, 40, 190, 199
  *See also* diversion; leisure; mechanical entertainments; novelty; pleasure
entr'acte divertissement. *See* theatre
Erasmus, 201
Essex, John, 191
*An Exact Description of Harlequin Doctor Faustus and The Necromancer*, 105
exhibitions. *See* advertising; entertainment; monstrosities

*The Fair in an Uproar*, 45, *46*, 234n.36
fairs, 18, 22, 28, 39, 44, 45, 55, 57, 58, 106, 112, 125, 130, 134, 155, 192, 214
  Bartholomew Fair, 7, 14, 44, 125, 128, 146, 148, 155, 160, 163, 175, 182, 235n.36, 259n.48
  fairground theatricals, 14, 135
  May Fair, 44
  monstrosities at, 9, 24, 123, 128, 154, 155, 157, 165, 175, 177, 261n.55
  Southwark Fair, 30, 182
  *See also* monstrosities; *individiual performers*
Fanning, Christopher, 274n.7
fashion. *See* aesthetics; commercialization; curiosity; novelty
Fawkes, Isaac, 39, 40–44, *41*, 47, 52, 76, 94, 105, 112, 178, 188, 191, 233n.23, 235n.40
festivities. *See* pastimes
Fielding, Henry, 14, 94, 269n.14, 272n.39
  *The Author's Farce*, 13, 14, 188, 189, 190, 270n.22
  *The Champion*, 188
  *The Covent-Garden Journal*, 178, 188
  *The Covent-Garden Tragedy*, 192
  and digression, 14, 190, 191, 203–13, 270n.23
  and diversion, 25, 36, 37, 49, 54, 187, 188–91, 200, 208, 213, 269n.17
  *Enquiry into the Causes of the Late Increase of Robbers*, 36, 37, 54, 188, 189
  and entertainment, 6, 37, 111, 186, 187, 191, 200, 201, 209, 210, 211, 212, 213, 269n.8, 273n.49
  and James Ralph, 201, 270n.22
  *Joseph Andrews*, 187, 189, 270n.23

*The Masquerade*, 187
  and mimesis, 208, 209, 272n.39
*The Mock Doctor*, 192
  and the "new species of writing," 25, 187, 202
*The Old Debauchees*, 192
  and self-consciousness, 25, 189, 190, 205, 210
*Tom Jones*, 6, 25, 185, 190–213, 219, 240n.1, 270n.23, 273n.45
*Tumble-Down Dick*, 111–13, 249n.69
Flint, Christopher, 5, 71, 72, 238n.78, 265n.92
Florio, John, 262n.71
*Fog's Weekly Journal*, 44
Foote, Samuel, 197, 272n.37
Formalism, 13
freak-shows. *See* monstrosities
Freeman, Arthur, 230n.1, 231n.2

Garrick, David, 3, 191, 198, 200, 203, 272n.37
Garth, Samuel, 250n.76
Gay, John
  *The Beggar's Opera*, 51
*The General Advertiser*, 192
Genette, Gérard, 12, 266n.97
George I, 123
George II, 254n.20, 271n.30
George III, 3
Gerard, Alexander, 217
giants, 22, 111, 123, 125, 133, 135, 142, 144, 147, 253n.18, 254n.20, 260n.49, 264n.87
  *See also* monstrosities
Gildon, Charles, 270n.25
  *All for the Better*, 6, 14
  *The Complete Art of Poetry*, 73, 239n.80
  *The Post-Boy Robbed of his Mail*, 72
  *The Post-Man Robb'd of his Mail*, 65–66, 71, 72, 183, 238n.72
Goldsmith, Oliver, 122
Graille, Patrick, 175
Granville, George (Lord Lansdowne)
  "Concerning Unnatural Flights in Poetry," 100, 122, 154
Grove, Henry
  *The Regulation of Diversions*, 77–79
Grub Street, 2, 14, 18, 155, 156, 230n.50, 256n.31, 263n.79
  and hack writing, 71, 161, 181, 265n.92, 270n.22
  as portrayed in literature, 14, 157, 159, 160, 163, 166, 170, 181, 263n.81, 265n.90, 270n.22
*The Grub Street Journal*, 42, 88
Gubar, Susan, 256n.33
Guerinot, J.V., 156

Habermas, Jürgen
  and bourgeois public sphere, 11, 232n.13

hack writing. *See* Grub Street
Hammond, Brean, 2
Handel, George Frederic, 191
Harlequin
  antics of, 9, 22, 28, 104, 108, 113, 118, 241n.6
  and corporeality, 22, 84, 87, 110, 120
  *See also* O'Brien, John; pantomime; Rich, John
harlequinades. *See* pantomime
Harte, Walter, 249n.70
Hawley, Judith, 153, 259n.48, 261n.60
Haymarket, 11, 25, 39, 57, 188, 195, 197, 209, 253n.15
  King's Theatre, 30, 187, 194, 196
  Little Theatre, 6, 230n.50
Haywood, Eliza, 53, 77, 141, 189, 208
  *The Female Spectator*, 52
Heidegger, Johann Jakob, 11, 39, 47, 55, 57, 114, 191, 194, 195, 196, 271n.30
Helena and Judith. *See* conjoined twins
Henley, John, 39, 44, 55, 188, 228n.36, 230n.1
Hill, Aaron, 109
  *The British Apollo*, 139, 254n.22
Historical Formalism, 12, 227n.29
Hobbes, Thomas, 257n.37
Hockley-in-the-Hole, 18, 38, 253n.15
Hogarth, William, 241n.4
  *Industry and Idleness*, 49
holidays. *See* pastimes
Hopkins, Hopkin, 150
Horace, 14, 115, 118, 170, 227n.33, 267n.106
  *Ars Poetica*, 153, 154, 160, 262n.69
Howell, James, 20
Hume, Robert D., 233n.23
Hunter, J. Paul, 2, 5, 125, 191, 252n.8, 269n.9, 270n.23
Hutcheson, Francis, 136
hyperbaton, 4, 101

idleness. *See* time
imagination, 4, 16, 19, 66, 140, 219, 242n.10, 269n.14
  and the monstrous, 10, 128, 137, 140, 147, 154, 251n.1
  pleasures of the, 3, 56, 58, 136, 137, 175
  and wit, 97, 98, 99

James I, 32, 33, 232n.15
James, Susan, 54
Johns, Adrian, 157
Johnson, Samuel
  *A Dictionary of the English Language*, 7, 152, 262n.67
  *The Prince of Abissinia*, 217
Johnson, Samuel, of Cheshire, 39, 191

Jonson, Ben
    *Bartholomew Fair*, 154
judgement. *See* wit

Keen, Paul, 7, 226n.17, 252n.6, 255n.23, 274n.3
Kenny, Shirley Strum, 198
Kerby-Miller, Charles, 140, 258n.45, 259n.47
Keymer, Thomas, 216, 218, 236n.50, 274n.1, 275n.9
Klein, Lawrence, 2
Kroll, Richard W.F., 264n.85

Laroon, Marcellus, 38
Law, William, 28, 230n.1
Lee, Nathaniel, 101
leisure, 17, 27, 49, 54, 57, 123, 195, 211, 221, 222,
        237n.64
    commercialization and consumption of, 2, 3,
        4, 8, 10, 13, 15, 16, 20, 21, 30, 31, 32, 37, 43, 44,
        48, 54, 59, 71, 79, 80, 104, 184, 186, 191, 210,
        214, 216, 220, 228n.36
    conceptualization of, 8, 31–33
    and digression, 8, 75, 80
    and effects on literary production, 14, 34, 35, 58,
        69, 79, 185, 186, 187, 213, 219
    function of, 47
    genealogy of, 74
    and identity, 9, 11
    and novelty, 178, 184
    and self-consciousness in literature, 8, 21, 59,
        79, 215, 220
    *See also* Plumb, J.H.
*Letters from a Moor at London*, 94
*A Letter to My Lord ******* On the Present
        Diversions of the Town*, 44, 199
Licensing Act (1695), 3, 155, 159, 263n.79
*The Life, Travels, and Adventures of Christopher
        Wagstaff*, 3, 221, 275n.11
Lincoln's Inn Fields, 30, 81, 120, 188
    competition with Drury Lane, 107, 242n.13
    management of, 39
    and pantomime, 9, 86, 94, 96, 107, 115,
        234n.30, 241n.4, 242n.13
Lindgren, Lowell, 231n.2
Locke, John, 110, 218, 262n.67
    *An Essay Concerning Human Understanding*,
        84, 96–97, 98, 119, 246n.36
London
    history of, 16–17
    and topography of pleasure, 17–19
    urbanization of, 10, 16–18, 37
    writing about, 18–20
*The London Journal*, 42
Longinus, 101
Love, Harold, 2
Lucian, 90

Lund, Roger D., 98, 134, 246n.38
Lupton, Christina, 5, 225n.12, 237n.67, 274n.5
Luttrell, Narcissus, 235n.36

Mackie, Erin, 2, 23, 230n.51
Macklin, Charles, 191
magic, 40, 103, 111, 135
    *See also* Fawkes, Isaac
Mandeville, Bernard, 48
Manley, Delarivière, 186
Marcus, Leah, 33
marketing. *See* advertising
Marshall, Ashley, 238n.77
Marvell, Andrew, 268n.3
    *Upon Appleton House*, 4
Mary II, 254n.20
Mary of Godliman. *See* Toft, Mary
masquerades, 8, 11, 14, 25, 28, 36, 39, 47, 52, 57, 58,
        179, 180, 183, 188, 194, 195, 196, 197, 205, 209,
        214, 230n.1, 272n.34
    *See also* Heidegger, Johann Jakob
McEwan, Gilbert D., 255n.28, 256n.30
McKendrick, Neil, 15, 17, 223n.1
mechanical entertainments, 9, 11, 39, 44, 198
    *See also* advertising; Cox, James; Fawkes, Isaac;
        Pinchbeck, Christopher; Pinkethman,
        William
*The Memoirs of Martinus Scriblerus*. *See* Pope,
        Alexander; Scriblerians; Swift, Jonathan
menageries, 123, 142, 251n.2
metaphor, 53, 54, 60, 98, 99, 101, 102, 103, 105,
        120, 167, 188, 202, 220, 245n.32
    extravagant or strained use of, 5, 7, 22, 60, 62,
        74, 75, 80, 85, 96, 100, 101, 114, 119, 215,
        247n.49
    and monstrosity, 133, 147, 152, 153, 154, 155, 160,
        161, 163, 256n.33, 265n.87
    and pantomime, 86, 91, 110, 114
Milburn, D. Judson, 96, 245n.34
Miller, Christopher R., 232n.6
Miller, James
    *Harlequin-Horace*, 81, 113–18, *116*, 249n.70,
        250n.71
Mills, William, 191
Milton, John, 268n.3
    *Paradise Lost*, 4
mime, 65, 241n.6
mimesis, 3, 11, 24, 66, 77, 82, 85, 86, 87, 89, 90, 93,
        95, 96, 97, 98, 99, 102, 104, 110, 115, 119, 154,
        169, 181, 208, 209, 215, 272n.39
    and monsters, 151, 152, 153
*Mist's Weekly Journal*, 42, 44
monsters. *See* monstrosities
monstrosities, 255n.29, 259n.46
    and aesthetics, 125, 128, 134, 136, 137, 138, 140

artistic and literary, 126, 152, 163
and beauty, 136
causes of, 127, 129, 251n.1
compared to beauty, 134, 135, 137, 140, 141, 142, 257n.37
craze for, 123, 160
and credulity, 127, 128, 137, 138, 157, 254n.21
and curiosity, 125, 126, 127, 128, 137, 138, 141, 142, 157, 163
defects and excesses in, 22, 23, 24, 127, 149, 150, 151, 152, 153, 161, 163, 171, 176
definitions of, 152, 262n.66
and ethics, 127, 130
exhibitions of, 6, 9, 10, 21, 22, 23, 24, 122, 123, 125, 127, 128, 130, 131, 135, 138, 139, 141, 144, 145, 146, 147, 148, 149, 154, 155, 156, 157, 163, 167, 175, 176, 177, 178, 182, 252n.7, 253n.10, 254n.20, 259n.48, 260n.52, 261n.55
and identity, 9, 123, 251n.1, 261n.55
and imagination, 128, 136, 137, 138, 140, 147, 154
literary representations of, 22, 23, 126, 128, 129, 130, 131, 138, 262n.69
and metaphor, 133, 152, 153, 154, 155, 156, 160, 161, 256n.33, 265n.87
and mimesis, 153, 154
and nature, 127, 129, 136, 152, 262n.68
and novelty, 126, 136, 137, 158
and satire, 22, 23, 125, 126, 128, 131, 133, 138, 140–48, 159, 160, 161, 163, 252n.7, 253n.18, 256n.33, 257n.37, 263n.83
and teratology, 125
textual, 23, 24, 125, 140, 146, 147, 148, 154, 156, 157, 158, 160, 161, 163, 164, 165, 170, 171, 174, 177, 181
Montaigne, Michael de, 4, 98
  *Essais*, 153, 262n.71
Montgomery, Robert L., 8
Morris, Corbyn, 97
Motteux, Peter, 4
Muir, Edward, 49

neoclassicism, 3, 85, 86, 90, 91, 105, 119, 152, 153, 154
New Historicism, 9, 13
New Science, 85, 96, 123, 150, 241n.7
newspapers, 12, 22, 39, 40, 42, 43, 44, 45, 52, 62, 149, 234n.28, 254n.22
  *See also individual titles*
Norris, John, 255n.26
  *An Essay Towards the Theory of the Intelligible World*, 257n.36
novel, 236n.55
  and amusement, 186, 187, 188, 194
  and audience, 209
  and digression, 185, 203–5, 206, 209–13, 218–20, 270n.23

and diversion, 24, 185–201, 208, 213, 216, 217, 219, 220, 221, 269n.17
  emergence as a genre, 10, 189, 216, 252n.8
  and interest, 25, 201–8, 209, 210, 213
  and leisure, 185, 186, 187
  and modes of entertainment, 24, 185, 187, 189, 200, 213, 216
  and novelty, 185, 186, 187, 189, 274n.5
  and pleasure, 2, 185, 194, 198, 199, 201, 209, 210, 211, 269n.9
  and satiety, 185, 187, 190
  and self-consciousness, 24, 72, 73, 186, 189, 190, 205, 208, 210, 211, 216, 217, 219, 274n.5
  *See also individual authors*

O'Brien, John, 2, 9, 10, 35, 86, 87, 108, 109, 110, 241n.4, 250n.74
oddities. *See* monstrosities
Oldmixon, John, 84, 99, 100
opera. *See* Heidegger, Johann Jakob; Senesino, Francesco
ornamentation. *See* rhetoric
Ovid, 81, 200, 248n.61, 250n.76
  *Ars Amatoria*, 206

pantomime, 9, 21, 22, 23, 51, 58, 84, 87, 89, 91, 92, 93, 108, 109, 110, 112, 113, 120, 156, 182, 210, 240n.1, 241n.6, 242n.13, 244n.26, 247n.50, 249n.65, 250n.71, 268n.5
  apologetics for, 22, 47, 82, 86, 90, 105, 107, 110
  critiqued, 65, 82, 84, 87, 89, 91, 94, 96, 99, 103, 106, 109, 110, 113, 118, 195, 250n.74
  defining characteristics of, 9, 82, 94, 104, 105, 118
  as diversion, 28, 42, 85, 107, 118, 188, 198, 214
  etymology of, 240n.3
  history and development of, 9, 81, 82, 85, 89, 93, 120, 241n.6, 243n.18
  and mimesis, 82, 89, 90, 93, 94, 95, 96, 104, 110
  and poetics, 82, 83, 84, 85, 89, 90, 91, 95, 103, 104, 113, 114, 115, 119, 120
  popularity of, 9, 22, 87, 105, 106, 107, 109, 118, 248n.57
  and rhetoric, 23, 82, 83, 85, 86, 87, 91, 107
  *See also* Harlequin; theatre; *individual productions*
"pantomimic poetics," 24, 85, 104–18, 216
paratext, 6, 22, 24, 71, 165, 166, 174, 175, 187, 266n.97
parenthesis, 4, 74, 221
  *See also* digression
Park, Julie, 10, 11
Park, Katherine, 151
Parker, Blanford, 247n.43
Parks, Stephen, 266n.101

parody, 7, 14, 19, 30, 77, 86, 101, 188, 193, 198, 215, 257n.37
  linguistic, 85
  and monsters, 138, 148, 153, 158, 161
  and the novel, 219, 270n.23
  of pantomime, 110, 111–18, 249n.65
  *See also* satire
Pasanek, Brad, 236n.56
*Pasquin*, 42, 43
passions. *See* "unbending the mind"
pastimes, 7, 32–37, 45, 54, 59, 65, 74, 192, 233n.15
  festivities, 9, 32, 34
  old holiday, 32, 33, 34, 35, 40, 50, 179
  sports, 6, 7, 9, 32, 34, 35, 37, 57, 59, 230n.1
  *See also* amusements; carnivalesque; entertainment; recreations
Paulson, Ronald, 13, 136
Pausanias, 131
Pepys, Samuel, 149, 253n.10, 259n.46
Phillips, Edward, 152
*The Philosophical Transactions*, 140, 149, 150, *151*, 254n.22, 255n.28, 258n.43, 261n.60
Pinchbeck, Christopher, 39, 40, 44, 45, 52, 178
Pinkethman, William, 38, 44, 45, 46, 188
Pinkus, Philip, 263n.79
Plato, 131
pleasure, 7, 8, 11, 12, 15, 17, 18, 19, 21, 22, 23, 27, 31, 34, 36, 48, 49, 50, 53, 57, 67, 72, 73, 75, 97, 103, 106, 107, 110, 119, 136, 145, 155, 156, 158, 163, 183, 188, 198, 218, 227n.29, 231n.1, 236n.49, 242n.13, 245n.33, 268n.5
  and aesthetics, 22, 35, 120, 136, 182, 217
  and digression, 2, 7, 20, 62, 79, 204, 209, 210, 268n.3
  and diversion, 2, 7, 9, 19, 21, 28, 31, 36, 44, 50, 52, 56, 59, 60, 66, 67, 73, 74, 76, 77, 118, 184, 211, 239n.81, 250n.71, 261n.55, 268n.6
  and the imagination, 3, 56, 58, 136, 137, 175
  material, 8, 15, 56, 216
  and the novel, 2, 185, 194, 198, 199, 201, 209, 210, 211, 269n.9
  and novelties, 11, 50, 57, 136, 137, 183, 217, 268n.6
  pursued for its own sake, 4, 31
Plumb, J.H., 2, 16
Plutarch, 131, 155
Pope, Alexander, 14, 16, 22, 72, 138, 175, 238n.79, 262n.67, 263n.81
  *The Dunciad*, 13, 14, 23, 39, 125, 159, 160, 161, 163, 249n.70, 265n.90, 274n.7
  *An Essay on Criticism*, 86, 90, 93, 101, 152
  *An Essay on Man*, 258n.42
  *The Memoirs of Martinus Scriblerus*, 126, 138, 140–42, 153, 258n.45, 259n.47, 260n.49, 264n.83

*Peri Bathous*, 6, 101, 103, 104, 112, 247n.48
  translation of the *Iliad*, 201
  *See also* Scriblerians
Popple, William, 109
Porter, Roy, 18
*The Post Boy*, 235n.36
Powell, Martin, 40, 44
Punch's Theatre, 13, 37, 44, 192, 253n.15, 270n.25
Preston, Christopher, 37
print culture, 2, 5, 23
  and advertising, 41, 43
  and attitudes towards reading, 12, 155
  and commercialization, 18, 157
  democratization of, 10
  and dissemination of knowledge, 157, 159
  ephemerality of, 159
  and lapse of Licensing Act, 3, 155, 159, 263n.79
  and monstrosity, 125, 163, 171, 175, 265n.93
  and novelty, 175, 176
  rapid expansion of, 7, 155, 156, 160, 263n.79, 265n.92, 268n.3
  and satire, 157–66, 169, 170
Prior, Matthew, 98, 115
prodigies. *See* monstrosities
*The Prompter*, 109, 118
public sphere. *See* Habermas, Jürgen
puppet shows, 9, 10, 11, 14, 20, 25, 28, 37, 40, 60, 81, 85, 111, 126, 183, 188, 195, 214, 230n.1, 253n.15, 271n.28
  as diversion, 58, 188, 190, 192–94, 205, 221
  *See also* Powell, Martin
Puttenham, George, 4
  *The Arte of English Poesie*, 154

Ralph, James, 16, 21, 230n.50
  *The Case of Authors by Profession or Trade*, 230n.50
  contributions to *The Champion*, 231n.2
  *The Fashionable Lady*, 231n.2
  *Sawney*, 230n.50
  *See also The Touch-Stone*
Ralph, Richard, 94, 250n.73
Ramsay, Allan, 98
Rapin, René, 98
raree-show, 6, 81, 109, 126, 135, 167, 170, 195, 253n.14
Raven, James, 216
reading, history of, 12–13
recreations, 6, 7, 18, 31, 32, 33, 34, 48, 54, 59, 64, 76, 78, 79, 183, 221
  *See also* amusements; entertainment; pastimes
reflexivity. *See* self-consciousness
refreshment. *See* Addison, Joseph; diversion; novelty; "unbending the mind"

rhetoric, 23, 63, 75, 79, 84, 86, 96, 97, 98, 147, 148, 157, 163, 180, 181, 187, 198, 208, 211, 216, 228n.36, 236n.50, 243n.23, 252n.6, 268n.3, 270n.22
*actio*, 86, 92
in advertising, 43, 234n.28
*ars rhetorica*, 83, 101, 120
critical attitudes towards, 4, 22, 75, 83, 96, 97, 119, 138
and disruption, 5, 60, 103, 104, 114, 189
and diversion, 8, 14, 22, 23, 24, 56, 59, 76, 210, 211, 212, 213, 214, 216, 217, 219, 220, 221, 222
*elocutio*, 86, 88, 92
excesses of, 83, 85, 100, 101
and pantomime, 22, 84, 85, 86, 90, 91, 92, 96, 108, 119
"silent Rhetorick," 82, 83, 86, 93, 99, 107, 120
*See also* catachresis; digression; hyperbaton; metaphor; parenthesis; simile
Rich, John, 7, 39, 47, 55, 76, 94, 105, 107, 113, 178, 188, 191, 210, 249n.69
*Jupiter and Europa*, 43, 107, 113, 234n.30, 240n.1
*The Necromancer*, 43, 87, 104, 234n.30, 242n.13
*Orpheus and Eurydice*, 105
*Perseus and Andromeda*, 107, 108, 109, 113, 114, 115, 248n.60, 250n.72
*The Rape of Proserpine*, 105, 107
in role as Harlequin, 9, 87, *88*, 109, 110, 115
*See also* Harlequin; pantomime; Theobald, Lewis
Richardson, Samuel, 53, 208, 209, 236n.55, 265n.92
*The Apprentice's Vade Mecum*, 51, 77, 236n.50
ridotto, 28, 36, 58, 179, 188, 214
Roger, Monsieur, 248n.58
Rogers, Pat, 13, 14, 233n.16, 263n.79
Royal Society, 4, 86, 97, 139, 149, 150, 241n.7, 253n.10
Rymer, Thomas, 98

Saccamano, Neil, 245n.32
Sackville, Charles, 34
Salmon, Mrs, 38
Samber, Robert, 231n.2
satiety, 24, 56, 75, 76, 182, 184, 185, 187, 190, 199, 210, 214, 239n.82
satire, 100, 257n.36, 263n.81
and commercialization, 16, 45, 48, 64, 159, 188
and digression, 181, 212, 218
and entertainment, 15, 44, 45, 48, 134, 135
history and development of, 34
Menippean, 5, 141
and monstrosities, 23, 125, 128–34, 138, 140–48, 157, 158, 160–63, 252n.7, 256n.33, 257n.41, 263n.83, 265n.93

and pantomime, 84, 106, 110, 113–18, 195, 250n.74
and print culture, 157–66, 169, 170, 265n.92
*See also* parody; *individual authors*
Sault, Richard, 255n.26, 256n.31
Saussure, Cesar de, 105
Savage, Richard
*An Author to be Lett*, 155, 156, 263n.81
Sawyer, Paul, 247n.50
Scriblerians, 138–48, 153, 159, 252n.7, 258n.43, 264n.83, 274n.1
*See also* Pope, Alexander; Swift, Jonathan; *individual authors*
*See and Seem Blind*, 178
self-consciousness, 12, 255n.26, 274n.3
apologetics for, 73
critical approaches towards, 79, 225n.12
and digression, 67, 69, 74, 76, 77, 79, 179, 208, 211, 214
and diversion, 59, 62, 79, 179, 190
literary, 3, 5, 6, 8, 21, 25, 34, 63, 80, 213, 215, 216, 218, 220, 224n.4
and the novel, 24, 25, 72, 181, 186, 190, 205, 208, 210, 211, 216, 217, 219, 274n.5
and rhetoric, 5, 79, 195, 213
*See also* Booth, Wayne; Hunter, J. Paul; Lupton, Christina
Seneca, 36, 55, 189
Senesino, Francesco, 30
sentimentalism, 194, 199, 220, 221, 274n.7, 275n.8
Shaftesbury. *See* Cooper, Anthony Ashley
Shakespeare, William, 4, 203, 262n.67, 263n.74
*Hamlet*, 25, 197, 198–200, 203, 209
*The Tempest*, 252n.4
Shelton, Thomas, 4
Shenstone, William, 204
Sheppard, Jack, 248n.57
Sherbert, Garry, 5, 257n.37
Sherman, Sandra, 210
sightseeing, 52, 123, 126, 127, 128, 130, 131, 134, 143, 146, 148, 149, 155, 156, 175
psychology of, 10, 23, 24, 125, 128, 146
and reading, 23, 125, 137, 138, 139, 146, 147, 157, 163, 164, 165, 166, 167, 170, 171, 174, 177, 215
simile, 6, 22, 78, 96, 98, 119, 187, 195, 206, 208, 210
Sitter, John, 121
Sloane, Hans, 139, 149, 163, 253n.10, 254n.20, 259n.46
Smith, Adam, 217
Smith, William, 101
Spacks, Patricia Meyer, 3
Speaight, George, 193
*The Spectator. See* Addison, Joseph; Steele, Richard
sports. *See* pastimes

Steele, Richard
  *The Spectator*, 44, 175, 182, 191, 192, 201,
    232n.13, 243n.21
  *The Tatler*, 44, 54, 191, 232n.13, 239n.81
Sterne, Laurence, 3
  and commercialism, 218, 219, 220
  and diversion, 217, 218, 219, 220
  and Henry Fielding, 219, 220
  and John Dunton, 224n.5
  and John Locke, 218
  and the "new species of writing," 218
  and self-consciousness, 217, 218, 219, 274n.6
  *Tristram Shandy*, 3, 217–21, 223n.4, 274n.7,
    275n.8
  and typography, 217, 218, 274n.7
Stow(e), John, 20
  *Chronicles of England*, 200, 201
sublime, 91, 93, 100, 101, 104, 114, 135, 158, 170,
  210, 217, 220
Swift, Jonathan, 14, 18, 23, 126, 127, 138, 175,
  229n.46, 263n.81
  *Gulliver's Travels*, 138, 142–47, 185, 254n.18,
    260n.49
  "An Ode to the Athenian Society," 256n.31
  *On Poetry*, 171
  *A Tale of a Tub*, 6, 13, 14, 125, 157, 158, 160, 161,
    162, 163, 170, 254n.18, 266n.100, 270n.22,
    274n.7
  *See also* Pope, Alexander; Scriblerians

Talbot, William, 249n.71
taste. *See* Addison, Joseph; aesthetics; novelty;
  sentimentalism
*The Tatler. See* Addison, Joseph; Steele, Richard
Taylor, Aline Mackenzie, 144, 260n.52
Taylor, Nancy, 244n.27
teratology. *See* monstrosities
theatre, 3, 27, 39, 40, 43, 45, 185, 190, 197–200,
  230n.1, 268n.7
  and audience expectations, 44, 45, 57, 191
  comedy, 4, 14, 51, 118, 128, 194, 198
  critiqued, 48, 51, 55, 178
  and entr'acte divertissements, 15, 39, 111, 198,
    199, 204
  *See also* pantomime; tragedy; *individual per-
    formances and venues*
Theobald, Lewis, 94
  *Perseus and Andromeda*, 9, 83, 104, 107, 109,
    240n.4, 250n.74
  *The Rape of Proserpine*, 83
Thomas à Kempis, 201
Thurmond, John, 7, 94
  *Apollo and Daphne*, 13, 83, 104
  *Harlequin Doctor Faustus*, 104, 242n.13, 243n.16
  *Harlequin Sheppard*, 248n.57

time
  anxieties over the use of, 52
  idleness versus industry, 49
  and leisure, 8, 31–33
Todd, Dennis, 9, 10, 127, 144, 145, 251n.1, 253n.10,
  254n.21, 260n.52, 261n.55
Toft, Mary, 122, 138, 177, 251n.1, 254n.21
Tonson, Jacob, 18
  *The Odes and Satyrs of Horace*, 115, *117*
*The Touch-Stone*
  on amusement, 1, 6, 26, 28–31, 33, 43, 53, 57, 60,
    62, 122, 179, 180, 182, 185, 231n.2
  and copiousness, 58, 60, 61, 176, 181
  and digression, 6, 7, 8, 57, 62, 76, 79, 180
  and diversion, 7, 12, 15, 26–31, *29*, 32, 34, 37, 47,
    48, 49, 53, 57–62, 122, 179, 180, 181, 184, 185,
    214, 230n.1, 231n.2
  on masquerade, 194
  on monstrosities, 186
  and the novel, 185
  and novelty, 39, 55, 56, 176, 178, 179, 182,
    184, 186
  on pantomime, 81–83, 85–86, 240n.3, 241n.6,
    268n.5
  and pleasure, 7, 15, 37, 48, 49, 56, 58, 59, 79
  on puppet shows, 60
  on reading, 58
  reissued as *The Taste of the Town*, 76
  and satiety, 182, 184
  and self-consciousness, 6, 58, 59, 62, 76, 184
  and time, 49
  tragedy, 1, 14, 47, 51, 60, 118, 198, 200, 204, 215,
    271n.28
  *See also* theatre
*The Tricks of the Town Laid Open*, 23, 26, 48, 183,
  268n.6
*A Trip Through the Town*, 229n.46
Troyer, Howard William, 64
typography, 3, 5, 75, 80, 163, 166, 169, 215, 217, 221
  and advertising, 163, *164*, 165
  asterisked ellipses, 5, 14, 22, 24, 60, *61*, 161, 169,
    171, 172, 175, 176, 177, 207, 215, 218, 221,
    267n.104
  blanks and lacunae, 7, 62, 158, 161, 171, 172, 177,
    218, 267n.104
  dashes and lacunae, 215
  manicules, 165
  and monstrosity, 23, 163, 171, 172, 174, 176, 177
  *See also* ellipses

"unbending the mind," 1, 15, 19, 21, 24, 25, 34, 54,
  63, 74, 75, 76, 80, 127, 176, 184, 202, 211, 212,
  214, 219
  as justification for diversion, 7, 50, 53, 55, 62, 191
  and passions, 54

*The Universal Journal*, 89
universal language, 85, 86, 91, 94, 96, 241n.9, 242n.10
Urquhart, Thomas, 4

Vanbrugh, John, 194
variety. *See* Addison, Joseph; advertising; aesthetics; copiousness; entertainment; novelty
Voltaire, 230n.50
  *Candide*, 217

Wanley, Nathaniel, 252n.8
Ward, Edward, 14, 238n.77
  *The Dancing Devils*, 94, 106
  *The London Spy*, 125, 128, 171, 175, 229n.46, 256n.32
  *The London Terræfilius*, 64
  *Writings*, 63, 64, 72, 73
Warner, William B., 2, 24, 185, 186, 237n.64, 269n.8, 272n.42, 273n.49
Watt, Ian, 208
Weaver, John, 22, 23, 89, 90, 91, 93, 94, 96, 104, 110, 243n.23
  *An Essay Towards the History of Dancing*, 90, 91, 93, 95, 103, 104, 244n.25
  *The History of the Mimes and Pantomimes*, 90, 93, 95, 96, 99, 104, 243n.18, 245n.33
  *The Loves of Mars and Venus*, 89, 91–93, 94, 104, 243n.18, 244n.27
  *Orpheus and Eurydice*, 250n.73
  *Tavern Bilkers*, 243n.18
*The Weekly Journal*, 42, 107, 109, 195
*The Weekly Oracle*, 106
Welsted, Leonard, 114
  "Acon and Lavinia," 101

Werenfels, Samuel
  *A Dissertation Concerning Meteors of Stile, or False Sublimity*, 100, 119
Wesley, John, 255n.26, 256n.31
Whyman, Susan E., 19
Wilks, Robert, 87, 191
William III, 254n.20
wit, 6, 22, 27, 65, 76, 79, 84, 85, 91, 94, 95, 96, 97, 98, 99, 100, 102, 103, 109, 111, 113, 119, 120, 121, 140, 170, 171, 172, 190, 193, 195, 196, 207, 218, 240n.82, 245n.34, 251n.76, 259n.47, 264n.83, 268n.7, 274n.3, 275n.9
  "Age of," 84
  corporeal, 87, 110, 120, 121, 195
  digressive, 4, 5, 7, 20, 22, 30, 62, 76, 77, 181, 182, 204, 205, 206, 208, 213, 214, 217, 219, 220
  dumb, 22, 82, 83, 87, 89, 93, 94, 95, 96, 104, 106, 110, 113, 118, 120, 182, 185, 244n.26, 245n.33
  false, 3, 22, 23, 24, 76, 83, 84, 95, 96, 98, 100, 103, 104, 107, 110, 113, 114, 118, 120, 121, 155, 181, 195, 221, 244n.31, 245n.32, 246n.38
  metaphysical, 135, 154
  rhetorical, 84, 93, 97, 99, 102, 103, 119
  true, 23, 76, 83, 84, 90, 93, 95, 99, 244n.31, 246n.35
  verbal, 82, 83, 85, 87, 93, 104, 110, 113, 120
  versus knowledge and judgement, 44, 93, 97, 100
wonder literature, 125, 252n.8
wonders. *See* monstrosities
Wormberg, John, 144

Young, Edward
  *Conjectures on Original Composition*, 217

CPSIA information can be obtained
at www.ICGtesting.com
Printed in the USA
LVHW052227070119
603029LV00022B/314